Y0-BQC-121

Building Secure Microsoft® ASP.NET Applications

Authentication, Authorization,
and Secure Communication

patterns & practices

PUBLISHED BY
Microsoft Press
A Division of Microsoft Corporation
One Microsoft Way
Redmond, Washington 98052-6399

Library of Congress Cataloging-in-Publication Data pending.

Printed and bound in the United States of America.

1 2 3 4 5 6 7 8 9   QWT   8 7 6 5 4 3

Distributed in Canada by H.B. Fenn and Company Ltd.

A CIP catalogue record for this book is available from the British Library.

Microsoft Press books are available through booksellers and distributors worldwide. For further information about international editions, contact your local Microsoft Corporation office or contact Microsoft Press International directly at fax (425) 936-7329. Visit our Web site at www.microsoft.com/mspress. Send comments to *mspinput@microsoft.com*.

Acquisitions Editor: Danielle Bird Voeller
Project Editor: Lynn Finnel

Body Part No. X09-38995

Contents at a Glance

Chapter 1
Introduction. 1

Chapter 2
Security Model for ASP.NET 7
Applications

Chapter 3
Authentication and Authorization. . . 27
Design

Chapter 4
Secure Communication 53

Chapter 5
Intranet Security 63

Chapter 6
Extranet Security. 101

Chapter 7
Internet Security 117

Chapter 8
ASP.NET Security. 135

Chapter 9
Enterprise Services Security. 193

Chapter 10
Web Services Security 225

Chapter 11
.NET Remoting Security 259

Chapter 12
Data Access Security 291

Chapter 13
Troubleshooting Security Issues . . . 327

Index of How Tos. 345

How To:
Create a Custom Account. 347
to Run ASP.NET

How To:
Use Forms Authentication with . . . 353
Active Directory

How To:
Use Forms Authentication with . . . 363
SQL Server 2000

How To:
Create GenericPrincipal Objects. . . 373
with Forms Authentication

How To:
Implement Kerberos Delegation . . 381
for Windows 2000

How To:
Implement IPrincipal 385

How To:
Create a DPAPI Library. 395

How To:
Use DPAPI (Machine Store) 405
from ASP.NET

How To:
Use DPAPI (User Store) from 411
ASP.NET with Enterprise Services

How To:
Create an Encryption Library 425

How To:
Store an Encrypted Connection . . . 435
String in the Registry

How To:
Use Role-based Security with 441
Enterprise Services

How To:
Call a Web Service Using Client . . . 449
Certificates from ASP.NET

How To:
Call a Web Service Using SSL 463

How To:
Host a Remote Object in 469
a Windows Service

How To:
Set Up SSL on a Web Server 475

How To:
Set Up Client Certificates 481

How To:
Use IPSec to Provide Secure 485
Communication Between
Two Servers

How To:
Use SSL to Secure 495
Communication with
SQL Server 2000

Base Configuration 505

Configuration Stores and Tools . . . 507

Reference Hub 513

How Does It Work? 523

ASP.NET Identity Matrix. 533

Cryptography and Certificates 537

.NET Web Application Security . . . 545

Contents

Acknowledgements xxiii
Preface xxv

Chapter 1

Introduction   1

The Connected Landscape 1
The Foundations 2
    Authentication 2
    Authorization 2
    Secure Communication 3
Tying the Technologies Together 3
Design Principles 4
Summary 6

Chapter 2

Security Model for ASP.NET Applications   7

.NET Web Applications 7
    Logical Tiers 8
    Physical Deployment Models 9
Implementation Technologies 10
Security Architecture 11
    Security Across the Tiers 12
    Authentication 13
    Authorization 16
    Gatekeepers and Gates 17
Introducing .NET Framework Security 20
    Code Access Security 20
    Principals and Identities 21
    WindowsPrincipal and WindowsIdentity 23
    GenericPrincipal and Associated Identity Objects 23
    ASP.NET and HttpContext.User 24
    Remoting and Web Services 24
Summary 25

Chapter 3

Authentication and Authorization Design   27

Designing an Authentication and Authorization Strategy 28
    Identify Resources 28
    Choose an Authorization Strategy 28
    Choose the Identities Used for Resource Access 29
    Consider Identity Flow 30
    Choose an Authentication Approach 31
    Decide How to Flow Identity 31
Authorization Approaches 32
    Role Based Authorization 32
    Resource Based Authorization 33
    Resource Access Models 33
    The Trusted Subsystem Model 33
    The Impersonation / Delegation Model 35
    Choosing a Resource Access Model 36
Flowing Identity 38
    Application vs. Operating System Identity Flow 38
    Impersonation and Delegation 38
Role-Based Authorization 40
    .NET Roles 40
    Enterprise Services (COM+) Roles 42
    SQL Server User Defined Database Roles 42
    SQL Server Application Roles 42
    .NET Roles versus Enterprise Services (COM+) Roles 43
    Using .NET Roles 44
Choosing an Authentication Mechanism 47
    Internet Scenarios 49
    Intranet / Extranet Scenarios 50
    Authentication Mechanism Comparison 51
Summary 51

Chapter 4

Secure Communication   53

Know What to Secure 54
SSL/TLS 55
    Using SSL 55
IPSec 56
    Using IPSec 56
RPC Encryption 57
    Using RPC Encryption 57
Point to Point Security 58
    Browser to Web Server 58
    Web Server to Remote Application Server 59
    Application Server to Database Server 59

Choosing Between IPSec and SSL 61
Farming and Load Balancing 61
    More Information 61
Summary 61

Chapter 5

Intranet Security   63

ASP.NET to SQL Server. 64
    Characteristics 64
    Secure the Scenario 65
    The Result 65
    Security Configuration Steps 66
    Analysis 68
    Q&A 69
    Related Scenarios. 70
ASP.NET to Enterprise Services to SQL Server. 71
    Characteristics 72
    Secure the Scenario 72
    The Result 73
    Security Configuration Steps 74
    Analysis 76
    Pitfalls 77
ASP.NET to Web Services to SQL Server 77
    Characteristics 78
    Secure the Scenario 78
    The Result 79
    Security Configuration Steps 79
    Analysis 82
    Pitfalls 84
    Q&A 84
ASP.NET to Remoting to SQL Server 85
    Characteristics 85
    Secure the Scenario 85
    The Result 86
    Security Configuration Steps 87
    Analysis 89
    Pitfalls 90
Flowing the Original Caller to the Database 91
    ASP.NET to SQL Server. 92
    ASP.NET to Enterprise Services to SQL Server 93
    The Result 94
    Analysis 98
    Pitfalls 99
Summary 99

Chapter 6

Extranet Security   **101**

Exposing a Web Service 102
    Characteristics 102
    Secure the Scenario 103
    The Result 103
    Security Configuration Steps 104
    Analysis 107
    Pitfalls 108
    Q&A 108
Exposing a Web Application 109
    Scenario Characteristics 109
    Secure the Scenario 110
    The Result 111
    Analysis 113
    Pitfalls 115
Summary 115

Chapter 7

Internet Security   **117**

ASP.NET to SQL Server. 118
    Characteristics 118
    Secure the Scenario 119
    The Result 120
    Security Configuration Steps 120
    Analysis 122
    Pitfalls 124
    Related Scenarios. 124
ASP.NET to Remote Enterprise Services to SQL Server 125
    Characteristics 126
    Secure the Scenario 127
    The Result 128
    Security Configuration Steps 128
    Analysis 132
    Pitfalls 133
    Related Scenarios. 133
Summary. 134

Chapter 8
ASP.NET Security   **135**

ASP.NET Security Architecture 135
  Gatekeepers 137
Authentication and Authorization Strategies 139
  Available Authorization Options 140
  Windows Authentication with Impersonation 141
  Windows Authentication without Impersonation 143
  Windows Authentication Using a Fixed Identity 145
  Forms Authentication 145
  Passport Authentication 147
Configuring Security 147
  Configure IIS Settings 149
  Configure ASP.NET Settings 149
  Secure Resources 152
  Secure Communication 155
Programming Security 155
  An Authorization Pattern 156
  Creating a Custom IPrincipal class 158
Windows Authentication 159
Forms Authentication 160
  Development Steps for Forms Authentication 162
  Forms Implementation Guidelines 165
  Hosting Multiple Applications Using Forms Authentication 166
  Cookieless Forms Authentication 166
Passport Authentication 167
Custom Authentication 168
Process Identity for ASP.NET 168
  Use a Least Privileged Account 168
  Avoid Running as SYSTEM 169
  Using the Default ASPNET Account 169
Impersonation 172
  Impersonation and Local Resources 172
  Impersonation and Remote Resources 172
  Impersonation and Threading 172
Accessing System Resources 173
  Accessing the Event Log 173
  Accessing the Registry 174
Accessing COM Objects 174
  Apartment Model Objects 174
Accessing Network Resources 176
  Using the ASPNET Process Identity 176
  Using a Serviced Component 177
  Using the Anonymous Internet User Account 178

Using LogonUser and Impersonating a Specific Windows Identity 180
Using the Original Caller 180
Accessing Files on a UNC File Share 181
Accessing Non-Windows Network Resources 181
Secure Communication 182
Storing Secrets 182
Options for Storing Secrets in ASP.NET 184
Consider Storing Secrets in Files on Separate Logical Volumes 184
Securing Session and View State 185
Securing View State 185
Securing Cookies 185
Securing SQL Session State 185
Web Farm Considerations 188
Session State 188
DPAPI 188
Using Forms Authentication in a Web Farm 188
The <machineKey> Element 189
Summary 190

Chapter 9

Enterprise Services Security   193

Security Architecture 193
Gatekeepers and Gates 195
Use Server Applications for Increased Security 196
Security for Server and Library Applications 197
Code Access Security Requirements 197
Configuring Security 198
Configuring a Server Application 198
Configuring an ASP.NET Client Application 205
Configuring Impersonation Levels for an Enterprise Services Application 206
Programming Security 207
Programmatic Role-Based Security 207
Identifying Callers 208
Choosing a Process Identity 208
Avoid Running as the Interactive User 208
Use a Least-Privileged Custom Account 209
Accessing Network Resources 209
Using the Original Caller 210
Using the Current Process Identity 210
Using a Specific Service Account 211
Flowing the Original Caller 211
Calling ColmpersonateClient 212
RPC Encryption 213
More Information 213

Building Serviced Components 213
DLL Locking Problems 213
Versioning 214
QueryInterface Exceptions 215
DCOM and Firewalls 215
More Information 215
Calling Serviced Components from ASP.NET 216
Caller's Identity 216
Use Windows Authentication and Impersonation Within
   the Web-based Application 216
Configure Authentication and Impersonation within Machine.config 216
Configuring Interface Proxies 216
Security Concepts 219
Enterprise Services (COM+) Roles and .NET Roles 220
Authentication 221
Impersonation 222
Summary 224

Chapter 10

Web Services Security   225

Web Service Security Model 225
Platform/Transport Level (Point-to-Point) Security 226
Application Level Security 227
Message Level (End-to-End) Security 227
Platform/Transport Security Architecture 229
Gatekeepers 230
Authentication and Authorization Strategies 231
Windows Authentication with Impersonation 231
Windows Authentication without Impersonation 233
Windows Authentication Using a Fixed Identity 235
Configuring Security 236
Configure IIS Settings 236
Configure ASP.NET Settings 237
Secure Resources 237
Disable HTTP-GET, HTTP-POST 237
Secure Communication 238
Passing Credentials for Authentication to Web Services 238
Specifying Client Credentials for Windows Authentication 239
Calling Web Services from Non-Windows Clients 241
Proxy Server Authentication 242
Flowing the Original Caller 242
Default Credentials with Kerberos Delegation 243
Explicit Credentials with Basic or Forms Authentication 245

Trusted Subsystem 248
   Flowing the Caller's Identity 249
   Configuration Steps 249
Accessing System Resources 250
Accessing Network Resources 250
Accessing COM Objects. 251
   More Information 251
Using Client Certificates with Web Services 251
   Authenticating Web Browser Clients with Certificates 252
   Using the Trusted Subsystem Model 252
Secure Communication 255
   Transport Level Options. 256
   Message Level Options 256
Summary 256

Chapter 11

.NET Remoting Security   259

.NET Remoting Architecture 259
   Remoting Sinks. 260
   Anatomy of a Request When Hosting in ASP.NET 262
   ASP.NET and the HTTP Channel 263
.NET Remoting Gatekeepers 264
Authentication. 265
   Hosting in ASP.NET 265
   Hosting in a Windows Service 266
Authorization. 267
   Using File Authorization 267
Authentication and Authorization Strategies 268
   More Information 269
Accessing System Resources 269
Accessing Network Resources 270
Passing Credentials for Authentication to Remote Objects 270
   Specifying Client Credentials 270
Flowing the Original Caller 273
   Default Credentials with Kerberos Delegation. 274
   Explicit Credentials with Basic or Forms Authentication. 276
Trusted Subsystem 280
   Flowing the Caller's Identity 281
   Choosing a Host 282
   Configuration Steps 282
Secure Communication 284
   Platform Level Options 284

Choosing a Host Process 285
   Recommendation 285
   Hosting in ASP.NET 285
   Hosting in a Windows Service 286
   Hosting in a Console Application 287
Remoting vs. Web Services 288
Summary 289

Chapter 12
Data Access Security

291

Introducing Data Access Security 291
   SQL Server Gatekeepers 293
   Trusted Subsystem vs. Impersonation/Delegation 293
Authentication 295
   Windows Authentication 295
   SQL Authentication 301
   Authenticating Against Non-SQL Server Databases 303
Authorization 304
   Using Multiple Database Roles 304
Secure Communication 305
   The Options 306
   Choosing an Approach 306
Connecting with Least Privilege 307
   The Database Trusts the Application 307
   The Database Trusts Different Roles 307
   The Database Trusts the Original Caller 308
Creating a Least Privilege Database Account 308
Storing Database Connection Strings Securely 310
   The Options 310
   Using DPAPI 310
   Using Web.config and Machine.config 314
   Using UDL Files 314
   Using Custom Text Files 316
   Using the Registry 316
   Using the COM+ Catalog 316
Authenticating Users against a Database 317
   Store One-way Password Hashes (with Salt) 317
SQL Injection Attacks 319
Auditing 323
Process Identity for SQL Server 324
Summary 325

Chapter 13

Troubleshooting Security Issues   327

Process for Troubleshooting. 327
    Searching for Implementation Solutions 328
Troubleshooting Authentication Issues 329
    IIS Authentication Issues. 329
    Using Windows Authentication 330
    Using Forms Authentication 331
    Kerberos Troubleshooting 331
Troubleshooting Authorization Issues 331
    Check Windows ACLs 331
    Check Identity 331
    Check the <authorization> Element 332
ASP.NET 333
    Enable Tracing 333
    Configuration Settings 333
Determining Identity 334
    Determining Identity in a Web Page 334
    Determining Identity in a Web service 336
    Determining Identity in a Visual Basic 6 COM Object 336
.NET Remoting 337
    More Information 337
SSL 338
    More Information 338
IPSec 338
Auditing and Logging 339
    Windows Security Logs 339
    SQL Server Auditing 339
    IIS Logging 340
Troubleshooting Tools 341
    File Monitor (FileMon.exe) 341
    Fusion Log Viewer (Fuslogvw.exe). 341
    ISQL.exe 342
    Windows Task Manager 342
    Network Monitor (NetMon.exe) 343
    Registry Monitor (regmon.exe) 343
    WFetch.exe 343
    Visual Studio .NET Tools 344
    WebServiceStudio 344
    Windows 2000 Resource Kit 344

Index of How Tos   345

ASP.NET 345
Authentication and Authorization 345
Cryptography. 345
Enterprise Services Security 345
Web Services Security 346
Remoting Security 346
Secure Communication 346

How To:

Create a Custom Account to Run ASP.NET   347

ASP.NET Worker Process Identity 347
Impersonating Fixed Identities 348
Notes 348
Summary 349
1. Create a New Local Account 349
2. Assign Minimum Privileges 349
3. Assign NTFS Permissions 350
4. Configure ASP.NET to Run Using the New Account 352

How To:

Use Forms Authentication with Active Directory   353

Requirements 353
Summary 353
1. Create a Web Application with a Logon Page 354
2. Configure the Web Application for Forms Authentication 355
3. Develop LDAP Authentication Code to Look Up the User in Active Directory 356
4. Develop LDAP Group Retrieval Code to Look Up the User's Group
    Membership 357
5. Authenticate the User and Create a Forms Authentication Ticket. 358
6. Implement an Authentication Request Handler to Construct a GenericPrincipal
    Object 360
7. Test the Application. 362

How To:

Use Forms Authentication with SQL Server 2000   363

Requirements 364
Summary 364
1. Create a Web Application with a Logon Page 364
2. Configure the Web Application for Forms Authentication 365
3. Develop Functions to Generate a Hash and Salt value 366
4. Create a User Account Database 367
5. Use ADO.NET to Store Account Details in the Database 368

6. Authenticate User Credentials Against the Database 369
7. Test the Application 371
Additional Resources 372

How To:

Create GenericPrincipal Objects with Forms Authentication 373

Requirements 374
Summary 374
1. Create a Web Application with a Logon Page 374
2. Configure the Web Application for Forms Authentication 375
3. Generate an Authentication Ticket for Authenticated Users 375
4. Construct GenericPrincipal and FormsIdentity Objects 378
5. Test the Application 379
Additional Resources 380

How To:

Implement Kerberos Delegation for Windows 2000 381

Notes 381
Requirements 382
Summary 382
1. Confirm that the Client Account is Configured for Delegation 382
2. Confirm that the Server Process Account is Trusted for Delegation 382
References 383

How To:

Implement IPrincipal 385

Requirements 386
Summary 386
1. Create a Simple Web Application 386
2. Configure the Web Application for Forms Authentication 387
3. Generate an Authentication Ticket for Authenticated Users 388
4. Create a Class that Implements and Extends IPrincipal 390
5. Create the CustomPrincipal Object 391
5. Test the Application 393
Additional Resources 394

How To:

Create a DPAPI Library 395

Notes 395
Requirements 396
Summary 396
1. Create a C# Class Library 396
2. Strong Name the Assembly (Optional) 402
References 403

How To:

Use DPAPI (Machine Store) from ASP.NET   **405**

Notes 405
    Requirements 406
Summary 406
1. Create an ASP.NET Client Web Application 406
2. Test the Application 408
3. Modify the Web Application to Read an Encrypted Connection String from
    Web.Config 409
References 410

How To:

Use DPAPI (User Store) from ASP.NET with Enterprise Services   **411**

Notes 411
    Why Use Enterprise Services? 412
    Why Use a Windows Service? 413
Requirements 414
Summary 414
1. Create a Serviced Component that Provides Encrypt and Decrypt Methods 414
2. Call the Managed DPAPI Class Library 415
3. Create a Dummy Class that will Launch the Serviced Component 416
4. Create a Windows Account to Run the Enterprise Services Application and
    Windows Service 416
5. Configure, Strong Name, and Register the Serviced Component 417
6. Create a Windows Service Application that will Launch the Serviced
    Component 418
7. Install and Start the Windows Service Application 420
8. Write a Web Application to Test the Encryption and Decryption Routines 420
9. Modify the Web Application to Read an Encrypted Connection String from
    an Application Configuration File 423
References 424

How To:

Create an Encryption Library   **425**

Requirements 425
Summary 425
1. Create a C# Class Library 426
2. Create a Console Test Application 433
References 434

How To:

Store an Encrypted Connection String in the Registry   **435**
Notes 435
Requirements 435
Summary 436
1. Store the Encrypted Data in the Registry 436
2. Create an ASP.NET Web Application 439
References 440

How To:

Use Role-based Security with Enterprise Services   **441**
Notes 441
Requirements 441
Summary 442
1. Create a C# Class Library Application to Host the Serviced Component 442
2. Create the Serviced Component 442
3. Configure the Serviced Component 443
4. Generate a Strong Name for the Assembly 444
5. Build the Assembly and Add it to the Global Assembly Cache 445
6. Manually Register the Serviced Component 445
7. Examine the Configured Application 445
8. Create a Test Client Application 446

How To:

Call a Web Service Using Client Certificates from ASP.NET   **449**
Why Use a Serviced Component? 449
    Why is a User Profile Required? 450
Requirements 451
Summary 451
1. Create a Simple Web Service 451
2. Configure the Web Service Virtual Directory to Require Client Certificates 452
3. Create a Custom Account for Running the Serviced Component 453
4. Request a Client Certificate for the Custom Account 453
5. Test the Client Certificate Using a Browser 455
6. Export the Client Certificate to a File 455
7. Develop the Serviced Component Used to Call the Web Service 456
8. Configure and Install the Serviced Component 459
9. Develop a Web Application to Call the Serviced Component 460
Additional Resources 462

How To:

Call a Web Service Using SSL   463

Requirements 463
Summary 463
1. Create a Simple Web Service 464
2. Configure the Web Service Virtual Directory to Require SSL 464
3. Test the Web Service Using a Browser 465
4. Install the Certificate Authority's Certificate on the Client Computer 466
5. Develop a Web Application to Call the Web Service. 467
Additional Resources 468

How To:

Host a Remote Object in a Windows Service   469

Notes 469
Requirements 469
Summary 470
1. Create the Remote Object Class 470
2. Create a Windows Service Host Application 470
3. Create a Windows Account to Run the Service 473
4. Install the Windows Service. 473
5. Create a Test Client Application 474
References 474

How To:

Set Up SSL on a Web Server   475

Requirements 475
Summary 475
1. Generate a Certificate Request 475
2. Submit a Certificate Request. 477
3. Issue the Certificate 478
4. Install the Certificate on the Web Server 478
5. Configure Resources to Require SSL Access 479

How To:

Set Up Client Certificates   481

Requirements 481
Summary 481
1. Create a Simple Web Application 482
2. Configure the Web Application to Require Client Certificates 482
3. Request and Install a Client Certificate 483
4. Verify Client Certificate Operation 484
Additional Resources 484

How To:

Use IPSec to Provide Secure Communication Between Two Servers   **485**

Notes 487
Requirements 487
Summary 488
1. Create an IP Filter 488
2. Create Filter Actions 489
3. Create Rules 490
4. Export the IPSec Policy to the Remote Computer 491
5. Assign Policies 491
6. Verify that it Works 492
Additional Resources 494

How To:

Use SSL to Secure Communication with SQL Server 2000   **495**

Notes 495
Requirements 496
Summary 496
1. Install a Server Authentication Certificate 496
2. Verify that the Certificate Has Been Installed 497
3. Install the Issuing CA's Certificate on the Client 498
4. Force All Clients to Use SSL 498
5. Allow Clients to Determine Whether to Use SSL 499
6. Verify that Communication is Encrypted 500
Additional Resources 503

Base Configuration   **505**

Configuration Stores and Tools   **507**

Reference Hub   **513**

Searching the Knowledge Base 513
    Tips 514
.NET Security 514
    Hubs 514
Active Directory 514
    Hubs 514
    Key Notes 515
    Articles 515
ADO.NET 515
    Roadmaps and Overviews 515
    Seminars and WebCasts 515

ASP.NET 515
 Hubs 515
 Roadmaps and Overviews 516
 Knowledge Base 516
 Articles 516
 How Tos 516
 Seminars and WebCasts 517
Enterprise Services 517
 Knowledge Base 517
 Roadmaps and Overviews 517
 How Tos 518
 FAQs 518
 Seminars and WebCasts 518
IIS (Internet Information Server) 518
 Hubs 518
Remoting 518
 Roadmaps and Overviews 518
 How Tos 519
 Seminars and WebCasts 519
SQL Server 519
 Hubs 519
 Seminars and WebCasts 519
Visual Studio .NET 519
 Hubs 519
 Roadmaps and Overviews: 519
Web Services 520
 Hubs 520
 Roadmaps and Overviews 520
 How Tos 520
 Seminars and WebCasts 520
Windows 2000 521
 Hubs 521

How Does It Work?   523

IIS and ASP.NET Processing 523
 Application Isolation 524
 The ASP.NET ISAPI Extension 524
 IIS 6.0 and Windows .NET Server 524
ASP.NET Pipeline Processing 525
 The Anatomy of a Web Request 526
 Event Handling 530
 Implementing a Custom HTTP Module 531
 Implementing a Custom HTTP Handler 531

ASP.NET Identity Matrix   533

Cryptography and Certificates   537
Keys and Certificates 537
    X.509 Digital Certificates 538
    Certificate Stores 538
    More Information 539
Cryptography 539
    Technical Choices 539
    Cryptography in .NET 540
Summary 543

.NET Web Application Security   545

Glossary   547

Index   565

Acknowledgements

Many thanks to the following contributors and reviewers:

- Thanks to external reviewers – Keith Brown (DevelopMentor) for review and feedback on the ASP.NET chapter, Andy Eunson for providing scenarios on middleware applications, John Langley (KANA Software) for bringing J2EE and .NET perspectives to the table, Kurt Dillard and Christof Sprenger for reviewing application scenarios and the authentication and authorization process, J.K.Meadows and David Alberto for reviewing application scenarios and individual chapters and Bernard Chen (Sapient) for reviewing the authentication and authorization process

- Product Group–Thanks to Manish Prabhu, Jesus Ruiz-Scougall, Jonathan Hawkins and Doug Purdy from the .NET Remoting team; Keith Ballinger Yann Christensen and Alexei Vopilov from the Web Services team; Laura Barsan from the ASP.NET team; Greg Fee (.NET Roles / Principal permission checks), Greg Singleton and Sebastian Lange (CAS); Tarik Soulami from the CLR team; Erik Olson (extensive validation and recommendations on ASP.NET); Caesar Samsi (for sharing in depth e-commerce Internet facing application scenarios), Riyaz Pishori, Shannon Pahl and Ron Jacobs (Enterprise Services), Dave McPherson (Windows security architecture and authorization strategies), Christopher Brown (helping resolve cross product issues), John Banes (DPAPI), Joel Scambray, Girish Chander (SQL Server security)

- MCS / Field–William Zentmayer (Remote application tier scenarios with Enterprise Services), Shantanu Sarkar (validation of application architecture scenarios), Carl Nolan (Web services), Samuel Melendez and Jacquelyn Schmidt (infrastructure and deployment scenarios), Steve Busby, Len Cardinal, Monica DeZulueta, Paula Paul (Data Access and Web application security), Ed Draper, Sean Finnegan (pushing Active Directory and Windows authentication with technical depth and practical scenarios), David Alberto, Kenny Jones (for bringing real world field issues to the table and helping to involve the field), Doug Orange (real world Extranet authorization scenarios), Alexey Yeltsov (SQL Injection), Martin Kohlleppel (Architecture review), Joel Yoker (firewalls and IPSec)

- Special thanks to Jay Nanduri (Microsoft.com) for reviewing and sharing real world experiences, Ilia Fortunov (Senior Architect) for providing continuous and diligent feedback and Aaron Margosis (MCS) for thoroughly reviewing several chapters and making excellent suggestions at various stages of the project.

- Special thanks to Product Support Services folks for contributing and reviewing various portions of the guide – Venkat Chilakala (Troubleshooting section), John Allen and Jeremy Bostron (ASP.NET), Martin Petersen-Frey (simplifying and helping to structure the Remoting and Web Service portions of the guide), Karl Westerholm (SSL), Jayaprakasam Siddian Thirunavukkarasu (SQL Roles and ADO), Wade Mascia (valuable feedback on Enterprise Services, COM threading, ASP.NET and Web services), Ryan Kivett (IIS6 and ASP.NET), Sarath Mallavarapu (Data Access), Jerry Bryant (bringing community issues to the table) and Peter Kyte for resources

- Thanks also, to Philip Teale, Ram Sunkara, Shaun Hayes, Eric Schmidt, Michael Howard, Rich Benack, Carlos Lyons, Ted Kehl. Thanks to Peter Dampier, Mike Sherrill and Devendra Tiwari from the Enterprise Alliance team for validating our application scenarios. Thanks to Tavi Siochi (IT Audit) for feedback on SQL Injection.

- Finally, thanks to our colleagues on the *patterns & practices* team: Per Vonge Nielsen, Andrew Mason, Edward Jezierski, Sandy Khaund, Tina Burden, Edward Lafferty, Peter M. Clift, John Munyon, Mohammad Al-Sabt, Anandha Murukan and Chris Sfanos.

J.D.Meier

Alex Mackman

Michael Dunner

Srinath Vasireddy

October 2002

Preface

Why We Wrote This Book

This book is not an introduction to security, nor is it a security reference for the Microsoft .NET Framework—for that you have the .NET Framework Software Development Kit (SDK) available from MSDN. This book picks up where the documentation leaves off and presents a scenario-based approach to sharing recommendations and proven techniques. We wanted the book to be as real world as possible and as a result it is packed full of insight, recommendations and best practices obtained from field experience, customer experience, and insight from the product teams at Microsoft.

There are many technologies used to build .NET Web applications. To build effective application-level authentication and authorization strategies, you need to understand how to fine-tune the various security features within each product and technology area, and how to make them work together to provide an effective, defense-in-depth security strategy. The focus of the book is on security and identity management across the tiers of distributed ASP.NET applications.

Specifically we have chosen to focus on authentication, authorization, and secure communication. Security is a broad topic but research has shown that early design of authentication and authorization eliminates a high percentage of application vulnerabilities. Secure communication is an integral part of securing your distributed application to protect sensitive data, including credentials, passed to and from your application, and between application tiers.

Who Should Read This Book?

If you are a middleware developer or architect, who plans to build, or is currently building .NET Web applications using one or more of the following technologies, you should read this book.

- ASP.NET
- Web Services
- Enterprise Services
- Remoting
- ADO.NET

To most effectively use this book to help you design and build secure .NET Web applications, you should already have some familiarity and experience with .NET development techniques and technologies. You should be familiar with distributed application architecture and if you have already implemented .NET Web application solutions, you should know your own application architecture and deployment pattern.

How You Should Read This Book

The book has been developed to be modular. This allows you to pick and choose which chapters to read. For example, if you are interested in learning about the in-depth security features provided by a specific technology, you can jump straight to Part III of the book (Chapters 8 through 12), which contains in-depth material covering ASP.NET, Enterprise Services, Web Services, .NET Remoting, and data access.

However, you are encouraged to read the early chapters (Chapters 1 through 4) in Part I of the book first, because these will help you understand the security model and identify the core technologies and security services at your disposal. Application architects should make sure they read Chapter 3, which provides some key insights into designing an authentication and authorization strategy that spans the tiers of your Web application. Part I will provide you with the foundation materials, which will allow you to extract maximum benefit from the remainder of the book.

The intranet, extranet, and Internet chapters (Chapters 5 through 7) in Part II of the book will show you how to secure specific application scenarios. If you know the architecture and deployment pattern that is or will be adopted by your application, use this part of the book to understand the security issues involved and the basic configuration steps required to secure specific scenarios.

Finally, additional information and reference material in Part IV of the book will help further your understanding of specific technology areas. It also contains a library of "How To" articles, which enable you to develop working security solutions in the shortest possible time.

Organization of this Book

This book is divided into four parts. The aim is to provide a logical partitioning, which will help you to more easily digest the content.

Part I, Security Models

Part I provides a foundation for the rest of the book. Familiarity with the concepts, principles, and technologies introduced in Part I will enable you to extract maximum value from the remainder of the book. Part I contains the following chapters:

- Chapter 1, "Introduction"
- Chapter 2, "Security Model for ASP.NET Applications"
- Chapter 3, "Authentication and Authorization Design"
- Chapter 4, "Secure Communication"

Part II, Application Scenarios

Most applications can be categorized as intranet, extranet, or Internet applications. This part of the book presents a set of common application scenarios, each of which falls into one of the aforementioned categories. The key characteristics of each scenario are described and the potential security threats analyzed.

You are then shown how to configure and implement the most appropriate authentication, authorization, and secure communication strategy for each application scenario. Each scenario also contains sections that include a detailed analysis, common pitfalls to watch out for, and frequently asked questions (FAQ). Part II contains the following chapters:

- Chapter 5, "Intranet Security"
- Chapter 6, "Extranet Security"
- Chapter 7, "Internet Security"

Part III, Securing the Tiers

This part of the book contains detailed information that relates to the individual tiers and technologies associated with secure .NET-connected Web applications. Part III contains the following chapters:

- Chapter 8, "ASP.NET Security"
- Chapter 9, "Enterprise Services Security"
- Chapter 10, "Web Services Security"
- Chapter 11, ".NET Remoting Security"
- Chapter 12, "Data Access Security"

Within each chapter, a brief overview of the security architecture as it applies to the particular technology in question is presented. Authentication and authorization strategies are discussed for each technology along with configurable security options, programmatic security options, and actionable recommendations of when to use the particular strategy.

Each chapter offers guidance and insight that will allow you to choose and implement the most appropriate authentication, authorization, and secure communication option for each technology. In addition, each chapter presents additional information specific to the particular technology. Finally, each chapter concludes with a concise recommendation summary.

Part IV, Reference

This reference part of the book contains supplementary information to help further your understanding of the techniques, strategies, and security solutions presented in earlier chapters. Detailed How Tos provide step-by-step procedures that enable you to implement specific security solutions. It contains the following information:

- Chapter 13, "Troubleshooting Security"
- "How Tos"
- "Base Configuration"
- "Configuration Stores and Tools"
- "Reference Hub"
- "How Tos"
- "How Does It Work?"
- "ASP.NET Identity Matrix"
- "Cryptography and Certificates"
- "ASP.NET Security Model"
- "Glossary"

System Requirements

This book will help you design and build secure ASP.NET applications for Windows 2000 using the .NET Framework. We targeted version 1 of the .NET Framework (with service pack 2) although the concepts and code will run with the next version of the .NET Framework. The book prepares you for new security features that will be provided with the next version and also for the additional features that will be provided with Windows .NET Server 2003, Microsoft's next generation Windows server operating system.

To use this book, you need at least one computer running Windows XP Professional or Windows 2000 Server SP3. In addition you require Visual Studio .NET, the .NET Framework SP2 and SQL Server 2000 SP2.

To implement some of the solutions discussed, you also need a second computer running Windows 2000 Server SP3, Windows 2000 Advanced Server SP3 or Windows 2000 DataCenter Server SP3.

Installing the Sample Files

The sample files can be downloaded from the book's Web site at *http://www.microsoft.com/mspress/books/6501.asp*. To download the sample files, click the "Companion Content" link in the More Information menu on the right side of the Web page. This will load the Companion Content page, which includes a link for downloading the sample files.

Building Secure ASP.NET Applications—Online Version

This guide is also available online. To read online go to: *http://msdn.microsoft.com /library/default.asp?url=/library/en-us/dnnetsec/html/secnetlpMSDN.asp*. To download the PDF go to

http://www.microsoft.com/downloads/release.asp?ReleaseID=44047.

Support

Every effort has been made to ensure the accuracy of this book and the companion content. If you have questions or feedback on the content, send e-mail to secguide@microsoft.com.

1

Introduction

Building secure distributed Web applications is challenging. Your application is only as secure as its weakest link. With distributed applications, you have a lot of moving parts and making those parts work together in a secure fashion requires a working knowledge that spans products and technologies.

You already have a lot to consider; integrating various technologies, staying current with technology, and keeping a step ahead of the competition. If you don't already know how to build secure applications, can you afford the time and effort to learn? More to the point, can you afford not to?

The Connected Landscape

If you already know how to build secure applications, are you able to apply what you know when you build .NET Web applications? Are you able to apply your knowledge in today's landscape of Web-based distributed applications, where Web services connect businesses to other business and business to customers and where applications offer various degrees of exposure; for example, to users on intranets, extranets, and the Internet?

Consider some of the fundamental characteristics of this connected landscape:

- Web services use standards such as SOAP, Extensible Markup Language (XML), and Hypertext Transport Protocol (HTTP), but fundamentally they pass potentially sensitive information using plain text.
- Internet business-to-consumer applications pass sensitive data over the Web.
- Extranet business-to-business applications blur the lines of trust and allow applications to be called by other applications in partner companies.
- Intranet applications are not without their risks considering the sensitive nature of payroll and Human Resource (HR) applications. Such applications are particularly vulnerable to rogue administrators and disgruntled employees.

The Foundations

Any successful application security strategy is built on the foundations of a solid approach to authentication and authorization together with secure communication to provide privacy and integrity for sensitive data. Before we go on, it is important to define these core concepts. In Chapter 3, we will show you how the various authentication and authorization mechanisms can be combined to provide a solid security design.

Authentication

Authentication is the process of positively identifying the clients of your application; clients might include end-users, services, processes or computers. In security parlance, authenticated clients are referred to as principals.

Authentication occurs across the tiers of a distributed Web application. End users are initially authenticated by the Web application, typically by a username and password. Subsequently, as the end-user's request is processed by middle tier application servers (if your architecture has one) and the database server, they perform authentication in order to validate and process the request.

In many applications, the downstream servers and components do not authenticate the end user. Instead they authenticate the entity that is the upstream application, having trusted that application to correctly authenticate and authorize the request prior to forwarding it.

The many authentication mechanisms that apply to ASP.NET application development are discussed further in Chapter 2.

Authorization

The authorization process governs which resources and operations the authenticated client is allowed to access. Resources include files, databases, tables, rows and so on, together with system level resources such as registry keys and configuration data.

Primarily for reasons of scalability and manageability, many Web applications authorize access to operations exposed via methods, rather than directly to the underlying resources. That said it is still essential to secure system level resources using platform level security such as Windows ACLs and so on. Many of the most common application level authorization schemes use roles to categorize groups of users who share the same privileges within the application.

The various authorization options and gatekeepers available to ASP.NET application developers are discussed further in Chapter 2.

Secure Communication

Many applications pass sensitive data among the application tiers, from database server to browser and vice-versa. Examples of sensitive data include bank account details, credit card numbers, payroll data and so on. Additionally, applications must secure logon credentials as they are passed across the network.

Secure communication provides the following two features:

- **Privacy**. Privacy is concerned with ensuring that data remains private and confidential, and cannot be viewed by eavesdroppers who may be armed with network monitoring software. Privacy is usually provided by means of encryption.

- **Integrity**. Secure communication channels must also ensure that data is protected from accidental or deliberate (malicious) modification while in transit. Integrity is usually provided by using Message Authentication Codes (MACs).

It's important to apply secure communication techniques both inside and outside of the firewall as many unwanted forms of information disclosure and security breeches occur internally on corporate networks.

Secure communication and the various approaches available are discussed further in Chapter 4.

Tying the Technologies Together

ASP.NET Web applications are developed using many different technologies and products. Various approaches to authentication, authorization and secure communication are required throughout your application's multiple tiers to ensure a defense in depth security strategy.

Figure 1 on the next page summarizes the various technologies together with the primary authentication and authorization options provided by each one.

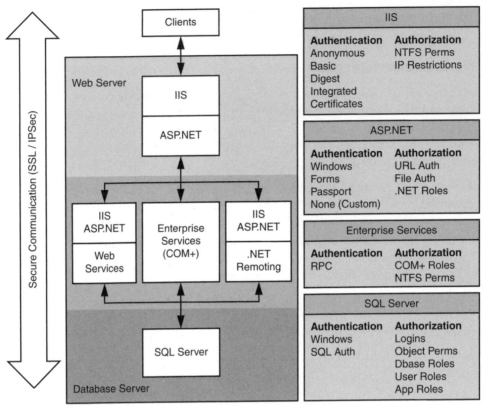

Figure 1
.NET Web Application Security

Design Principles

There are a number of overarching principles that apply to the guidance presented in later chapters. You should learn these principles and apply them to your application designs:

- **Adopt the principle of least privilege**. Processes that run script or execute code should run under a least privileged account to limit the potential damage that can be done if the process is compromised. If a malicious user manages to inject code into a server process, the privileges granted to that process determine to a large degree the types of operations the user is able to perform. Code that requires additional trust (and raised privileges) should be isolated within separate processes.

The ASP.NET team made a conscious decision to run the ASP.NET account with least privileges (using the ASPNET account). This change was implemented for the initial release of the .NET Framework. During beta releases, ASP.NET ran as SYSTEM, an inherently less secure setting.

- **Use defense in depth**. Place check points within each of the layers and sub-systems within your application. The check points are the gatekeepers that ensure that only authenticated and authorized users are able to access the next down-stream layer.

- **Don't trust user input**. Applications should thoroughly validate all user input before performing operations with that input. The validation may include filtering out special characters. This preventive measure protects the application against accidental misuse or deliberate attacks by people who are attempting to inject malicious commands into the system. Common examples include SQL injection attacks, script injection, and buffer overflow.

- **Use secure defaults**. A common practice among developers is to use reduced security settings, simply to make an application work. If your application demands features that force you to reduce or change default security settings, test the effects and understand the implications before making the change.

- **Don't rely on security by obscurity**. Trying to hide secrets by using misleading variable names or storing them in odd file locations does not provide security. In a game of hide-and-seek, it's better to use platform features or proven techniques for securing your data.

- **Check at the gate**. You don't always need to flow a user's security context to the back end for authorization checks. Often, in a distributed system, this is not the best choice. Checking the client at the gate refers to authorizing the user at the first point of authentication (for example, within the Web application on the Web server), and determining which resources and operations (potentially provided by downstream services) the user should be allowed to access.

  If you design solid authentication and authorization strategies at the gate, you can circumvent the need to delegate the original caller's security context all the way through to your application's data tier.

- **Assume external systems are insecure**. If you don't own it, don't assume security is taken care of for you.

- **Reduce surface area**. Avoid exposing information that is not required. By doing so, you are potentially opening doors that can lead to additional vulnerabilities. Also, handle errors gracefully; don't expose any more information than is required when returning an error message to the end user.

- **Fail to a secure mode**. If your application fails, make sure it does not leave sensitive data unprotected. Also, do not provide too much detail in error messages; in other words, don't include details that could help an attacker exploit a vulnerability in your application. Write detailed error information to the Windows event log.

- **Remember you are only as secure as your weakest link**. Security is a concern across all of your application tiers.

- **If you don't use it, disable it**. You can remove potential points of attack by disabling modules and components that your application does not require. For example, if your application doesn't use output caching, then you should disable the ASP.NET output cache module. If a future security vulnerability is found in the module, your application is not threatened.

Summary

This chapter has provided some foundation material to prepare you for the rest of the book. Make sure you are familiar with the core concepts and principles introduced in this chapter, because these are used and referenced extensively throughout the forthcoming chapters.

2

Security Model for
ASP.NET Applications

This chapter introduces .NET Web application security. It provides an overview of the security features and services that span the tiers of a typical .NET Web application. It also introduces .NET Framework security and explains which elements are most significant for ASP.NET Web application developers. The core concepts of principal and identity objects are also introduced.

The goal of the chapter is to:

- Provide a frame of reference for typical .NET Web applications.
- Identify the authentication, authorization, and secure communication security features provided by the various implementation technologies used to build .NET Web applications.
- Identify gatekeepers and gates that can be used in your application to enforce trust boundaries.
- Introduce identities and principals.

.NET Web Applications

This section provides a brief introduction to .NET Web applications and describes their characteristics both from a logical and physical viewpoint. It also provides an introduction to the various implementation technologies used to build .NET Web applications.

Logical Tiers

Logical application architecture views any system as a set of cooperating services grouped in the following layers:

- User Services
- Business Services
- Data Services

The value of this logical architecture view is to identify the generic types of services invariably present in any system, to ensure proper segmentation, and to drive the definition of interfaces between tiers. This segmentation allows you to make more discreet architecture and design choices when implementing each layer, and to build a more maintainable application.

The layers can be described as follows:

- **User Services** are responsible for the client interaction with the system and provide a common bridge into the core business logic encapsulated by components within the Business Services layer. Traditionally, User Services are associated most often with interactive users. However, they also perform the initial processing of programmatic requests from other systems, where no visible user interface is involved. Authentication and authorization, the precise nature of which varies depending upon the client type, are typically performed within the User Services layer.

- **Business Services** provide the core functionality of the system and encapsulate business logic. They are independent from the delivery channel and back-end systems or data sources. This provides the stability and flexibility necessary to evolve the system to support new and different channels and back-end systems. Typically, to service a particular business request involves a number of cooperating components within the Business Services layer.

- **Data Services** provide access to data (hosted within the boundaries of the system), and to other (back-end) systems through generic interfaces, which are convenient to use from components within the Business Services layer. Data Services abstract the multitude of back-end systems and data sources, and encapsulate specific access rules and data formats.

The logical classification of service types within a system may correlate with, but is relatively independent from, the possible physical distribution of the components implementing the services.

It is also important to remember that the logical tiers can be identified at any level of aggregation; that is, the tiers can be identified for the system as a whole (in the context of its environment and external interactions) and for any contained subsystem. For example, each remote node that hosts a Web service consists of User Services (handling incoming requests and messages), Business Services, and Data Services.

Physical Deployment Models

The three logical service layers described earlier, in no way imply specific numbers of physical tiers. All three logical services may be physically located on the same computer, or they may be spread across multiple computers.

The Web Server as an Application Server

A common deployment pattern for .NET Web applications is to locate business and data access components on the Web server. This minimizes the network hops, which can help performance. This model is shown in Figure 2.1.

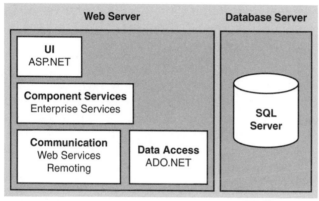

Figure 2.1
The Web server as an application server

Remote Application Tier

The remote application tier is a common deployment pattern, particularly for Internet scenarios where the Web tier is self-contained within a perimeter network (also known as DMZ, demilitarized zone, and screened subnet) and is separated from end users and the remote application tier with packet filtering firewalls. The remote application tier is shown in Figure 2.2.

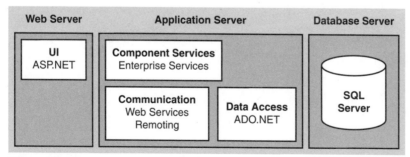

Figure 2.2
The introduction of a remote application tier

Implementation Technologies

.NET Web applications typically implement one or more of the logical services by using the following technologies:

- **ASP.NET**

  ASP.NET is typically used to implement User Services. ASP.NET provides a pluggable architecture that can be used to build Web pages. ASP.NET security is discussed in detail in Chapter 8.

- **Enterprise Services**

  Enterprise Services provide infrastructure-level services to applications. These include distributed transactions and resource management services such as object pooling for .NET components. Enterprise Services security is discussed in detail in Chapter 9.

- **Web Services**

  Web Services enable the exchange of data and the remote invocation of application logic using SOAP-based message exchanges to move data through firewalls and between heterogeneous systems. Web Service security is discussed in detail in Chapter 10.

- **.NET Remoting**

  .NET Remoting provides a framework for accessing distributed objects across process and machine boundaries..NET Remoting security is discussed in detail in Chapter 11.

- **ADO.NET and Microsoft® SQL Server™ 2000**

  ADO.NET provides data access services. It is designed from the ground up for distributed Web applications, and it has rich support for the disconnected scenarios inherently associated with Web applications. SQL Server provides integrated security that uses the operating system authentication mechanisms (Kerberos or NTLM). Authorization is provided by logons and granular permissions that can be applied to individual database objects. Data access security is discussed in detail in Chapter 12.

- **Internet Protocol Security (IPSec)**

  IPSec provides point-to-point, transport level encryption and authentication services. For more information about IPSec, refer to Chapter 4.

- **Secure Sockets Layer (SSL)**

  SSL provides a point-to-point secure communication channel. Data sent over the channel is encrypted. For more information about SSL, refer to Chapter 4.

Security Architecture

Figure 2.3 shows the remote application tier model together with the set of security services provided by the various technologies introduced earlier. Authentication and authorization occurs at many individual points throughout the tiers. These services are provided primarily by Internet Information Services (IIS), ASP.NET, Enterprise Services, and SQL Server. Secure communication channels are also applied throughout the tiers and stretch from the client browser or device, right through to the database. Channels are secured with a combination of Secure Sockets Layer (SSL) or IPSec.

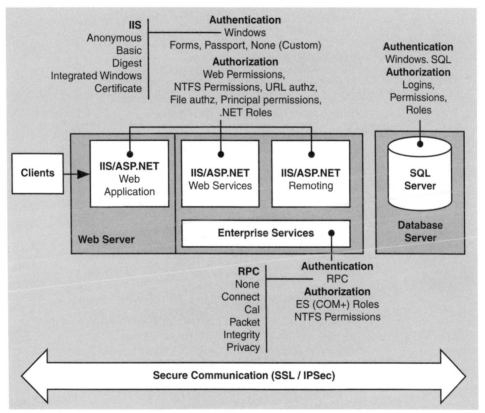

Figure 2.3
Security architecture

Security Across the Tiers

The authentication, authorization, and secure communication features provided by the technologies discussed earlier are summarized in Table 2.1.

Table 2.1: Security features

Technology	Authentication	Authorization	Secure Communication
IIS	Anonymous Basic Digest Windows Integrated (Kerberos/NTLM) Certificate	IP/DNS Address Restrictions Web Permissions NTFS Permissions; Windows Access Control Lists (ACLs) on requested files	SSL
ASP.NET	None (Custom) Windows Forms Passport	File Authorization URL Authorization Principal Permissions .NET Roles	
Web Services	Windows None (Custom) Message level authentication	File Authorization URL Authorization Principal Permissions .NET Roles	SSL and Message level encryption
Remoting	Windows	File Authorization URL Authorization Principal Permissions .NET Roles	SSL and message level encryption
Enterprise Services	Windows	Enterprise Services (COM+) Roles NTFS Permissions	Remote Procedure Call (RPC) Encryption
SQL Server 2000	Windows (Kerberos/NTLM) SQL authentication	Server logins Database logins Fixed database roles User defined roles Application roles Object permissions	SSL
Windows 2000	Kerberos NTLM	Windows ACLs	IPSec

Authentication

The .NET Framework on Windows 2000 provides the following authentication options:

- ASP.NET Authentication Modes
- Enterprise Services Authentication
- SQL Server Authentication

ASP.NET Authentication Modes

ASP.NET authentication modes include Windows, Forms, Passport, and None.

- **Windows authentication**. With this authentication mode, ASP.NET relies on IIS to authenticate users and create a Windows access token to represent the authenticated identity. IIS provides the following authentication mechanisms:

  - **Basic authentication**. Basic authentication requires the user to supply credentials in the form of a user name and password to prove their identity. It is a proposed Internet standard based on RFC 2617: *http://www.faqs.org/rfcs /rfc2617.html*. Both Netscape Navigator and Microsoft Internet Explorer support Basic authentication. The user's credentials are transmitted from the browser to the Web server in an unencrypted Base64 encoded format. Because the Web server obtains the user's credentials unencrypted, the Web server can issue remote calls (for example, to access remote computers and resources) using the user's credentials.

    Note: Basic authentication should only be used in conjunction with a secure channel (typically established by using SSL). Otherwise, user names and passwords can be easily stolen with network monitoring software. If you use Basic authentication you should use SSL on all pages (not just a logon page), because credentials are passed on all subsequent requests. For more information about using Basic authentication with SSL, see Chapter 8, "ASP.NET Security."

  - **Digest authentication**. Digest authentication, introduced with IIS 5.0, is similar to Basic authentication except that instead of transmitting the user's credentials unencrypted from the browser to the Web server, it transmits a hash of the credentials. As a result it is more secure, although it requires an Internet Explorer 5.0 or later client and specific server configuration.

  - **Integrated Windows authentication**. Integrated Windows Authentication (Kerberos or NTLM depending upon the client and server configuration) uses a cryptographic exchange with the user's Internet Explorer Web browser to confirm the identity of the user. It is supported only by Internet Explorer (and not by Netscape Navigator), and as a result tends to be used only in intranet scenarios, where the client software can be controlled. It is used only by the Web server if either anonymous access is disabled or if anonymous access is denied through Windows file system permissions.

- **Certificate authentication**. Certificate authentication uses client certificates to positively identify users. The client certificate is passed by the user's browser (or client application) to the Web server. (In the case of Web services, the Web services client passes the certificate by means of the ClientCertificates property of the HttpWebRequest object). The Web server then extracts the user's identity from the certificate. This approach relies on a client certificate being installed on the user's computer and as a result tends to be used mostly in intranet or extranet scenarios where the user population is well known and controlled. IIS, upon receipt of a client certificate, can map the certificate to a Windows account.

- **Anonymous authentication**. If you do not need to authenticate your clients (or you implement a custom authentication scheme), IIS can be configured for Anonymous authentication. In this event, the Web server creates a Windows access token to represent all anonymous users with the same anonymous (or guest) account. The default anonymous account is IUSR_MACHINENAME, where MACHINENAME is the NetBIOS name of your computer specified at install time.

- **Passport authentication**. With this authentication mode, ASP.NET uses the centralized authentication services of Microsoft Passport. ASP.NET provides a convenient wrapper around functionality exposed by the Microsoft Passport Software Development Kit (SDK), which must be installed on the Web server.

- **Forms authentication**. This approach uses client-side redirection to forward unauthenticated users to a specified HTML form that allows them to enter their credentials (typically user name and password). These credentials are then validated and an authentication ticket is generated and returned to the client. The authentication ticket maintains the user identity and optionally a list of roles that the user is a member of for the duration of the user's session.

  Forms authentication is sometimes used solely for Web site personalization. In this case, you need write little custom code because ASP.NET handles much of the process automatically with simple configuration. For personalization scenarios, the cookie needs to hold only the user name.

  Note: Forms authentication sends the user name and password to the Web server in plain text. As a result, you should use Forms authentication in conjunction with a channel secured by SSL. For continued protection of the authentication cookie transmitted on subsequent requests, you should consider using SSL for all pages within your application and not just the logon page.

- **None**. None indicates that you either don't want to authenticate users or that you are using a custom authentication protocol.

More Information

For more details about ASP.NET authentication, see Chapter 8, "ASP.NET Security."

Enterprise Services Authentication

Enterprises services authentication is performed by using the underlying Remote Procedure Call (RPC) transport infrastructure, which in turn uses the operating system Security Service Provider Interface (SSPI). Clients of Enterprise Services applications may be authenticated using Kerberos or NTLM authentication.

A serviced component can be hosted in a Library application or Server application. Library applications are hosted within client processes and as a result assume the client's identity. Server applications run in separate server processes under their own identity. For more information about identity, see the "Identities and Principals" section later in this chapter.

The incoming calls to a serviced component can be authenticated at the following levels:

- **Default**: The default authentication level for the security package is used.
- **None**: No authentication occurs.
- **Connect**: Authentication occurs only when the connection is made.
- **Call**: Authenticates at the start of each remote procedure call.
- **Packet**: Authenticates and verifies that all call data is received.
- **Packet Integrity**: Authenticates and verifies that none of the data has been modified in transit.
- **Packet Privacy**: Authenticates and encrypts the packet, including the data and the sender's identity and signature.

More Information

For more information about Enterprise Services authentication, see Chapter 9, "Enterprise Services Security."

SQL Server Authentication

SQL Server can authenticate users by using Windows authentication (NTLM or Kerberos) or can use its own built-in authentication scheme referred to as SQL authentication. The following two options are available:

- **SQL Server and Windows**. Clients can connect to an instance of Microsoft SQL Server by using either SQL Server authentication or Windows authentication. This is sometimes referred to as mixed mode authentication.
- **Windows Only**. The user must connect to the instance of Microsoft SQL Server by using Windows authentication.

More Information

The relative merits of each approach are discussed in Chapter 12, "Data Access Security."

Authorization

The .NET Framework on Windows 2000 provides of the following authorization options:

- ASP.NET Authorization Options
- Enterprise Services Authorization
- SQL Server Authorization

ASP.NET Authorization Options

ASP.NET authorization options can be used by ASP.NET Web applications, Web services and remote components. ASP.NET provides the following authorization options:

- **URL Authorization**. This is an authorization mechanism, configured by settings within machine and application configuration files. URL Authorization allows you to restrict access to specific files and folders within your application's Uniform Resource Identifier (URI) namespace. For example, you can selectively deny or allow access to specific files or folders (addressed by means of a URL) to nominated users. You can also restrict access based on the user's role membership and the type of HTTP verb used to issue a request (GET, POST, and so on).

  URL Authorization requires an authenticated identity. This can be obtained by a Windows or ticket-based authentication scheme.

- **File Authorization**. File authorization applies only if you use one of the IIS-supplied Windows authentication mechanisms to authenticate callers and ASP.NET is configured for Windows authentication.

  You can use it to restrict access to specified files on a Web server. Access permissions are determined by Windows ACLs attached to the files.

- **Principal Permission Demands**. Principal permission demands can be used (declaratively or programmatically) as an additional fine-grained access control mechanism. They allow you to control access to classes, methods, or individual code blocks based on the identity and group membership of individual users.

- **.NET Roles**. .NET roles are used to group together users who have the same permissions within your application. They are conceptually similar to previous role-based implementations, for example Windows groups and COM+ roles. However, unlike these earlier approaches, .NET roles do not require authenticated Windows identities and can be used with ticket-based authentication schemes such as Forms authentication.

  .NET roles can be used to control access to resources and operations and they can be configured both declaratively and programmatically.

More Information

For more information about ASP.NET authorization, see Chapter 8, "ASP.NET Security."

Enterprise Services Authorization

Access to functionality contained in serviced components within Enterprise Services applications is governed by Enterprise Services role membership. These are different from .NET roles and can contain Windows group or user accounts. Role membership is defined within the COM+ catalog and is administered by using the Component Services tool.

More Information

For more information about Enterprise Services authorization, see Chapter 9, "Enterprise Services Security."

SQL Server Authorization

SQL Server allows fine-grained permissions that can be applied to individual database objects. Permissions may be based on role membership (SQL Server provides fixed database roles, user defined roles, and application roles), or permission may be granted to individual Windows user or group accounts.

More Information

For more information about SQL Server authorization, see Chapter 12, "Data Access Security."

Gatekeepers and Gates

Throughout the remainder of this book, the term *gatekeeper* is used to identify the technology that is responsible for a *gate*. A gate represents an access control point (guarding a resource) within an application. For example, a resource might be an operation (represented by a method on an object) or a database or file system resource.

Each of the core technologies listed earlier provide gatekeepers for access authorization. Requests must pass through a series of gates before being allowed to access the requested resource or operation. The following describes the gates the requests must pass through:

- IIS provides a gate when you authenticate users (that is, you disable Anonymous authentication). IIS Web permissions can be used as an access control mechanism to restrict the capabilities of Web users to access specific files and folders. Unlike NTFS file permissions, Web permissions apply to all Web users, as opposed to individual users or groups. NTFS file permissions provide further restrictions on Web resources such as Web pages, images files, and so on. These restrictions apply to individual users or groups.

IIS checks Web permissions, followed by NTFS file permissions. A user must be authorized by both mechanisms for them to be able to access the file or folder. A failed Web permission check results in IIS returning an HTTP 403 – Access Forbidden response, whereas a failed NTFS permission check results in IIS returning an HTTP 401 – Access Denied.

- ASP.NET provides various configurable and programmatic gates. These include URL Authorization, File Authorization, Principal Permission demands, and .NET Roles.

- The Enterprise Services gatekeeper uses Enterprise Services roles to authorize access to business functionality.

- SQL Server 2000 includes a series of gates that include server logins, database logins, and database object permissions.

- Windows 2000 provides gates using ACLs attached to secure resources.

The bottom line is that gatekeepers perform authorization based on the identity of the user or service calling into the gate and attempting to access a specific resource. The value of multiple gates is in-depth security with multiple lines of defense. Table 2.2 summaries the set of gatekeepers and identifies for each one the gates that they are responsible for.

Table 2.2: Gatekeepers responsibilities and the gates they provide

Gatekeeper	Gates
Windows Operating System	Logon rights (positive and negative, for example "Deny logon locally") Other privileges (for example "Act as part of the operating system") Access checks against secured resources such as the registry and file system. Access checks use ACLs attached to the secure resources, which specify who is and who is not allowed to access the resource and also the types of operation that may be permitted. TCP/IP filtering IP Security
IIS	Authentication (Anonymous, Basic, Digest, Integrated, Certificate) IP address and domain name restrictions (these can be used as an additional line of defense, but should not be relied upon due to the relative ease of spoofing IP addresses). Web permissions NTFS permissions
ASP.NET	URL Authorization File Authorization Principal Permission Demands .NET Roles
Enterprise Services	Windows (NTLM / Kerberos) authentication Enterprise Services (COM+) roles Impersonation levels

Gatekeeper	Gates
Web Services	Uses gates provided by IIS and ASP.NET
Remoting	Uses gates provided by the host. If hosted in ASP.NET it uses the gates provided by IIS and ASP.NET. If hosted in a Windows service, then you must develop a custom solution.
ADO.NET	Connection strings. Credentials may be explicit or you may use Windows authentication (for example, if you connect to SQL Server)
SQL Server	Server logins Database logins Database object permissions

By using the various gates throughout the tiers of your application, you can filter out users that should be allowed access to your back-end resources. The scope of access is narrowed by successive gates which become more and more granular as the request proceeds through the application to the back-end resources.

Consider the Internet-based application example using IIS that is shown in Figure 2.4.

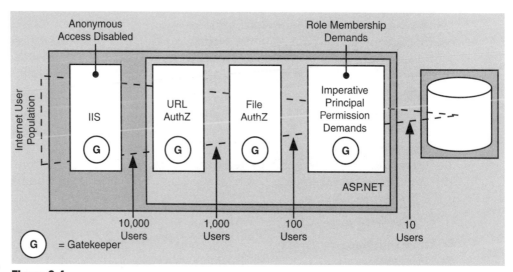

Figure 2.4
Filtering users with gatekeepers

Figure 2.4 illustrates the following:

- You can disable Anonymous authentication in IIS. As a result, only accounts that IIS is able to authenticate are allowed access. This might reduce the potential number of users to 10,000.

- Next, in ASP.NET you use URL Authorization which might reduce the user count to 1,000 users.
- File authorization might further narrow access down to 100 users.
- Finally, your Web application code might allow only 10 users to access your restricted resource, based on specific role membership.

Introducing .NET Framework Security

.NET Framework security is layered on top of Windows security; it does not replace it in any way but provides additional security features. The success or otherwise of all resource access performed by your .NET applications is ultimately determined by operating system security.

For example, if an ASP.NET Web application attempts to open a file, the access attempt is subject to the Windows ACLs associated with file. The identity used for resource access is either the ASP.NET application's process identity or the impersonated identity if the application is currently impersonating.

Code Access Security

The .NET Framework provides an additional security mechanism called Code Access Security (CAS). Conventional security such as that provided by Windows is principal-oriented and authorization decisions are based on the identity of an authenticated principal, for example the user running code, or the user logged into a Web application.

CAS adds another dimension to security by supporting authorization decisions based on the identity of code; not the user who runs the code. This is particularly important for mobile code such as controls and applications downloaded from the Internet through Internet Explorer. Just because you may be logged into your computer as an administrator, do you really want such code to have administrative privileges? – probably not if you are concerned about the integrity and security of your machine.

Evidence and Security Policy

Code is authenticated and its identity is determined using attributes of the code called evidence. Evidence can include an assembly's public key, which is part of its strong name, its download URL, its installed application directory and others. Once the code identity has been established, the gathered evidence is passed through security policy which ultimately governs the capabilities of the code and what permissions it is granted to access secure resources.

Default policy ensures that all code installed on a local machine is fully trusted and is granted an unrestricted set of permissions to access secure resources. As a result any resource access is only subject to operating system security. Code installed on the local machine is fully trusted because a conscious decision is required by an administrator to install the software in the first place.

CAS and ASP.NET Web Applications

ASP.NET Web applications are installed onto the local Web server and as a result default policy grants Web applications full trust on the server. The implication of this for server-side Web application developers is that CAS has limited use. In fact, ASP.NET Web applications built on version 1 of the .NET Framework must run as fully trusted applications.

Note: Version 1.1 of the .NET Framework adds support for partial trust Web applications, which effectively enables CAS for server-side Web applications. The main benefit that this introduces is that it becomes easier to isolate applications from one another and from critical system resources; an important consideration for Internet Service Providers (ISPs) and Application Service Provides (ASPs) who host multiple Web applications developed by different organizations.

Principals and Identities

While CAS is code-centric, other aspects of .NET Framework security are principal-centric. This principal-centric aspect of .NET Framework security is central to ASP.NET application security.

The user centric concept of Windows security is based on security context provided by a logon session while .NET security is based on principal and identity objects.

With traditional Windows programming when you want to know the security context code is running under, the identity of the process owner or currently executing thread is consulted. With .NET programming, if you want to query the security context of the current user, you retrieve the current principal object which is associated with the current thread and accessed through **Thread.CurrentPrincipal**.

The .NET Framework uses principal objects, which contain identity objects to represent users when .NET code is running and together they provide the backbone of .NET role-based authorization. For ASP.NET Web applications, the authenticated user is represented by a principal and identity object attached to the current thread and Web request.

The IPrincipal and IIdentity Interfaces

Identity and principal objects must implement the **IIdentity** and **IPrincipal** interfaces respectively. These interfaces are defined within the **System.Security.Principal** namespace. Common interfaces allow the .NET Framework to treat identity and principal objects in a polymorphic fashion, regardless of the underlying implementation details.

The **IPrincipal** interface allows you to test role membership through an **IsInRole** method and also provides access to an associated **IIdentity** object.

```
public interface IPrincipal
{
  bool IsInRole( string role );
  IIdentity Identity {get;}
}
```

The **IIdentity** interface provides additional authentication details such as the name and authentication type.

```
public interface IIdentity
{
  string authenticationType {get;}
  bool IsAuthenticated {get;}
  string Name {get;}
}
```

The .NET Framework supplies a number of concrete implementations of **IPrincipal** and **IIdentity** as shown in Figure 2.5 and described in the following sections.

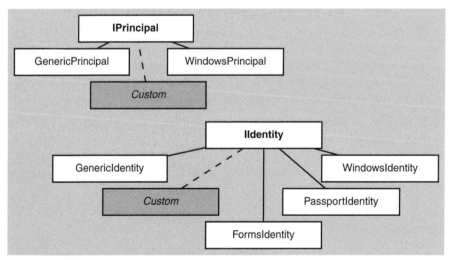

Figure 2.5
IPrincipal and IIdentity implementation classes

WindowsPrincipal and WindowsIdentity

The .NET version of a Windows security context is divided between two classes:

- **WindowsPrincipal**. This class stores the roles associated with the current Windows user. The **WindowsPrincipal** implementation treats Windows groups as roles. The **IPrncipal.IsInRole** method returns true or false based on the user's Windows group membership.

- **WindowsIdentity**. This class holds the identity part of the current user's security context and can be obtained from the static **WindowsIdentity.GetCurrent()** method. This returns a **WindowsIdentity** object that has a **Token** property that returns an **IntPtr** that represents a Windows handle to the access token associated with the current execution thread. This token can then be passed to native Win32® application programming interface (API) functions such as **GetTokenInformation**, **SetTokenInformation**, **CheckTokenMembership** and so on, to retrieve security information about the token.

Note: The static **WindowsIdentity.GetCurrent()** method returns the identity of the currently executing thread, which may or may not be impersonating. This is similar to the Win32 **GetUserName** API.

GenericPrincipal and Associated Identity Objects

These implementations are very simple and are used by applications that do not use Windows authentication and where the application does not need complex representations of a principal. They can be created in code very easily and as a result a certain degree of trust must exist when an application deals with a **GenericPrincipal**.

If you are relying upon using the **IsInRole** method on the **GenericPrincipal** in order to make authorization decisions, you must trust the application that sends you the **GenericPrincipal**. This is in contrast to using **WindowsPrincipal** objects, where you must trust the operating system to provide a valid **WindowsPrincipal** object with an authenticated identity and valid group/role names.

The following types of identity object can be associated with the **GenericPrincipal** class:

- **FormsIdentity**. This class represents an identity that has been authenticated with Forms authentication. It contains a **FormsAuthenticationTicket** which contains information about the user's authentication session.

- **PassportIdentity**. This class represents an identity that has been authenticated with Passport authentication and contains Passport profile information.

- **GenericIdentity**. This class represents a logical user that is not tied to any particular operating system technology and is typically used in association with custom authentication and authorization mechanisms.

ASP.NET and HttpContext.User

Typically, **Thread.CurrentPrincipal** is checked in .NET code before any authorization decisions are made. ASP.NET, however, provides the authenticated user's security context using **HttpContext.User**.

This property accepts and returns an **IPrincipal** interface. The property contains an authenticated user for the current request. ASP.NET retrieves **HttpContext.User** when it makes authorization decisions.

When you use Windows authentication, the Windows authentication module automatically constructs a **WindowsPrincipal** object and stores it in **HttpContext.User**. If you use other authentication mechanisms such as Forms or Passport, you must construct a **GenericPrincipal** object and store it in **HttpContext.User**.

ASP.NET Identities

At any given time during the execution of an ASP.NET Web application, there may be multiple identities present during a single request. These identities include:

- **HttpContext.User** returns an **IPrincipal** object that contains security information for the current Web request. This is the authenticated Web client.

- **WindowsIdentity.GetCurrent()** returns the identity of the security context of the currently executing Win32 thread. By default, this identity is ASPNET; the default account used to run ASP.NET Web applications. However, if the Web application has been configured for impersonation, the identity represents the authenticated user (which if IIS Anonymous authentication is in effect, is IUSR_MACHINE).

- **Thread.CurrentPrincipal** returns the principal of the currently executing .NET thread which rides on top of the Win32 thread.

More Information

- For a detailed analysis of ASP.NET identity for a combination of Web application configurations (both with and without impersonation), see "ASP.NET Identity Matrix" within the "Reference" section of this book.

- For more information about creating your own **IPrincipal** implementation, see Chapter 8, "ASP.NET Security," and "How to implement IPrincipal" in the "Reference" section of this book.

Remoting and Web Services

In the current version of the .NET Framework, Remoting and Web services do not have their own security model. They both inherit the security feature of IIS and ASP.NET.

Although there is no security built into the remoting architecture, it was designed with security in mind. It is left up to the developer and/or administrator to incorporate certain levels of security in remoting applications. Whether or not principal objects are passed across remoting boundaries depends on the location of the client and remote object, for example:

- **Remoting within the same process**. When remoting is used between objects in the same or separate application domain(s), the remoting infrastructure copies a reference to the **IPrincipal** object associated with the caller's context to the receiver's context.

- **Remoting across processes**. In this case, **IPrincipal** objects are not transmitted between processes. The credentials used to construct the original **IPrincipal** must be transmitted to the remote process, which may be located on a separate computer. This allows the remote computer to construct an appropriate **IPrincipal** object based on the supplied credentials.

Summary

This chapter has introduced the full set of authentication and authorization options provided by the various .NET related technologies. It also introduced .NET Framework security together with principal and identity objects which are central to ASP.NET authorization.

By using multiple gatekeepers throughout your .NET Web application, you will be able to implement a defense-in-depth security strategy. To summarize:

- ASP.NET applications can use the existing security features provided by Windows and IIS.

- A combination of SSL and IPSec can be used to provide secure communications across the layers of a .NET Web application; for example, from browser to database.

- Use SSL to protect the clear text credentials passed across the network when you use Basic or Forms authentication.

- ASP.NET Web applications built on version 1 of the .NET Framework must run as fully trusted applications, which means that Code Access Security is of limited use for server-side Web application developers. Version 1.1 of the .NET Framework will enable partial trust Web applications, at which point CAS will become more significant.

- .NET represents users who have been identified with Windows authentication using a combination of the **WindowsPrincipal** and **WindowsIdentity** classes.

- The **GenericPrincipal** and **GenericIdentity** or **FormsIdentity** classes are used to represent users who have been identified with non-Windows authentication schemes, such as Forms authentication.

- You can create your own principal and identity implementations by creating classes that implement **IPrincipal** and **IIdentity**.

- Within ASP.NET Web applications, the **IPrincipal** object that represents the authenticated user is associated with the current HTTP Web request using the **HttpContext.User** property.

- Gates are access control points within your application through which authorized users can access resources or services. Gatekeepers are responsible for controlling access to gates.

- Use multiple gatekeepers to provide a defense-in-depth strategy.

- Web services and .NET remoting rely on the underlying security services provided by ASP.NET and IIS.

The next chapter, Chapter 3, "Authentication and Authorization Design," provides additional information to help you choose the most appropriate authentication and authorization strategy for your particular application scenario.

3

Authentication and Authorization Design

Designing an authentication and authorization strategy for distributed Web applications is a challenging task. The good news is that proper authentication and authorization design during the early phases of your application development helps to mitigate many top security risks.

This chapter will help you design an appropriate authorization strategy for your application and will also help answer the following key questions:

- Where should I perform authorization and what mechanisms should I use?
- What authentication mechanism should I use?
- Should I use Active Directory® directory service for authentication or should I validate credentials against a custom data store?
- What are the implications and design considerations for heterogeneous and homogenous platforms?
- How should I represent users who do not use the Microsoft® Windows® operating system within my application?
- How should I flow user identity throughout the tiers of my application? When should I use operating system level impersonation/delegation?

When you consider authorization, you must also consider authentication. The two processes go hand in hand for two reasons:

- First, any meaningful authorization policy requires authenticated users.
- Second, the way in which you authenticate users (and specifically the way in which the authenticated user identity is represented within your application) determines the available gatekeepers at your disposal.

  Some gatekeepers such as ASP.NET file authorization, Enterprise Services (COM+) roles, and Windows ACLs, require an authenticated Windows identity (in the form of a **WindowsIdentity** object that encapsulates a Windows access token, which defines the caller's security context). Other gatekeepers, such as ASP.NET URL authorization and .NET roles, do not. They simply require an authenticated identity; one that is not necessarily represented by a Windows access token.

Designing an Authentication and Authorization Strategy

The following steps identify a process that will help you develop an authentication and authorization strategy for your application:

1. Identify resources
2. Choose an authorization strategy
3. Choose the identities used for resource access
4. Consider identity flow
5. Choose an authentication approach
6. Decide how to flow identity

Identify Resources

Identify resources that your application needs to expose to clients. Typical resources include:

- Web Server resources such as Web pages, Web services, static resources (HTML pages and images).
- Database resources such as per-user data or application-wide data.
- Network resources such as remote file system resources and data from directory stores such as Active Directory.

You must also identify the system resources that your application needs to access. This is in contrast to resources that are exposed to clients. Examples of system resources include the registry, event logs, and configuration files.

Choose an Authorization Strategy

The two basic authorization strategies are:

- **Role based**. Access to operations (typically methods) is secured based on the role membership of the caller. Roles are used to partition your application's user base into sets of users that share the same security privileges within the application; for example, Senior Managers, Managers and Employees. Users are mapped to roles and if the user is authorized to perform the requested operation, the application uses fixed identities with which to access resources. These identities are trusted by the respective resource managers (for example, databases, the file system, and so on).

- **Resource based**. Individual resources are secured using Windows ACLs. The application impersonates the caller prior to accessing resources, which allows the operating system to perform standard access checks. All resource access is performed using the original caller's security context. This impersonation approach severely impacts application scalability, because it means that connection pooling cannot be used effectively within the application's middle tier.

In the vast majority of .NET Web applications where scalability is essential, a role-based approach to authorization represents the best choice. For certain smaller scale intranet applications that serve per-user content from resources (such as files) that can be secured with Windows ACLs against individual users, a resource-based approach may be appropriate.

The recommended and common pattern for role-based authorization is:

- Authenticate users within your front-end Web application.
- Map users to roles.
- Authorize access to operations (not directly to resources) based on role membership.
- Access the necessary back-end resources (required to support the requested and authorized operations) by using fixed service identities. The back-end resource managers (for example, databases) *trust* the application to authorize callers and are willing to grant permissions to the trusted service identity or identities.

  For example, a database administrator may grant access permissions exclusively to a specific HR application (but not to individual users).

More Information

- For more information about the two contrasting authorization approaches, see "Authorization Approaches" later in this chapter.
- For more information about role-based authorization and the various types of roles that can be used, see "Role-Based Authorization" later in this chapter.

Note: An application level role-based authorization approach still requires the use of resource-based authorization to secure system level resource, for example configuration files, registry keys and so on.

Choose the Identities Used for Resource Access

Answer the question, "who will access resources?"

Choose the identity or identities that should be used to access resources across the layers of your application. This includes resources accessed from Web-based applications, and optionally Web services, Enterprise Services, and .NET Remoting components. In all cases, the identity used for resource access can be:

- **Original caller's identity**. This assumes an impersonation/delegation model in which the original caller identity can be obtained and then flowed through each layer of your system. The delegation factor is a key criteria used to determine your authentication mechanism.

- **Process identity**. This is the default case (without specific impersonation). Local resource access and downstream calls are made using the current process identity. The feasibility of this approach depends on the boundary being crossed, because the process identity must be recognized by the target system.

  This implies that calls are made in one of the following ways:

  - Within the same Windows security domain

  - Across Windows security domains (using trust and domain accounts, or duplicated user names and passwords where no trust relationship exists)

- **Service account**. This approach uses a (fixed) service account. For example:

  - For database access this might be a fixed SQL user name and password presented by the component connecting to the database.

  - When a fixed Windows identity is required, use an Enterprise Services server application.

- **Custom identity**. When you don't have Windows accounts to work with, you can construct your own identities (using **IPrincipal** and **IIdentity** implementations) that can contain details that relate to your own specific security context. For example, these could include role lists, unique identifiers, or any other type of custom information.

  By implementing your custom identity with **IPrincipal** and **IIdentity** types and placing them in the current Web context (using **HttpContext.User**), you immediately benefit from built-in gatekeepers such as .NET roles and **PrincipalPermission** demands.

Consider Identity Flow

To support per-user authorization, auditing, and per-user data retrieval you may need to flow the original caller's identity through various application tiers and across multiple computer boundaries. For example, if a back-end resource manager needs to perform per-caller authorization, the caller's identity must be passed to that resource manager.

Based on resource manager authorization requirements and the auditing requirements of your system, identify which identities need to be passed through your application.

Choose an Authentication Approach

Two key factors that influence the choice of authentication approach are first and foremost the nature of your application's user base (what types of browsers are they using and do they have Windows accounts), and secondly your application's impersonation/delegation and auditing requirements.

More Information

For more detailed considerations that help you to choose an authentication mechanism for your application, see "Choosing an Authentication Mechanism" later in this chapter.

Decide How to Flow Identity

You can flow identity (to provide security context) at the application level or you can flow identity and security context at the operating system level.

To flow identity at the application level, use method and stored procedure parameters. Application identity flow supports:

- Per-user data retrieval using trusted query parameters

```
SELECT x,y FROM SomeTable WHERE username="bob"
```

- Custom auditing within any application tier

Operating system identity flow supports:

- Platform level auditing (for example, Windows auditing and SQL Server auditing)
- Per-user authorization based on Windows identities

To flow identity at the operating system level, you can use the impersonation/delegation model. In some circumstances you can use Kerberos delegation, while in others (where perhaps the environment does not support Kerberos) you may need to use other approaches such as, using Basic authentication. With Basic authentication, the user's credentials are available to the server application and can be used to access downstream network resources.

More Information

For more information about flowing identity and how to obtain an impersonation token with network credentials (that is, supports delegation), see "Flowing Identity" later in this chapter.

Authorization Approaches

There are two basic approaches to authorization:

- **Role based**. Users are partitioned into application-defined, logical roles. Members of a particular role share the same privileges within the application. Access to operations (typically expressed by method calls) is authorized based on the role-membership of the caller.

  Resources are accessed using fixed identities (such as a Web application's or Web service's process identity). The resource managers trust the application to correctly authorize users and they authorize the *trusted* identity.

- **Resource based**. Individual resources are secured using Windows ACLs. The ACL determines which users are allowed to access the resource and also the types of operation that each user is allowed to perform (read, write, delete, and so on).

  Resources are accessed using the original caller's identity (using impersonation).

Role Based Authorization

With a role (or operations) based approach to security, access to operations (not back-end resources) is authorized based on the role membership of the caller. Roles (analyzed and defined at application design time) are used as logical containers that group together users who share the same security privileges (or capabilities) within the application. Users are mapped to roles within the application and role membership is used to control access to specific operations (methods) exposed by the application.

Where within your application this role mapping occurs is a key design criterion; for example:

- On one extreme, role mapping might be performed within a back-end resource manager such as a database. This requires the original caller's security context to flow through your application's tiers to the back-end database.

- On the other extreme, role mapping might be performed within your front-end Web application. With this approach, downstream resource managers are accessed using fixed identities that each resource manager authorizes and is willing to trust.

- A third option is to perform role mapping somewhere in between the front-end and back-end tiers; for example, within a middle tier Enterprise Services application.

In multi-tiered Web applications, the use of trusted identities to access back-end resource managers provides greater opportunities for application scalability (thanks to connection pooling). Also, the use of trusted identities alleviates the need to flow the original caller's security context at the operating system level, something that can be difficult (if not impossible in certain scenarios) to achieve.

Resource Based Authorization

The resource-based approach to authorization relies on Windows ACLs and the underlying access control mechanics of the operating system. The application impersonates the caller and leaves it to the operating system in conjunction with specific resource managers (the file system, databases, and so on) to perform access checks.

This approach tends to work best for applications that provide access to resources that can be individually secured with Windows ACLs, such as files. An example would be an FTP application or a simple data driven Web application. The approach starts to break down where the requested resource consists of data that needs to be obtained and consolidated from a number of different sources; for example, multiple databases, database tables, external applications, or Web services.

The resource-based approach also relies on the original caller's security context flowing through the application to the back-end resource managers. This can require complex configuration and significantly reduces the ability of a multi-tiered application to scale to large numbers of users, because it prevents the efficient use of pooling (for example, database connection pooling) within the application's middle tier.

Resource Access Models

The two contrasting approaches to authorization can be seen within the two most commonly used resource-access security models used by .NET Web applications (and distributed multi-tier applications in general). These are:

- The trusted subsystem model
- The impersonation/delegation model

Each model offers advantages and disadvantages both from a security and scalability perspective. The next sections describe these models.

The Trusted Subsystem Model

With this model, the middle tier service uses a fixed identity to access downstream services and resources. The security context of the original caller does not flow through the service at the operating system level, although the application may choose to flow the original caller's identity at the application level. It may need to do so to support back-end auditing requirements, or to support per-user data access and authorization.

The model name stems from the fact that the downstream service (perhaps a database) trusts the upstream service to authorize callers. Figure 3.1 on the next page shows this model. Pay particular attention to the trust boundary. In this example, the database *trusts* the middle tier to authorize callers and allow only authorized callers to access the database using the trusted identity.

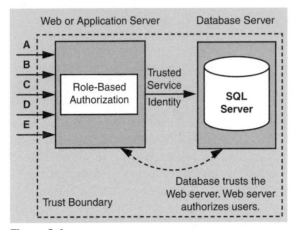

Figure 3.1
The Trusted Subsystem model

The pattern for resource access in the trusted subsystem model is the following:

- Authenticate users
- Map users to roles
- Authorize based on role membership
- Access downstream resource manager using a fixed trusted identity

Fixed Identities

The fixed identity used to access downstream systems and resource managers is often provided by a preconfigured Windows account, referred to as a service account. With a Microsoft SQL Server™ resource manager, this implies Windows authentication to SQL Server.

Alternatively, some applications use a nominated SQL account (specified by a user name and password in a connection string) to access SQL Server. In this scenario, the database must be configured for SQL authentication.

For more information about the relative merits of Windows and SQL authentication when communicating with SQL Server, see Chapter 12, "Data Access Security."

Using Multiple Trusted Identities

Some resource managers may need to be able to perform slightly more fine-grained authorization, based on the role membership of the caller. For example, you may have two groups of users, one who should be authorized to perform read/write operations and the other read-only operations.

Consider the following approach with SQL Server:

- Create two Windows accounts, one for read operations and one for read/write operations.

  More generally, you have separate accounts to mirror application-specific roles. For example, you might want to use one account for Internet users and another for internal operators and/or administrators.

- Map each account to a SQL Server user-defined database role, and establish the necessary database permissions for each role.

- Map users to roles within your application and use role membership to determine which account to impersonate before connecting to the database.

This approach is shown in Figure 3.2.

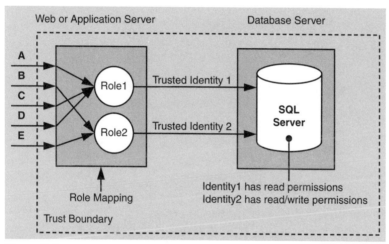

Figure 3.2

Using multiple identities to access a database to support more fine-grained authorization

The Impersonation / Delegation Model

With this model, a service or component (usually somewhere within the logical business services layer) impersonates the client's identity (using operating system-level impersonation) before it accesses the next downstream service. If the next service in line is on the same computer, impersonation is sufficient. Delegation is required if the downstream service is located on a remote computer.

As a result of the delegation, the security context used for the downstream resource access is that of the client. This model is typically used for a couple of reasons:

- It allows the downstream service to perform per-caller authorization using the original caller's identity.

- It allows the downstream service to use operating system-level auditing features.

As a concrete example of this technique, a middle-tier Enterprise Services component might impersonate the caller prior to accessing a database. The database is accessed using a database connection tied to the security context of the original caller. With this model, the database authenticates each and every caller and makes authorization decisions based on permissions assigned to the individual caller's identity (or the Windows group membership of the caller). The impersonation/ delegation model is shown in Figure 3.3.

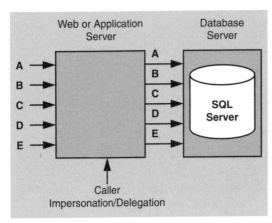

Figure 3.3
The impersonation/delegation model

Choosing a Resource Access Model

The trusted subsystem model is used in the vast majority of Internet applications and large scale intranet applications, primarily for scalability reasons. The impersonation model tends to be used in smaller-scale applications where scalability is not the primary concern and those applications where auditing (for reasons of non-repudiation) is a critical concern.

Advantage of the Impersonation / Delegation Model

The primary advantage of the impersonation / delegation model is auditing (close to the data). Auditing allows administrators to track which users have attempted to access specific resources. Generally auditing is considered most authoritative if the audits are generated at the precise time of resource access and by the same routines that access the resource.

The impersonation / delegation model supports this by maintaining the user's security context for downstream resource access. This allows the back-end system to authoritatively log the user and the requested access.

Disadvantages of the Impersonation / Delegation Model

The disadvantages associated with the impersonation / delegation model include:

- **Technology challenges**. Most security service providers don't support delegation, Kerberos is the notable exception.

    Processes that perform impersonation require higher privileges (specifically the Act *as part of the operating system* privilege). (This restriction applies to Windows 2000 and will not apply to Windows .NET Server).

- **Scalability**. The impersonation / delegation model means that you cannot effectively use database connection pooling, because database access is performed by using connections that are tied to the individual security contexts of the original callers. This significantly limits the application's ability to scale to large numbers of users.

- **Increased administration effort**. ACLs on back-end resources need to be maintained in such a way that each user is granted the appropriate level of access. When the number of back-end resources increases (and the number of users increases), a significant administration effort is required to manage ACLs.

Advantages of the Trusted Subsystem Model

The trusted subsystem model offers the following advantages:

- **Scalability**. The trusted subsystem model supports connection pooling, an essential requirement for application scalability. Connection pooling allows multiple clients to reuse available, pooled connections. It works with this model because all back-end resource access uses the security context of the service account, regardless of the caller's identity.

- **Minimizes back-end ACL management**. Only the service account accesses back-end resources (for example, databases). ACLs are configured against this single identity.

- **Users can't access data directly**. In the trusted-subsystem model, only the middle-tier service account is granted access to the back-end resources. As a result, users cannot directly access back-end data without going through the application (and being subjected to application authorization).

Disadvantages of the Trusted Subsystem Model

The trusted-subsystem model suffers from a couple of drawbacks:

- **Auditing**. To perform auditing at the back end, you can explicitly pass (at the application level) the identity of the original caller to the back end, and have the auditing performed there. You have to trust the middle-tier and you do have a potential repudiation risk. Alternatively, you can generate an audit trail in the middle tier and then correlate it with back-end audit trails (for this you must ensure that the server clocks are synchronized).

- **Increased risk from server compromise**. In the trusted-subsystem model, the middle-tier service is granted broad access to back-end resources. As a result, a compromised middle-tier service potentially makes it easier for an attacker to gain broad access to back-end resources.

Flowing Identity

Distributed applications can be divided into multiple secure subsystems. For example, a front-end Web application, a middle-tier Web service, a remote component, and a database represent four different security subsystems. Each performs authentication and authorization.

You must identify those subsystems that must flow the caller's identity (and associated security context) to the next downstream subsystem in order to support authorization against the original caller.

Application vs. Operating System Identity Flow

Strategies for flowing identities include using the delegation features of the operating system or passing tickets and/or credentials at the application level. For example:

- To flow identity at the application level, you typically pass credentials (or tickets) using method arguments or stored procedure parameters.

Note: GenericPrincipal objects that carry the authenticated caller's identity do not automatically flow across processes. This requires custom code.

You can pass parameters to stored procedures that allow you to retrieve and process user-specific data. For example:

```
SELECT CreditLimit From Table Where UserName="Bob"
```

This approach is sometimes referred to as a *trusted query parameter* approach.

- Operating system identity flow requires an extended form of impersonation called delegation.

Impersonation and Delegation

Under typical circumstances, threads within a server application run using the security context of the server process. The attributes that comprise the process' security context are maintained by the process' logon session and are exposed by the process level Windows access token. All local and remote resource access is performed using the process level security context that is determined by the Windows account used to run the server process.

Impersonation

When a server application is configured for impersonation, an impersonation token is attached to the thread used to process a request. The impersonation token represents the security context of the authenticated caller (or anonymous user). Any local resource access is performed using the thread impersonation token that results in the use of the caller's security context.

Delegation

If the server application thread attempts to access a remote resource, delegation is required. Specifically, the impersonated caller's token must have network credentials. If it doesn't, all remote resource access is performed as the anonymous user (AUTHORITY\ANONYMOUS LOGON).

There are a number of factors that determine whether or not a security context can be delegated. Table 3.1 shows the various IIS authentication types and for each one indicates whether or not the security context of the authenticated caller can be delegated.

Table 3.1: IIS Authentication types

Authentication Type	Can Delegate	Notes
Anonymous	Depends	If the anonymous account (by default IUSR_MACHINE) is configured in IIS as a local account, it cannot be delegated unless the local (Web server) and remote computer have identical local accounts (with matching usernames and passwords). If the anonymous account is a domain account it can be delegated.
Basic	Yes	If Basic authentication is used with local accounts, it can be delegated if the local accounts on the local and remote computers are identical. Domain accounts can also be delegated.
Digest	No	
Integrated Windows	Depends	Integrated Windows authentication either results in NTLM or Kerberos (depending upon the version of operating system on client and server computer). NTLM does not support delegation. Kerberos supports delegation with a suitably configured environment. For more information, see "How To: Implement Kerberos Delegation for Windows 2000" in the References section of this book.

(continued)

Authentication Type	Can Delegate	Notes
Client Certificates	Depends	Can be delegated if used with IIS certificate mapping and the certificate is mapped to a local account that is duplicated on the remote computer or is mapped to a domain account. This works because the credentials for the mapped account are stored on the local server and are used to create an Interactive logon session (which has network credentials). Active Directory certificate mapping does not support delegation.

Important: Kerberos delegation under Windows 2000 is unconstrained. In other words, a user may be able to make multiple network hops across multiple remote computers. To close this potential security risk, you should limit the scope of the domain account's reach by removing the account from the Domain Users group and allow the account to be used only to log on to specific computers.

Role-Based Authorization

Most .NET Web applications will use a role-based approach to authorization. You need to consider the various role types and choose the one(s) most appropriate for your application scenario. You have the following options:

- .NET roles
- Enterprise Services (COM+) roles
- SQL Server User Defined Database roles
- SQL Server Application roles

.NET Roles

.NET roles are extremely flexible and revolve around **IPrincipal** objects that contain the list of roles that an authenticated identity belongs to. .NET roles can be used within Web applications, Web services, or remote components hosted within ASP.NET (and accessed using the HttpChannel).

You can perform authorization using .NET roles either declaratively using **PrincipalPermission** demands or programmatically in code, using imperative **PrincipalPermission** demands or the **IPrincipal.IsInRole** method.

.NET Roles with Windows Authentication

If your application uses Windows authentication, ASP.NET automatically constructs a **WindowsPrincipal** that is attached to the context of the current Web request (using **HttpContext.User**). After the authentication process is complete and ASP.NET has attached to object to the current request, it is used for all subsequent .NET role-based authorization.

The Windows group membership of the authenticated caller is used to determine the set of roles. With Windows authentication, .NET roles are the same as Windows groups.

.NET Roles with non-Windows Authentication

If your application uses a non-Windows authentication mechanism such as Forms or Passport, you must write code to create a **GenericPrincipal** object (or a custom **IPrincipal** object) and populate it with a set of roles obtained from a custom authentication data store such as a SQL Server database.

Custom IPrincipal Objects

The .NET Role-based security mechanism is extensible. You can develop your own classes that implement **IPrincipal** and **IIdentity** and provide your own extended role-based authorization functionality.

As long as the custom **IPrincipal** object (containing roles obtained from a custom data store) is attached to the current request context (using **HttpContext.User**), basic role-checking functionality is ensured.

By implementing the **IPrincipal** interface, you ensure that both the declarative and imperative forms of **PrincipalPermission** demands work with your custom identity. Furthermore, you can implement extended role semantics; for example, by providing an additional method such as **IsInMultipleRoles(string [] roles)** which would allow you to test and assert for membership of multiple roles.

More Information

- For more information about .NET role-based authorization, see Chapter 8, "ASP.NET Security."
- For more information about creating **GenericPrincipal** objects, see "How to use Forms authentication with GenericPrincipal objects" in the Reference section of this book.

Enterprise Services (COM+) Roles

Using Enterprise Services (COM+) roles pushes access checks to the middle tier and allows you to use database connection pooling when connecting to back-end databases. However, for meaningful Enterprise Services (COM+) role-based authorization, your front-end Web application must impersonate and flow the original caller's identity (using a Windows access token) to the Enterprise Services application. To achieve this, the following entries must be placed in the Web application's Web.config file.

```
<authentication mode="Windows" />
<identity impersonate="true" />
```

If it is sufficient to use declarative checks at the method level (to determine which users can call which methods), you can deploy your application and update role membership using the Component Services administration tool.

If you require programmatic checks in method code, you lose some of the administrative and deployment advantages of Enterprise Services (COM+) roles, because role logic is hard-coded.

SQL Server User Defined Database Roles

With this approach, you create roles in the database, assign permissions based on the roles and map Windows group and user accounts to the roles. This approach requires you to flow the caller's identity to the back end (if you are using the preferred Windows authentication to SQL Server).

SQL Server Application Roles

With this approach, permissions are granted to the roles within the database, but SQL Server application roles contain no user or group accounts. As a result, you lose the granularity of the original caller.

With application roles, you are authorizing access to a specific application (as opposed to a set of users). The application activates the role using a built-in stored procedure that accepts a role name and password. One of the main disadvantages of this approach is that it requires the application to securely manage credentials (the role name and associated password).

More Information

For more information about SQL Server user defined database roles and application roles, see Chapter 12, "Data Access Security."

.NET Roles versus Enterprise Services (COM+) Roles

The following table presents a comparison of the features of .NET roles and Enterprise Services (COM+) roles.

Table 3.2: Comparing Enterprise Services roles with .NET roles

Feature	Enterprise Services Roles	.NET Roles
Administration	Component Services Administration Tool	Custom
Data Store	COM+ Catalog	Custom data store (for example, SQL Server or Active Directory)

Declarative	Yes
	[SecurityRole("Manager")]
		Yes
		[PrincipalPermission(
		    SecurityAction.Demand,
		    Role="Manager")]

Imperative	Yes ContextUtil.IsCallerInRole()	Yes IPrincipal.IsInRole
Class, Interface and Method Level Granularity	Yes	Yes
Extensible	No	Yes (using custom IPrincipal implementation)
Available to all .NET components	Only for components that derive from ServicedComponent base class	Yes
Role Membership	Roles contain Windows group or user accounts	When using WindowsPrincipals, roles ARE Windows groups – no extra level of abstraction
Requires explicit Interface implementation	Yes To obtain method level authorization, an interface must be explicitly defined and implemented	No

Using .NET Roles

You can secure the following items with .NET roles:

- Files
- Folders
- Web pages (.aspx files)
- Web services (.asmx files)
- Objects
- Methods and properties
- Code blocks within methods

The fact that you can use .NET roles to protect operations (performed by methods and properties) and specific code blocks means that you can protect access to local and remote resources accessed by your application.

Note: The first four items in the preceding list (Files, folders, Web pages, and Web services) are protected using the **UrlAuthorizationModule**, which can use the role membership of the caller (and the caller's identity) to make authorization decisions.

If you use Windows authentication, much of the work required to use .NET roles is done for you. ASP.NET constructs a **WindowsPrincipal** object and the Windows group membership of the user determines the associated role set.

To use .NET roles with a non-Windows authentication mechanism, you must write code to:

- Capture the user's credentials.
- Validate the user's credentials against a custom data store such as a SQL Server database.
- Retrieve a role list, construct a **GenericPrincipal** object and associate it with the current Web request.

  The **GenericPrincipal** object represents the authenticated user and is used for subsequent .NET role checks, such as declarative **PrincipalPermission** demands and programmatic **IPrincipal.IsInRole** checks.

More Information

For more information about the process involved in creating a **GenericPrincipal** object for Forms authentication, see Chapter 8, "ASP.NET Security."

Checking Role Membership

The following types of .NET role checks are available:

> **Important:** .NET role checking relies upon an **IPrincipal** object (representing the authenticated user) being associated with the current request. For ASP.NET Web applications, the **IPrincipal** object must be attached to **HttpContext.User**. For Windows Forms applications, the **IPrincipal** object must be attached to **Thread.CurrentPrincipal**.

- **Manual role checks**. For fine-grained authorization, you can call the **IPrincipal.IsInRole** method to authorize access to specific code blocks based on the role membership of the caller. Both AND and OR logic can be used when checking role membership.

- **Declarative role checks (gates to your methods)**. You can annotate methods with the **PrincipalPermissionAttribute** class (which can be shortened to **PrincipalPermission**), to declaratively demand role membership. These support OR logic only. For example you can demand that a caller is in at least one specific role (for example, the caller must be a teller or a manager). You cannot specify that a caller must be a manager and a teller using declarative checks.

- **Imperative role checks (checks within your methods)**. You can call **PrincipalPermission.Demand** within code to perform fine-grained authorization logic. Logical AND and OR operations are supported.

Role Checking Examples

The following code fragments show some example role checks using programmatic, declarative, and imperative techniques.

Authorizing Bob to perform an operation:

> **Note:** Although you can authorize individual users, you should generally authorize based on role membership which allows you to authorize sets of users who share the same privileges within your application.

- Direct user name check

```
GenericIdentity userIdentity = new GenericIdentity("Bob");
if (userIdentity.Name=="Bob")
{
}
```

- Declarative check

```
[PrincipalPermissionAttribute(SecurityAction.Demand, User="Bob")]
public void DoPrivilegedMethod()
{
}
```

- Imperative check

```
PrincipalPermission permCheckUser = new PrincipalPermission(
                                          "Bob", null);
permCheckUser.Demand();
```

Authorizing tellers to perform an operation:

- Direct role name check

```
GenericIdentity userIdentity = new GenericIdentity("Bob");
// Role names would be retrieved from a custom data store
string[] roles = new String[]{"Manager", "Teller"};
GenericPrincipal userPrincipal = new GenericPrincipal(userIdentity,
                                                      roles);
if (userPrincipal.IsInRole("Teller"))
{
}
```

- Declarative check

```
[PrincipalPermissionAttribute(SecurityAction.Demand, Role="Teller")]
void SomeTellerOnlyMethod()
{
}
```

- Imperative check

```
public SomeMethod()
{
  PrincipalPermission permCheck = new PrincipalPermission(
                                          null,"Teller");
  permCheck.Demand();
  // Only Tellers can execute the following code
  // Non members of the Teller role result in a security exception
  . . .
}
```

Authorize managers OR tellers to perform operation:

- Direct role name check

```
if (Thread.CurrentPrincipal.IsInRole("Teller") ||
    Thread.CurrentPrincipal.IsInRole("Manager"))
{
  // Perform privileged operations
}
```

- Declarative check

```
[PrincipalPermissionAttribute(SecurityAction.Demand, Role="Teller"),
 PrincipalPermissionAttribute(SecurityAction.Demand, Role="Manager")]
public void DoPrivilegedMethod()
{
  ...
}
```

- Imperative check

```
PrincipalPermission permCheckTellers = new PrincipalPermission(
                                           null,"Teller");
PrincipalPermission permCheckManagers = new PrincipalPermission(
                                           null,"Manager");
(permCheckTellers.Union(permCheckManagers)).Demand();
```

Authorize only those people who are managers AND tellers to perform operation:

- Direct role name check

```
if (Thread.CurrentPrincipal.IsInRole("Teller") &&
    Thread.CurrentPrincipal.IsInRole("Manager"))
{
  // Perform privileged operation
}
```

- Declarative check

  It is not possible to perform AND checks with .NET roles declaratively. Stacking **PrincipalPermission** demands together results in a logical OR.

- Imperative check

```
PrincipalPermission permCheckTellers = new PrincipalPermission(
                                           null,"Teller");
permCheckTellers.Demand();
PrincipalPermission permCheckManagers = new PrincipalPermission(
                                           null, "Manager");
permCheckManagers.Demand();
```

Choosing an Authentication Mechanism

This section presents guidance which is designed to help you choose an appropriate authentication mechanism for common application scenarios. You should start by considering the following issues:

- **Identities**. A Windows authentication mechanism is appropriate only if your application's users have Windows accounts that can be authenticated by a trusted authority accessible by your application's Web server.

- **Credential management**. One of the key advantages of Windows authentication is that it enables you to let the operating system take care of credential management. With non-Windows approaches, such as Forms authentication, you must carefully consider where and how you store user credentials. The two most common approaches are to use:

- SQL Server databases
- User objects within Active Directory

For more information about the security considerations of using SQL Server as a credential store, see Chapter 12, "Data Access Security."

For more information about using Forms authentication against custom data stores (including Active Directory), see Chapter 8, "ASP.NET Security."

- **Identity flow**. Do you need to implement an impersonation/delegation model and flow the original caller's security context at the operating system level across tiers? For example, to support auditing or per-user (granular) authorization. If so, you need to be able to impersonate the caller and delegate their security context to the next downstream subsystem, as described in the "Delegation" section earlier in this chapter.

- **Browser type**. Do your users all have Internet Explorer or do you need to support a user base with mixed browser types? Table 3.3 illustrates which authentication mechanisms require Internet Explorer browsers, and which support a variety of common browser types.

Table 3.3: Authentication browser requirements

Authentication Type	Requires Internet Explorer	Notes
Forms	No	
Passport	No	
Integrated Windows (Kerberos or NTLM)	Yes	Kerberos also requires Windows 2000 or later operating systems on the client and server computers and accounts configured for delegation. For more information, see "How To: Implement Kerberos Delegation for Windows 2000" in the Reference section of this book.
Basic	No	Basic authentication is part of the HTTP 1.1 protocol that is supported by virtually all browsers
Digest	Yes	
Certificate	No	Clients require X.509 certificates

Internet Scenarios

The basic assumptions for Internet scenarios are:

- Users do not have Windows accounts in the server's domain or in a trusted domain accessible by the server.
- Users do not have client certificates.

Figure 3.4 shows a decision tree for choosing an authentication mechanism for Internet scenarios.

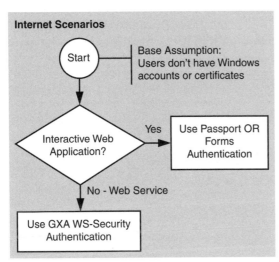

Figure 3.4
Choosing an authentication mechanism for Internet applications

For more information about Web service security and the WS-Security specification, part of the Global XML Architecture (GXA) initiative, see Chapter 10, "Web Services Security."

Forms / Passport Comparison

This section summarizes the relative merits of Forms and Passport authentication.

Advantages of Forms Authentication

- Supports authentication against a custom data store; typically a SQL Server database or Active Directory.
- Supports role-based authorization with role lookup from a data store.
- Smooth integration with Web user interface.
- ASP.NET provides much of the infrastructure. Relatively little custom code is required in comparison to classic ASP.

Advantages of Passport Authentication

- Passport is a centralized solution.
- It removes credential management issues from the application.
- It can be used with role-based authorization schemes.
- It is very secure as it is built on cryptography technologies.

More Information

- For more information about Web service authentication approaches, see Chapter 10, "Web Services Security."
- For more information about using Forms Authentication with SQL Server, see "How To: Use Forms authentication with SQL Server 2000" in the Reference section of this book.

Intranet / Extranet Scenarios

Figure 3.5 shows a decision tree that can be used to help choose an authentication mechanism for intranet and extranet application scenarios.

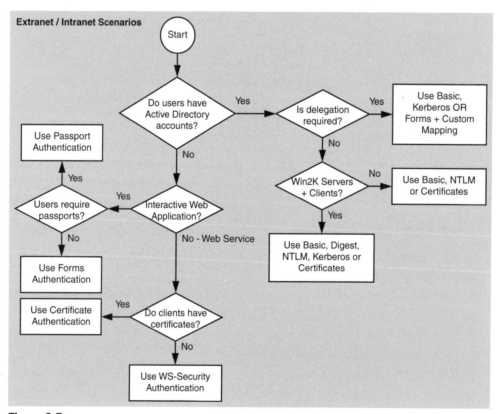

Figure 3.5

Choosing an authentication mechanism for intranet and extranet applications

Authentication Mechanism Comparison

The following table presents a comparison of the available authentication mechanisms.

Table 3.4: Available authentication methods

	Basic	Digest	NTLM	Kerberos	Certs	Forms	Passport
Users need Windows accounts in server's domain	Yes	Yes	Yes	Yes	No	No	No
Supports delegation*	Yes	No	No	Yes	Can do	Yes	Yes
Requires Win2K clients and servers	No	Yes	No	Yes	No	No	No
Credentials passed as clear text (requires SSL)	Yes	No	No	No	No	Yes	No
Supports non-IE browsers	Yes	No	No	No	Yes	Yes	Yes

* Refer to the "Delegation" topic in the "Flowing Identity" section earlier in this chapter for details.

Summary

Designing distributed application authentication and authorization approaches is a challenging task. Proper authentication and authorization design during the early design phases of your application development helps mitigate many of the top security risks. The following summarizes the information in this chapter:

- Use the trusted subsystem resource access model to gain the benefits of database connection pooling.

- If your application does not use Windows authentication, use .NET role checking to provide authorization. Validate credentials against a custom data store, retrieve a role list and create a **GenericPrincipal** object. Associate it with the current Web request (**HttpContext.User**).

- If your application uses Windows authentication and doesn't use Enterprise Services, use .NET roles. Remember that for Windows authentication, .NET roles are Windows groups.

- If your application uses Windows authentication and Enterprise Services, consider using Enterprise Services (COM+) roles.

- For meaningful role-based authorization using Enterprise Services (COM+) roles, the original caller's identity must flow to the Enterprise Services application. If the Enterprise Services application is called from an ASP.NET Web application, this means that the Web application must use Windows authentication and be configured for impersonation.

- Annotate methods with the **PrincipalPermission** attribute to declaratively demand role membership. The method is not called if the caller is not in the specified role and a security exception is generated.

- Call **PrincipalPermission.Demand** within method code (or use **IPrincipal.IsInRole**) for fine-grained authorization decisions.

- Consider implementing a custom **IPrincipal** object to gain additional role-checking semantics.

4

Secure Communication

Many applications pass security sensitive data across networks to and from end users and between intermediate application nodes. Sensitive data might include credentials used for authentication, or data such as credit card numbers or bank transaction details. To guard against unwanted information disclosure and to protect the data from unauthorized modification while in transit, the channel between communication end points must be secured.

Secure communication provides the following two features:

- **Privacy**. Privacy is concerned with ensuring that data remains private and confidential, and cannot be viewed by eavesdroppers who may be armed with network monitoring software. Privacy is usually provided by means of encryption.

- **Integrity**. Secure communication channels must also ensure that data is protected from accidental or deliberate (malicious) modification while in transit. Integrity is usually provided by using Message Authentication Codes (MACs).

This chapter covers the following secure communication technologies:

- **Secure Sockets Layer / Transport Layer Security (SSL/TLS)**. This is most commonly used to secure the channel between a browser and Web server. However, it can also be used to secure Web service messages and communications to and from a database server running Microsoft® SQL Server™ 2000.

- **Internet Protocol Security (IPSec)**. IPSec provides a transport level secure communication solution and can be used to secure the data sent between two computers; for example, an application server and a database server.

- **Remote Procedure Call (RPC) Encryption**. The RPC protocol used by Distributed COM (DCOM) provides an authentication level (packet privacy) that results in the encryption of every packet of data sent between client and server.

Know What to Secure

When a Web request flows across the physical deployment tiers of your application, it crosses a number of communication channels. A commonly used Web application deployment model is shown in Figure 4.1.

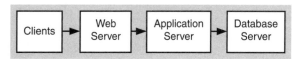

Figure 4.1
A typical Web deployment model

In this typical deployment model, a request passes through three distinct channels. The client-to-Web server link may be over the Internet or corporate intranet and typically uses HTTP. The remaining two links are between internal servers within your corporate domain. Nonetheless, all three links represent potential security concerns. Many purely intranet-based applications convey security sensitive data between tiers; for example, HR and payroll applications that deal with sensitive employee data.

Figure 4.2 shows how each channel can be secured by using a combination of SSL, IPSec and RPC encryption.

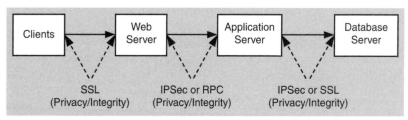

Figure 4.2
A typical Web deployment model, with secure communications

The choice of technology depends on a number of factors including the transport protocol, end point technologies, and environmental considerations (such as hardware, operating system versions, firewalls, and so on).

SSL/TLS

SSL/TLS is used to establish an encrypted communication channel between client and server. The handshake mechanism used to establish the secure channel is well documented and details can be found in the following articles in the Microsoft Knowledge Base:

- Q257591, "Description of the Secure Sockets Layer (SSL) Handshake"
- Q257587, "Description of the Server Authentication Process During the SSL Handshake"
- Q257586, "Description of the Client Authentication Process During the SSL Handshake"

Using SSL

When you use SSL you should be aware of the following:

- When SSL is applied, the client uses the HTTPS protocol (and specifies an https:// URL) and the server listens on TCP port 443.
- You should monitor your application's performance when you enable SSL.

  SSL uses complex cryptographic functions to encrypt and decrypt data and as a result impacts the performance of your application. The largest performance hit occurs during the initial handshake, where asymmetric public/private-key encryption is used. Subsequently (after a secure session key is generated and exchanged), faster, symmetric encryption is used to encrypt application data.

- You should optimize pages that use SSL by including less text and simple graphics in those pages.
- Because the performance hit associated with SSL is greatest during session establishment, ensure that your connections do not time out.

  You can fine tune this by increasing the value of the **ServerCacheTime** registry entry. For more information, see article Q247658, "HOW TO: Configure Secure Sockets Layer Server and Client Cache Elements" in the Microsoft Knowledge Base.

- SSL requires a server authentication certificate to be installed on the Web server (or database server if you are using SSL to communicate with SQL Server 2000). For more information about installing server authentication certificates, see "How to setup SSL on a Web server" within the Reference section of this book.

IPSec

IPSec can be used to secure the data sent between two computers; for example, an application server and a database server. IPSec is completely transparent to applications as encryption, integrity, and authentication services are implemented at the transport level. Applications continue to communicate with one another in the normal manner using TCP and UDP ports.

Using IPSec you can:

- Provide message confidentiality by encrypting all of the data sent between two computers.
- Provide message integrity between two computers (without encrypting data).
- Provide mutual authentication between two computers (not users). For example, you can help secure a database server by establishing a policy that permits requests only from a specific client computer (for example, an application or Web server).
- Restrict which computers can communicate with one another. You can also restrict communication to specific IP protocols and TCP/UDP ports.

Note: IPSec is not intended as a replacement for application level security. Today it is used as a defense-in-depth mechanism or to secure insecure applications without changing them, and to secure non-TLS protocols from network-wire attacks.

Using IPSec

When you use IPSec you should be aware of the following:

- IPSec can be used for both authentication and encryption.
- There are no IPSec APIs for developers to programmatically control settings. IPSec is completely controlled and configured through the IPSec snap-in, within the Local Security Policy Microsoft Management Console (MMC).
- IPSec in the Microsoft Windows® 2000 operating system cannot secure all types of IP traffic.

   Specifically, it cannot be used to secure Broadcast, Multicast, Internet Key Exchange, or Kerberos (which is already a secure protocol) traffic.

   For more information, see article Q253169, "Traffic That Can and Cannot Be Secured by IPSec," in the Microsoft Knowledge Base.

- You use IPSec filters to control when IPSec is applied.

   To test the IPSec policies, use IPSec Monitor. IPSec Monitor (Ipsecmon.exe) provides information about which IPSec policy is active and whether a secure channel between computers is established.

For more information, see these Microsoft Knowledge Base articles:

- Q313195, "HOW TO: Use IPSec Monitor in Windows 2000"
- Q231587, "Using the IP Security Monitor Tool to View IPSec Communications"

- To establish a trust between two servers, you can use IPSec with mutual authentication. This uses certificates to authenticate both computers.

  For more information, see the following Microsoft Knowledge Base articles:

  - Q248711, "Mutual Authentication Methods Supported for L2TP/IPSec"
  - Q253498, "HOW TO: Install a Certificate for Use with IP Security"

- If you need to use IPSec to secure communication between two computers that are separated by a firewall, make sure that the firewall does not use Network Address Translation (NAT). IPSec does not work with any NAT-based devices.

  For more information and configuration steps, see article Q233256, "HOW TO Enable IPSec Traffic through a Firewall" in the Microsoft Knowledge Base and "How To: Use IPSec to Provide Secure Communication between Two Servers" in the Reference section of this book.

RPC Encryption

RPC is the underlying transport mechanism used by DCOM. RPC provides a set of configurable authentication levels that range from no authentication (and no protection of data) to full encryption of parameter state.

The most secure level (RPC Packet Privacy) encrypts parameter state for every remote procedure call (and therefore every DCOM method invocation). The level of RPC encryption, 40-bit or 128-bit, depends on the version of the Windows operating system that is running on the client and server computers.

Using RPC Encryption

You are most likely to want to use RPC encryption when your Web-based application communicates with serviced components (within Enterprise Services server applications) located on remote computers.

In this event, to use RPC Packet Privacy authentication (and encryption) you must configure both the client and the server. A process of high-water mark negotiation occurs between client and server, which ensures that the higher of the two (client and server) settings are used.

The server settings can be defined at the (Enterprise Services) application level, either by using .NET attributes within your serviced component assembly, or by using the Component Services administration tool at deployment time.

If the client is an ASP.NET Web application or Web service, the authentication level used by the client is configured using the **comAuthenticationLevel** attribute on the **<processModel>** element within Machine.config. This provides the default authentication level for all ASP.NET applications that run on the Web server.

More Information

For more information about RPC authentication level negotiation and service component configuration, see Chapter 9, "Enterprise Services Security."

Point to Point Security

Point-to-point communication scenarios can be broadly categorized into the following topics:

- Browser to Web Server
- Web Server to Remote Application Server
- Application Server to Database Server

Browser to Web Server

To secure sensitive data sent between a browser and Web server, use SSL. You need to use SSL in the following situations:

- You are using Forms authentication and need to secure the clear text credentials submitted to a Web server from a logon form.

  In this scenario, you should use SSL to secure access to all pages (not just the logon page) to ensure that the authentication cookie, generated as a result on the initial authentication process, remains secure throughout the lifetime of the client's browser session with the application.

- You are using Basic authentication and need to secure the (Base64 encoded) clear text credentials.

  You should use SSL to secure access to all pages (not just the initial log on), as Basic authentication sends the clear text credentials to the Web server with all requests to the application (not just the initial one).

  Note: Base64 is used to encode binary data as printable ASCII text. Unlike encryption, it does not provide message integrity or privacy.

- Your application passes sensitive data between the browser and Web server (and vice-versa); for example, credit card numbers or bank account details.

Web Server to Remote Application Server

The transport channel between a Web server and a remote application server should be secured by using IPSec, SSL or RPC Encryption. The choice depends on the transport protocols, environmental factors (operating system versions, firewalls, and so on).

- **Enterprise Services**. If your remote server hosts one or more serviced components (in an Enterprise Services server application) and you are communicating directly with them (and as a result using DCOM), use RPC Packet Privacy encryption.

  For more information about how to configure RPC encryption between a Web application and remote serviced component, see Chapter 9, "Enterprise Services Security."

- **Web Services**. If your remote server hosts a Web Service, you can choose between IPSec and SSL.

  You should generally use SSL because the Web service already uses the HTTP transport. SSL also allows you to only encrypt the data sent to and from the Web service (and not all traffic sent between the two computers). IPSec results in the encryption of all traffic sent between the two computers.

Note: Message level security (including data encryption) is addressed by the Global XML Web Services Architecture (GXA) initiative and specifically the WS-Security specification. Microsoft provides the Web Services Development Toolkit to allow you to develop message level security solutions. This is available for download at *http://msdn.microsoft.com/webservices/building/wsdk/*.

- **.NET Components (using .NET Remoting)**. If your remote server hosts one or more .NET components and you connect to them over the TCP channel, you can use IPSec to provide a secure communication link. If you host the .NET components within ASP.NET, you can use SSL (configured using IIS).

Application Server to Database Server

To secure the data sent between an application server and database server, you can use IPSec. If your database server runs SQL Server 2000 (and the SQL Server 2000 network libraries are installed on the application server), you can use SSL. This latter option requires a server authentication certificate to be installed in the database server's machine store.

You may need to secure the link to the database server in the following situations:

- You are connecting to the database server and are not using Windows authentication. For example, you may be using SQL authentication to SQL Server or you may be connecting to a non-SQL Server database. In these cases, the credentials are passed in clear text, which can represent a significant security concern.

> **Note:** One of the key benefits of using Windows authentication to SQL Server is that it means that the credentials are not passed across the network. For more information about Windows and SQL authentication, see Chapter 12, "Data Access Security."

- Your application may be submitting and retrieving sensitive data to and from the database (for example, payroll data).

Using SSL to SQL Server

Consider the following points if you use SSL to secure the channel to a SQL Server database:

- For SSL to work, you must install a server authentication certificate in the machine store on the database server computer. The client computer must also have a root Certificate Authority certificate from the same (or trusting) authority that issued the server certificate.
- Clients must have the SQL Server 2000 connectivity libraries installed. Earlier versions or generic libraries will not work.
- SSL only works for TCP/IP (the recommended communication protocol for SQL Server) and named pipes.
- You can configure the server to force the use of encryption for all connections (from all clients).
- On the client, you can:
  - Force the use of encryption for all outgoing connections.
  - Allow client applications to choose whether or not to use encryption on a per-connection basis, by using the connection string.
- Unlike IPSec, configuration changes are not required if the client or server IP addresses change.

More Information

For more information about using SSL to SQL Server, see the following resources:

- "How To: Use SSL to Secure Communication with SQL Server 2000" in the Reference section of this book.
- Webcast: "Microsoft SQL Server 2000: How to Configure SSL Encryption (April 23, 2002)"

Choosing Between IPSec and SSL

Consider the following points when choosing between IPSec and SSL:

- IPSec can used to secure all IP traffic between computers; SSL is specific to an individual application.
- IPSec is a computer-wide setting and does not support the encryption of specific network connections. However, sites can be partitioned to use or not use SSL. Also, when you use SSL to connect to SQL Server, you can choose on a per connection basis (from the client application) whether or not to use SSL.
- IPSec is transparent to applications, so it can be used with secure protocols that run on top of IP such as HTTP, FTP, and SMTP. However, SSL/TLS is closely tied to the application.
- IPSec can be used for computer authentication in addition to encryption. This is particularly significant for trusted subsystem scenarios, where the database authorizes a fixed identity from a specific application (running on a specific computer). IPSec can be used to ensure that only the specific application server can connect to the database server, in order to prevent attacks from other computers.
- IPSec requires that both computers run Windows 2000 or later.
- SSL can work through a NAT-based firewall; IPSec cannot.

Farming and Load Balancing

If you use SSL in conjunction with multiple virtual Web sites, you need to use unique IP addresses or unique port numbers. You cannot use multiple sites with the same IP address and port number. If the IP address is combined with a server affinity setting in a load balancer, this will work fine.

More Information

For more information, see Q187504, "HTTP 1.1 Host Headers Are Not Supported When You Use SSL," in the Microsoft Knowledge Base.

Summary

This chapter described how a combination of SSL, IPSec, and RPC encryption can be used to provide an end-to-end secure communication solution for your distributed application. To summarize:

- Channel security is a concern for data passed over the Internet and on the corporate intranet.

- Consider the security requirements of the Web browser to Web server, Web server to application server, and application server to database server links.

- Secure communication provides privacy and integrity. It does not protect you from non-repudiation (for this use, client certificates)

- Channel security options include SSL, IPSec, and RPC Encryption. The latter option applies when your application uses DCOM to communicate with remote serviced components.

- If you use SSL to communicate with SQL Server, the application can choose (on a per-connection basis) whether or not to encrypt the connection.

- IPSec encrypts all IP traffic that flows between two computers.

- The choice of security mechanism is dependent upon transport protocol, operating system versions, and network considerations (including firewalls).

- There is always a trade-off between secure communication and performance. Choose the level of security that is appropriate to your application requirements.

5
Intranet Security

Access to intranet applications is restricted to a limited group of authorized users (such as employees that belong to a domain). While an intranet setting limits the exposure of your application, you may still face several challenges when you develop authentication, authorization, and secure communication strategies. For example, you may have non-trusting domains, which make it difficult to flow a caller's security context and identity through to the back-end resources within your system. You may also be operating within a heterogeneous environment with mixed browser types. This makes it more difficult to use a common authentication mechanism.

If you have a homogenous intranet where all computers run the Microsoft® Windows® 2000 operating system or later and you have a domain where users are trusted for delegation, delegation of the original caller's security context to the back end becomes an option.

You must also consider secure communication. Despite the fact that your application runs in an intranet environment, you cannot consider the data sent over the network secure. It is likely that you will need to secure the data sent between browsers and the Web server in addition to data sent between application servers and databases.

The following common intranet scenarios are used in this chapter to illustrate key authentication, authorization, and secure communication techniques:

- ASP.NET to SQL Server
- ASP.NET to Enterprise Services to SQL Server
- ASP.NET to Web Services to SQL Server
- ASP.NET to Remoting to SQL Server

In addition, this chapter describes a Windows 2000 delegation scenario (Flowing the Original Caller to the Database), in which the original caller's security context and identity flows at the operating system level from browser to database using intermediate Web and application servers.

Note: Several scenarios described in this chapter change the password of the default ASPNET account to allow duplicated accounts to be created on remote computers for network authentication purposes. This requires an update to the <**processModel**> element of Machine.config. <**processModel**> credentials should not be stored in plain text in machine.config. Instead use the aspnet_setreg.exe utility to store encrypted credentials in the registry. For more information, see Chapter 8, "ASP.NET Security" and article Q329290, "HOWTO: Use the ASP.NET Utility to Encrypt Credentials and Session State Connection Strings" in the Microsoft Knowledge Base.

ASP.NET to SQL Server

In this scenario, a HR database serves per-user data securely on a homogenous intranet. The application uses a trusted subsystem model and executes calls on behalf of the original callers. The application authenticates callers by using Integrated Windows authentication and makes calls to the database using the ASP.NET process identity. Due to the sensitive nature of the data, SSL is used between the Web server and clients.

The basic model for this application scenario is shown in Figure 5.1.

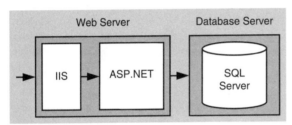

Figure 5.1
ASP.NET to SQL Server

Characteristics

This scenario has the following characteristics:

- Clients have Internet Explorer.
- User accounts are in Microsoft Active Directory® directory service.
- The application provides sensitive, per-user data.
- Only authenticated clients should access the application.
- The database trusts the application to authenticate users properly (that is, the application makes calls to the database on behalf of the users).
- Microsoft SQL Server™ is using a single database user role for authorization.

Secure the Scenario

In this scenario, the Web server authenticates the caller and restricts access to local resources by using the caller's identity. You don't have to impersonate within the Web application in order to restrict access to resources against the original caller. The database authenticates against the ASP.NET default process identity, which is a least privileged account (that is, the database trusts the ASP.NET application).

Table 5.1: Security measures

Category	Details
Authentication	• Provide strong authentication at the Web server to authenticate original callers by using Integrated Windows authentication in IIS. • Use Windows authentication within ASP.NET (no impersonation). • Secure connections to the database using SQL Server configured for Windows authentication. • The database trusts the ASP.NET worker process to make calls. Authenticate the ASP.NET process identity at the database.
Authorization	• Configure resources on the Web server using ACLs tied to the original callers. For easier administration, users are added to Windows groups and groups are used within the ACLs. • The Web application performs .NET role checks against the original caller to restrict access to pages.
Secure Communication	• Secure sensitive data sent between the Web server and the database • Secure sensitive data sent between the original callers and the Web application

The Result

Figure 5.2 shows the recommended security configuration for this scenario.

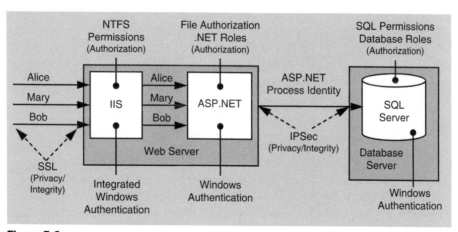

Figure 5.2

The recommended security configuration for the ASP.NET to SQL Server intranet scenario

Security Configuration Steps

Before you begin, you'll want to see the following:

- Creating custom ASP.NET accounts (see "How To: Create a Custom Account to Run ASP.NET" in the Reference section of this book)
- Creating a least privileged database account (see Chapter 12, "Data Access Security")
- Configuring SSL on a Web server (see "How To: Set Up SSL on a Web Server" in the Reference section of this book)
- Configuring IPSec (see "How To: Use IPSec to Provide Secure Communication Between Two Servers" in the Reference section of this book)

Configuring IIS

Step	More Information
Disable Anonymous access for your Web application's virtual root directory Enable Integrated Windows Authentication	To work with IIS authentication settings, use the IIS MMC snap-in. Right-click your application's virtual directory, and then click **Properties**. Click the **Directory Security** tab, and then click **Edit** within the **Anonymous access and authentication control** group.

Configuring ASP.NET

Step	More Information

Change the ASPNET password to a known strong password value	ASPNET is a least privileged local account used by default to run ASP.NET Web applications.
	Set the ASPNET account's password to a known value by using Local Users and Groups.
	Edit Machine.config located in %windir%\Microsoft.NET \Framework\ v1.0.3705\CONFIG
	and reconfigure the password attribute on the **<processModel>** element
	Default
	
	`<!-- userName="machine" password="AutoGenerate" -->`
	
	Becomes
	
	`<!-- userName="machine"`
	`password="YourNewStrongPassword" -->`

Configure your ASP.NET Web application to use Windows authentication	Edit Web.config in your application's virtual directory root Set the **<authentication>** element to: `<authentication mode="Windows" />`

Step	More Information
Make sure impersonation is off	Impersonation is off by default; however, double check to ensure that it's turned off in Web.config, as follows: `<identity impersonate="false" />` The same effect can be achieved by removing the <**identity**> element.

Configuring SQL Server

Step	More Information
Create a Windows account on your SQL Server computer that matches the ASP.NET process account (ASPNET)	The user name and password must match the ASPNET account. Give the account the following privileges: - Access this computer from the network - Deny logon locally - Log on as a batch job
Configure SQL Server for Windows authentication	
Create a SQL Server Login for the local ASPNET account	This grants access to the SQL Server
Create a new database user and map the login name to the database user	This grants access to the specified database
Create a new user-defined database role and add the database user to the role	
Establish database permissions for the database role	Grant minimum permissions For more information, see Chapter 12, "Data Access Security."

Configuring Secure Communication

Step	More Information
Configure the Web site for SSL	See "How To: Set Up SSL on a Web Server" in the Reference section of this book.
Configure IPSec between Web server and database server	See "How To: Use IPSec to Provide Secure Communication Between Two Servers" in the Reference section of this book.

Analysis

- Integrated Windows authentication in IIS is ideal in this scenario because all users have Windows accounts and are using Microsoft Internet Explorer. The benefit of Integrated Windows authentication is that the user's password is never sent over the network. Additionally, the logon is transparent for the user because Windows uses the current interactive user's logon session.

- ASP.NET is running as least privileged account, so potential damage from compromise is mitigated.

- You don't need to impersonate in ASP.NET to perform .NET role checks or to secure resources within Windows ACLs against the original caller. To perform .NET role checks against the original caller, the **WindowsPrincipal** object that represents the original caller is retrieved from the HTTP context as follows:

```
WindowsPrincipal wp = (HttpContext.Current.User as WindowsPrincipal);
if ( wp.IsInRole("Manager") )
{
  // User is authorized to perform manager-specific functionality
}
```

  The ASP.NET **FileAuthorizationModule** provides ACL checks against the original caller for ASP.NET file types that are mapped within IIS to the aspnet_isapi.dll. For static file types such as .jpg, .gif, and .htm files, IIS acts as the gatekeeper and performs access checks using the original caller's identity, based on the NTFS permissions associated with the file.

- Using Windows authentication to SQL Server means that you avoid storing credentials in files and passing credentials over the network to the database server.

- The use of a duplicated Windows account on the database server (one that matches the ASPNET local account) results in increased administration. If a password is changed on one computer, it must be synchronized and updated on the other. In some scenarios, you may be able to use a least-privileged domain account for easier administration.

- The duplicated local account approach also works in the presence of a firewall where the ports required for Windows authentication may not be open. The use of Windows authentication and domain accounts may not work in this scenario.

- You'll need to ensure that your Windows groups are as granular as your security needs. Because .NET role-based security is based on Windows group membership this solution relies on Windows groups being set up at the correct level of granularity to match the categories of users (sharing the same security privileges) who access the application. The Windows groups that you use here to manage roles could be local to that computer or domain groups

- SQL Server database user roles are preferred to SQL server application roles to avoid the associated password management and connection pooling issues associated with the use of SQL application roles.

    Applications activate SQL application roles by calling a built-in stored procedure with a role name and a password. Therefore, the password must be stored securely. Database connection pooling must also be disabled when you use SQL application roles, which severely impacts application scalability.

    For more information about SQL Server database user roles and SQL Server application roles, see Chapter 12, "Data Access Security."

- The database user is added to a database user role and permissions are assigned for the role so that if the database account changes; you don't have to change the permissions on all database objects.

Q&A

- **Why can't I enable impersonation for the Web application, so that I can secure the resources accessed by my Web application using ACLs configured against the original caller?**

    If you enable impersonation, the impersonated security context will not have network credentials (assuming delegation is not enabled and you are using Integrated Windows authentication). Therefore, the remote call to SQL Server will use a NULL session, which will result in a failed call. With impersonation disabled, the remote request will use the ASP.NET process identity.

    The preceding scenario uses the ASP.NET **FileAuthorizationModule**, which performs authorization using Windows ACLs against the original caller identity and does not require impersonation.

    If you use Basic authentication instead of Integrated Windows authentication (NTLM) and you do enable impersonation, each call to the database would use the original caller's security context. Each user account (or the Windows groups to which the user belongs) would require SQL Server logins. Permissions on database objects would need to be secured against the Windows group (or original caller).

- **The database doesn't know who the original caller is. How can I create an audit trail?**

    Audit end user activity within the Web application or pass the identity of the user explicitly as a parameter of the data access call.

Related Scenarios

Non-Internet Explorer Browsers

Integrated Windows authentication to IIS requires Internet Explorer. In a mixed browser environment, your typical options would include:

- **Basic authentication and SSL**. Basic authentication is supported by most browsers. Since the user's credentials are passed over the network, you must use SSL to secure the scenario.
- **Client certificates**. Individual client certificates can either be mapped to a unique Windows account or a single Windows account can be used to represent all clients. The use of client certificates also requires SSL.
- **Forms Authentication**. Forms authentication can validate credentials against a custom data store such as a database or against Active Directory.

  If you authenticate against Active Directory, make sure that you retrieve only the necessary groups that are pertinent to your application. Just like you shouldn't issue queries against a database using SELECT * clauses, you shouldn't blindly retrieve all groups from Active Directory.

  If you authenticate against a database, you need to carefully parse the input used in SQL commands to protect against SQL injection attacks, and you should store password hashes (with salt) in the database instead of clear text or encrypted passwords.

  For more information about using SQL Server as a credential store and storing passwords in the database, see Chapter 12, "Data Access Security."

Notice that in all cases, if you don't use Integrated Windows authentication, where the platform manages credentials for you, you end up using SSL. However, this benefit pertains strictly to the authentication process. If you are passing security sensitive data over the network, you must still use IPSec or SSL.

SQL Authentication to the Database

In some scenarios you may be forced to use SQL authentication instead of the preferred Windows authentication. For example, there may be a firewall between the Web application and database, or the Web server may not be a member of your domain for security reasons. This also prevents Windows authentication. In this case, you might use SQL authentication between the database and Web server. To secure this scenario, you should:

- Use the Data Protection API (DPAPI) to secure database connection strings that contain usernames and passwords. For more information, see the following resources:

- "Storing Database Connection Strings Securely", in Chapter 12, "Data Access Security"
- "How To: Use DPAPI (Machine Store) from ASP.NET" in the Reference section of this book
- "How To Use DPAPI (User Store) from ASP.NET with Enterprise Services" in the Reference section of this book
- "How To: Create a DPAPI Library" in the Reference section of this book
- Use IPSec or SSL between the Web server and database server to protect the clear text credentials passed over the network.

Flowing the Original Caller to the Database

In this scenario, calls are made from the Web application to the database using the security context of the original caller. With this approach, it's important to note the following:

- If you choose this approach, you need to use either Kerberos authentication (with accounts configured for delegation) or Basic authentication.

  A delegation scenario is discussed in the "Flowing the Original Caller to the Database" section later in this chapter.
- You must also enable impersonation in ASP.NET. This means that local system resource access is performed using the original caller's security context and as a result, ACLs on local resources such as the registry and event log require appropriate configuration.
- Database connection pooling is limited because original callers won't be able to share connections. Each connection is associated with the caller's security context.
- An alternate approach to flowing the user's security context is to flow the original caller's identity at the application level (for example, by using method and stored procedure parameters).

ASP.NET to Enterprise Services to SQL Server

In this scenario, ASP.NET pages call business components hosted in an Enterprise Services application that in turn connects to a database. As an example, consider an internal purchase order system that uses transactions over the intranet and allows internal departments to place orders. This scenario is shown in Figure 5.3 on the next page.

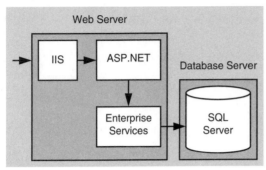

Figure 5.3
ASP.NET calls a component within Enterprise Services which calls the database

Characteristics

This scenario has the following characteristics:

- Users have Internet Explorer.
- Components are deployed on the Web server.
- The application handles sensitive data which must be secured while in transit.
- Business components connect to SQL Server using Windows authentication.
- Business functionality within these components is restricted based on the identity of the caller.
- Serviced components are configured as a server application (out-of-process).
- Components connect to the database using the server application's process identity.
- Impersonation is enabled within ASP.NET (to facilitate Enterprise Services role-based security).

Secure the Scenario

In this scenario, the Web server authenticates the original caller and flows the caller's security context to the serviced component. The serviced component authorizes access to business functionality based on the original caller's identity. The database authenticates against the Enterprise Service application's process identity (that is,. the database trusts the serviced components within the Enterprise Services application). When the serviced component makes calls to the database, it passes the user's identity at the application level (by using trusted query parameters).

Table 5.2: Security measures

Category	Detail
Authentication	• Provide strong authentication at the Web server using Integrated Windows authentication. • Flow the original caller's security context to the serviced component to support Enterprise Services (COM+) role checks. • Secure connections to the database use Windows authentication. • The database trusts the serviced component's identity to make the database calls. The database authenticates the Enterprise Services application process identity.
Authorization	• Authorize access to business logic using Enterprise Services (COM+) roles.
Secure Communication	• Secure sensitive data sent between the users and the Web application by using SSL. • Secure sensitive data sent between the Web server and the database by using IPSec.

The Result

Figure 5.4 shows the recommended security configuration for this scenario.

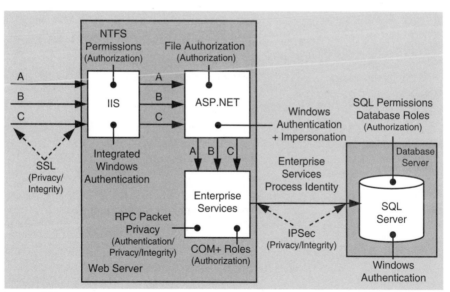

Figure 5.4
The recommended security configuration for the ASP.NET to local Enterprise Services to SQL Server intranet scenario

Security Configuration Steps

Before you begin, you'll want to see the following:

- Creating a least privileged database account (see Chapter 12, "Data Access Security")
- Configuring SSL on a Web server (see "How To: Set Up SSL on a Web Server" in the Reference section of this book)
- Configuring IPSec (see "How To: Use IPSec to Provide Secure Communication Between Two Servers" in the Reference section of this book)
- Configuring Enterprise Services security (see "How To: Use Role-Based Security with Enterprise Services" in the Reference section of this book)

Configuring IIS

Step	More Information
Disable Anonymous access for your Web application's virtual root directory Enable Integrated Windows Authentication	

Configuring ASP.NET

Step	More Information
Configure your ASP.NET Web application to use Windows authentication	Edit Web.config in your application's virtual directory root Set the <**authentication**> element to: `<authentication mode="Windows" />`
Configure your ASP.NET Web application for impersonation	Edit Web.config in your Web application's virtual directory Set the <**identity**> element to: `<identity impersonate="true" />`

Configure ASP.NET DCOM security to ensure that calls to Enterprise Services support caller impersonation	Edit Machine.config and locate the <**processModel**> element. Confirm that the **comImpersonationLevel** attribute is set to **Impersonate** (this is the default setting)
	
	`<processModel`
	`        comImpersonationLevel="Impersonate"`

Configuring Enterprise Services

Step	More Information
Create a custom account for running Enterprise Services	**Note**: If you use a local account, you must also create a duplicate account on the SQL Server computer.

Configure the Enterprise Services application as a server application	This can be configured using the Component Services tool, or via the following .NET attribute placed in the service component assembly.
	
	`[assembly:`
	`ApplicationActivation(ActivationOption.Server)]`

Configure Enterprise Services (COM+) roles	Use the Component Services tool or script to add Windows users and/or groups to roles. Roles can be defined using .NET attributes within the serviced component assembly.
Configure Enterprise Services to run as your custom account	This must be configured using the Component Services tool or script. You cannot use .NET attributes within the serviced component assembly.

Configuring SQL Server

Step	More Information
Create a Windows account on your SQL Server computer that matches the Enterprise Services process account	The user name and password must match your custom Enterprise Services account. Give the account the following privileges: - Access this computer from the network - Deny logon locally - Log on as a batch job
Configure SQL Server for Windows authentication	
Create a SQL Server Login for your Enterprise Services account	This grants access to the SQL Server.
Create a new database user and map the login name to the database user	This grants access to the specified database.
Create a new database user role and add the database user to the role	
Establish database permissions for the database user role	Grant minimum permissions For details, see Chapter 12, "Data Access Security"

Configuring Secure Communication

Step	More Information
Configure the Web site for SSL	See "How To: Set Up SSL on a Web Server" in the Reference section of this book.
Configure IPSec between Web server and database server	See "How To: Use IPSec to Provide Secure Communication Between Two Servers" in the Reference section of this book.

Analysis

- ASP.NET and Enterprise Services are running as least privileged accounts, so potential damage from compromise is mitigated. If either process identity were compromised, the account's limited privileges reduce the scope of damage. Also, in the case of ASP.NET, if malicious script were injected, potential damage is constrained.

- The ASP.NET application must be configured for impersonation in order to flow the security context of the original caller to the Enterprise Services components (to support Enterprise Services (COM+) role-based authorization). If you do not impersonate, role checks are made against the process identity (that is, the ASP.NET worker process). Impersonation affects who you authorize resources against.

  Without impersonation, system resource checks are against the ASP.NET process identity. With impersonation, system resource checks are made against the original caller. For more information about accessing system resources from ASP.NET, see "Accessing System Resources" in Chapter 8, "ASP.NET Security."

- By using Enterprise Services (COM+) roles, access checks are pushed to the middle tier, where the business logic is located. In this case, callers are checked at the gate, mapped to roles, and calls to business logic are based on roles. This avoids unnecessary calls to the back end. Another advantage of Enterprise Services (COM+) roles is that you can create and administer roles at deployment rime, using the Component Services Manager.

- Windows authentication to SQL means you avoid storing credentials in files and sending them across the network.

- The use of a local account to run the Enterprise Services application, together with a duplicated account on the database server, also works in the presence of a firewall where the ports required for Windows authentication may not be open. The use of Windows authentication and domain accounts may not work in this scenario.

Pitfalls

- The use of a duplicated Windows account on the database server (one that matches the Enterprise Services process account) results in increased administration. Passwords should be manually updated and synchronized on a periodic basis.

- Because .NET role-based security is based on Windows group membership, this solution relies on Windows groups being set up at the correct level of granularity to match the categories of users (sharing the same security privileges) who access the application.

ASP.NET to Web Services to SQL Server

In this scenario, a Web server that runs ASP.NET pages connects to a Web service on a remote server. This server in turn connects to a remote database server. As an example, consider a HR Web application that provides sensitive data specific to a user. The application relies on the Web service for data retrieval. The basic model for this application scenario is shown in Figure 5.5.

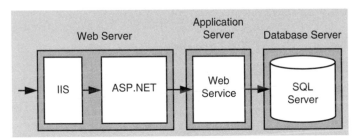

Figure 5.5
ASP.NET to remote Web Service to SQL Server

The Web service exposes a method that allows an individual employee to retrieve his or her own personal details. Details must be provided only to authenticated individuals using the Web application. The Web service also provides a method that supports the retrieval of any employee details. This functionality must be available only to members of the HR or payroll department. In this scenario, employees are categorized into three Windows groups:

- **HRDept** (members of the HR department)

    Members of this group can retrieve details about any employee.

- **PayrollDept** (members of the Payroll department)

    Members of this group can retrieve details about any employee.

- **Employees** (all employees)

    Members of this group can only retrieve their own details.

Due to the sensitive nature of the data, the traffic between all nodes should be secure.

Characteristics

- Users have Internet Explorer 5.x or later.
- All computers run Windows 2000 or later.
- User accounts are in Active Directory within a single forest.
- The application flows the original caller's security context all the way to the database.
- All tiers use Windows authentication.
- Domain user accounts are configured for delegation.
- The database does not support delegation.

Secure the Scenario

In this scenario, the Web server that hosts the ASP.NET Web application authenticates the original caller's identity and flows their security context to the remote server that hosts the Web service. This enables authorization checks to be applied to Web methods to either allow or deny access to the original caller. The database authenticates against the Web service process identity (the database trusts the Web service). The Web service in turn makes calls to the database and passes the user's identity at the application level using stored procedure parameters.

Table 5.3: Security measures

Category	Detail
Authentication	• The Web application authenticates users by using Integrated Windows authentication from IIS. • The Web service uses Integrated Windows authentication from IIS. It authenticates the original caller's security context delegated by the Web application. • The Kerberos authentication protocol is used to flow the original caller security context from the Web application to the Web service using delegation. • Windows authentication is used to connect to the database using the ASP.NET process account.
Authorization	• The Web application performs role checks against the original caller to restrict access to pages. • Access to the Web service methods is controlled by using .NET roles based on the original caller's Windows group membership.
Secure Communication	• Sensitive data sent between the original callers and the Web application and Web service is secured by using SSL. • Sensitive data sent between the Web service and the database is secure by using IPSec.

The Result

Figure 5.6 shows the recommended security configuration for this scenario.

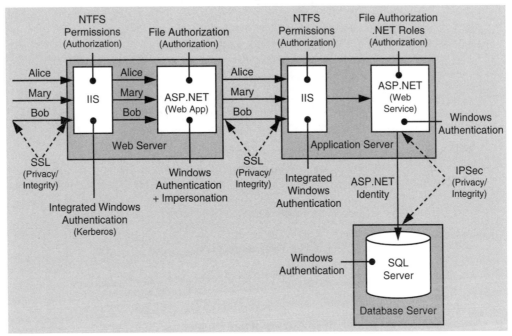

Figure 5.6
The recommended security configuration for the ASP.NET to Web Service to SQL Server intranet scenario

Security Configuration Steps

Before you begin, you'll want to see the following:

- Configuring SSL on a Web server (see "How To: Set Up SSL on a Web Server" in the Reference section of this book)
- Configuring IPSec (see "How To: Use IPSec to Provide Secure Communication Between Two Servers" in the Reference section of this book)

Configuring the Web Server (that Hosts the Web Application)

Configure IIS Step	More Information
Disable Anonymous access for your Web application's virtual root directory Enable Windows Integrated Authentication for your Web application's virtual root	

Configure ASP .NET Step	More Information
Configure your ASP.NET Web application to use Windows authentication	Edit Web.config in your Web application's virtual directory Set the <**authentication**> element to: `<authentication mode="Windows" />`
Configure your ASP.NET Web application for impersonation	Edit Web.config in your Web application's virtual directory Set the <**identity**> element to: `<identity impersonate="true" />`

Configuring the Application Server (that Hosts the Web Service)

Configure IIS Step	More Information
Disable Anonymous access for your Web service's virtual root directory Enable Windows Integrated Authentication for your Web service's virtual root directory	

Configure ASP .NET

Step	More Information

Change the ASPNET password to a known value	ASPNET is a least privileged local account used by default to run the ASPNET Web applications.
	Set the ASPNET account's password to a know value by using Local Users and Groups.
	Edit Machine.config located in %windir%\Microsoft.NET\Framework\ v1.0.3705\CONFIG and reconfigure the password attribute on the **\<processModel\>** element:
	Default
	
	`<!-- userName="machine" password="AutoGenerate" -->`
	
	Becomes
	
	`<!-- userName="machine" password="YourNewStrongPassword" -->`

Configure your ASP.NET Web service to use Windows authentication	Edit Web.config in your Web service's virtual directory Set the **\<authentication\>** element to: `<authentication mode="Windows" />`
Make sure impersonation is off	Impersonation is off by default; however, double check to ensure that it's turned off in Web.config, as follows: `<identity impersonate="false" />` Note that because impersonation is disabled by default, the same effect can be achieved by removing the **\<identity\>** element.

Configure SQL Server

Step	More Information
Create a Windows account on your SQL Server computer that matches the ASPNET process account used to run the Web service	The user name and password must match your custom ASPNET account. Give the account the following privileges: - Access this computer from the network - Deny logon locally - Log on as a batch job
Configure SQL Server for Windows authentication	

(continued)

Configure SQL Server *(continued)*

Step	More Information
Create a SQL Server Login for your custom ASP.NET account	This grants access to the SQL Server.
Create a new database user and map the login name to the database user	This grants access to the specified database.
Create a new database user role and add the database user to the role	
Establish database permissions for the database user role	Grant minimum permissions

Configuring Secure Communication

Step	More Information
Configure the Web site on the Web server for SSL	See "How To: Set Up SSL on a Web Server" in the Reference section of this book.
Configure IPSec between Web server and database server	See "How To: Use IPSec to Provide Secure Communication Between Two Servers" in the Reference section of this book.

Analysis

- Integrated Windows authentication in IIS is ideal in this scenario because all users are using Windows 2000 or later, Internet Explorer 5.x or later, and have accounts in Active Directory, which makes it possible to use the Kerberos authentication protocol (which supports delegation). This allows you to flow the security context of the user across computer boundaries.

- End user accounts must be NOT marked as "Sensitive and cannot be delegated" in Active Directory. The Web server computer account must be marked as "Trusted for delegation" in Active Directory. For more details, see "How To: Implement Kerberos Delegation for Windows 2000" in the Reference section of this book.

- ASP.NET on the Web server and application server runs with a least privileged local account (the local ASPNET account), so potential damage from compromise is mitigated.

- The Web service and Web application are both configured for Windows authentication. IIS on both computers is configured for Integrated Windows authentication.

- When making a call to the Web service from the Web application, no credentials are passed by default. They are required in order to respond to the network authentication challenge issued by IIS on the downstream Web server. You must specify this explicitly by setting the **Credentials** property of the Web service proxy as shown in the following:

```
wsproxy.Credentials = CredentialCache.DefaultCredentials;
```

For more information about calling Web services with credentials, see Chapter 10, "Web Services Security."

- The Web application is configured for impersonation. As a result, calls from the Web application to the Web service flow the original caller's security context and allow the Web service to authenticate (and authorize) the original caller.

- .NET roles are used within the Web service to authorize the users based on the Windows group to which they belong (HRDept, PayrollDept and Employees). Members of HRDept and PayrollDept can retrieve employee details for any employee, while members of the Employees group are authorized to retrieve only their own details.

  Web methods can be annotated with the **PrincipalPermissionAttribute** class to demand specific role membership, as shown in the following code sample. Notice that **PrincipalPermission** can be used instead of **PrincipalPermissionAttribute**. This is a common feature of all .NET attribute types.

```
[WebMethod]
[PrincipalPermission(SecurityAction.Demand,
                     Role=@"DomainName\HRDept)]
public DataSet RetrieveEmployeeDetails()
{
}
```

  The attribute shown in the preceding code means that only members of the DomainName\HRDept Windows group are allowed to call the **RetrieveEmployeeDetails** method. If any nonmember attempts to call the method, a security exception is thrown.

- ASP.NET File Authorization (within the Web application and Web service) performs ACL checks against the caller for any file type for which a mapping exists in the IIS Metabase that maps the file type to Aspnet_isapi.dll. Static file types (such as .jpg, .gif, .htm, and so on), for which an ISAPI mapping does not exist are checked by IIS (again using the ACL attached to the file).

- Because the Web application is configured for impersonation, resources accessed by the application itself must be configured with an ACL that grants at least read access to the original caller.

- The Web service does not impersonate or delegate; therefore, it accesses local system resources and the database using the ASP.NET process identity. As a result, all calls are made using the single process account. This enables database connection pooling to be used. If the database doesn't support delegations (such as SQL Server 7.0 or earlier), this scenario is a good option.

- Windows authentication to SQL Server means you avoid storing credentials on the Web server and it also means that credentials are not sent across the network to the SQL Server computer.

- SSL between the original caller and Web server protects the data passed to and from the Web application.

- IPSec between the downstream Web server and database protects the data passed to and from the database.

Pitfalls

- The use of a duplicated Windows account on the database server (one that matches the ASP.NET process account) results in increased administration. Passwords should be manually updated and synchronized on a periodic basis.

  As an alternative, consider using least-privileged domain accounts. For more information about choosing an ASP.NET process identity, see Chapter 9, "ASP.NET Security."

- Because .NET role-based security is based on Windows group membership, this solution relies on Windows groups being set up at the correct level of granularity to match the categories of users (sharing the same security privileges) who will access the application.

- Kerberos delegation is unrestricted and as a result you must carefully control which applications identities run on the Web server. To raise the bar on security, limit the scope of the domain account's reach by removing the account from Domain Users group and provide access only from appropriate computers. For more information, see the white paper on the Microsoft Web site at *http://www.microsoft.com/windows2000/techinfo/planning/security/secdefs.asp*.

Q&A

- **The database doesn't know who the original caller is. How can I create an audit trail?**

Audit end user activity within the Web service or pass the identity of the user explicitly as a parameter of the data access call.

Related Scenarios

If you need to connect to non SQL Server databases, or you currently use SQL authentication, you must pass database account credentials explicitly using the connection string. If you do so, make sure that you securely store the connection string.

For more information, see "Storing Database Connection Strings Securely" within Chapter 10, "Data Access Security."

ASP.NET to Remoting to SQL Server

In this scenario, a Web server that runs ASP.NET pages makes secure connections to a remote component on a remote application server. The Web server communicates with the component by using .NET Remoting over the HTTP channel. The remote component is hosted by ASP.NET. This is shown in Figure 5.7.

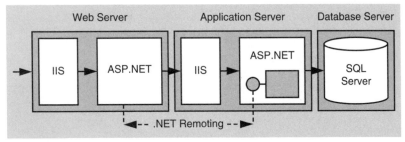

Figure 5.7
ASP.NET to remoting using .NET Remoting to SQL Server

Characteristics

- Users have various types of Web browsers.
- The remote component is hosted by ASP.NET.
- The Web application communicates with the remote component using the HTTP channel.
- The ASP.NET application calls the .NET remote component and passes the original caller's credentials for authentication. These are available from Basic authentication.
- The data is sensitive and therefore must be secured between processes and computers.

Secure the Scenario

In this scenario, the Web server that hosts the ASP.NET Web application authenticates the original callers. The Web application is able to retrieve the caller's authentication credentials (user name and password) from HTTP server variables. It can then use them to connect to the application server that hosts the remote component, by configuring the remote component proxy. The database uses Windows authentication to authenticate against the ASP.NET process identity (that is, the database trusts the remote component). The remote component in turn calls the database and passes the original caller's identity at the application level using stored procedure parameters.

Table 5.4: Security measures

Category	Detail
Authentication •	• Authenticate users using Basic authentication from IIS (in addition to SSL). • Use Windows authentication from remote component (ASP.NET/IIS). Use Windows authentication to connect to the database using a least privileged ASP.NET account.
Authorization	• ACL checks against original caller on the Web server. • Role checks within the remote component against original caller. • Database permissions against the ASP.NET (remote component) identity.
Secure Communication	• Secure sensitive data sent between the users and the Web application and remote objects hosted in IIS using SSL. • Secure sensitive data sent between the Web server and the database using IPSec.

The Result

Figure 5.8 shows the recommended security configuration for this scenario.

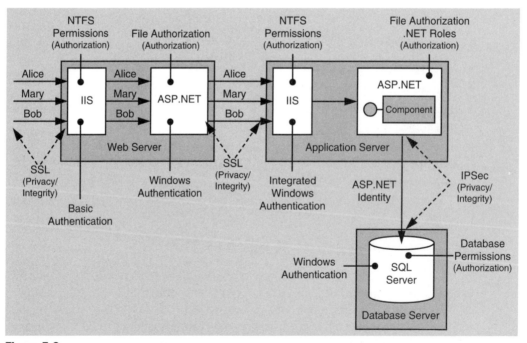

Figure 5.8
The recommended security configuration for the ASP.NET to remote Web Service to SQL Server intranet scenario

Security Configuration Steps

Before you begin, you'll want to see the following:

- Creating a least privileged database account (see Chapter 12, "Data Access Security")
- Configuring SSL on a Web server (see "How To: Set Up SSL on a Web Server" in the Reference section of this book)
- Configuring IPSec (see "How To: Use IPSec to Provide Secure Communication Between Two Servers" in the Reference section of this book)

Configuring the Web Server

Configure IIS Step	More Information
Disable Anonymous access for your Web application's virtual root directory	
Enable Basic authentication	Use SSL to protect the Basic authentication credentials.

Configure ASP.NET Step	More Information
Configure your ASP.NET Web application to use Windows authentication	Edit Web.config in your application's virtual directory root Set the **<authentication>** element to: `<authentication mode="Windows" />`

Configure the Application Server

Configure IIS Step	More Information
Disable Anonymous access for your Web application's virtual root directory	
Enable Integrated Windows authentication	

Configure ASP .NET Step	More Information
Configure your remote component (within ASP.NET) to use Windows authentication	Edit Web.config in your remote component's virtual directory root Set the **\<authentication\>** element to: `<authentication mode="Windows" />`

Change the ASPNET password to a known value	ASPNET is a least privileged local account used by default to run ASP.NET Web applications (and in this case the remote component host process).
	Set the ASPNET account's password to a know value by using Local Users and Groups.
	Edit Machine.config located in %windir%\Microsoft.NET\Framework\ v1.0.3705\CONFIG and reconfigure the password attribute on the **\<processModel\>** element
	Default
	
	`<!-- userName="machine" password="AutoGenerate" -->`
	
	Becomes
	
	`<!-- userName="machine"`
	`password="YourNewStrongPassword" -->`

Make sure impersonation is off	Impersonation is off by default; however, double check to ensure that it's turned off in web.config, as shown below: `<identity impersonate="false" />` The same effect can be achieved by removing the **\<identity\>** element.

Configure SQL Server

Step	More Information
Create a Windows account on your SQL Server computer that matches the ASPNET process account used to run the Web service	The user name and password must match your custom ASP.NET account. Give the account the following privileges: - Access this computer from the network - Deny logon locally - Log on as a batch job
Configure SQL Server for Windows authentication	

Step	More Information
Create a SQL Server Login for your custom ASP.NET account	This grants access to the SQL Server
Create a new database user and map the login name to the database user	This grants access to the specified database
Create a new database user role and add the database user to the role	
Establish database permissions for the database user role	Grant minimum permissions

Configuring Secure Communication

Step	More Information
Configure the Web site on the Web server for SSL	See "How To: Set Up SSL on a Web Server" in the Reference section of this book.
Configure the Web site on the application server for SSL	See "How To: Set Up SSL on a Web Server" in the Reference section of this book.
Configure IPSec between application server and database server	See "How To: Use IPSec to Provide Secure Communication Between Two Servers in the Reference section of this book."

Analysis

- ASP.NET on the Web server and application sever is running as a least privileged local account, so potential damage from compromise is mitigated. The default ASP.NET account is used in both cases.

  Use of the ASP.NET local account (duplicated on the SQL Server computer) further reduces the potential security risk. A duplicated Windows account on the database server allows the remote component to run with a least privilege ASP.NET account on the application server.

- Basic authentication at the Web server allows the user's credentials to be used by the Web application to respond to Windows authentication challenges from the application server.

  To call the remote component using the caller's credentials, the Web application configures the remote component proxy as shown in the code fragment on the next page.

```
string pwd = Request.ServerVariables["AUTH_PASSWORD"];
string uid = Request.ServerVariables["AUTH_USER"];
IDictionary channelProperties =
                        ChannelServices.GetChannelSinkProperties(proxy);
NetworkCredential credentials;
credentials = new NetworkCredential(uid, pwd);
ObjRef objectReference = RemotingServices.Marshal(proxy);
Uri objectUri = new Uri(objectReference.URI);
CredentialCache credCache = new CredentialCache();
credCache.Add(objectUri, "Negotiate", credentials);
channelProperties["credentials"] = credCache;
channelProperties["preauthenticate"] = true;
```

For more information about flowing security credentials to a remote component, see Chapter 11, ".NET Remoting Security."

- Impersonation is not enabled within the ASP.NET Web application, because the remoting proxy is specifically configured using the user's credentials obtained by Basic authentication. Any other resource accessed by the Web application uses the security context provided by the ASP.NET process account.

- SSL between the user and Web server protects the data passed to and from the Web server and also protects the Basic credentials passed in clear text during the authentication process.

- Integrated Windows authentication at the application server provides .NET role checks against the original caller. The roles correspond to Windows groups.

  Role-based checks can be performed, even without impersonation.

- ASP.NET File Authorization performs ACL checks against the caller for any file type for which a mapping exists in the IIS Metabase that maps the file type to aspnet_isapi.dll. IIS performs access checks for static files (not mapped to an ISAPI extension within IIS).

- Because impersonation is not enabled on the application server, any local or remote resource access performed by the remote component does so using the ASPNET security context. ACLs should be set accordingly.

- Windows authentication to SQL Server means you avoid storing credentials on the application server and it also means that credentials are not sent across the network to the SQL Server computer.

Pitfalls

- The use of a duplicated Windows account on the database server (one that matches the ASP.NET process account) results in increased administration. Passwords should be manually updated and synchronized on a periodic basis.

- Because .NET role-based security is based on Windows group membership, this solution relies on Windows groups being set up at the correct level of granularity to match the categories of users (sharing the same security privileges) who will access the application.

Related Scenarios

The Web server uses Kerberos to authenticate callers. Kerberos delegation is used to flow the original caller's security context across to the remote component on the application server.

This approach requires that all user accounts be configured for delegation. The Web application would also be configured for impersonation and would use DefaultCredentials to configure the remote component proxy. This technique is discussed further in the "Flowing the Original Caller" section of Chapter 11, ".NET Remoting Security."

Flowing the Original Caller to the Database

The scenarios discussed earlier have used the trusted subsystem model and in all cases the database has trusted the application server or Web server to correctly authenticate and authorize users. While the trusted subsystem model offers many advantages, some scenarios (perhaps for auditing reasons) may require you to use the impersonation/delegation model and flow the original caller's security context across computer boundaries all the way to the database.

Typical reasons why you may need to flow the original caller to the database include:

- You need granular access in the database and permissions are restricted by object. Specific users or groups can read, while others can write to individual objects.

  This is in contrast to less granular task-based authorization, where role membership determines read and write capabilities for specific objects.

- You may want to use the auditing capabilities of the platform, rather than flow identity and perform auditing at the application level.

If you do choose an impersonation/delegation model (or are required to do so due to corporate security policy) and flow the original caller's context through the tiers of your application to the back end, you must design with delegation and network access in mind (which is nontrivial when spanning multiple computers). The pooling of shared resources (such as database connections) also becomes a key issue and can significantly reduce application scalability.

This section shows you how to implement the impersonation/delegation for two of the most common application scenarios:

- ASP.NET to SQL Server
- ASP.NET to Enterprise Services to SQL Server

For more information about the trusted subsystem and impersonation/delegation models and their relative merits, see Chapter 3, "Authentication and Authorization Design."

ASP.NET to SQL Server

In this scenario, calls to the database are made using the security context of the original caller. Authentication options described in this section include Basic and Integrated Windows authentication. A Kerberos delegation scenario is described within the "ASP.NET to Enterprise Services to SQL Server" section.

Using Basic Authentication at the Web Server

The following configuration settings for Basic authentication enable you to flow the original caller all the way to the database.

Table 5.5: Security measures

Category	Detail
Authentication	• Authenticate users by using Basic authentication from IIS. • Use Windows authentication within ASP.NET. • Turn on impersonation in ASP.NET. • Use Windows authentication to communicate with SQL Server.
Authorization	• Use ACL checks against the original caller on the Web server. • If the original callers are mapped to Windows groups (based on application requirements, for example, Managers, Tellers, and so on) then you can use .NET role checks against the original caller to restrict access to methods.
Secure Communication	• Secure the clear text credentials sent between the Web server and the database by using SSL. • To secure all sensitive data sent between the Web application and database, use IPSec.

With this approach, it's important to note the following points:

- Basic authentication prompts the user with a pop-up dialog box into which they can type credentials (user name and password).
- The database must recognize the original caller. If the Web server and database are in different domains, appropriate trust relationships must be enabled to allow it to authenticate the original caller.

Using Integrated Windows Authentication at the Web Server

Integrated Windows authentication results in either NTLM or Kerberos authentication and is dependent upon the client and server computer configurations.

NTLM authentication does not support delegation and as a result does not allow you to flow the original caller's security context from the Web server to a physically remote database. The single network hop allowed for NTLM authentication is used between the browser and Web server. To use NTLM authentication, the SQL Server must be installed on the Web server, which is likely to be appropriate only for very small intranet applications.

ASP.NET to Enterprise Services to SQL Server

In this scenario, ASP.NET pages call business components hosted in a remote Enterprise Services application that in turn talk to a database. The original caller's security context flows all the way from the browser to the database. This is shown in Figure 5.9.

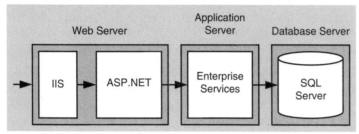

Figure 5.9
ASP.NET calls a component within Enterprise Services which calls the database

Characteristics

- Users have Internet Explorer 5.x or later.
- All computers are Windows 2000 or later.
- User accounts are maintained in Active Directory within a single forest.
- The application flows the original caller's security context (at the operating system level) all the way to the database.
- All tiers use Windows authentication.
- Domain user accounts are configured for delegation and the account used to run the Enterprise Services application must be marked as "Trusted for delegation" within Active Directory.

Secure the Scenario

In this scenario, the Web server authenticates the caller. You must then configure ASP.NET for impersonation in order to flow the original caller's security context to the remote Enterprise Services application. Within the Enterprise Services application, component code must explicitly impersonate the caller (using **CoImpersonateClient**) in order to ensure the caller's context flows to the database.

Table 5.6: Security measures

Category	Detail
Authentication	• All tiers support Kerberos authentication (the Web server, the application server, and database server).
Authorization	• Authorization checks are performed in the middle tier with Enterprise Services (COM+) roles against the original caller's identity.
Secure Communication	• SSL is used between the browser and the Web server to secure sensitive data. • RPC Packet Privacy (providing encryption) is used between ASP.NET and the serviced components within the remote Enterprise Services application. • IPSec is used between the serviced components and the database.

The Result

Figure 5.10 shows the recommended security configuration for this scenario.

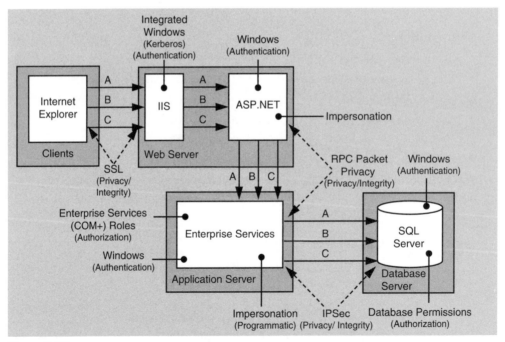

Figure 5.10
ASP.NET calls a component within Enterprise Services which calls the database. The original caller's security context flows to the database.

Security Configuration Steps

Before you begin, you should be aware of the following configuration issues:

- The Enterprise Services process account must be marked "Trusted for delegation" in Active Directory and end user accounts must not be marked "Sensitive and cannot be delegated." For more information, see "How To: Implement Kerberos Delegation for Windows 2000" in the Reference section of this book.

- Windows 2000 or later is required on all computers. This includes client (browser) computers and all servers.

- All computers must be in the Active Directory and must be part of a single forest.

- The application server that hosts Enterprise Services must be running Windows 2000 SP3.

- If you are using Internet Explorer 6.0 on Windows 2000, it defaults to NTLM authentication instead of the required Kerberos authentication. To enable Kerberos delegation, see article Q299838, "Can't Negotiate Kerberos Authentication After Upgrading to Internet Explorer 6," in the Microsoft Knowledge Base.

Configure the Web Server (IIS)

Step	More Information
Disable Anonymous access for your Web application's virtual root directory Enable Windows Integrated authentication	

Configure the Web Server (ASP.NET)

Step	More Information
Configure your ASP.NET Web application to use Windows authentication	Edit Web.config in your Web application's virtual directory root Set the <**authentication**> element to: `<authentication mode="Windows" />`
Configure your ASP.NET Web application for impersonation	Edit Web.config in your Web application's virtual directory Set the <**identity**> element to: `<identity impersonate="true" />`

(continued)

Configure the Web Server (ASP.NET) *(continued)*	
Step	**More Information**
Configure the DCOM impersonation level used by the ASP.NET Web application for outgoing calls	The ASP.NET Web application calls the remote serviced components over DCOM. The default impersonation level used for outgoing calls from ASP.NET is Impersonate. This must be changed to Delegate in Machine.config. Edit Machine.config, locate the **<processModel>** element, and set the **comImpersonateLevel** attribute to "Delegate" as shown below. `<processModel comImpersonationLevel="Delegate"`
Configure the DCOM authentication level at the client	DCOM authentication levels are determined by both client and server. The DCOM client in this case is ASP.NET. Edit Machine.config, locate the **<processModel>** element and set the **comAuthenitcationLevel** attribute to "**PktPrivacy**" as shown below. `<processModel comAuthenticationLevel="PktPrivacy"`

Configure Serviced Components (and the Application Server)	
Step	**More Information**
Managed class(es) must inherit from the Serviced Component class	See article Q306296, "HOW TO: Create a Serviced .NET Component in Visual C# .NET," in the Microsoft Knowledge Base.

Add code to the serviced component to impersonate the caller by calling the **ColmpersonateClient()** and **CoRevertToSelf()** APIs from OLE32.DLL before accessing remote resources (for example, a database) in order for the caller's context to be used. By default, the Enterprise Services process context is used for outgoing calls.	Add references to OLE32.DLL:
	
	```class COMSec```
	```{```
	```[DllImport("OLE32.DLL", CharSet=CharSet.Auto)]```
	```public static extern long CoImpersonateClient();```
	
	```[DllImport("OLE32.DLL", CharSet=CharSet.Auto)]```
	```public static extern long CoRevertToSelf();```
	```}```
	
	Call these external functions before calling remote resources:
	
	```COMSec.CoImpersonateClient();```
	```COMSec.CoRevertToSelf();```
	
	For more information, see Chapter 9, "Enterprise Services Security."

Configure Serviced Components (and the Application Server)	
Step	**More Information**

Configure the Enterprise Services application as a server application	This can be configured using the Component Services tool, or via the following .NET attribute placed in the service component assembly.
	
	`[assembly:`
	`ApplicationActivation(ActivationOption.Server)]`

Configure the Enterprise Services application to use packet privacy authentication (to provide secure communication with encryption)	Add the following .NET attribute to the serviced component assembly.
	
	`[assembly: ApplicationAccessControl(`
	`        Authentication =`
	`            AuthenticationOption.Privacy)]`

Configure the Enterprise Services application for component level role-based security `AccessChecksLevelOption.`	To configure role checks at the process and component level (including interfaces and classes) use the following attribute.
	
	`[assembly: ApplicationAccessControl(AccessChecksLevel=ApplicationComponent)]`
	
	Decorate classes with the following attribute:
	
	`[ComponentAccessControl(true)]`
	
	For more information about configuring interface and method level role checks, see "Configuring Security" in Chapter 9, "Enterprise Services Security."

Create a custom account for running Enterprise Services and mark it as Trusted for delegation in Active Directory	The Enterprise Services application needs to run as domain account marked as Trusted for Delegation in Active Directory. For more information, see "How To: Implement Kerberos Delegation for Windows 2000" in the Reference section of this book.
Configure Enterprise Services to run as your custom account	This must be configured using the Component Services tool or script. You can not use .NET attributes within the serviced component assembly.

Configure the Database Server (SQL Server)	
Step	**More Information**
Configure SQL Server for Windows authentication	
Create SQL Server Logins for the Windows groups that the users belong to.	This grants access to the SQL Server. The access control policy treats Windows groups as roles. For example, you may have groups such as **Employees**, **HRDept** and **PayrollDept**.
Create new database users for each SQL Server login	This grants access to the specified database.
Establish database permissions for the database users	Grant minimum permissions For more information, see Chapter 12, "Data Access Security."

Analysis

- The key to flowing the original caller's security context is Kerberos authentication, which generates a delegate-level token. After the server process (IIS) receives the delegate-level token, it can pass it to any other process, running under any account on the same computer, without changing its delegation level. It does not matter whether the worker process is running as a local or domain account. It *does* matter what IIS is running as. If it's running as something other than **LocalSystem**, the account it is running under needs to be marked as "Trusted for delegation" in Active Directory.

  If IIS is running as **LocalSystem**, the computer account must be marked as "Trusted for delegation". For more information, see "How To: Implement Kerberos Delegation for Windows 2000" in the Reference section of this book.

- Integrated Windows authentication (with Kerberos) in IIS is ideal in this scenario because all users have Windows accounts and they are using Internet Explorer 5.x or later. The benefit of Integrated Windows authentication is that the user's password is never sent over the wire. Additionally, the logon will be transparent because Windows will use the current interactive user's logon session.

- ASP.NET constructs a **WindowsPrincipal** object and attaches it to the current Web request context (**HttpContext.User**). If you need to perform authorization checks within the Web application you can use the following code.

```
WindowsPrincipal wp = (HttpContext.Current.User as WindowsPrincipal);
if ( wp.IsInRole("Manager") )
{
  // User is authorized to perform manager-specific functionality
}
```

The ASP.NET **FileAuthorizationModule** provides ACL checks against the original caller for ASP.NET file types that are mapped within IIS to the Aspnet_isapi.dll. For static file types such as .jpg, .gif and .htm files, IIS acts as the gatekeeper and performs access checks using the original caller's identity.

- By using Windows authentication to SQL, you avoid storing credentials in files on the application server and avoid passing them across the network. For example include the Trusted_Connection attribute in the connection string:

```
ConStr="server=YourServer; database=yourdatabase; Trusted_Connection=Yes;"
```

- The original caller's context flows across all tiers, which makes auditing extremely easy. You can use platform-level auditing (for example, auditing features provided by Windows and SQL Server).

Pitfalls

- If you are using Internet Explorer 6.0 on Windows 2000, the default authentication mechanism that is negotiated is NTLM (and not Kerberos). For more information, see article Q299838, "Can't Negotiate Kerberos Authentication After Upgrading to Internet Explorer 6," in the Microsoft Knowledge Base.
- Delegating users across tiers is expensive in terms of performance and application scalability compared to using the trusted subsystem model. You cannot take advantage of connection pooling to the database, because connections to the database are tied to original caller's security context and therefore cannot be efficiently pooled.
- This approach also relies on the granularity of Windows groups matching your application's security needs. That is, Windows groups must be set up at the correct level of granularity to match the categories of users (sharing the same security privileges) who access the application.

Summary

This chapter has described how to secure a set of common intranet application scenarios.

For Extranet and Internet application scenarios, see Chapter 6, "Extranet Security" and Chapter 7, "Internet Security."

6

Extranet Security

Extranet applications are those that share resources or applications across two different companies or divisions. The applications and resources are exposed over the Internet. One of the main challenges associated with extranet applications is developing an authentication approach that both parties agree to. Your choices may be limited in this respect because you may need to interoperate with existing authentication mechanisms.

Extranet applications generally share some common characteristics:

- You have tighter control over user accounts, compared to Internet scenarios.
- You may have a higher level of trust for the user accounts, compared to applications that have Internet users.

The scenarios presented in this chapter that are used to illustrate recommended authentication, authorization, and secure communication techniques include:

- Exposing a Web Service
- Exposing a Web Application

Note: The scenarios described in this chapter change the password of the default ASPNET account used to run ASP.NET applications to allow duplicated accounts to be created on remote computers for network authentication purposes. This requires an update to the <**processModel**> element of Machine.config. <**processModel**> credentials should not be stored in plain text in machine.config. Instead use the aspnet_setreg.exe utility to store encrypted credentials in the registry. For more information, see Chapter 8, "ASP.NET Security" and article Q329290, "HOWTO: Use the ASPNET Utility to Encrypt Credentials and Session State Connection Strings" in the Microsoft Knowledge Base.

Exposing a Web Service

Consider a business to business partner exchange scenario where a publisher company publishes and sells its services over the Internet. It exposes information to selected partner companies using a Web service. Users within each partner company access the Web service using an Intranet-based internal Web application. This scenario is shown in Figure 6.1.

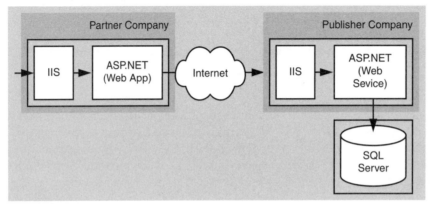

Figure 6.1
Extranet Web service business to business partner exchange

Characteristics

This scenario has the following characteristics:

- The publisher company exposes a Web service over the Internet.
- Partner company (not individual user) credentials (X.509 client certificates) are validated by the publisher to authorize access to resources. The publisher does not need to know about the user's individual logins in the partner company.
- Client certificates are mapped to Active Directory® directory service accounts within the publisher company.
- The extranet contains a separate Active Directory from the (internal) corporate Active Directory. The extranet Active Directory is in a separate forest, which provides a separate trust boundary.
- Web service authorization is based on the mapped Active Directory account. You can use separate authorization decisions based on partner company identity (represented by separate Active Directory accounts per company).
- The database is accessed by a single trusted connection that corresponds to the ASP.NET Web service process identity.

- The data retrieved from the Web service is sensitive and must be secured while in transit (internally within the publisher company and externally while flowing over the Internet).

Secure the Scenario

In this scenario, each partner company's internal Web application retrieves data from the publisher company through the Web service and then presents the retrieved data to its users. The publisher requires a secure mechanism to authenticate partner companies, although the identity of individual users within partner companies is not relevant.

Due to the sensitive nature of the data sent between the two companies over the Internet, it must be secured using SSL while in transit.

A firewall that permits only inbound connections from the IP address of extranet partner companies is used to prevent other unauthorized Internet users from opening network connections to the Web service server.

Table 6.1: Security measures

Category	Detail
Authentication	<ul><li>Partner applications use client certificates with each request to the Web service.</li><li>Client certificates from partner companies are mapped to individual Active Directory accounts.</li><li>Windows® authentication is used at the database. The ASP.NET Web service process identity is used to connect. The database trusts the Web service.</li></ul>
Authorization	<ul><li>The Web service uses .NET role-based authorization to check that authenticated Active Directory accounts are members of a Partner group.</li></ul>
Secure Communication	<ul><li>SSL is used to secure the communication between the partner Web application and publisher's Web service.</li><li>IPSec is used to secure all communication between the Web service and the database.</li></ul>

The Result

Figure 6.2 on the next page shows the recommended security configuration for this scenario.

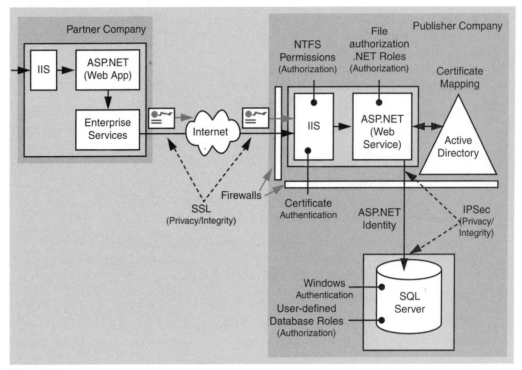

Figure 6.2
The recommended security configuration for the Web service business to business partner exchange scenario

Security Configuration Steps

Before you begin, you'll want to see the following:

- Creating custom ASP.NET accounts (see "How To: Create a Custom Account to Run ASP.NET" in the Reference section of this book)

- Creating a least privileged database account (see Chapter 12, "Data Access Security")

- Configuring SSL on a Web server (see "How To: Set Up SSL on a Web Server" in the Reference section of this book)

- Configuring IPSec (see "How To: Use IPSec to Provide Secure Communication Between Two Servers" in the Reference section of this book)

- Configuring IPSec through firewalls (see article Q233256, "How to Enable IPSec Traffic Through a Firewall," in the Microsoft Knowledge Base).

- Calling a Web service using SSL (see "How To: Call a Web Service Using SSL" in the Reference section of this book); this solution technique is required within the partner company
- The discussion of certificate management and the infrastructure is beyond the scope of this topic, for more information search for "Certificates and Authenticode" on Microsoft TechNet.

Configuring the Partner Application

This chapter does not go into details about the partner application and its security configuration. However, the following points needs to be considered to facilitate communication between the partner application and Web service:

- The partner company's Web application can choose an authentication mechanism that allows it to authenticate and authorize its internal users. Those users are not passed to the Web service for further authentication.
- The partner company's Web application makes calls on behalf of its user to the Web service. Users cannot directly call the Web service.
- The partner company's Web application uses a client certificate to prove its identity to the Web service.
- If the partner application is an ASP.NET Web application, then it must use an intermediate out of process component (an Enterprise Services application or Windows service) to load the certificate and forward it to the Web service.

   For more information about why this is necessary and the steps to achieve this, see "How to call a Web service using client certificates from ASP.NET" in the Reference section of this book.

Configuring the Extranet Web Server

Configure IIS Step	More Information
Disable Anonymous access for the Web service's virtual root directory	To work with IIS authentication settings, use the IIS MMC snap-in. Select your application's virtual directory, right-click and then click **Properties**. Click the **Directory Security** tab, and then click **Edit** within the **Anonymous access and authentication control** group.
Enable certificate Authentication for your Web application's and Web service's virtual root	See "How To: Set Up SSL on a Web Server" in the Reference section of this book. See "How To: Call a Web Service Using Client Certificates from ASP.NET" in the Reference section of this book.

Configure Active Directory (Extranet)

Step	More Information
Set up Active Directory accounts to represent partner companies	A separate extranet Active Directory is used. This is located in its own forest, and is completely separate from the corporate Active Directory.
Configure certificate mapping	See the "Step-by-Step Guide to Mapping Certificates to User Accounts" on Microsoft TechNet. Also see article Q313070, "HOW TO: Configure Client Certificate Mappings in IIS 5.0," in the Microsoft Knowledge Base.

Configure ASP.NET (Web Service)

Step	More Information
Configure the ASP.NET Web service to use Windows authentication	Edit Web.config in the Web service's virtual root directory Set the **<authentication>** element to: `<authentication mode="Windows" />`

Reset the password of the ASPNET account (used to run ASP.NET) to a known strong password	This allows you to create a duplicate local account (with the same username and password) on the database server. This is required to allow the ASPNET account to respond to network authentication challenges from the database server when it connects using Windows authentication.
	
	An alternative here is to use a least privileged domain account (if Windows authentication is permitted through the firewall). For more information, see "Process Identity for ASP.NET" in Chapter 8, "ASP.NET Security."
	
	Edit Machine.config located in %windir%\Microsoft.NET\Framework\v1.0.3705\CONFIG
	
	Set your custom account username and password attributes on the **<processModel>** element
	
	Default
	
	`<!-- userName="machine" password="AutoGenerate" -->`
	
	Becomes
	
	`<!-- userName="machine"`
	`        password="YourStrongPassword" -->`

Configuring SQL Server

Step	More Information
Create a Windows account on the computer running Microsoft SQL Server™ that matches the ASP.NET process account used to run the Web service (by default ASPNET)	The user name and password must match your ASP.NET process account. Give the account the following privileges: - Access this computer from the network - Deny logon locally - Log on as a batch job
Configure SQL Server for Windows authentication	
Create a SQL Server Login for the ASPNET account	This grants access to the SQL Server.
Create a new database user and map the login name to the database user	This grants access to the specified database.
Create a new user-defined database role within the database and place the database user into the role	
Establish database permissions for the database role	Grant minimum permissions See Chapter 12, "Data Access Security."

Configuring Secure Communication

Step	More Information
Configure the Web site on the Web server for SSL	See "How To: Set Up SSL on a Web Server" in the Reference section of this book.
Configure IPSec between Web server and database server	See "How To: Use IPSec to Provide Secure Communication Between Two Servers" in the Reference section of this book.

Analysis

- ASP.NET on the Web server is running as a least privileged local account (the default ASPNET account), so potential damage from compromise is mitigated.
- The ASP.NET Web applications within the partner companies use Windows Integrated authentication and perform authorization to determine who can access the Web service.

- The ASP.NET Web application within the partner company uses an intermediate Enterprise Services application to retrieve client certificates and make calls to the Web service.

- The publisher company uses the partner organization name (contained in the certificate) to perform certificate mapping within IIS.

- The Web service uses the mapped Active Directory account to perform authorization, using **PrincipalPermission** demands and .NET role checks.

- Windows authentication to SQL Server means you avoid storing credentials on the Web server and it also means that credentials are not sent across the internal network to the SQL Server computer. If you use SQL authentication, it is important to secure the connection string (containing a user name and password) within the application and as it is passed across the network. Use DPAPI or one of the alternative secure storage strategies discussed in Chapter 12, "Data Access Security," to store connection strings and use IPSec to protect the connection string (and sensitive application data) as it is passed between the Web service and database.

- SSL between partner companies and Web service protects the data passed across the Internet.

- IPSec between the Web service and database protects the data passed to and from the database on the corporate network. In some scenarios where the partner and publisher communicate over a private network, it may be possible to use IPSec for machine authentication in addition to secure communication.

Pitfalls

- The use of a duplicated local Windows account on the database server (one that matches the ASP.NET process account local to IIS) results in increased administration. Passwords must be manually updated and synchronized on a periodic basis.

- Because .NET role-based security is based on Windows group membership, this solution relies on Windows groups being set up at the correct level of granularity to match the categories of users (sharing the same security privileges) who will access the application. In this scenario, Active Directory accounts must be a member of a Partner group.

Q&A

- **The database doesn't know who the original caller is. How can I create an audit trail?**

  Audit end user (partner company) activity within the Web service. Pass the partner company identity at the application level to the database using stored procedure parameters.

Related Scenarios

The publisher company might publish non sensitive data such as soft copies of magazines, newspapers, and so on. In this scenario, the publisher can provide a unique username and password for each partner to connect with to retrieve the data from the Web service.

In this related scenario, the publisher's Web site is configured to authenticate users with Basic authentication. The partner application uses the username and password to explicitly set the credentials for the Web service proxy.

More Information

For more information about configuring Web service proxies, see Chapter 10, "Web Services Security."

Exposing a Web Application

In this scenario the publisher company gives its partners exclusive access to its application over the Internet and provides a partner-portal application; for example, to sell services, keep partners updated with product information, and provide online collaboration and so on. This scenario is shown in Figure 6.3.

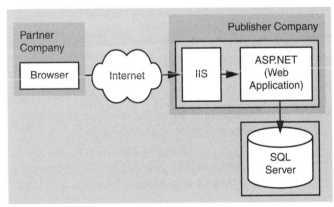

Figure 6.3
Partner portal scenario

Scenario Characteristics

This scenario has the following characteristics:

- The partner Web application accepts credentials either by using a Forms login page or it presents a login dialog using Basic authentication in IIS.

- The credentials are validated against a separate Active Directory within the extranet perimeter network (also known as DMZ, demilitarized zone, and screened subnet). The extranet Active Directory is in a separate forest, which provides a separate trust boundary.

- The database is accessed by a single trusted connection that corresponds to the ASP.NET Web application process identity.

- Web application authorization is based on either a **GenericPrincipal** object (created as part of the Forms authentication process) or a **WindowsPrincipal** object (if Basic authentication is used).

- The data retrieved from the Web application is sensitive and must be secured while in transit (internally within the publisher company and externally while flowing over the Internet).

Secure the Scenario

Due to the sensitive nature of the data sent between the two companies over the Internet, it must be secured using SSL while in transit.

A firewall that permits only inbound connections from the IP address of extranet partner companies is used to prevent other unauthorized Internet users from opening network connections to the Web server.

Table 6.2: Security measures

Category	Detail
Authentication	<ul><li>Users within partner companies are authenticated by the Web application using either Basic or Forms authentication against the extranet Active Directory.</li><li>Windows authentication is used at the database. The ASP.NET Web application process identity is used to connect. The database trusts the Web application.</li></ul>
Authorization	<ul><li>The Web application uses .NET role-based authorization to check that the authenticated user (represented by either a **GenericPrincipal** object or a **WindowsPrincipal** object, for Forms and Basic authentication respectively) are members of a Partner group.</li></ul>
Secure Communication	<ul><li>SSL is used to secure the communication between the partner Web browser and publisher's Web application.</li><li>IPSec is used to secure all communication between the Web application and the database.</li></ul>

The Result

Figure 6.4 shows the recommended security configuration for this scenario.

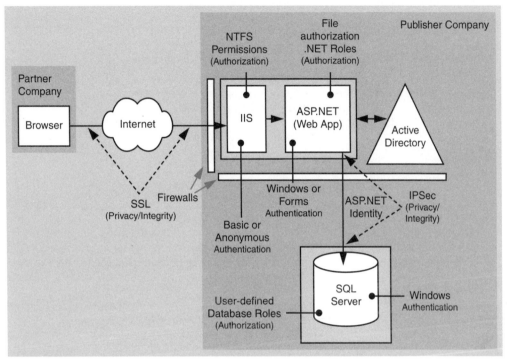

Figure 6.4
The recommended security configuration for the partner portal scenario

Configuring the Extranet Web Server

Configure IIS Step	More Information
To use Forms authentication, enable Anonymous access for the Web application's virtual root directory - or - To use Basic authentication, disable Anonymous access and select Basic authentication	

(continued)

Configure Active Directory (Extranet)	
Step	**More Information**
Set up Active Directory accounts to represent partner users	A separate extranet Active Directory is used. This is located in its own forest and is completely separate from the corporate Active Directory.

Configure ASP.NET	
Step	**More Information**

Configure the ASP.NET Web application to use Windows authentication (for IIS Basic) - or - Configure ASP.NET to use Forms authentication	Edit Web.config in the Web service's virtual root directory Set the <**authentication**> element to either:
	
	`<authentication mode="Windows" />`
	
	- or -
	
	`<authentication mode="Forms" />`

Reset the password of the ASPNET account (used to run ASP.NET) to a known strong password	This allows you to create a duplicate local account (with the same user name and password) on the database server. This is required to enable the ASPNET account to respond to network authentication challenges from the database server, when it connects using Windows authentication.
	
	An alternative here is to use a least privileged domain account (if Windows authentication is permitted through the firewall). For more information, see "Process Identity for ASP.NET" in Chapter 8, "ASP.NET Security."
	
	Edit Machine.config located in %windir%\Microsoft.NET\Framework\v1.0.3705\CONFIG
	
	Set your custom account username and password attributes on the <**processModel**> element
	
	Default
	
	`<!-- userName="machine" password="AutoGenerate" -->`
	
	Becomes
	
	`<!-- userName="machine"`
	`   password="YourStrongPassword" -->`

Configuring SQL Server

Step	More Information
Create a Windows account on the SQL Server computer that matches the ASP.NET process account used to run the Web service (by default ASPNET)	The user name and password must match your ASP.NET process account. Give the account the following privileges: - Access this computer from the network - Deny logon locally - Log on as a batch job
Configure SQL Server for Windows authentication	
Create a SQL Server Login for the ASPNET account	This grants access to the SQL Server.
Create a new database user and map the login name to the database user	This grants access to the specified database.
Create a new user-defined database role within the database and place the database user into the role	
Establish database permissions for the database role	Grant minimum permissions See Chapter 12, "Data Access Security."

Configuring Secure Communication

Step	More Information
Configure the Web site on the Web server for SSL	See "How To: Set Up SSL on a Web Server" in the Reference section of this book.
Configure IPSec between Web server and database server	See "How To: Use IPSec to Provide Secure Communication Between Two Servers" in the Reference section of this book.

Analysis

- ASP.NET on the Web server is running as a least privileged local account (the default ASPNET account), so potential damage from compromise is mitigated.
- SSL is used between browser and Web application to protect the Forms or Basic authentication credentials (both passed in clear text, although Basic uses Base64 encoding). SSL also protects the application-specific data returned from the Web application.

- For Forms authentication, SSL is used on all pages (not just the logon page) to protect the authentication cookie passed on all subsequent Web requests after the initial authentication.

- If SSL is used only on the initial logon page to encrypt the credentials passed for authentication, you should ensure that the Forms authentication ticket (contained within a cookie) is protected, because it is passed between client and server on each subsequent Web request. To encrypt the Forms authentication ticket, configure the **protection** attribute of the **<forms>** element as shown below and use the **Encrypt** method of the **FormsAuthentication** class to encrypt the ticket.

```
<authentication mode="Forms">
  <forms name="MyAppFormsAuth"
      loginUrl="login.aspx"
      protection="All"
      timeout="20"
      path="/" >
  </forms>
</authentication>
```

The **protection="All"** attribute specifies that when the application calls **FormsAuthentication.Encrypt**, the ticket should be validated (integrity checked) and encrypted. Call this method when you create the authentication ticket, typically within the application's Login button event handler.

```
string encryptedTicket = FormsAuthentication.Encrypt(authTicket);
```

For more information about Forms authentication and ticket encryption, see Chapter 8, "ASP.NET Security."

- Similarly, SSL is used on all pages for Basic authentication because the Basic credentials are passed on all Web page requests and not just the initial one where the Basic credentials are supplied by the user.

- For Basic authentication, ASP.NET automatically creates a **WindowsPrincipal** object to represent the authenticated caller and associates it with the current Web request (**HttpContext.User**) where it is used by .NET authorization including **PrincipalPermission** demands and .NET roles.

- For Forms authentication, you must develop code to validate the supplied credentials against Active Directory and construct a **GenericPrincipal** to represent the authenticated user.

- Windows authentication to SQL Server means you avoid storing credentials on the Web server and it also means that credentials are not sent across the internal network to the SQL Server computer.

- IPSec between the Web service and database protects the data passed to and from the database on the corporate network.

Pitfalls

- The use of a duplicated local Windows account on the database server (one that matches the ASP.NET process account local to IIS) results in increased administration. Passwords must be manually updated and synchronized on a periodic basis.

- Basic authentication results in a pop-up dialog within the browser. To provide a more seamless logon experience, use Forms authentication.

Related Scenarios

No Connectivity from Extranet to Corporate Network

For additional security, the extranet application can be built to require no connectivity back into the corporate network. In this scenario:

- A separate SQL Server database is located in the extranet and replication of data occurs from the internal database to the extranet database.

- Routers are used to refuse connections from the extranet to the corporate network. Connections can be established the other way using specific high ports.

- Connections from the corporate network to the extranet should be performed through a dedicated server that has strong auditing and logging and through which users must authenticate before accessing the extranet.

More Information

- See the following Microsoft TechNet articles:
  - "Extending Your Network to Business Partners"
  - "Deploying SharePoint Portal Server in an Extranet Environment"
- For more information about using Forms authentication with Active Directory, see "How To: Use Forms Authentication with Active Directory" in the Reference section of this book.

Summary

This chapter has described how to secure two common extranet application scenarios.

For intranet and Internet application scenarios, see Chapter 5, "Intranet Security," and Chapter 7, "Internet Security."

7

Internet Security

Internet applications have large audiences, many potential uses, and varied security requirements. They range from portal applications that require no user authentication, through Web applications that provide content for registered users, to large scale e-commerce applications that require full authentication, authorization, credit card validation, and secure communication of sensitive data over public and internal networks.

As Internet application developers, you face a challenge to ensure that your application uses appropriate defense mechanisms and is designed to be scalable, high performance, and secure. Some of the challenges you face include:

- Choosing an appropriate user credential store, for example, a custom database or Active Directory® directory service.
- Making your application work through firewalls.
- Flowing security credentials across the multiple tiers of your application.
- Performing authorization.
- Ensuring the integrity and privacy of data as it flows across public and internal networks.
- Securing your application's state with a database.
- Ensuring the integrity of your application's data.
- Implementing a solution that can scale to potentially huge numbers of users.

The two common Internet application scenarios presented in this chapter, which are used to illustrate recommended authentication, authorization, and secure communication techniques are:

- ASP.NET to SQL Server
- ASP.NET to Remote Enterprise Services to SQL Server

> **Note:** Several scenarios described in this chapter change the password of the default ASPNET account to allow duplicated accounts to be created on remote computers for network authentication purposes. This requires an update to the <**processModel**> element of Machine.config. <**processModel**> credentials should not be stored in plain text in machine.config. Instead use the aspnet_setreg.exe utility to store encrypted credentials in the registry. For more information, see Chapter 8, "ASP.NET Security" and article Q329290, "HOWTO: Use the ASP.NET Utility to Encrypt Credentials and Session State Connection Strings" in the Microsoft Knowledge Base.

ASP.NET to SQL Server

In this scenario with two physical tiers, registered users securely log in to the Web-based application using a Web browser. The ASP.NET-based Web application makes secure connections to a Microsoft® SQL Server™ database to manage predominantly data retrieval tasks. An example is a portal application that provides news content to registered subscribers. This is shown in Figure 7.1.

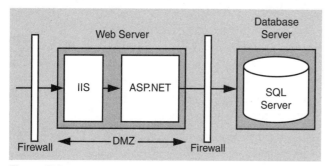

Figure 7.1
An ASP.NET Web application to SQL Server Internet scenario

Characteristics

This scenario has the following characteristics:

- Users have a number of different browser types.
- Anonymous users can browse the application's unrestricted pages.
- Users must register or log on (through an HTML form) before being allowed to view restricted pages.
- User credentials are validated against a SQL Server database.
- All user input (such as user credentials) that is used in database queries is validated to mitigate the threat of SQL injection attacks.

- The front-end Web application is located within a perimeter network (also known as DMZ, demilitarized zone, and screened subnet), with firewalls separating it from the Internet and the internal corporate network (and the SQL Server database).
- The application requires strong security, high levels of scalability, and detailed auditing.
- The database trusts the application to authenticate users properly (that is, the application makes calls to the database on behalf of the users).
- The Web application connects to the database by using the ASP.NET process account.
- A single user-defined database role is used within SQL Server for database authorization.

Secure the Scenario

In this scenario, the Web application presents a logon page to accept credentials. Successfully validated users are allowed to proceed, all others are denied access. The database authenticates against the ASP.NET default process identity, which is a least privileged account (that is, the database trusts the ASP.NET application).

Table 7.1: Security summary

Category	Detail
Authentication	• IIS is configured to allow anonymous access; the ASP.NET Web application authenticates users with Forms authentication to acquire credentials. Validation is against a SQL Server database. • Users' passwords are not stored in the database. Instead password hashes with salt values are stored. The salt mitigates the threat associated with dictionary attacks. • Windows® authentication is used to connect to the database using the least privileged Windows account used to run the ASP.NET Web application.
Authorization	• The ASP.NET process account is authorized to access system resources on the Web server. Resources are protected with Windows ACLs. • Access to the database is authorized using the ASP.NET application identity.
Secure Communication	• Secure sensitive data sent between the users and the Web application by using SSL. • Secure sensitive data sent between the Web server and the database server by using IPSec.

The Result

Figure 7.2 shows the recommended security configuration for this scenario.

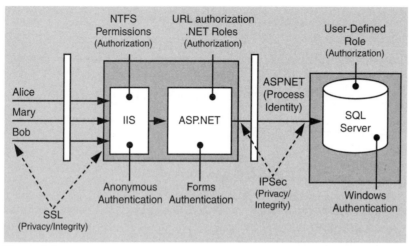

Figure 7.2
The recommended security configuration for the ASP.NET to SQL Server Internet scenario

Security Configuration Steps

Before you begin, you'll want to see the following:

- Creating custom ASP.NET accounts (see "How To: Create a Custom Account to Run ASP.NET" in the Reference section of this book)

- Creating a least privileged database account (see Chapter 12, "Data Access Security")

- Configuring SSL on a Web server (see "How To: Set Up SSL on a Web Server" in the Reference section of this book)

- Configuring IPSec (see "How To: Use IPSec to Provide Secure Communication Between Two Servers" in the Reference section of this book)

Configure the Web Server

Configure IIS Step	More Information
Enable Anonymous access for your Web application's virtual root directory	To work with IIS authentication settings, use the IIS MMC snap-in. Right-click your application's virtual directory, and then click **Properties**. Click the **Directory Security** tab, and then click **Edit** within the **Anonymous access and authentication control** group.

Configure ASP.NET Step	More Information

Reset the password of the ASPNET account (used to run ASP.NET) to a known strong password	This allows you to create a duplicate local account (with the same user name and password) on the database server. This is required to allow the ASPNET account to respond to network authentication challenges from the database server when it connects using Windows authentication.
	
	An alternative here is to use a least privileged domain account (if Windows authentication is permitted through the firewall). For more information, see "Process Identity for ASP.NET" in Chapter 8, "ASP.NET Security."
	
	Edit Machine.config located in %windir%\Microsoft.NET\Framework\v1.0.3705\CONFIG
	
	Set your custom account user name and password attributes on the <**processModel**> element
	
	Default
	
	`<!-- userName="machine" password="AutoGenerate" -->`
	
	Becomes
	
	`<!-- userName="machine"`
	`        password="YourStrongPassword" -->`

Configure your ASP.NET Web application to use Forms authentication (with SSL)	Edit Web.config in your application's virtual directory root
	Set the <**authentication**> element to:
	
	`<authentication mode="Forms" >`
	`  <forms name="MyAppFormsAuth"`
	`          loginUrl="login.aspx"`
	`          protection="All"`
	`          timeout="20"`
	`          path="/" >`
	`  </forms>`
	`</authentication>`
	
	For more information about using Forms authentication against a SQL Server database, see "How To: Use Forms Authentication with SQL Server 2000" in the Reference section of this book.

Configuring SQL Server

Step	More Information
Create a Windows account on your SQL Server computer that matches the ASP.NET process account	The user name and password must match your custom ASP.NET application account or must be ASPNET if you are using the default account.
Configure SQL Server for Windows authentication	
Create a SQL Server Login for your custom ASP.NET application account	This grants access to SQL Server.
Create a new database user and map the login name to the database user	This grants access to the specified database.
Create a new user-defined database role within the database and place the database user into the role	
Establish database permissions for the database role	Grant minimum permissions. For more information, see Chapter 12, "Data Access Security."

Configuring Secure Communication

Step	More Information
Configure the Web site for SSL	See "How To: Setup SSL on a Web Server" in the Reference section of this book.
Configure IPSec between application server and database server	See "How To: Use IPSec to Provide Secure Communication Between Two Servers" in the Reference section of this book.

Analysis

- Forms authentication is ideal in this scenario because the users do not have Windows accounts. The Forms login page is used to acquire user credentials. Credential validation must be performed by application code. Any data store can be used. A SQL Server database is the most common solution, although Active Directory provides an alternate credential store.

- With Forms authentication, you must protect the initial logon credentials with SSL. The Forms authentication ticket (passed as a cookie on subsequent Web requests from the authenticated client) must also be protected. You could use SSL for all pages in order to protect the ticket, or alternatively you can encrypt the Forms authentication ticket by configuring the **protection** attribute of the <**forms**> element (to **All** or **Encrypt**) and use the **Encrypt** method of the **FormsAuthentication** class to encrypt the ticket.

  The **protection="All"** attribute specifies that when the application calls **FormsAuthentication.Encrypt**, the ticket should be validated (integrity checked) and encrypted. Call this method when you create the authentication ticket, typically within the application's Login button event handler.

  ```
  string encryptedTicket = FormsAuthentication.Encrypt(authTicket);
  ```

  For more information about Forms authentication and ticket encryption, see Chapter 8, "ASP.NET Security."

- ASP.NET runs as the least privileged local ASPNET account, so potential damage from compromise is mitigated.

- URL authorization on the Web server allows unauthenticated users to browse unrestricted Web pages and forces authentication for restricted pages.

- Because impersonation is not enabled, any local or remote resource access performed by the Web-based application is performed using the ASPNET account security context. Windows ACLs on secure resources should be set accordingly.

- User credentials are validated against a custom SQL Server database. Password hashes (with salt) are stored within the database. For more information, see "Authenticating Users against a Database" in Chapter 12, "Data Access Security."

- By using Windows authentication to SQL Server, you avoid storing credentials in files on the Web server and also passing them over the network.

- If your application currently uses SQL authentication, you must securely store the database connection string as it contains user names and passwords. Consider using DPAPI. For more details, see "Storing Database Connection Strings Securely", in Chapter 12, "Data Access Security."

- The use of a duplicated Windows account on the database server (one that matches the ASP.NET process account) results in increased administration. If a password is changed on one computer, it must be synchronized and updated on all computers. In some scenarios, you may be able to use a least-privileged domain account for easier administration.

- IPSec between the Web server and database server ensures the privacy of the data sent to and from the database.

- SSL between browser and Web server protects credentials and any other security sensitive data such as credit card numbers.

- If you use a Web farm, ensure that the encryption keys, for example those used to encrypt the Forms authentication ticket (and specified by the **<machineKey>** element in Machine.config), are consistent across all servers in the farm. See Chapter 8, "ASP.NET Security," for further details about using ASP.NET in a Web farm scenario.

Pitfalls

The application must flow the original caller's identity to the database to support auditing requirements. Caller identity may be passed using stored procedure parameters.

Related Scenarios

Forms Authentication against Active Directory

The user credentials that are accepted from the Forms login page can be authenticated against various stores. Active Directory is an alternate to using a SQL Server database.

More Information

For more information, see "How To: Use Forms Authentication with Active Directory" in the Reference section of this book.

.NET Roles for Authorization

The preceding scenario doesn't take into consideration the different types of users accessing the application. For example, a portal server could have different subscription levels such as Standard, Premier, and Enterprise.

If role information is maintained in the user store (SQL Server database), the application can create a **GenericPrincipal** object in which role and identity information can be stored. After the **GenericPrincipal** is created and added to the Web request context (using **HttpContext.User**), you can add programmatic role checks to method code or you can decorate methods and pages with **PrincipalPermission** attributes to demand role membership.

More Information

- For more information about creating **GenericPrincipal** objects that contain role lists, see "How To: Use Forms Authentication with GenericPrincipal Objects" in the Reference section of this book.

- For more information about **PrincipalPermission** demands and programmatic role checks, see Chapter 8, "ASP.NET Security."

Using a Domain Anonymous Account at the Web Server

In this scenario variation, the default anonymous Internet user account (a local account called IUSR_MACHINE) is replaced by a domain account. The domain account is configured with the minimum privileges necessary to run the application (you can start with no privilege and incrementally add privileges). If you have multiple Web-based applications, you can use different domain accounts (one for each Web-based application or virtual directory).

In order to flow the security context of the anonymous domain account from IIS to ASP.NET, turn on impersonation for the Web-based application by using the following web.config file setting

```
<identity impersonate="true" />
```

If the Web-based application communicates with a remote resource such as a database, the domain account must be granted the necessary permissions to the resource. For example, if the application accesses a remote file system, ACLs must be configured appropriately to give (at minimum) read access to the domain account. If the application accesses a SQL Server database, the domain account must be mapped using a SQL login to a database login.

As the security context that flows through the application is that of the anonymous account, the original caller's identity (captured through Forms authentication) must be passed at the application level from tier to tier; for example, through method and stored procedure parameters.

More Information

- For more information regarding this approach, see "Using the Anonymous Internet User Account" within Chapter 8, "ASP.NET Security."
- Before implementing this scenario, see article Q259353, "Must Enter Password Manually After You Set Password Synchronization" in the Microsoft Knowledge Base.

ASP.NET to Remote Enterprise Services to SQL Server

In this scenario, a Web server running ASP.NET pages makes secure connections to serviced components, located on a remote application server that in turn connects to a SQL Server database. In common with many Internet application infrastructures, the Web server and application server are separated by a firewall (and the Web server is located within a perimeter network). Serviced components make secure connections to SQL Server.

As an example, consider an Internet banking application that provides sensitive data, (for example, private financial details) to users. All banking transactions from the client to the database must be secured and data integrity is critical. Not only does the traffic to and from the user need to be secured but the traffic to and from the database needs to be secured as well. This is shown in Figure 7.3.

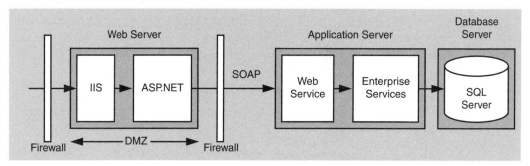

Figure 7.3
An ASP.NET to remote Enterprise Services to SQL Server Internet scenario

Characteristics

- Users have a number of different browser types.
- Anonymous users can browse the application's unrestricted pages.
- Users must register or log on (through an HTML form) before being allowed to view restricted pages.
- The front-end Web-based application is located within a perimeter network, with firewalls separating it from the Internet and the internal corporate network (and the application server).
- The application requires strong security, high levels of scalability, and detailed auditing.
- The Web-based application uses SOAP to connect to a Web services layer, which provides an interface to the serviced components that run within an Enterprise Services application on the application server. SOAP is preferred to DCOM due to firewall restrictions.
- SQL Server is using a single user-defined database role for authorization.
- Data is security sensitive and integrity and privacy must be secured over the network and in all persistent data stores.
- Enterprise Services (COM+) transactions are used to enforce data integrity.

Secure the Scenario

In this scenario, the Web service accepts credentials from a Forms login page and then authenticates the caller against a SQL Server database. The login page uses SSL to protect the user's credentials passed over the Internet.

The Web-based application communicates with a Web service, which provides an interface to the business services implemented within serviced components. The Web service trusts the Web-based application (inside the perimeter network) and authenticates the ASP.NET process identity. The user's identity is passed through all tiers at the application level using method and stored procedure parameters. This information is used for auditing the users' actions across the tiers.

Table 7.2: Security measures

Category	Detail
Authentication	<ul><li>Provide strong authentication at the Web server.</li><li>Authenticate the Enterprise Services application identity at the database.</li><li>IIS is configured for anonymous access and the Web-based application authenticates users with Forms authentication (against a SQL Server database).</li><li>The Web service's virtual directory is configured for Integrated Windows authentication. Web services authenticate the Web-based application's process identity.</li><li>Windows authentication is used to connect to the database. The database authenticates the least privileged Windows account used to run the Enterprise Services application.</li></ul>
Authorization	<ul><li>The trusted subsystem model is used and per-user authorization occurs only within the Web application.</li><li>User access to pages on the Web server is controlled with URL authorization.</li><li>The ASP.NET process account is authorized to access system resources on the Web server. Resources are protected with ACLs.</li><li>Permissions within the database are controlled by a user-defined role. The Enterprise Services application identity is a member of the role.</li><li>The Enterprise Services process account is authorized to access system resources on the application server. Resources are protected ACLs.</li></ul>
Secure Communication	<ul><li>Sensitive data sent between the users and the Web-based application is secured with SSL.</li><li>Sensitive data sent between the Web server and Web service is secured with SSL.</li><li>Sensitive data sent between serviced components and the database is secured with IPSec.</li></ul>

The Result

Figure 7.4 shows the recommended security configuration for this scenario.

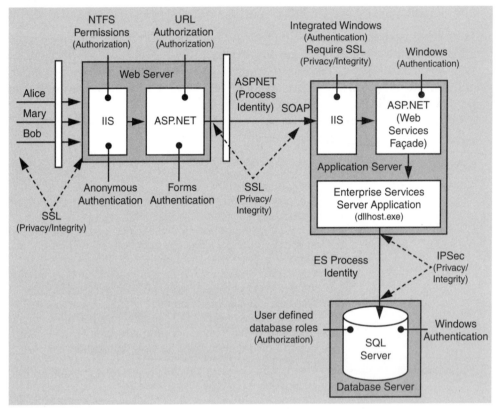

Figure 7.4
The recommended security configuration for the ASP.NET to remote Enterprise Services to SQL Server Internet scenario

Security Configuration Steps

Before you begin, you'll want to see the following:

- Creating a least privileged database account (see Chapter 12, "Data Access Security")
- Configuring SSL on a Web server (see "How To: Set Up SSL on a Web Server" in the Reference section of this book)
- Configuring IPSec (see "How To: Use IPSec to Provide Secure Communication Between Two Servers" in the Reference section of this book)
- Configuring Enterprise Services security (see "How To: Use Role-based Security with Enterprise Services" in the Reference section of this book)

Configure the Web Server

Configure IIS Step	More Information
Enable Anonymous access for your Web-based application's virtual root directory	

Configure ASP.NET Step	More Information

Reset the password of the ASPNET account (used to run ASP.NET) to a known strong password	This allows you to create a duplicate local account (with the same user name and password) on the application server. This is required to enable the ASPNET account to respond to network authentication challenges from the application server.
	
	An alternative is to use a least privileged domain account (if Windows authentication is permitted through the firewall).
	
	For more information, see "Process Identity for ASP.NET" in Chapter 8, "ASP.NET Security."
	
	Edit Machine.config located in %windir%\Microsoft.NET\Framework\v1.0.3705\CONFIG
	
	Set your custom account username and password attributes on the <**processModel**> element.
	
	Default
	
	`<!-- userName="machine" password="AutoGenerate" -->`
	
	Becomes
	`<!-- userName="machine"`
	`        password="YourStrongPassword" -->`

(continued)

Configure ASP.NET *(continued)*	
Step	**More Information**

Configure your Web-based application to use Forms authentication (with SSL)	Edit Web.config in your application's virtual directory root
	Set the <**authentication**> element to:
	
	```<authentication mode="Forms" >```
	``` <forms name="MyAppFormsAuth"```
	``` loginUrl="login.aspx"```
	``` protection="All"```
	``` timeout="20"```
	``` path="/" >```
	``` </forms>```
	```</authentication>```
	
	For more information about using Forms authentication against a SQL Server database, see "How To: Use Forms Authentication with SQL Server 2000" in the Reference section of this book.

Configure the Application Server

Configure IIS	
Step	**More Information**
Disable anonymous access	
Configure Integrated Windows authentication	IIS authenticates the ASP.NET process identity from the Web-based application on the Web server.

Configure ASP.NET	
Step	**More Information**
Use Windows authentication	Edit Web.config in your Web service's virtual directory root. Set the <**authentication**> element to: ``` <authentication mode="Windows" />```

Configure Enterprise Services	
Step	**More Information**
Create a least privileged custom account for running the Enterprise Services server application	**Note**: If you use a local account, you must also create a duplicate account on the database server computer.
Configure the Enterprise Services application to use the custom account	Refer to "Configuring Security" within Chapter 9, "Enterprise Services Security."
Enable role-based access checking	Refer to "Configuring Security" within Chapter 9, "Enterprise Services Security."

Configure Enterprise Services	
Step	**More Information**
Add a single Enterprise Services (COM+) role to the application called (for example Trusted Web Service)	Full end-user authorization is performed by the Web-based application. The Web service (and serviced components) only allows access to members of the Trusted Web Service role.
Add the local ASPNET account to the Trusted Web Service role	Refer to "Configuring Security" within Chapter 9, "Enterprise Services Security."

Configuring SQL Server

Step	**More Information**
Create a Windows account on your SQL Server computer that matches the Enterprise Services application account	The user name and password must match your custom Enterprise Services account.
Configure SQL Server for Windows authentication	
Create a SQL Server Login for your custom Enterprise Services account	This grants access to the SQL Server.
Create a new database user and map the login name to the database user	This grants access to the specified database.
Create a new user-defined database role and add the database user to the role	
Establish database permissions for the database role	Grant minimum permissions For details, see Chapter 12, "Data Access Security."

Configuring Secure Communication

Step	**More Information**
Configure the Web site for SSL	See "How To: Setup SSL on a Web Server" in the Reference section of this book.
Configure SSL between the Web server and application server.	See "How To: Call a Web Service Using SSL" in the Reference section of this book.
Configure IPSec between application server and database server	See "How To: Use IPSec to Provide Secure Communication Between Two Servers" in the Reference section of this book.

Analysis

- Forms authentication is ideal in this scenario because the users do not have Windows accounts. The Forms login page is used to acquire user credentials. Credential validation must be performed by application code. Any data store can be used. A SQL Server database is the most common solution, although Active Directory provides an alternate credential store.

- The Web-based application is running as the least privileged local ASPNET account, so potential damage from compromise is mitigated.

- URL authorization on the Web server allows unauthenticated users to browse unrestricted Web pages and forces authentication for restricted pages.

- Because impersonation is not enabled, any local or remote resource access performed by the Web-based application does so using the ASPNET account security context. ACLs should be configured accordingly.

- User credentials are validated against a custom SQL Server database. Password hashes (with salt) are stored within the database. For more information, see "Authenticating Users against a Database" in Chapter 12, "Data Access Security."

- Windows authentication to SQL Server means you avoid storing credentials in files on the application server and avoid passing them across the network.

- The use of a duplicated Windows account on the database server (one that matches the Enterprise Services process account) results in increased administration. If a password is changed on one computer, it must be synchronized and updated on all computers. In some scenarios, you may be able to use a least-privileged domain account for easier administration.

- When the Web application calls the Web service, it must configure the Web service proxy using DefaultCredentials (that is, the ASP.NET process account; ASPNET).

```
proxy.Credentials = System.Net.CredentialCache.DefaultCredentials;
```

  For more information, see "Passing Credentials For Authentication to Web Services" in Chapter 10, "Web Services Security."

- SSL between the Web server and Web service layer (that fronts the serviced components on the application server) ensures the privacy of the data sent between the two servers.

- The Enterprise Services application is configured for application-level role-based security. The configuration permits only the local ASPNET account (used to run the Web service) to access the serviced components.

- IPSec between the application server and database server ensures the privacy of the data sent to and from the database.
- SSL between browser and Web server protects credentials and bank account details.

Pitfalls

The application must flow the original caller's identity to the database to support auditing requirements. Caller identity may be passed using stored procedure parameters.

Related Scenarios

Forms Authentication Against Active Directory

The user credentials that are accepted from the Forms login page can be authenticated against various stores. Active Directory is an alternate to using a SQL Server database.

More Information

For more information, see "How To: Use Forms Authentication with Active Directory" in the Reference section of this book.

Using DCOM

Windows 2000 (SP3 or SP2 with QFE 18.1) or Windows .NET Server allows you to configure Enterprise Services applications to use a static endpoint. If a firewall separates the client from the server, this means that you need to open only two ports in the firewall. Specifically, you must open port 135 for RPC and a port for your Enterprise Services application.

This enhancement to DCOM makes it a valid choice of communication protocol between Web server and application server and removes the requirement to have a Web services layer.

Important: If your application requires distributed transactions to flow between the two servers, DCOM must be used. Transactions cannot flow over SOAP. In the SOAP scenario, transactions must be initiated by the serviced components on the application server.

More Information

For more information, see Chapter 9, "Enterprise Services Security."

Using .NET Remoting

Remoting can be a valid choice when you don't need services provided by Enterprise Services such as transactions, queued components, object pooling, and so on. .NET Remoting solutions also support network load balancing at the middle tier. Note the following when you use .NET Remoting:

- For ultimate performance, use the TCP channel and host in a Windows service. Note that this channel provides no authentication and authorization mechanism by default. The TCP channel is designed for trusted subsystem scenarios. You can use an IPSec policy to establish a secure channel and to ensure that only the Web server communicates with the application server.

- If you need authentication and authorization checks using **IPrincipal** objects, you should host the remote objects in ASP.NET and use the HTTP channel. This allows you use the IIS and ASP.NET security features.

- The remote object can connect to the database using Windows authentication and can use the host process identity (either ASP.NET or a Windows service identity).

More Information

For more information about .NET Remoting security, see Chapter 11, ".NET Remoting Security."

Summary

This chapter has described how to secure a set of common Internet application scenarios.

For Intranet and extranet application scenarios, see Chapter 5, "Intranet Security," and Chapter 6, "Extranet Security."

8

ASP.NET Security

This chapter presents guidance and recommendations that will help you build secure ASP.NET Web applications. Much of the guidance and many of the recommendations presented in this chapter also apply to the development of ASP.NET Web services and .NET Remoting objects hosted by ASP.NET.

ASP.NET Security Architecture

ASP.NET works in conjunction with IIS, the .NET Framework, and the underlying security services provided by the operating system, to provide a range of authentication and authorization mechanisms. These are summarized in Figure 8.1 on the next page.

Figure 8.1 illustrates the authentication and authorization mechanisms provided by IIS and ASP.NET. When a client issues a Web request, the following sequence of authentication and authorization events occurs:

1. The HTTP(S) Web request is received from the network. SSL can be used to ensure the server identity (using server certificates) and, optionally, the client identity.

   Note: SSL also provides a secure channel to protect sensitive data passed between client and server (and vice-versa).

2. IIS authenticates the caller by using Basic, Digest, Integrated (NTLM or Kerberos), or Certificate authentication. If all or part of your site does not require authenticated access, IIS can be configured for anonymous authentication. IIS creates a Windows access token for each authenticated user. If anonymous authentication is selected, IIS creates an access token for the anonymous Internet user account (which, by default, is IUSR_MACHINE).

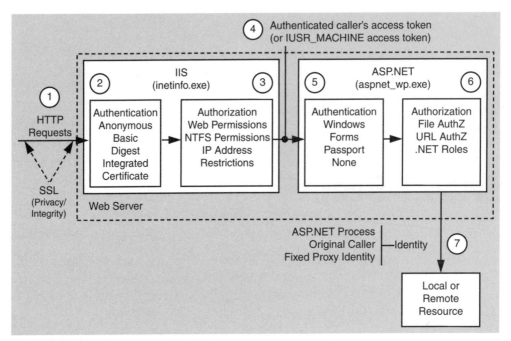

Figure 8.1
ASP.NET security services

3. IIS authorizes the caller to access the requested resource. NTFS permissions defined by ACLs attached to the requested resource are used to authorize access. IIS can also be configured to accept requests only from client computers with specific IP addresses.

4. IIS passes the authenticated caller's Windows access token to ASP.NET (this may be the anonymous Internet user's access token, if anonymous authentication is being used).

5. ASP.NET authenticates the caller.

   If ASP.NET is configured for Windows authentication, no additional authentication occurs at this point. ASP.NET will accept any token it receives from IIS.

   If ASP.NET is configured for Forms authentication, the credentials supplied by the caller (using an HTML form) are authenticated against a data store; typically a Microsoft® SQL Server™ database or Active Directory® directory service. If ASP.NET is configured for Passport authentication, the user is redirected to a Passport site and the Passport authentication service authenticates the user.

6. ASP.NET authorizes access to the requested resource or operation.

   The **UrlAuthorizationModule** (a system provided HTTP module) uses authorization rules configured in Web.config (specifically, the **<authorization>** element) to ensure that the caller can access the requested file or folder.

With Windows authentication, the **FileAuthorizationModule** (another HTTP module) checks that the caller has the necessary permission to access the requested resource. The caller's access token is compared against the ACL that protects the resource.

.NET roles can also be used either declaratively or programmatically to ensure that the caller is authorized to access the requested resource or perform the requested operation.

7. Code within your application accesses local and/or remote resources by using a particular identity. By default, ASP.NET performs no impersonation and as a result, the configured ASP.NET process account provides the identity. Alternate options include the original caller's identity if impersonation is enabled, or a configured service identity.

Gatekeepers

The authorization points or gatekeepers within an ASP.NET Web application are provided by IIS and ASP.NET:

IIS

With anonymous authentication turned off, IIS permits requests only from users that it can authenticate either in its domain or in a trusted domain.

For static file types (for example .jpg, .gif and .htm files—files that are not mapped to an ISAPI extension), IIS uses the NTFS permissions associated with the requested file to perform access control.

ASP.NET

The ASP.NET gatekeepers include the **UrlAuthorizationModule**, **FileAuthorizationModule** and principal permission demands and role checks.

UrlAuthorizationModule

You can configure <**authorization**> elements within your application's Web.config file to control which users and groups of users should have access to the application. Authorization is based on the **IPrincipal** object stored in **HttpContext.User**.

FileAuthorizationModule

For file types mapped by IIS to the ASP.NET ISAPI extension (Aspnet_isapi.dll), automatic access checks are performed using the authenticated user's Windows access token (which may be IUSR_MACHINE) against the ACL attached to the requested ASP.NET file.

Note: Impersonation is not required for file authorization to work.

The **FileAuthorizationModule** class only performs access checks against the re-quested file, and not for files accessed by the code in the requested page, although these are access checked by IIS.

For example, if you request Default.aspx and it contains an embedded user control (Usercontrol.ascx), which in turn includes an image tag (pointing to Image.gif), the **FileAuthorizationModule** performs an access check for Default.aspx and Usercontrol.ascx, because these file types are mapped by IIS to the ASP.NET ISAPI extension.

The **FileAuthorizationModule** does not perform a check for Image.gif, because this is a static file handled internally by IIS. However, as access checks for static files are performed by IIS, the authenticated user must still be granted read permission to the file with an appropriately configured ACL.

This scenario is shown in Figure 8.2.

Note to system administrators: The authenticated user requires NTFS read permissions to all of the files involved in the scenario. The only variable is regarding which gatekeeper is used to enforce access control. The ASP.NET process account only requires read access to the ASP.NET registered file types.

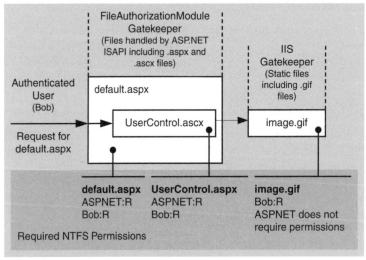

Figure 8.2
IIS and ASP.NET gatekeepers working together

In this scenario you can prevent access at the file gate. If you configure the ACL attached to Default.aspx and deny access to a particular user, the user control or any embedded images will not get a chance to be sent to the client by the code in Default.aspx. If the user requests the images directly, IIS performs the access checks itself.

Principal Permission Demands and Explicit Role Checks

In addition to the IIS and ASP.NET configurable gatekeepers, you can also use principal permission demands (declaratively or programmatically) as an additional fine-grained access control mechanism. Principal permission checks (performed by the **PrincipalPermissionAttribute** class) allow you to control access to classes, methods, or individual code blocks based on the identity and group membership of individual users, as defined by the **IPrincipal** object attached to the current thread.

Note: Principal permission demands used to demand role membership are different from calling **IPrincipal.IsInRole** to test role membership; the former results in an exception if the caller is not a member of the specified role, while the latter simply returns a Boolean value to confirm role membership.

With Windows authentication, ASP.NET automatically attaches a **WindowsPrincipal** object that represents the authenticated user to the current Web request (using **HttpContext.User**). Forms and Passport authentication create a **GenericPrincipal** object with the appropriate identity and no roles and attaches it to the **HttpContext.User**.

More Information

- For more information about configuring security, see "Configuring Security" later in this chapter.

- For more information about programming security (and **IPrincipal** objects), see "Programming Security" later in this chapter.

Authentication and Authorization Strategies

ASP.NET provides a number of declarative and programmatic authorization mechanisms that can be used in conjunction with a variety of authentication schemes. This allows you to develop an in depth authorization strategy and one that can be configured to provide varying degrees of granularity; for example, per-user or per-user group (role-based).

This section shows you which authorization options (both configurable and programmatic) are available for a set of commonly used authentication options.

The authentication options that follow are summarized here:

- Windows authentication with impersonation
- Windows authentication without impersonation
- Windows authentication using a fixed identity
- Forms authentication
- Passport authentication

Available Authorization Options

The following table shows you the set of available authorization options. For each one the table indicates whether or not Windows authentication and/or impersonation are required. If Windows authentication is not required, the particular authorization option is available for all other authentication types. Use the table to help refine your authentication/authorization strategy.

Table 8.1: Windows authentication and impersonation requirements

Authorization Option	Requires Windows Authentication	Requires Impersonation
FileAuthorizationModule	Yes	No
UrlAuthorizationModule	No	No
Principal Permission Demands	No	No
.NET Roles	No	No
Enterprise Services Roles application)	Yes	Yes (within the ASP.NET Web
NTFS Permissions (for directly requested static files types; not mapped to an ISAPI extension)	N/A – These files are not handled by ASP.NET. With any (non-Anonymous) IIS authentication mechanism, permissions should be configured for individual authenticated users. With Anonymous authentication, permissions should be configured for IUSR_MACHINE.	No (IIS performs the access check.)
NTFS Permissions (for files accessed by Web application code)	No	No If impersonating, configure ACLs against the impersonated Windows identity, which is either the original caller or the identity specified on the <identity> element in Web.config*.

Windows Authentication with Impersonation

The following configuration elements show you how to enable Windows (IIS) authentication and impersonation declaratively in Web.config or Machine.config.

Note: You should configure authentication on a per-application basis in each application's Web.config file.

```
<authentication mode="Windows" />
<identity impersonate="true" />
```

With this configuration, your ASP.NET application code impersonates the IIS-authenticated caller.

Configurable Security

When you use Windows authentication together with impersonation, the following authorization options are available to you:

- **Windows ACLs**
  - **Client Requested Resources**. The ASP.NET **FileAuthorizationModule** performs access checks for requested file types that are mapped to the ASP.NET ISAPI. It uses the original caller's access token and ACL attached to requested resources in order to perform access checks.

    For static files types (not mapped to an ISAPI extension), IIS performs access checks using the caller's access token and ACL attached to the file.
  - **Resources Accessed by Your Application**. You can configure Windows ACLs on resources accessed by your application (files, folders, registry keys, Active Directory objects, and so on) against the original caller.
- **URL Authorization**. Configure URL authorization in Web.config. With Windows authentication, user names take the form DomainName\UserName and roles map one-to-one with Windows groups.

  ```
  <authorization>
    <deny user="DomainName\UserName" />
    <allow roles="DomainName\WindowsGroup" />
  </authorization>
  ```

- **Enterprise Services (COM+) Roles**. Roles are maintained in the COM+ catalog. You can configure roles with the Component Services administration tool or script.

Programmatic Security

Programmatic security refers to security checks located within your Web application code. The following programmatic security options are available when you use Windows authentication and impersonation:

- **PrincipalPermission Demands**
  - Imperative (in-line within a method's code)

    ```
    PrincipalPermission permCheck = new PrincipalPermission(
                                    null, @"DomainName\WindowsGroup");
    permCheck.Demand();
    ```

  - Declarative (attributes preceding interfaces, classes and methods)

    ```
    [PrincipalPermission(SecurityAction.Demand,
                         Role=@"DomainName\WindowsGroup")]
    ```

- **Explicit Role Checks**. You can perform role checking using the **IPrincipal** Sinterface.

  ```
  IPrincipal.IsInRole(@"DomainName\WindowsGroup");
  ```

- **Enterprise Services (COM+) Roles**. You can perform role checking programmatically using the **ContextUtil** class.

  ```
  ContextUtil.IsCallerInRole("Manager")
  ```

When to Use

Use Windows authentication and impersonation when:

- Your application's users have Windows accounts that can be authenticated by the server.
- You need to flow the original caller's security context to the middle tier and/or data tier of your Web application to support fine-grained (per-user) authorization.
- You need to flow the original caller's security context to the downstream tiers to support operating system level auditing.

Before using impersonation within your application, make sure you understand the relative trade-offs of this approach in comparison to using the trusted subsystem model. These were elaborated upon in "Choosing a Resource Access Model" in Chapter 3, "Authentication and Authorization Design."

The disadvantages of impersonation include:

- Reduced application scalability due to the inability to effectively pool database connections.
- Increased administration effort as ACLs on back-end resources need to be configured for individual users.
- Delegation requires Kerberos authentication and a suitably configured environment.

More Information

- For more information about Windows authentication, see "Windows Authentication" later in this chapter.
- For more information about impersonation, see "Impersonation" later in this chapter.
- For more information about URL authorization, see "URL Authorization Notes" later in this chapter.
- For more information about Enterprise Services (COM+) roles, see Chapter 9, "Enterprise Services Security."
- For more information about **PrincipalPermission** demands, see "Identities and Principals" in Chapter 2, "Security Model for ASP.NET Application."

Windows Authentication without Impersonation

The following configuration elements show how you enable Windows (IIS) authentication with no impersonation declaratively in Web.config.

```
<authentication mode="Windows" />
<!-- The following setting is equivalent to having no identity element -->
<identity impersonate="false" />
```

Configurable Security

When you use Windows authentication without impersonation, the following authorization options are available to you:

- **Windows ACLs**
  - **Client Requested Resources.** The ASP.NET **FileAuthorizationModule** performs access checks for requested file types that are mapped to the ASP.NET ISAPI. It uses the original caller's access token and ACL attached to requested resources in order to perform access checks. Impersonation is not required.

    For static files types (not mapped to an ISAPI extension) IIS performs access checks using the caller's access token and ACL attached to the file.

- **Resources accessed by your application**. Configure Windows ACLs on resources accessed by your application (files, folders, registry keys, Active Directory objects) against the ASP.NET process identity.

- **URL Authorization**. Configure URL Authorization in Web.config. With Windows authentication, user names take the form DomainName\UserName and roles map one-to-one with Windows groups.

```
<authorization>
  <deny user="DomainName\UserName" />
  <allow roles="DomainName\WindowsGroup" />
</authorization>
```

Programmatic Security

The following programmatic security options are available:

- **Principal Permission Demands**
  - Imperative

    ```
    PrincipalPermission permCheck = new PrincipalPermission(
                                    null,
    @"DomainName\WindowsGroup");
      permCheck.Demand();
    ```

  - Declarative

    ```
    [PrincipalPermission(SecurityAction.Demand,
                        Role=@"DomainName\WindowsGroup")]
    ```

- **Explicit Role Checks**. You can perform role checking using the **IPrincipal** interface.

  ```
  IPrincipal.IsInRole(@"DomainName\WindowsGroup");
  ```

When to Use

Use Windows authentication without impersonation when:

- Your application's users have Windows accounts that can be authenticated by the server.
- You want to use a fixed identity to access downstream resources (for example, databases) in order to support connection pooling.

More Information

- For more information about Windows authentication, see "Windows Authentication" later in this chapter.

- For more information about URL authorization, see "URL Authorization Notes", later in this chapter.

- For more information about **PrincipalPermission** demands, see "Principals" within the "Getting Started" section of this book.

Windows Authentication Using a Fixed Identity

The <**identity**> element in Web.config supports optional user name and password attributes, which allows you to configure a specific fixed identity for your application to impersonate. This is shown in the following configuration file fragment.

```
<identity impersonate="true"
          userName="registry:HKLM\SOFTWARE\YourSecureApp\
                    identity\ASPNET_SETREG,userName"
          password="registry:HKLM\SOFTWARE\YourSecureApp\
                    identity\ASPNET_SETREG,password" />
```

This example shows the <**identity**> element where the credentials are encrypted in the registry using the aspnet_setreg.exe utility. The clear text **userName** and **password** attribute values have been replaced with pointers to the secured registry key and named values that contain the encrypted credentials. For details about this utility and to download it, see article Q329290, "HOWTO: Use the ASP.NET Utility to Encrypt Credentials and Session State Connection Strings" in the Microsoft Knowledge Base.

When to Use

Using a fixed impersonated identity is not recommended when using the .NET Framework 1.0 on Windows 2000 servers. This is because you would need to give the ASP.NET process account the powerful "Act as part of the operating system" privilege. This privilege is required by the ASP.NET process because it performs a **LogonUser** call using the credentials that you have provided.

Note: The .NET Framework version 1.1 will provide an enhancement for this scenario on Windows 2000. The logon will be performed by the IIS process, so that ASP.NET does not require the "Act as part of the operating system" privilege.

Forms Authentication

The following configuration elements show how you enable Forms authentication declaratively in Web.config.

```
<authentication mode="Forms">
  <forms loginUrl="logon.aspx" name="AuthCookie" timeout="60" path="/">
  </forms>
</authentication>
```

Configurable Security

When you use Forms authentication, the following authorization options are available to you:

- **Windows ACLs**
  - **Client Requested Resources**. Requested resources require ACLs that allow read access to the anonymous Internet user account. (IIS should be configured to allow anonymous access when you use Forms authentication).

    ASP.NET File authorization is not available because it requires Windows authentication.

  - **Resources Accessed by Your Application**. Configure Windows ACLs on resources accessed by your application (files, folders, registry keys, and Active Directory objects) against the ASP.NET process identity.

- **URL Authorization**

  Configure URL Authorization in Web.config. With Forms authentication, the format of user names is determined by your custom data store; a SQL Server database, or Active Directory.

  - If you are using a SQL Server data store:

    ```
    <authorization>
    <deny users="?" />
      <allow users="Mary,Bob,Joe" roles="Manager,Sales" />
    </authorization>
    ```

  - If you are using Active Directory as your data store, user names, and group names appear in X.500 format:

    ```
    <authorization>
      <deny users="someAccount@domain.corp.yourCompany.com" />
      <allow roles ="CN=Smith James,CN=FTE_northamerica,CN=Users,
                  DC=domain,DC=corp,DC=yourCompany,DC=com" />
    </authorization>
    ```

Programmatic Security

The following programmatic security options are available:

- **Principal Permission Demands**
  - Imperative

    ```
    PrincipalPermission permCheck = new PrincipalPermission(
                                    null, "Manager");
    permCheck.Demand();
    ```

- Declarative

```
[PrincipalPermission(SecurityAction.Demand,
                     Role="Manager")]
```

- **Explicit Role Checks**. You can perform role checking using the **IPrincipal** interface.

```
IPrincipal.IsInRole("Manager");
```

When to Use

Forms authentication is most ideally suited to Internet applications. Use Forms authentication when:

- Your application's users do not have Windows accounts.
- You want users to log on to your application by entering credentials using an HTML form.

More Information

- For more information about Forms authentication, see "Forms Authentication" later in this chapter.
- For more information about URL authorization, see "URL Authorization Notes" later in this chapter.

Passport Authentication

The following configuration elements show how you enable Passport authentication declaratively in Web.config.

```
<authentication mode="Passport" />
```

When to Use

Passport authentication is used on the Internet when application users do not have Windows accounts and you want to implement a single-sign-on solution. Users who have previously logged on with a Passport account at a participating Passport site will not have to log on to your site configured with Passport authentication.

Configuring Security

This section shows you the practical steps required to configure security for an ASP.NET Web application. These are summarized in Figure 8.3 on the next page.

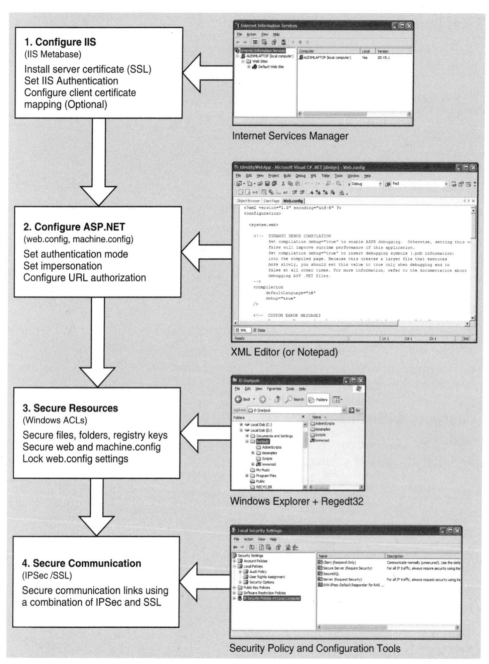

Figure 8.3
Configuring ASP.NET application security

Configure IIS Settings

To configure IIS security, you must perform the following steps:

1. Optionally install a Web server certificate (if you need SSL).

   For more information, see "How To: Set Up SSL on a Web Server" in the Reference section of this book.

2. Configure IIS authentication.

3. Optionally configure client certificate mapping (if using certificate authentication).

   For more information about client certificate mapping, see article Q313070, "How to Configure Client Certificate Mappings in Internet Information Services (IIS) 5.0" in the Microsoft Knowledge Base.

4. Set NTFS permissions on files and folders. Between them, IIS and the ASP.NET **FileAuthorizationModule** check that the authenticated user (or the anonymous Internet user account) has the necessary access rights (based on ACL settings) to access the requested file.

Configure ASP.NET Settings

Application level configuration settings are maintained in Web.config files, which are located in your application's virtual root directory and optionally within additional subfolders (these settings can sometimes override the parent folder settings).

1. **Configure authentication**. This should be set on a per-application basis (not in Machine.config) in the Web.config file located in the application's virtual root directory.

   ```
   <authentication mode="Windows|Forms|Passport|None" />
   ```

2. **Configure Impersonation**. By default, ASP.NET applications do not impersonate. The applications runs using the configured ASP.NET process identity (usually ASPNET) and all resource access performed by your application uses this identity. You only need impersonation in the following circumstances:

   - You are using Enterprise Services and you want to use Enterprise Services (COM+) roles to authorize access to functionality provided by serviced components.

   - IIS is configured for Anonymous authentication and you want to use the anonymous Internet user account for resource access. For details about this approach, see "Accessing Network Resources" later in this chapter.

   - You need to flow the authenticated user's security context to the next tier (for example, the database).

- You have ported a classic ASP application to ASP.NET and want the same impersonation behavior. Classic ASP impersonates the caller by default.

To configure ASP.NET impersonation use the following <**identity**> element in your application's Web.config.

```
<identity impersonate="true" />
```

3. **Configure Authorization**. URL authorization determines whether a user or role can issue specific HTTP verbs (for example, GET, HEAD, and POST) to a specific file. To implement URL authorization, you perform the following tasks.

   a. Add an <**authorization**> element to the Web.config file located in your application's virtual root directory.

   b. Restrict access to users and roles by using **allow** and **deny** attributes. The following example from Web.config uses Windows authentication and allows Bob and Mary access but denies everyone else.

   ```
   <authorization>
     <allow users="DomainName\Bob, DomainName\Mary" />
     <deny users="*" />
   </authorization>
   ```

Important: You need to add either <**deny users**="?"/> or <**deny users**="*"/> at the end of the <**authorization**> element, otherwise access is granted to all authenticated identities.

URL Authorization Notes

Take note of the following when you configure URL authorization:

- "*" refers to all identities.
- "?" refers to unauthenticated identities (that is, the anonymous identity).
- You don't need to impersonate for URL authorization to work.
- Authorization settings in Web.config usually refer to all of the files in the current directory and all subdirectories (unless a subdirectory contains its own Web.config with an <**authorization**> element. In this case the settings in the subdirectory override the parent directory settings).

Note: URL authorization only applies to file types that are mapped by IIS to the ASP.NET ISAPI extension, aspnet_isapi.dll.

You can use the <**location**> tag to apply authorization settings to an individual file or directory. The following example shows how you can apply authorization to a specific file (Page.aspx).

```
<location path="page.aspx" />
  <authorization>
    <allow users="DomainName\Bob, DomainName\Mary" />
    <deny users="*" />
  </authorization>
</location>
```

- Users and roles for URL authorization are determined by your authentication settings:

  - When you have <**authentication mode**="Windows" /> you are authorizing access to Windows user and group accounts.

    User names take the form "DomainName\WindowsUserName"

    Role names take the form "DomainName\WindowsGroupName"

    Note: The local administrators group is referred to as "BUILTIN\Administrators". The local users group is referred to as "BUILTIN\Users".

  - When you have <**authentication mode**="Forms" /> you are authorizing against the user and roles for the **IPrincipal** object that was stored in the current HTTP context. For example, if you used Forms to authenticate users against a database, you will be authorizing against the roles retrieved from the database.

  - When you have <**authentication mode**="Passport" /> you authorize against the Passport User ID (PUID) or roles retrieved from a store. For example, you can map a PUID to a particular account and set of roles stored in a SQL Server database or Active Directory.

    Note: This functionality will be built into the Microsoft Windows .NET Server 2003 operating system.

  - When you have <**authentication mode**="None" /> you may not be performing authorization. "None" specifies that you don't want to perform any authentication or that you don't want to use any of the .NET authentication modules and want to use your own custom mechanism.

    However, if you use custom authentication, you should create an **IPrincipal** object with roles and store it into the **HttpContext.User**. When you subsequently perform URL authorization, it is performed against the user and roles (no matter how they were retrieved) maintained in the **IPrincipal** object.

URL Authorization Examples

The following list shows the syntax for some typical URL authorization examples:

- Deny access to the anonymous account

```
<deny users="?" />
```

- Deny access to all users

```
<deny users="*"/>
```

- Deny access to Manager role

```
<deny roles="Manager"/>
```

- Forms authentication example

```
<configuration>
  <system.web>
      <authentication mode="Forms">
        <forms name=".ASPXUSERDEMO"
               loginUrl="login.aspx"
               protection="All" timeout="60" />
      </authentication>
      <authorization>
        <deny users="jdoe@somewhere.com" />
        <deny users="?" />
      </authorization>
  </system.web>
</configuration>
```

Note: The <**authorization**> element works against the current **IPrincipal** object stored in **HttpContext.User** and also the HTTP data transfer method stored in **HttpContext.Request.RequestType**.

Secure Resources

1. Use Windows ACLs to secure resources that include files, folders, and registry keys.

   If you are not impersonating, any resource your application is required to access must have an ACL that grants at least read access to the ASP.NET process account.

   If you are impersonating, files and registry keys must have an ACL that grants at least read access to the authenticated user (or the anonymous Internet user account, if anonymous authentication is in effect).

2. Secure Web.config and Machine.config:

- **Use the Correct ACLs**. If ASP.NET is impersonating, the impersonated identity requires read access. Otherwise, the ASP.NET process identity requires
  read access. Use the following ACL on Web.config and Machine.config.

  System: Full Control

  Administrators: Full Control

  Process Identity or Impersonated Identity : Read

  If you are not impersonating the anonymous Internet user account
  (IUSR_MACHINE), you should deny access to this account.

  Note: If your application is mapped to a UNC share then the UNC identity requires read
  access to the configuration files as well.

- Remove Unwanted HTTP Modules. Machine.config contains a set of default
  HTTP modules (within the **<httpModules>** element. These include:
  - WindowsAuthenticationModule
  - FormsAuthenticationModule
  - PassportAuthenticationModule
  - UrlAuthorizationModule
  - FileAuthorizationModule
  - OutputCacheModule
  - SessionStateModule

  If your application doesn't use a specific module, remove it to prevent any
  potential future security issues associated with a particular module from being
  exploited within your application.

3. Optionally, lock configuration settings by using the **<location>** element together
with the **allowOverride="false"** attribute as described below.

Locking Configuration Settings

Configuration settings are hierarchical. Web.config file settings in subdirectories
override Web.config settings in parent directories. Also, Web.config settings override
Machine.config settings.

You can lock configuration settings to prevent them being overridden at lower
levels, by using the <location> element coupled with the **allowOverride** attribute.
For example:

```
<location path="somepath" allowOverride="false" />
 . . . arbitrary configuration settings . . .
</location>
```

Note that the path may refer to a Web site or virtual directory and it applies to the nominated directory and all subdirectories. If you set **allowOverride** to false, you prevent any lower level configuration file from overriding the settings specified in the **<location>** element. The ability to lock down configuration settings applies to all types of setting and not just security settings such as authentication modes.

In the context of machine.config, the path must be fully qualified and include the Web site, virtual directory name and optionally a sub directory and filename. For example:

```
<location path="Web Site Name/VDirName/SubDirName/PageName.aspx" >
. . .
</location>
```

In the context of web.config, the path is relative from the application's virtual directory. For example:

```
<location path="SubDirName/PageName.aspx" >
. . .
</location>
```

Preventing Files from Being Downloaded

You can use the **HttpForbiddenHandler** class to prevent certain file types from being downloaded over the Web. This class is used internally by ASP.NET to prevent the download of certain system level files (for example, configuration files including web.config). For a complete list of file types restricted in this way, see the <httpHandlers> section in machine.config.

You should consider using the **HttpForbiddenHandler** for files that your application uses internally, but are not intended for download.

Note: You must also secure the files with Windows ACLs to control which users can access the files, when logged on to the Web server.

▶ **To use the HttpForbiddenHandler to prevent a particular file type from being downloaded**

1. Create an application mapping in IIS for the specified file type to map it to Aspnet_isapi.dll.

   a. On the taskbar, click the **Start** button, click **Programs**, click **Administrative Tools**, and then select Internet Information Services.

   b. Select your application's virtual directory, right-click, and then click **Properties**.

   c. Select **Application Settings**, click **Configuration**.

d. Click **Add** to create a new application mapping.

e. Click **Browse,** and select
c:\winnt\Microsoft.NET\Framework\v1.0.3705\aspnet_isapi.dll.

f. Enter the file extension for the file type you want to prevent being down-loaded (for example, .abc) in the **Extension** field.

g. Ensure **All Verbs** and **Script engine** is selected and **Check that file exists** is not selected.

h. Click **OK** to close the **Add/Edit Application Extension Mapping** dialog box.

i. Click **OK** to close the **Application Configuration** dialog box, and then click **OK** again to close the **Properties** dialog box.

2. Add an **<HttpHandler>** mapping in Web.config for the specified file type.

An example for the .abc file type is shown below.

```
<httpHandlers>
  <add verb="*" path="*.abc"
    type="System.Web.HttpForbiddenHandler"/>
</httpHandlers>
```

Secure Communication

Use a combination of SSL and Internet Protocol Security (IPSec) to secure communication links.

More information

- For information about using SSL to secure the link to the database server, see "How To: Use SSL to Secure Communication with SQL Server 2000."

- For information about using IPSec between two computers, see "How To: Use IPSec to Provide Secure Communication Between Two Servers."

Programming Security

After you establish your Web application's configurable security settings, you need to further enhance and fine-tune your application's authorization policy program-matically. This includes using declarative .NET attributes within your assemblies and performing imperative authorizing checks within code.

This section highlights the key programming steps required to perform authorization within an ASP.NET Web application.

An Authorization Pattern

The following summarizes the basic pattern for authorizing users within your Web application:

1. Retrieve credentials

2. Validate credentials

3. Put users in roles

4. Create an **IPrincipal** object

5. Put the **IPrincipal** object into the current HTTP context

6. Authorize based on the user identity / role membership

Important: Steps 1 to 5 are performed automatically by ASP.NET if you have configured Windows authentication. For other authentication mechanisms (Forms, Passport and custom approaches), you must write code to perform these steps, as discussed below.

Retrieve Credentials

You must start by retrieving a set of credentials (user name and password) from the user. If your application does not use Windows authentication, you need to ensure that clear text credentials are properly secured on the network by using SSL.

Validate Credentials

If you have configured Windows authentication, credentials are validated automatically using the underlying services of the operating system.

If you use an alternate authentication mechanism, you must write code to validate credentials against a data store such as a SQL Server database or Active Directory.

For more information about how to securely store user credentials in a SQL Server database, see "Authenticating Users Against a Database" within Chapter 12, "Data Access Security."

Put Users in Roles

Your user data store should also contain a list of roles for each user. You must write code to retrieve the role list for the validated user.

Create an IPrincipal Object

Authorization occurs against the authenticated user, whose identity and role list is maintained within an **IPrincipal** object (which flows in the context of the current Web request).

If you have configured Windows authentication, ASP.NET automatically constructs a **WindowsPrincipal** object. This contains the authenticated user's identity together with a role list, which equates to the list of Windows groups to which the user belongs.

If you are using Forms, Passport, or custom authentication, you must write code within the **Application_AuthenticateRequest** event handler in Global.asax to create an **IPrincipal** object. The **GenericPrincipal** class is provided by the .NET Framework, and should be used in most scenarios.

Put the IPrincipal Object into the Current HTTP Context

Attach the **IPrincipal** object to the current HTTP context (using the Http**Context.User** variable). ASP.NET does this automatically when you use Windows authentication. Otherwise, you must attach the object manually.

Authorize Based on the User Identity and/or Role Membership

Use .NET roles either declaratively (to obtain class or method level authorization), or imperatively within code if your application requires more fine-grained authorization logic.

You can use declarative or imperative principal permission demands (using the **PrincipalPermission** class), or you can perform explicit role checks by calling the **IPrincipal.IsInRole()** method.

The following example assumes Windows authentication and shows a declarative principal permission demand. The method that follows the attribute will only be executed if the authenticated user is a member of the **Manager** Windows group. If the caller is not a member of this group, a **SecurityException** is thrown.

```
[PrincipalPermission(SecurityAction.Demand,
                     Role=@"DomainName\Manager")]
public void SomeMethod()
{
}
```

The following example shows an explicit role check within code. This example assumes Windows authentication. If a non-Windows authentication mechanism is used, the code remains very similar. Instead of casting the **User** object to a **WindowsPrincipal** object, it should be cast to a **GenericPrincipal** object.

```
// Extract the authenticated user from the current HTTP context.
// The User variable is equivalent to HttpContext.Current.User if you are
// using an .aspx or .asmx page
WindowsPrincipal authenticatedUser = User as WindowsPrincipal;
if (null != authenticatedUser)
{
```

```
// Note: To retrieve the authenticated user's username, use the
// following line of code
// string username = authenticatedUser.Identity.Name;

// Perform a role check
if (authenticatedUser.IsInRole(@"DomainName\Manager") )
{
  // User is authorized to perform manager functionality
}
}
else
{
  // User is not authorized to perform manager functionality
}
```

More Information

For a practical implementation of the above pattern for Forms authentication, see the "Forms Authentication" section later in this chapter.

Creating a Custom IPrincipal class

The **GenericPrincipal** class provided by the .NET Framework should be used in most circumstances when you are using a non-Windows authentication mechanism. This provides role checks using the **IPrincipal.IsInRole** method.

On occasion, you may need to implement your own **IPrincipal** class. Reasons for implementing your own **IPrincipal** class include:

- You want extended role checking functionality. You might want methods that allow you to check whether a particular user is a member of multiple roles. For example:

```
CustomPrincipal.IsInAllRoles( "Role", "Role2", "Role3" )
CustomPrincipal.IsInAnyRole( "Role1", "Role2", "Role3" )
```

- You may want to implement an extra method or property that returns a list of roles in an array. For example:

```
string[] roles = CustomPrincipal.Roles;
```

- You want your application to enforce role hierarchy logic. For example, a Senior Manager may be considered higher up in the hierarchy than a Manager. This could be tested using methods like the ones shown below.

```
CustomPrincipal.IsInHigherRole("Manager");
CustomPrincipal.IsInLowerRole("Manager");
```

- You may want to implement lazy initialization of the role lists. For example, you could dynamically load the role list only when a role check is requested.

- You may want to implement the **IIdentity** interface to have the user identified by an **X509ClientCertificate**. For example:

```
CustomIdentity id = CustomPrincipal.Identity;
X509ClientCertificate cert = id.ClientCertificate;
```

More Information

For more information about creating your own **IPrincipal** class, see "How To: Implement IPrincipal" in the Reference section of this book.

Windows Authentication

Use Windows authentication when the users of your application have Windows accounts that can be authenticated by the server (for example, in intranet scenarios).

If you configure ASP.NET for Windows authentication, IIS performs user authentication by using the configured IIS authentication mechanism. This is shown in Figure 8.4.

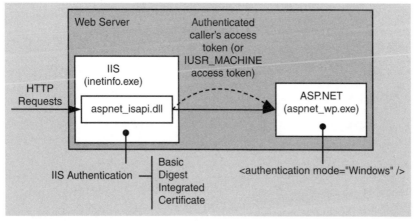

Figure 8.4
ASP.NET Windows authentication uses IIS to authenticate callers

The access token of the authenticated caller (which may be the Anonymous Internet user account if IIS is configured for Anonymous authentication) is made available to the ASP.NET application. Note the following:

- This allows the ASP.NET **FileAuthorizationModule** to perform access checks against requested ASP.NET files using the original caller's access token.

> **Important:** ASP.NET File authorization only performs access checks against file types that are mapped to Aspnet_isapi.dll.

- File authorization does not require impersonation. With impersonation enabled any resource access performed by your application uses the impersonated caller's identity. In this event, ensure that the ACLs attached to resources contain an Access Control Entry (ACE) that grants at least read access to the original caller's identity.

Identifying the Authenticated User

ASP.NET associates a **WindowsPrincipal** object with the current Web request. This contains the identity of the authenticated Windows user together with a list of roles that the user belongs to. With Windows authentication, the role list consists of the set of Windows groups to which the user belongs.

The following code shows how to obtain the identity of the authenticated Windows user and to perform a simple role test for authorization.

```
WindowsPrincipal user = User as WindowsPrincipal;
if (null != user)
{
  string username = user.Identity.Name;
  // Perform a role check
  if ( user.IsInRole(@"DomainName\Manager") )
  {
    // User is authorized to perform manager functionality
  }
}
else
{
  // Throw security exception as we don't have a WindowsPrincipal
}
```

Forms Authentication

When you are using Forms authentication, the sequence of events triggered by an unauthenticated user who attempts to access a secured file or resource (where URL authorization denies the user access), is shown in Figure 8.5.

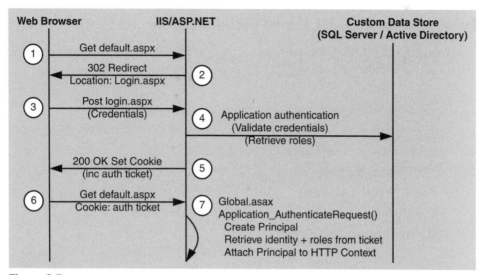

Figure 8.5

Forms authentication sequence of events

The following describes the sequence of events shown in Figure 8.5:

1. The user issues a Web request for Default.aspx.

   IIS allows the request because Anonymous access is enabled. ASP.NET checks the **<authorization>** elements and finds a **<deny users**=?" /> element.

2. The user is redirected to the login page (Login.aspx) as specified by the **loginUrl** attribute of the **<forms>** element.

3. The user supplies credentials and submits the login form.

4. The credentials are validated against a store (SQL Server or Active Directory) and roles are optionally retrieved. You must retrieve a role list if you want to use role-based authorization.

5. A cookie is created with a **FormsAuthenticationTicket** and sent back to the client. Roles are optionally stored in the ticket. By storing the role list in the ticket, you avoid having to access the database to re-retrieve the list for each successive Web request from the same user.

6. The user is redirected with client-side redirection to the originally requested page (Default.aspx).

7. In the **Application_AuthenticateRequest** event handler (in Global.asax), the ticket is used to create an **IPrincipal** object and it is stored in **HttpContext.User**.

   ASP.NET checks the **<authorization>** elements and finds a **<deny users**=?" /> element. However, this time the user is authenticated.

   ASP.NET checks the **<authorization>** elements to ensure the user is in the **<allow>** element.

   The user is granted access to Default.aspx.

Development Steps for Forms Authentication

The following list highlights the key steps that you must perform to implement Forms authentication:

1. Configure IIS for anonymous access.
2. Configure ASP.NET for Forms authentication.
3. Create a logon Web form and validate the supplied credentials.
4. Retrieve a role list from the custom data store.
5. Create a Forms authentication ticket (store roles in the ticket).
6. Create an **IPrincipal** object.
7. Put the **IPrincipal** object into the current HTTP context.
8. Authorize the user based on user name/role membership.

Configure IIS for Anonymous Access

Your application's virtual directory must be configured in IIS for anonymous access.

▶ **To configure IIS for anonymous access**

1. Start the Internet Information Services administration tool.
2. Select your application's virtual directory, right-click, and then click **Properties**.
3. Click **Directory Security**.
4. In the **Anonymous access and authentication control** group, click **Edit**.
5. Select **Anonymous access**.

Configure ASP.NET for Forms Authentication

A sample configuration is shown below.

```
<authentication mode="Forms">
  <forms name="MyAppFormsAuth"
       loginUrl="login.aspx"
       protection="Encryption"
       timeout="20"
       path="/" >
  </forms>
</authentication>
```

Create a Logon Web Form and Validate the Supplied Credentials

Validate credentials against a SQL Server database, or Active Directory.

More Information

- See "How To: Use Forms Authentication with SQL Server 2000" in the Reference section of this book.
- See "How To: Use Forms Authentication with Active Directory" in the Reference section of this book.

Retrieve a Role List from the Custom Data Store

Obtain roles from a table within a SQL Server database, or groups/distribution lists configured within Active Directory. Refer to the preceding resources for details.

Create a Forms Authentication Ticket

Store the retrieved roles in the ticket. This is illustrated in the following code.

```
// This event handler executes when the user clicks the Logon button
// having supplied a set of credentials
private void Logon_Click(object sender, System.EventArgs e)
{
  // Validate credentials against either a SQL Server database
  // or Active Directory
  bool isAuthenticated = IsAuthenticated( txtUserName.Text,
                                           txtPassword.Text );
  if (isAuthenticated == true )
  {
    // Retrieve the set of roles for this user from the SQL Server
    // database or Active Directory. The roles are returned as a
    // string that contains pipe separated role names
    // for example "Manager|Employee|Sales|"
    // This makes it easy to store them in the authentication ticket

    string roles = RetrieveRoles( txtUserName.Text, txtPassword.Text );

    // Create the authentication ticket and store the roles in the
    // custom UserData property of the authentication ticket
    FormsAuthenticationTicket authTicket = new
        FormsAuthenticationTicket(
                    1,                          // version
                    txtUserName.Text,           // user name
                    DateTime.Now,               // creation
                    DateTime.Now.AddMinutes(20),// Expiration
                    false,                      // Persistent
                    roles );                    // User data
    // Encrypt the ticket.
     string encryptedTicket = FormsAuthentication.Encrypt(authTicket);
    // Create a cookie and add the encrypted ticket to the
    // cookie as data.
    HttpCookie authCookie =
            new HttpCookie(FormsAuthentication.FormsCookieName,
                           encryptedTicket);

    // Add the cookie to the outgoing cookies collection.
    Response.Cookies.Add(authCookie);
    // Redirect the user to the originally requested page
    Response.Redirect( FormsAuthentication.GetRedirectUrl(
                    txtUserName.Text,
                    false ));
  }
}
```

Create an IPrincipal Object

Create the **IPrincipal** object in the **Application_AuthenticationRequest** event handler in Global.asax. Use the **GenericPrincipal** class, unless you need extended role-based functionality. In this case create a custom class that implements **IPrincipal**.

Put the IPrincipal Object into the Current HTTP Context

The creation of a **GenericPrincipal** object is shown below.

```
protected void Application_AuthenticateRequest(Object sender, EventArgs e)
{
  // Extract the forms authentication cookie
  string cookieName = FormsAuthentication.FormsCookieName;
  HttpCookie authCookie = Context.Request.Cookies[cookieName];
  if(null == authCookie)
  {
    // There is no authentication cookie.
    return;
  }
  FormsAuthenticationTicket authTicket = null;
  try
  {
    authTicket = FormsAuthentication.Decrypt(authCookie.Value);
  }
  catch(Exception ex)
  {
    // Log exception details (omitted for simplicity)
    return;
  }
  if (null == authTicket)
  {
    // Cookie failed to decrypt.
    return;
  }
  // When the ticket was created, the UserData property was assigned a
  // pipe delimited string of role names.
  string[] roles = authTicket.UserData.Split(new char[]{'|'});

  // Create an Identity object
  FormsIdentity id = new FormsIdentity( authTicket );
  // This principal will flow throughout the request.
  GenericPrincipal principal = new GenericPrincipal(id, roles);
  // Attach the new principal object to the current HttpContext object
  Context.User = principal;
}
```

Authorize the User Based on User Name or Role Membership

Use declarative principal permission demands to restrict access to methods. Use imperative principal permission demands and/or explicit role checks (**IPrincipal.IsInRole**) to perform fine-grained authorization within methods.

Forms Implementation Guidelines

- Use SSL when capturing credentials using an HTML form.

  In addition to using SSL for the login page, you should also use SSL for other pages, whenever the credentials or the authentication cookie is sent across the network. This is to mitigate the threat associated with cookie replay attacks.

- Authenticate users against a custom data store. Use SQL Server or Active Directory.

- Retrieve a role list from the custom data store and store a delimited list of roles within the **UserData** property of the **FormsAuthenticationTicket** class. This improves performance by eliminating repeated access to the data store for each Web request and also saves you from storing the user's credentials in the authentication cookie.

- If the list of roles is extensive and there is a danger of exceeding the cookie size limit, store the role details in the ASP.NET cache object or database and retrieve them on each subsequent request.

- For each request after initial authentication:

  - Retrieve the roles from the ticket in the **Application_AuthenticateRequest** event handler.

  - Create an **IPrincipal** object and store it in the HTTP context (**HttpContext.User**). The .NET Framework also associates it with the current .NET thread (**Thread.CurrentPrincipal**).

  - Use the **GenericPrincipal** class unless you have a specific need to create a custom **IPrincipal** implementation; for example, to support enhanced role-based operations.

- Use two cookies; one for personalization and one for secure authentication and authorization. Make the personalization cookie persistent (make sure it does not contain information that would permit a request to perform a restricted operation; for example, placing an order within a secure part of a site).

- Use a separate cookie name (using the **Forms** attribute of the <**forms**> element) and path for each Web application. This will ensure that users who are authenticated against one application are not treated as authenticated when using a second application hosted by the same Web server.

- Ensure cookies are enabled within client browsers. For a Forms authentication approach that does not require cookies, see "Cookieless Forms Authentication" later in this chapter.

More Information

- See "How To: Use Forms Authentication with SQL Server 2000" in the Reference section of this book.
- See "How To: Use Forms Authentication with Active Directory" in the Reference section of this book.
- See "How To: Use Forms Authentication with GenericPrincipal Objects" in the Reference section of this book.

Hosting Multiple Applications Using Forms Authentication

If you are hosting multiple Web applications that use Forms authentication on the same Web server, it is possible for a user who is authenticated in one application to make a request to another application without being redirected to that application's logon page. The URL authorization rules within the second application may deny access to the user, without providing the opportunity to supply logon credentials using the logon form.

This only happens if the name and path attributes on the **<forms>** element are the same across multiple applications and each application uses a common **<machineKey>** element in Web.config.

More Information

For more information about this issue, and for resolution techniques, see the following Knowledge Base articles:

- Q313116, "PRB: Forms Authentication Requests Are Not Directed to loginUrl Page"
- Q310415, "PRB: Mobile Forms Authentication and Different Web Applications"

Cookieless Forms Authentication

If you need a cookieless Forms authentication solution, consider using the approach used by the Microsoft Mobile Internet Toolkit. Mobile Forms Authentication builds upon Forms Authentication but uses the query string to convey the authentication ticket instead of a cookie.

More Information

For more information about Mobile Forms Authentication, see article Q311568, "INFO: How To Use Mobile Forms Authentication with Microsoft Mobile Internet Toolkit," in the Microsoft Knowledge Base.

Passport Authentication

Use Passport authentication when the users of your application have Passport accounts and you want to implement a single-sign-on solution with other Passport enabled sites.

When you configure ASP.NET for Passport authentication, the user is prompted to log in and then is redirected to the Passport site. After successful credential validation, the user is redirected back to your site.

Configure ASP.NET for Passport authentication

To configure ASP.NET for Passport authentication, use the following Web.config settings.

```
<authentication mode="Passport">
  <passport redirectUrl="internal" />
</authentication>
<authorization>
  <deny users="?" />
  <allow users="*" />
</authorization>
```

Map a Passport Identity into Roles in Global.asax

To map a Passport identity into roles, implement the **PassportAuthentication_OnAuthentication** event handler in Global.asax as shown below.

```
void PassportAuthentication_OnAuthenticate(Object sender,
                                           PassportAuthenticationEventArgs e)
{
  if(e.Identity.Name == "0000000000000001")
  {
    string[] roles = new String[]{"Developer", "Admin", "Tester"};
    Context.User = new GenericPrincipal(e.Identity, roles);
  }
}
```

Test Role Membership

The following code fragment shows how to retrieve the authenticated Passport identity and check role membership within an aspx page.

```
PassportIdentity passportId = Context.User.Identity as PassportIdentity;
if (null == passportId)
{
  Response.Write("Not a PassportIdentity<br>");
  return;
}
Response.Write("IsInRole: Develeoper? " + Context.User.IsInRole("Developer"));
```

Custom Authentication

If none of the authentication modules supplied with the .NET Framework meet your precise authentication needs, you can use custom authentication and implement your own authentication mechanism. For example, your company may already have a custom authentication strategy that is widely used by other applications.

To implement custom authentication in ASP.NET:

- Configure the authentication mode in Web.config as shown below. This notifies ASP.NET that it should not invoke any of its built-in authentication modules.

  ```
  <authentication mode="None" />
  ```

- Create a class that implements the **System.Web.IHttpModule** interface to create a custom HTTP module. This module should hook into the **HttpApplication.AuthenticateRequest** event and provide a delegate to be called on each request to the application when authentication is required.

  An authentication module must:

  - Obtain credentials from the caller.
  - Validate the credentials against a store.
  - Create an **IPrincipal** object and store it in **HttpContext.User.**
  - Create and protect an authentication token and send it back to the user (typically in a query string, cookie, or hidden form field).
  - Obtain the authentication token on subsequent requests, validate it, and reissue it.

More Information

For more information about how to implement a custom HTTP Module, see article Q307996, "HOW TO: Create an ASP.NET HTTP Module Using Visual C# .NET," in the Microsoft Knowledge Base.

Process Identity for ASP.NET

Run ASP.NET (specifically the Aspnet_wp.exe worker process) by using a least privileged account.

Use a Least Privileged Account

Use a least privileged account to lessen the threat associated with a process compromise. If a determined attacker manages to compromise the ASP.NET process that runs your Web application, they can easily inherit and exploit the privileges and access rights granted to the process account. An account configured with minimum privileges restricts the potential damage that can be done.

Avoid Running as SYSTEM

Don't use the highly-privileged SYSTEM account to run ASP.NET and don't grant the ASP.NET process account the "Act as part of the operating system" privilege. You may be tempted to do one or the other to allow your code to call the **LogonUser** API to obtain a fixed identity (typically for network resource access). For alternate approaches, see "Accessing Network Resources" later in this chapter.

Reasons for not running as SYSTEM, or granting the "Act as part of the operating system privilege" include:

- It significantly increases the damage that an attacker can do when the system is compromised, but it doesn't affect the ability to be compromised.
- It defeats the principle of least privilege. The ASPNET account has been specifically configured as a least privileged account designed to run ASP.NET Web applications.

More Information

For more information about the "Act as part of the operating system" privilege, see the Microsoft Systems Journal August 1999 Security Briefs column.

Domain Controllers and the ASP.NET Process Account

In general, it is not advisable to run your Web server on a domain controller, because a compromise of the server is a compromise of the domain. If you need to run ASP.NET on a domain controller, you need to give the ASP.NET process account appropriate privileges as outlined in article Q315158, "BUG: ASP.NET Does Not Work with the Default ASPNET Account on a Domain Controller," in the Microsoft Knowledge Base.

Using the Default ASPNET Account

The local ASPNET account has been configured specifically to run ASP.NET Web applications with the minimum possible set of privileges. Use ASPNET whenever possible.

By default, ASP.NET Web applications run using this account, as configured by the **<processModel>** element within Machine.config.

```
<processModel userName="machine" password="AutoGenerate" />
```

Note: The *machine* user name indicates the ASPNET account. The account is created with a cryptographically strong password when you install the .NET Framework. In addition to being configured within the Security Account Manager (SAM) database, the password is stored within the Local System Authority (LSA) on the local computer. The system retrieves the password from the LSA, when it launches the ASPNET worker process.

If your application accesses network resources, the ASPNET account must be capable of being authenticated by the remote computer. You have two choices:

- Reset the ASPNET account's password to a known value and then create a duplicate account (with the same name and password) on the remote computer. This approach is the only option in the following circumstances:

  - The Web server and remote computer are in separate domains with no trust relationship.

  - The Web server and remote computer are separated by a firewall and you do not want to open the necessary ports to support Windows authentication.

- If ease of administration is your primary concern, use a least privileged, domain account.

  To avoid having to manually update and synchronize passwords, you can use a least privileged domain account to run ASP.NET. It is vital that the domain account is fully locked down to mitigate the process compromise threat. If an attacker manages to compromise the ASP.NET worker process, he or she will have the ability to access domain resources, unless the account is fully locked down.

Note: If you use a local account and the account becomes compromised, the only computers subject to attack are the computers on which you have created duplicate accounts. If you use a domain account, the account is visible to each computer on the domain. However, the account still needs to have permission to access those computers.

The <processModel> Element

The <**processModel**> element in the Machine.config file contains the **userName** and **password** attributes which specify the account that should be used to run the ASP.NET worker process (Aspnet_wp.exe).

Note: In contrast to the way classic ASP applications run, ASP.NET code never runs in the dllhost.exe process or as the IWAM_MACHINENAME account even when the application protection level is set to **High** (**Isolated**) in IIS.

ASP.NET requests sent to IIS are directly routed to the ASP.NET worker process (Aspnet_wp.exe). The ASP.NET ISAPI extension, Aspnet_isapi.dll, runs in the IIS (Inetinfo.exe) process address space. (This is controlled by the InProcessIsapiApps Metabase entry, which should not be modified). The ISAPI extension is responsible for routing requests to the ASP.NET worker process. ASP.NET applications then run in the ASP.NET worker process, where application domains provide isolation boundaries.

In IIS 6, you will be able to isolate ASP.NET applications by configuring application pools, where each pool will have its own application instance.

You have a number of options for configuring the <**processModel**> userName attribute. For example:

- **"machine"**. The worker process runs as the default least privileged ASPNET account. The account has network access but cannot be authenticated to any other computer on the network because the account is local to the computer and there is no authority to vouch for the account. On the network, this account is represented as "MachineName\ASPNET".

- **"system"**. The worker process runs as the local SYSTEM account. This account has extensive privileges on the local computer and also has the ability to access the network using the credentials of the computer. On the network, this account is represented as "DomainName\MachineName$".

- **Specific credentials**. When you supply credentials for **userName** and **password**, remember the principle of least privilege. If you specify a local account, the Web application cannot be authenticated on the network unless you create a duplicate account on the remote computer. If you elect to use a least privileged domain account, ensure it is not an account that has permission to access more computers on the network than it needs to.

  In the .NET Framework version 1.1 you will have the ability to store encrypted **userName** and **password** attributes in the registry.

Storing Encrypted <processModel> Credentials

If you use custom credentials, use the aspnet_setreg.exe utility to store encrypted credentials in the registry. Avoid storing plain text credentials in machine.config.

For details about this utility and to download it, see article Q329290, "HOWTO: Use the ASP.NET Utility to Encrypt Credentials and Session State Connection Strings" in the Microsoft Knowledge Base.

The following sample shows the format of the **userName** and **password** attributes before and after using this utility. Notice how the attribute values point to the secured registry key and named values that contain the encrypted credentials.

```
<!--Before -->
<processModel userName="SomeCustomAccount"
              password="ClearTextPassword" . . ./>

<!-- After -->
<processModel
        userName="registry:HKLM\SOFTWARE\YourSecureApp\processModel\
                  ASPNET_SETREG,userName"
        password="registry:HKLM\SOFTWARE\YourSecureApp\processModel\
                  ASPNET_SETREG,password" . . ./>
```

More Information

- For more information about accessing network resources from ASP.NET Web applications, see "Accessing Network Resources," later in this chapter.

- For detailed information about how to create a custom account for running ASP.NET, see "How To: Create a Custom Account to Run ASP.NET" in the Reference section of this book.

Impersonation

With the introduction of the **FileAuthorizationModule**, and with the efficient use of gatekeepers and trust boundaries, impersonation may prove more of a disadvantage than a benefit in ASP.NET.

Impersonation and Local Resources

If you use impersonation and access local resources from your Web application code, you must configure the ACLs attached to each secured resource to contain an ACE that grants at least read access to the authenticated user.

A better approach is to avoid impersonation, grant permissions to the ASP.NET process account, and use URL authorization, File authorization, and a combination of declarative and imperative role-based checks.

Impersonation and Remote Resources

If you use impersonation and then access remote resources from your Web application code, the access will fail unless you are using Basic, Forms, or Kerberos authentication. If you use Kerberos authentication, user accounts must be suitably configured for delegation. They must be marked as "Sensitive and cannot be delegated" within Active Directory.

More Information

For more information about how to configure Kerberos delegation, see:

- "Flowing the Original Caller to the Database" in Chapter 5, "Intranet Security."
- "How To: Implement Kerberos Delegation for Windows 2000" in the Reference section of this book.

Impersonation and Threading

If a thread that is impersonating creates a new thread, the new thread inherits the security context of the ASP.NET process account and not the impersonated account.

Accessing System Resources

ASP.NET performs no impersonation by default. As a result, if your Web application accesses local system resources, it does so using the security context associated with the Aspnet_wp.exe worker process. The security context is determined by the account used to run the worker process.

Accessing the Event Log

Least privileged accounts have sufficient permissions to be able to write records to the event log by using existing event sources. However, they do not have sufficient permissions to create new event sources, This requires a new entry to be placed beneath the following registry hive.

```
HKEY_LOCAL_MACHINE\SYSTEM\CurrentControlSet\Services\Eventlog\<log>
```

To avoid this issue, create the event sources used by your application at installation time, when administrator privileges are available. A good approach is to use a .NET installer class which can be instantiated by the Windows Installer (if you are using .msi deployment) or by the InstallUtil.exe system utility if you are not.

If you are unable to create event sources at installation time, you must add permission to the following registry key and grant access to the ASP.NET process account (of any impersonated account if your application uses impersonation).

```
HKEY_LOCAL_MACHINE\SYSTEM\CurrentControlSet\Services\Eventlog
```

The account(s) must have the following minimum permissions:

- Query key value
- Set key value
- Create subkey
- Enumerate subkeys
- Notify
- Read

The following code can be used to write to the Application event log from ASP.NET once permissions have been applied to the registry:

```csharp
string source = "Your Application Source";
string logToWriteTo = "Application";
string eventText = "Sample Event";

if (!EventLog.SourceExists(source))
{
   EventLog.CreateEventSource(source, logToWriteTo);
}
EventLog.WriteEntry(source, eventText, EventLogEntryType.Warning, 234);
```

Accessing the Registry

Any registry key accessed by your application requires an ACE in the ACL that grants (at minimum) read access to the ASP.NET process account.

More Information

For more information about installer classes and the InstallUtil.exe utility, see the ".NET Framework Tools" section of the .NET Framework SDK on MSDN.

Accessing COM Objects

In classic ASP, requests are processed using threads from the Single Threaded Apartment (STA) thread pool. In ASP.NET, requests are processed using threads from the Multithreaded Apartment (MTA) thread pool. This has implications for ASP.NET Web applications that call Apartment model objects.

Apartment Model Objects

When an ASP.NET Web application calls an Apartment model object (such as a Visual Basic 6 COM object) there are two issues to note:

- You must mark your ASP.NET page with the **AspCompat** directive, as shown below.

```
<%@ Page Language="C#" AspCompat="True" %>
```

- Don't create your COM objects outside of specific Page event handlers. Create COM objects in Page event handlers (such as **Page_Load** and **Page_Init**). Don't create COM objects in the page's constructor.

The AspCompat Directive is Required

By default, ASP.NET uses MTA threads to process requests. This results in a thread-switch when an Apartment model object is called from ASP.NET, because the Apartment model object can't be accessed directly by MTA threads (COM would use an STA thread).

Specifying **AspCompat** causes the page to be processed by an STA thread. This avoids a thread switch from MTA to STA. This is important from a security perspective if your Web application is impersonating because a thread switch results in a lost impersonation token. The new thread would not have the impersonation token associated with it.

The **AspCompat** directive is not supported for ASP.NET Web services. This means that when you call Apartment model objects from Web service code, a thread switch does occur and you lose the thread impersonation token. This typically results in an Access Denied exception.

More Information

- See the following Knowledge Base articles for more information:
  - Article Q303375, "INFO: XML Web Services and Apartment Objects"
  - Article Q325791, "PRB: Access Denied Error Message Occurs When Impersonating in ASP.NET and Calling STA COM Components"
- For more information about how to determine the identity of the currently executing code, see the "Determining Identity" section of Chapter 13, "Troubleshooting."

Don't Create COM Objects Outside of Specific Page Events

Don't create COM object outside of specific Page event handlers. The following code fragment illustrates what not to do.

```
<%@ Page Language="C#" AspCompat="True" %>
<script runat="server">
  // COM object created outside of Page events
  YourComObject obj = new apartmentObject();
  public void Page_Load()
  {
    obj.Foo()
  }
</script>
```

When you use Apartment model objects, it is important to create the object within. specific Page events such as **Page_Load**, as shown below.

```
<%@ Page Language="C#" AspCompat="True" %>
<script runat="server">
public void Page_Load()
{
  YourComObject obj = new apartmentObject();
  obj.Foo()
}
</script>
```

More Information

For more information, see article Q308095, "PRB: Creating STA Components in the Constructor in ASP.NET ASPCOMPAT Mode Negatively Impacts Performance" in the Microsoft Knowledge Base.

C# and VB .NET Objects in COM+

Microsoft C#® development tool and Microsoft Visual Basic® .NET development system support all threading models (Free-threaded, Neutral, Both, and Apartment). By default, when hosted in COM+, C# and Visual Basic .NET objects are marked as Both. As a result, when they are called by ASP.NET, access is direct and you do not incur a thread switch.

Accessing Network Resources

Your application may need to access network resources. It is important to be able to identify:

- The resources your application needs to access.

  For example, files on file shares, databases, DCOM servers, Active Directory objects, and so on.

- The identity used to perform the resource access.

  If your application accesses remote resources, this identity must be capable of being authenticated by the remote computer.

Note: For information specific to accessing remote SQL Server databases, see Chapter 12, "Data Access Security."

You can access remote resources from an ASP.NET application by using any of the following techniques:

- Use the ASP.NET process identity.
- Use a serviced component.
- Use the Anonymous Internet user account (for example, IUSR_MACHINE).
- Use the **LogonUser** API and impersonating a specific Windows identity.
- Use the original caller.

Using the ASP.NET Process Identity

When the application is not configured for impersonation, the ASP.NET process identity provides the default identity when your application attempts to access remote resources. If you want to use the ASP.NET process account for remote resource access, you have three options:

- Use mirrored accounts.

  This is the simplest approach. You create a local account with a matching user name and password on the remote computer. You must change the ASPNET account password in User Manager to a known value (use a strong password). You must then explicitly set this on the <**processModel**> element in Machine.config, and replace the existing "**AutoGenerate**" value. Avoid clear text credentials. Use the aspnet_setreg.exe utility to store encrypted credentials in the registry as described earlier.

> **Important:** If you change the ASPNET password to a known value, the password in the LSA will no longer match the SAM account password. If you need to revert to the "**AutoGenerate**" default, you will need to do the following:
>
> Run Aspnet_regiis.exe, to reset ASP.NET to its default configuration. For more information, see article Q306005, "HOWTO: Repair IIS Mapping After You Remove and Reinstall IIS" in the Microsoft Knowledge Base.

- Create a custom, least privileged local account to run ASP.NET and create a duplicate account on the remote computer.
- Run ASP.NET using a least-privileged domain account.

  This assumes that client and server computers are in the same or trusting domains.

More Information

For more information about configuring an ASP.NET process account, see "How To: Create a Custom Account to Run ASP.NET" in the Reference section of this book.

Using a Serviced Component

You can use an out of process serviced component, configured to run as a fixed identity to access network resources. This approach is shown in Figure 8.6.

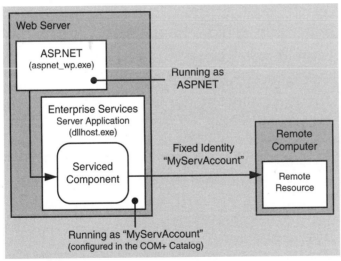

Figure 8.6
Using an out of process serviced component to provide a fixed identity for network resource access

Using an out of process serviced component (in an Enterprise Services server application) has the following advantages:

- Flexibility in terms of the identity used. You don't just rely on the ASP.NET identity.
- Trusted or higher-privileged code can be isolated from your main Web application.
- An additional process hop raises the bar from a security perspective. It makes it much tougher for an attacker to cross the process boundary to a process with raised privileges.
- If you need to hand-craft impersonation with **LogonUser** API calls, you can do so in a process that is separated from your main Web application.

> **Note:** To call **LogonUser** you must give the Enterprise Services process-account the "Act as part of the operating system" privilege. Raising the privileges for a process that is separate from your Web application is less of a security concern.

Using the Anonymous Internet User Account

You can use the anonymous Internet user account to access network resources if IIS is configured for Anonymous authentication. This is the case if one of the following is true:

- Your application supports anonymous access.
- Your application uses Forms, Passport, or Custom authentication (where IIS is configured for anonymous access).

▶ **To use the anonymous account for remote resource access**

1. Configure IIS for Anonymous authentication. You can set the ASP.NET authentication mode to Windows, Forms, Passport, or None, depending upon the authentication requirements of your application.

2. Configure ASP.NET for impersonation. Use the following setting in Web.config:

```
<identity impersonate="true" />
```

3. Configure the anonymous account as a least privileged domain account,

   –or–

   Duplicate the anonymous account by using the same user name and password on the remote computer. This approach is necessary when you are making calls across non-trusting domains or through firewalls where the necessary ports to support Integrated Windows authentication are not open.

To support this approach, you must also:

a. Use Internet Services Manager to clear the **Allow IIS to Control Password** checkbox for the anonymous account.

If you select this option, the logon session created using the specified anonymous account ends up with NULL network credentials (and therefore cannot be used to access network resources). If you don't select this option, the logon session is an interactive logon session with network credentials.

b. Set the account's credentials both in User Manager and in Internet Services Manager.

Important: If you impersonate the anonymous account (for example, IUSR_MACHINE), resources must be secured against this account by using appropriately configured ACLs. Resources that your application needs to access must grant read access (at minimum) to the anonymous account. All other resources should deny access to the anonymous account.

Hosting Multiple Web Applications

You can use a separate anonymous Internet user account for each virtual root within your Web site. In a hosted environment, this allows you to separately authorize, track, and audit requests that originate from separate Web applications. This approach is shown in Figure 8.7.

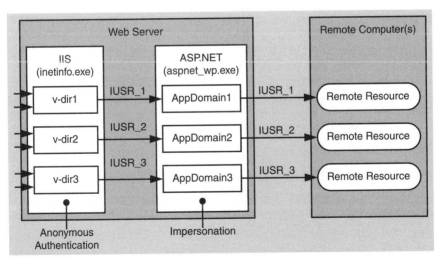

Figure 8.7
Impersonating separate anonymous Internet user accounts per application (v-dir)

▶ **To configure the anonymous Internet user account for a specific virtual directory**

1. Start **Internet Services Manager** from the **Administrative Tools** programs group.

2. Select the virtual directory you want to configure, right-click, and then click **Properties**.

3. Click the **Directory Security** tab.

4. Click **Edit** within the **Anonymous access and authentication control** group.

5. Select **Anonymous access,** and then click **Edit**.

6. Enter the user name and password of the account that you want IIS to use when anonymous users connect to the site.

7. Make sure that **Allow IIS to control password** is NOT selected.

Using LogonUser and Impersonating a Specific Windows Identity

You can impersonate a specific identity by configuring user name and password attributes on the <identity> element in Web.config, or by calling the Win32® **LogonUser** API in your application code.

Important: As mentioned earlier in this chapter, use of **LogonUser** or a fixed impersonated identity is not recommended when using the .NET Framework 1.0 on Windows 2000 servers because it forces you to give the ASP.NET process account the powerful "Act as part of the operating system" privilege.

Microsoft Windows .NET Server 2003 lifts this restriction. Additionally, the .NET Framework version 1.1 will provide an enhancement for this scenario on Windows 2000. The logon will be performed by the IIS process, so that ASP.NET does not require the "Act as part of the operating system" privilege.

Using the Original Caller

To use the original caller's identity for remote resource access, you must be able to delegate the caller's security context from the Web server to the remote computer.

Scalability Warning: If you access the data services tier of your application using the original caller's impersonated identity, you severely impact the application's ability to scale, because database connection pooling is rendered ineffective. The security context for database connections is different for each user.

The following authentication schemes support delegation:

- **Kerberos**. For more information, see "How To: Implement Kerberos Delegation for Windows 2000" within the Reference section of this book.

- **Client certificates mapped to Windows accounts**. The mapping must be performed by IIS.

- **Basic**. Basic authentication supports remote resource access because the original caller's credentials are available in clear text at the Web server. These can be used to respond to authentication challenges from remote computers.

  Basic authentication must be used in conjunction with an interactive or batch logon session. The type of logon session that results from Basic authentication is configurable in the IIS Metabase. For more information, see the Platform SDK: Internet Information Services 5.1 on MSDN.

Important: Basic authentication is the least secure of the approaches that support delegation. This is because a clear text user name and password are passed from the browser to the server over the network and they are cached in memory at the Web server. You can use SSL to protect credentials while in transit but you should avoid caching clear text credentials at the Web server where possible.

▶ To use the original caller for remote resource access

1. Configure IIS for Integrated Windows (Kerberos), Certificate (with IIS certificate mapping), or Basic authentication.

2. Configure ASP.NET for Windows authentication and impersonation.

```
<authentication mode="Window" />
<identity impersonate="true" />
```

3. If you use Kerberos delegation, configure Active Directory accounts for delegation.

More Information

- For more information about configuring Kerberos delegation, see "How To: Implement Kerberos Delegation for Windows 2000" in the Reference section of this book.

- For more information about IIS certificate mapping, see *http://www.microsoft.com /technet/treeview/default.asp?url=/technet/prodtechnol/ad/windows2000/howto /mapcerts.asp*.

- For more information about ASP.NET Impersonation, see the .NET Framework Developers Guide on MSDN.

Accessing Files on a UNC File Share

If your application needs to access files on a Universal Naming Convention (UNC) share using ASP.NET, it is important to add NTFS permissions to the share's folder. You will also need to set the share's permissions to grant at least read access to either the ASP.NET process account or the impersonated identity (if your application is configured for impersonation).

Accessing Non-Windows Network Resources

If your application needs to access non-Windows resources such as databases located on non-Windows platforms or mainframe applications, you need to consider the following questions:

- What are the gatekeepers and trust boundaries associated with the resource?

- What credentials are required for authentication?
- Does the resource need to know the original caller identity, or does it trust the calling application (using a fixed process or service identity)?
- What is the performance cost associated with establishing connections? If the cost is significant you may need to implement connection pooling; for example, by using the object pooling feature of Enterprise Services.

If the resource needs to be able to authenticate the original caller (and Windows authentication is not an option), you have the following options:

- Pass credentials using (method call) parameters.
- Pass credentials in a connection string. Use SSL or IPSec to secure clear text credentials passed over a network.

  Store credentials securely within your application, for example by using DPAPI. For more information about securely storing database connection strings, see "Storing Database Connection Strings Securely" in Chapter 12, "Data Access Security."

- Use a centralized data store for authentication that both platforms can access; for example, an LDAP directory.

Secure Communication

Use SSL to secure the communication link between browser and Web server. SSL provides message confidentiality and message integrity. Use SSL and/or IPSec to provide a secure channel from Web server to application server or database server.

More Information

For more information about secure communication, see "Chapter 4, "Secure Communication."

Storing Secrets

Web applications often need to store secrets. These need to be secured against rogue administrators and malicious Web users, such as:

- **Rogue administrators**. Rogue administrators and other unscrupulous users should not be able to view privileged information. For example, the administrator of the Web server should not be able to read the password of a SQL Server login account on a SQL Server computer located across the network.
- **Malicious Web users**. Even though there are components (such as the **FileAuthorizationModule**) that prevent users from accessing privileged files, if an attacker does gain access to a configuration file, the secret in the file should not be in plain text.

Typical examples of secrets include:

- **SQL connection strings**. A common mistake is to store the user name and password in plain text. The recommendation is to use Windows authentication instead of SQL authentication. If you can't use Windows authentication, see the following sections in Chapter 12, "Data Access Security," which present secure alternatives:
  - "Storing Database Connections Securely"
  - "Secure Communications"
- **Credentials used for SQL application roles**. SQL Application roles must be activated with a stored procedure that requires the role name and associated password. For more information, see "Authorization" in Chapter 12, "Data Access Security."
- **Fixed identities in Web.config**. For example:

```
<identity impersonate="true" userName="bob" password="inClearText"/>
```

The aspnet_setreg.exe utility allows you to replace clear text credentials with a pointer to a secured registry key that contains the encrypted credentials.

- **Process identity in Machine.config**. For example:

```
<process userName="cUsTuMUzerName" password="kUsTumPazzWerD" >
```

As per the **<identity>** element, you should use aspnet_setreg.exe to store encrypted credentials in the registry.

- **Keys used to store data securely**. It is impossible to safely store keys in software. However, certain tasks can mitigate the risk. An example is to create a custom configuration section handler which uses asymmetric encryption to encrypt a session key. The session key can then be stored in a configuration file.
- **SQL Server session state**. To use SQL server to manage ASP.NET Web application session state, use the following Web.config settings.

```
<sessionState … stateConnectionString="tcpip=127.0.0.1:42424"
               sqlConnectionString="data source=127.0.0.1;
               user id=UserName;password=MyPassword" />
```

The aspnet_setreg.exe also supports the **stateConnectionString** and **sqlConnectionString** attributes on the **<sessionState>** element, which allows you to store these values in encrypted format in the registry.

- **Passwords used for Forms authentication against a database**.

If your application validates authentication credentials against a database, don't store passwords in the database. Use a hash of the password with a salt value and compare hashes.

For more information, see "Authenticating Users Against a Database" in Chapter 12, "Data Access Security."

Options for Storing Secrets in ASP.NET

A number of approaches are available to .NET Web application developers to store secrets. These include:

- **.NET cryptography classes**. The .NET Framework includes classes that can be used for encryption and decryption. These approaches require that you safely store the encryption key.

- **Data Protection API (DPAPI)**. DPAPI is a pair of Win32 APIs that encrypt and decrypt data by using a key derived from the user's password. When using DPAPI, you do not deal with key management. The operating system manages the key which is the user's password.

- **COM+ Constructor Strings**. If your application uses serviced components, you can store the secret in an object construction string. The string is stored in the COM+ catalog in a clear text form.

- **CAPICOM**. This is a Microsoft COM object which provides COM-based access to the underlying Crypto API.

- **Crypto API**. These are low level Win32 APIs that perform encryption and decryption.

More Information

For more information, see the entry for Cryptography, CryptoAPI and CAPICOM in the Platform SDK on MSDN.

Consider Storing Secrets in Files on Separate Logical Volumes

Consider installing Web application directories on a separate logical volume from the operating system (for example, E: instead of C:). This means that Machine.config (located under C:\WINNT\Microsoft.NET) and potentially other files that contain secrets such as, Universal Data Link (UDL) files, are located on a separate logical volume from the Web application directories.

The rationale for this approach is to protect against possible file canonicalization and directory traversal bugs because:

- File canonicalization bugs can expose files in the Web application folders.

> **Note:** File canonicalization routines return the canonical form of a file path. This is usually the absolute pathname in which all relative references and references to the current directory have been completely resolved.

- Directory traversal bugs can expose files in other folders on the same logical volume.

No bugs of the sort described above have yet been published that exposed files on other logical volumes.

Securing Session and View State

Web applications must manage various types of state including view state and session state. This section discusses secure state management for ASP.NET Web applications.

Securing View State

If your ASP.NET Web applications use view state:

- Ensure the integrity of view state (to ensure it is not altered in any way while in transit) by setting the **enableViewStateMac** to true as shown below. This causes ASP.NET to generate a Message Authentication Code (MAC) on the page's view state when the page is posted back from the client.

  ```
  <% @ Page enableViewStateMac=true >
  ```

- Configure the **validation** attribute on the **<machineKey>** element in Machine.config, to specify the type of encryption to use for data validation. Consider the following:
  - Secure Hash Algorithm 1 (SHA1) produces a larger hash size than Message Digest 5 (MD5) so it is considered more secure. However, view state protected with SHA1 or MD5 can be decoded in transit or on the client side and can potentially be viewed in plain text.
  - Use 3 Data Encryption Standard (3DES) to detect changes in the view state and to also encrypt it while in transit. When in this state, even if view state is decoded, it cannot be viewed in plain text.

Securing Cookies

Cookies that contain authentication or authorization data or other sensitive data should be secured in transit by using SSL. For Forms authentication, the **FormsAuthentication.Encrypt** method can be used to encrypt the authentication ticket, passed between client and server in a cookie.

Securing SQL Session State

The default (in-process) ASP.NET session state handler has certain limitations. For example, it cannot work across computers in a Web farm. To overcome this limitation, ASP.NET allows session state to be stored in a SQL Server database or remote state service.

SQL session state can be configured either in Machine.config or Web.config. The default setting in machine.config is shown below.

```
<sessionState mode="InProc"
              stateConnectionString="tcpip=127.0.0.1:42424"
              stateNetworkTimeout="10"
              sqlConnectionString="data source=127.0.0.1;user id=sa;password="
              cookieless="false" timeout="20"/>
```

By default, the SQL script InstallSqlState.sql, which is used for building the database used for SQL session state is installed at the following location:

```
C:\WINNT\Microsoft.NET\Framework\v1.0.3705
```

When you use SQL session state there are two problems to consider.

- You must secure the database connection string.
- You must secure the session state as it crosses the network.

Securing the Database Connection String

If you use SQL authentication to connect to the server, the connection string specified on the **sqlConnectionString** attribute contains a user name and password. Use the aspnet_setreg.exe utility to store an encrypted connection string in the registry. The following example shows the **<sessionState>** element before and after using aspnet_setreg.exe.

```
<!-- Before -->
<sessionState
    mode="SQLServer",
    sqlConnectionString="data source=Server;user id=userID;password=pwd" . . . />
<!-- After -->
<sessionState mode="SQLServer"
              sqlConnectionString="registry:HKLM\SOFTWARE\YourSecureApp\
              sessionState\ASPNET_SETREG,sqlConnectionString" />
```

Note: You can also use aspnet_setreg.exe to encrypt the **stateConnectionString** attribute if you use the ASP.NET state service.

If possible, you should use Windows authentication to the SQL Server state database. This has the added advantages that the connection string doesn't contain credentials and credentials are not passed over the network to the database server.

▶ **To use Windows authentication, you can use the ASP.NET process identity (typically ASPNET)**

1. Create a duplicate account (with the same name and password) on the database server.

2. Create a SQL login for the account.

3. Create a database user in the **ASPState** database and map the SQL login to the new user.

   The **ASPState** database is created by the InstallSQLState.sql script.

5. Create a user defined database role and add the database user to the role.

6. Configure permissions in the database for the database role.

You can then change the connection string to use a trusted connection, as shown below:

```
sqlConnectionString="server=127.0.0.1;
                     database=StateDatabase;
                     Integrated Security=SSPI;"
```

Securing Session State Across the Network

You may need to protect the session state as it crosses the network to the SQL Server database. This depends on how secure the network hosting the Web server and data servers is. If the database is physically secured in a trusted environment, you may be able to do without this extra security measure.

You can use IPSec to protect all IP traffic between the Web servers and SQL Server, or alternatively, you can use SSL to secure the link to SQL Server. With this approach, you have the option of encrypting just the connection used for the session state, and not all traffic that passes between the computers.

More Information

- For more information about how to set up SQL Session State, see article Q317604, "HOW TO: Configure SQL Server to Store ASP.NET Session State," in the Microsoft Knowledge Base.

- For more information about using SSL to SQL Server, see "How To: Use SSL to Secure Communication with SQL Server 2000" in the Reference section of this book.

- For more information about using IPSec, see "How To: Use IPSec to Provide Secure Communication Between Two Servers" in the Reference section of this book.

Web Farm Considerations

In a Web farm scenario, there is no guarantee that successive requests from the same client are serviced by the same Web server. This has implications for state management and for any encryption that relies on attributes maintained by the <**machineKey**> element in Machine.config.

Session State

The default ASP.NET in-process session state handling (which mirrors previous ASP functionality) results in server affinity and cannot be used in a Web farm scenario. For Web farm deployments, session state must be stored out of process in either the ASP.NET State service or a SQL Server database as described earlier.

Note: You cannot rely on application state for maintaining global counters or unique values in Web farm (Web application configured to run on multiple servers) or Web garden (Web application configured to run on multiple processors) scenarios because application state is not shared across processes or computers.

DPAPI

DPAPI can work with either the machine store or user store (which requires a loaded user profile). If you use DPAPI with the machine store, the encrypted string is specific to a given computer and therefore you must generate the encrypted data on every computer. Do not copy the encrypted data across computers in a Web farm or cluster.

If you use DPAPI with the user store, you can decrypt the data on any computer with a roaming user profile.

More Information

For more information about DPAPI, see Chapter 12, "Data Access Security."

Using Forms Authentication in a Web Farm

If you are using Forms authentication, it is essential that all of the servers in the Web farm share a common machine key, which is used for encryption, decryption, and validation of the authentication ticket.

The machine key is maintained by the <**machineKey**> element within Machine.config. The default setting is shown below.

```
<machineKey validationKey="AutoGenerate"
            decryptionKey="AutoGenerate"
            validation="SHA1"/>
```

This setting results in every machine generating a different validation and decryption key. You must change the <**machineKey**> element and place common key values across all servers in the Web farm.

The <machineKey> Element

The <**machineKey**> element located in Machine.config is used to configure the keys used for encryption and decryption of Forms authentication cookie data and view state integrity checking and encryption.

When the **FormsAuthentication.Encrypt** or **FormsAuthentication.Decrypt** methods are called, and when view state is created or retrieved, the values in the <**machineKey**> element are consulted.

```
<machineKey validationKey="autogenerate|value"
            decryptionKey="autogenerate|value"
            validation="SHA1|MD5|3DES" />
```

The validationKey Attribute

The value of the **validationKey** attribute is used to create and validate MAC codes for view state and Forms authentication tickets. The validation attribute signifies what algorithm to use when performing the MAC generation. Note the following:

- With Forms authentication, this key works in conjunction with the <**forms**> **protection** attribute. When the protection attribute is set to **Validation**, and then when the **FormsAuthentication.Encrypt** method is called, the ticket value and the **validationKey** are used to compute a MAC which is appended to the cookie. When the **FormsAuthentication.Decrypt** method is called, the MAC is computed and compared to the MAC that is appended to the ticket.

- With view state, the value of a control's view state and the **validationKey** are used to compute a MAC, which is appended to the view state. When the view state is posted back from the client, the MAC is recomputed and compared to the MAC that is appended to the view state.

The decryptionKey Attribute

The value of the **decryptionKey** attribute is used to encrypt and decrypt Forms authentication tickets and view state. The DES or Triple DES (3DES) algorithms are used. The precise algorithm depends on whether or not the Windows 2000 High Encryption Pack is installed on the server. If it is installed 3DES is used, otherwise DES is used. Note the following:

- With Forms authentication, the key works in conjunction with the <**forms**> **protection** attribute. When the **protection** attribute is set to **Encryption**, and the **FormsAuthentication.Encrypt** or **Decrypt** methods are called, the ticket value is encrypted or decrypted with the specified **decryptionKey** value.

- With view state, the value of a controls view state is encrypted with the **decryptionKey** value when sent to the client and is decrypted when the client posts the data back to the server.

The Validation Attribute

This attribute dictates what algorithm to use when validating, encrypting, or decrypting. It can take the values SHA1, MD5, or 3DES. The following describes these values:

- **SHA1**. The HMACSHA1 algorithm is actually used when the setting is SHA1. It produces a 160 bit (20 byte) hash or digest of the input. HMACSHA1 is a keyed hashing algorithm. The key used as the input for this algorithm is specified by the **validationKey** attribute.

    SHA1 is a popular algorithm because of its larger digest size compared to other algorithms.

- **MD5**. This produces a 20 byte hash using the MD5 algorithm.
- **3DES**. This encrypts data using the Triple DES (3DES) algorithm.

Note: When the validation attribute is set to 3DES, it is not actually used by Forms authentication. SHA1 is used instead.

More Information

- For information about how to create keys suitable for placing in Machine.config, see article Q312906, "HOW TO: Create Keys w/ C# .NET for Use in Forms Authentication," in the Microsoft Knowledge Base.
- For more information about the Windows 2000 High Encryption Pack, see *http://www.microsoft.com/windows2000/downloads/recommended/encryption/*.

Summary

This chapter has described a variety of techniques and approaches for securing ASP.NET Web applications. Much of the guidance and many of the recommendations presented in this chapter also apply to the development of ASP.NET Web services and .NET Remoting objects hosted by ASP.NET. To summarize:

- If your application uses Forms authentication and if performance is an issue when authenticating the user, retrieve a list of roles and store them in the authentication ticket.
- If you use Forms authentication, create a principal and store it in the context on each request.
- If there are too many roles to store in an authentication cookie, then use the global application cache to store the roles.

- Don't create a custom least privileged account to run ASP.NET. Instead, change the ASPNET account password and create a duplicate account on any remote Windows server that your application needs to access.
- If you must create a custom account to run ASP.NET, use the principle of least privilege. For example:
  - Use a least privileged domain account if administration is the main concern.
  - If you use a local account. you must create a duplicated account on any remote computer that the Web application needs to access, You must use local accounts when your application needs to access resources in non-trusting domains, or where a firewall prevents Windows authentication.
  - Don't run ASP.NET using the local SYSTEM account.
  - Don't give the ASPNET account "Act as part of the operating system" privilege.
- Use SSL when:
  - Security sensitive information is passed between browser and Web server.
  - When Basic authentication is used (to protect credentials).
  - When Forms authentication is used for authentication (as opposed to personalization).
- Avoid storing secrets in plain text.
  - Don't store plain text credentials in machine.config or web.config. Use the aspnet_setreg.exe utility to store encrypted credentials in the registry for the <**identity**>, <**processModel**> and <**sessionState**> elements.

9

Enterprise Services Security

Traditional COM+ services such as distributed transactions, just-in-time activation, object pooling, and concurrency management are available to .NET components. With .NET, such services are referred to as Enterprise Services. They are essential for many middle-tier .NET components running within .NET Web applications.

To add services to a .NET component, you must derive the component class from the **EnterpriseServices.ServicedComponent** base class and then specify precise service requirements using .NET attributes compiled into the assembly that hosts the component.

This chapter describes how to build secure serviced components and how to call them from ASP.NET Web applications.

Security Architecture

The authentication, authorization, and secure communication features supported by Enterprise Services applications are shown in Figure 9.1 on the next page. The client application shown in Figure 9.1 is an ASP.NET Web application.

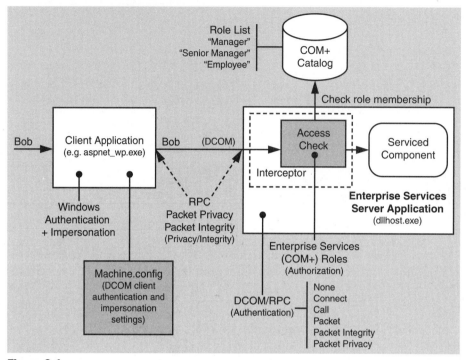

Figure 9.1
Enterprise Services role-based security architecture

Notice that authentication and secure communication features are provided by the underlying RPC transport used by Distributed COM (DCOM). Authorization is provided by Enterprise Services (COM+) roles.

The following summarizes the main elements of the Enterprise Services security architecture:

- Enterprise Services applications use RPC authentication to authenticate callers. This means that unless you have taken specific steps to disable authentication, the caller is authenticated using either Kerberos or NTLM authentication.

- Authorization is provided through Enterprise Services (COM+) roles, which can contain Microsoft® Windows® operating system group or user accounts. Role membership is defined within the COM+ catalog and is administered by using the Component Services tool.

Note: If the Enterprise Services application uses impersonation, caller authorization using Windows ACLs on secured resources is also available.

- When a client (for example, an ASP.NET Web application) calls a method on a serviced component, after the authentication process is complete, the Enterprise Services interception layer accesses the COM+ catalog to determine the client's role membership. It then checks whether membership of the role or roles permits authorized access to the current application, component, interface, and method.

- If the client's role membership permits access, the method is called. If the client doesn't belong to an appropriate role, the call is rejected, and a security event is optionally generated to reflect the failed access attempt.

Important: To implement meaningful role-based authorization within an Enterprise Services application called by an ASP.NET Web application, Windows authentication and imperson-ation must be used within the ASP.NET Web application in order to ensure that the original caller's security context flows through to the serviced component.

- To secure the DCOM communication link between client and server applications, either the RPC Packet Integrity authentication level can be used (to provide message integrity), or the RPC Packet Privacy authentication level can be used (to provide message confidentiality).

Gatekeepers and Gates

The Enterprise Services runtime acts as the gatekeeper for serviced components. The individual gates (authorization points) within an Enterprise Services application are shown in Figure 9.2. You configure these gates by using Enterprise Services roles, which you must populate with the appropriate Windows group and user accounts.

Note: You must also ensure that access checking (role-based security) is enabled for your Enterprise Services application and that the appropriate level of authentication is being used. For more information about how to configure security, see "Configuring Security" later in this chapter.

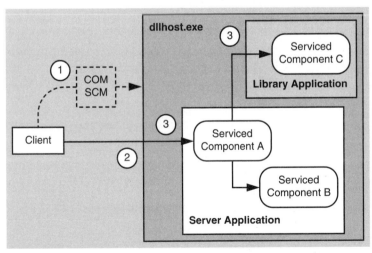

Figure 9.2

Gatekeepers within an Enterprise Services application

There are three distinct access checks performed in response to a client issuing a method call on a serviced component. These are illustrated in Figure 9.2 and described below:

1. An initial access check is performed by the subsystem responsible for activating Enterprise Services applications—the COM Service Control Manager (SCM)—when a call to a serviced component results in an activation request (and the creation of a new instance of the COM+ surrogate process, Dllhost.exe).

   To successfully pass this access check, the caller must be a member of at least one role defined within the application.

2. A second access check is performed when the client's call enters the Dllhost.exe process instance.

   Once again, if the caller is a member of at least one role defined within the application, this access check succeeds.

3. The final access check occurs when the client's call enters either a server or library application.

   To successfully pass this access check, the caller must be a member of a role that is associated with either, the interface, class, or method that is the target of the client's call.

Important: After a call invokes a method on a serviced component, no further access checks are made if the component communicates with other components located in the same application. However, access checks do occur if a component calls another component within a separate application (library or server).

Use Server Applications for Increased Security

If your application needs to enforce an authentication level, for example because it requires encryption to ensure that the data sent to a serviced component remains confidential and tamper proof while in transit across the network, you should use a server application.

The authentication level can be enforced for a server application, while library applications inherit their authentication level from the host process.

To configure the activation type of an Enterprise Services application, use the assembly level **ApplicationActivation** attribute as shown below.

```
[assembly: ApplicationActivation(ActivationOption.Server)]
```

This is equivalent to setting the **Activation Type** to **Server application** on the **Activation** page of the application's **Properties** dialog within Component Services.

Security for Server and Library Applications

Role-based security works in a similar fashion for in-process library applications and out-of-process server applications.

Note the following differences for library applications:

- **Privileges**. The privileges of a library application are determined by the privileges of the client (host) process. For example, if the client process runs with administrator privileges, the library application will also have administrator privileges.
- **Impersonation**. The impersonation level of a library application is inherited from the client process and cannot be set explicitly.
- **Authentication**. The authentication level of a library application is inherited from the client process. With library applications, you can explicitly enable or disable authentication. This option is available on the **Security** page of a library application's **Properties** dialog box.

   This option is typically used to support unauthenticated call-backs from other out-of-process COM components.

Assign Roles to Classes, Interfaces, or Methods

With library applications you should always assign roles at the class, interface, or method level. This is also best practice for server applications.

Users that are defined within library application roles cannot be added to the security descriptor of the client process. This means that you must use at least class-level security to allow a library application to perform role-based authorization.

Code Access Security Requirements

Code Access Security (CAS) requires that code have particular permissions to be able to perform certain operations and access restricted resources. CAS is most useful in a client environment where code is downloaded from the Internet. In this type of situation it is unlikely that the code is fully trusted.

Typically, applications that use serviced components are fully trusted, and as a result CAS has limited use. However, Enterprise Services does demand that the calling code have the necessary permission to call unmanaged code. This implies the following:

- Unmanaged code permission is required to activate and perform cross context calls on serviced components.
- If the client of a serviced component is an ASP.NET Web application, this application must have unmanaged code permission.
- If a reference to a serviced component is passed to untrusted code, methods defined on the serviced component cannot be called from the untrusted code.

Configuring Security

This section shows you how to configure security for:

- A serviced component running in an Enterprise Services server (out-of-process) application.
- An ASP.NET Web application client.

Configuring a Server Application

The steps required to configure an Enterprise Services server application are shown in Figure 9.3.

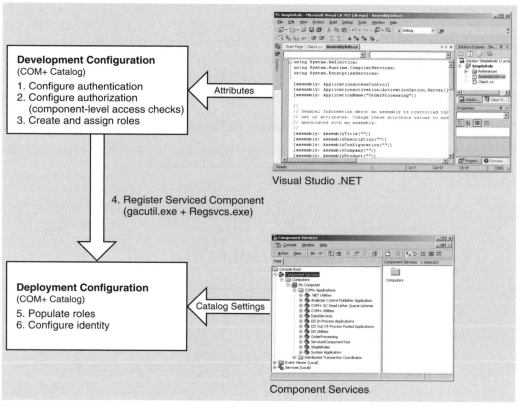

Figure 9.3
Configuring Enterprise Services security

Development Time vs. Deployment Time Configuration

You can configure most security settings within the COM+ catalog at development time by using .NET attributes within the assembly that contains the serviced component. These attributes are used to populate the COM+ catalog when the serviced component is registered with COM+ by using the Regsvcs.exe tool.

Other configuration steps such as populating roles with Windows group and user accounts and configuring a run-as identity for the server application (Dllhost.exe instance) must be configured using the Component Services administration tool (or programmatically using script) at deployment time.

Configure Authentication

To set the application authentication level declaratively, use the **ApplicationAccessControl** assembly level attribute as shown below.

```
[assembly: ApplicationAccessControl(
          Authentication = AuthenticationOption.Call)]
```

This is equivalent to setting the **Authentication Level for Calls** value on the **Security** page of the application's **Properties** dialog within Component Services.

Note: The client's authentication level also affects the authentication level used by the Enterprise Services application, because a process of high-water mark negotiation is employed, which always results in the higher of the two settings being used.

For more information about configuring the DCOM authentication level used by an ASP.NET client application, see "Configuring an ASP.NET Client Application," later in this section.

For more information about DCOM authentication levels and authentication level negotiation, see the "Security Concepts" section of this chapter.

Configure Authorization (Component-Level Access Checks)

To enable fine-grained authorization at the component, interface, or method level you must:

* Enable access checks at the application level.

  Use the following .NET attribute to enable application-wide access checks.

  ```
  [assembly: ApplicationAccessControl(true)]
  ```

  This is equivalent to selecting the **Enforce access checks for this application** check box on the **Security** page of the application's **Properties** dialog box within Component Services.

Important: Failure to set this attribute results in no access checks being performed.

● Configure the application's security level at the process and component level.

For meaningful role-based security, enable access checking at the process and component levels by using the following .NET attribute.

```
[assembly: ApplicationAccessControl(AccessChecksLevel=
                         AccessChecksLevelOption. ApplicationComponent)]
```

This is equivalent to selecting the **Perform access checks at the process and component levels** check box on the **Security** page of the application's **Properties** dialog box within Component Services.

Note: You should enable access checking at the process and component level for library applications.

● Enable component level access checks.

To enable component-level access checks, use the **ComponentAccessControl** class-level attribute as shown below.

```
[ComponentAccessControl(true)]
public class MyServicedComponent : ServicedComponent
{
}
```

This is equivalent to selecting the **Enforce Component Level Access Checks** check box on the **Security** page of the component **Properties** dialog box within Component Services.

Note: This setting is effective only if you have enabled application-level access checking and have configured process and component level access checks, as described previously.

Create and Assign Roles

Roles can be created and assigned at the application, component (class), interface, and method levels.

Adding Roles to an Application

To add roles to an application, use the **SecurityRole** assembly level attribute as shown below.

```
[assembly:SecurityRole("Employee")]
[assembly:SecurityRole("Manager")]
```

This is equivalent to adding roles to an application by using the Component Services tool.

Note: Using the **SecurityRole** attribute at the assembly level is equivalent to adding roles to the application, but not assigning them to individual components, interfaces, or methods. The result is that the members of these roles determine the composition of the security descriptor attached to the application. This is used solely to determine who is allowed to access (and launch) the application.

For more effective role-based authorization, apply roles to components, interfaces, and methods as described below.

Adding Roles to a Component (Class)

To add roles to a component apply the **SecurityRole** attribute above the class definition, as shown below.

```
[SecurityRole("Manager")]
public class Transfer : ServicedComponent
{
}
```

Adding Roles to an Interface

To apply roles at the interface level, you must create an interface definition and then implement it within your serviced component class. You can then associate roles with the interface by using the **SecurityRole** attribute.

Important: At development time, you must also annotate the class with the **SecureMethod** attribute. This informs Enterprise Services that method level security services may be used. At deployment time, administrators must also add users to the system defined **Marshaler** role, which is automatically created within the COM+ catalog, when a class that is marked with **SecureMethod** is registered with Component Services.

Use of the **Marshaler** role is discussed further in the next section.

The following example shows how to add the **Manager** role to a particular interface.

```
[SecurityRole("Manager")]
public interface ISomeInterface
{
  void Method1( string message );
  void Method2( int parm1, int parm2 );
}

[ComponentAccessControl]
[SecureMethod]
public class MyServicedComponent : ServicedComponent, ISomeInterface
{
  public void Method1( string message )
  {
```

```
    // Implementation
  }
  public void Method2( int parm1, int parm2 )
  {
    // Implementation
  }
}
```

Adding Roles to a Method

To ensure that the public methods of a class appear in the COM+ catalog, you must explicitly implement an interface that defines the methods. Then, to secure the methods, you must use the **SecureMethod** attribute on the class, or the **SecureMethod** or **SecurityRole** attribute at the method level.

Note: The **SecureMethod** and **SecurityRole** attributes must appear above the method implementation and not within the interface definition.

To enable method level security, perform the following steps:

a. Define an interface that contains the methods you want to secure. For example:

```
public interface ISomeInterface
{
  void Method1( string message );
  void Method2( int parm1, int parm2 );
}
```

b. Implement the interface on the serviced component class:

```
[ComponentAccessControl]
public class MyServicedComponent : ServicedComponent, ISomeInterface
{
  public void Method1( string message )
  {
    // Implementation
  }
  public void Method2( int parm1, int parm2 )
  {
    // Implementation
  }
}
```

c. If you want to configure roles administratively by using the Component Services tool, you must annotate the class with the **SecureMethod** attribute, as shown below.

```
[ComponentAccessControl]
[SecureMethod]
```

```
public class MyServicedComponent : ServicedComponent, ISomeInterface
{
}
```

d. Alternatively, if you want to add roles to methods at development time by using .NET attributes, apply the **SecurityRole** attribute at the method level. In this event, you do not need to apply the **SecureMethod** attribute at the class level (although the **ComponentAccessControl** attribute must still be present to configure component level access checks).

In the following example only members of the **Manager** role can call **Method1**, while members of the **Manager** and **Employee** roles can call **Method2**.

```
[ComponentAccessControl]
public class MyServicedComponent : ServicedComponent, ISomeInterface
{
   [SecurityRole("Manager")]
   public void Method1( string message )
   {
     // Implementation
   }
   [SecurityRole("Manager")]
   [SecurityRole("Employee")]
   public void Method2( int parm1, int parm2 )
   {
     // Implementation
   }
}
```

e. At deployment time, administrators must add any user that requires access to methods or interfaces of the class to the predefined **Marshaler** role.

Note: The Enterprise Services infrastructure uses a number of system-level interfaces that are exposed by all serviced components. These include **IManagedObject**, **IDisposable**, and **IServiceComponentInfo**. If access checks are enabled at the interface or method levels, the Enterprise Services infrastructure is denied access to these interfaces.

As a result, Enterprise Services creates a special role called **Marshaler** and associates the role with these interfaces. You can view this role (and the aforementioned interfaces) with the Component Services tool.

At deployment time, application administrators need to add all users to the **Marshaler** role who needs to access any methods or interface of the class. You can automate this in two different ways:

- Write a script that uses the Component Services object model to copy all users from other roles to the **Marshaler** role.
- Write a script which assigns all other roles to these three special interfaces and delete the **Marshaler** role.

Register Serviced Components

Register serviced components in:

- **The Global Assembly Cache**. Serviced components hosted in COM+ server applications require installation in the global assembly cache, while library applications do not.

  To register a serviced component in the global assembly cache, run the Gacutil.exe command line utility. To register an assembly called MyServicedComponent.dll in the global assembly cache, run the following command.

  ```
  gacutil -i MyServicedComponent.dll
  ```

  Note: You can also use the Microsoft .NET Framework Configuration Tool from the **Administrative Tools** program group to view and manipulate the contents of the global assembly cache.

- **The COM+ Catalog**. To register an assembly called MyServicedComponent.dll in the COM+ catalog, run the following command.

  ```
  regsvcs.exe MyServicedComponent.dll
  ```

  This command results in the creation of a COM+ application. The .NET attributes present within the assembly are used to populate the COM+ catalog.

Populate Roles

Populate roles by using the Component Services tool, or by using script to program the COM+ catalog using the COM+ administration objects.

Use Windows Groups

Add Windows 2000 group accounts to Enterprise Services roles for maximum flexibility. By using Windows groups, you can effectively use one administration tool (the Users and Computers Administration tool) to administer both Windows and Enterprise Services security.

- Create a Windows group for each role in the Enterprise Services application.
- Assign each group to its respective role.

  For example, if you have a role called **Manager**, create a Windows group called **Managers**. Assign the **Managers** group to the **Manager** role.

- After you assign groups to roles, use the Users and Computers Administration tool to add and remove users in each group.

For example, adding a Windows 2000 user account named **David** to the Windows 2000 group Managers effectively maps **David** to the **Manager** role.

▶ **To assign Windows groups to Enterprise Services roles by using Component Services**

1. Using the Component Services tool, expand the application that contains the roles to which you want to add Windows 2000 groups.
2. Expand the **Roles** folder and the specific role to which you want to assign Windows groups.
3. Select the **Users** folder under the specific role.
4. Right-click the folder, point to **New,** and then click **User**.
5. In the **Select Users or Groups** dialog box, add groups (or users) to the role.

More Information

For more information about programming the COM+ catalog by using the COM+ administration objects, see "Automating COM+ Administration" within the Component Development section of the MSDN Library.

Configure Identity

Use the Component Services tool (or script) to configure the identity of the Enterprise Services application. The identity property determines the account used to run the instance of Dllhost.exe that hosts the application.

▶ **To configure identity**

1. Using the Component Services tool, select the relevant application.
2. Right-click the name of the application, and then click **Properties**.
3. Click the **Identity** tab.
4. Click **This user** and specify the configured service account used to run the application.

More Information

For more information about choosing an appropriate identity to run an Enterprise Services application, see "Choosing a Process Identity" later in this chapter.

Configuring an ASP.NET Client Application

You must configure the DCOM authentication level and impersonation levels used by client applications when communicating with serviced components using DCOM.

Configure Authentication

To configure the default authentication level used by an ASP.NET Web application when it communicates with a serviced component, edit the **comAuthenticationLevel** attribute on the **<processModel>** element in Machine.config.

Machine.config is located in the following folder.

```
%windir%\Microsoft.NET\Framework\v1.0.3705\CONFIG
```

Set the **comAuthenticationLevel** attribute to one of the following values.

```
comAuthenticationLevel=
         "[Default|None|Connect|Call|Pkt|PktIntegrity|PktPrivacy]"
```

More Information

For more information about DCOM authentication levels, see "Authentication" within the "Security Concepts" section later in this chapter.

Configure Impersonation

The impersonation level set by the client determines the impersonation level capabilities of the server. To configure the default impersonation level used by a Web-based application when it communicates with a serviced component, edit the **comImpersonationLevel** attribute on the **<processModel>** element in Machine.config. Set it to one of the following values.

```
comImpersonationLevel="[Default|Anonymous|Identify|Impersonate|Delegate]"
```

More Information

For more information about DCOM impersonation levels, see "Impersonation" within the "Security Concepts" section later in this chapter.

Configuring Impersonation Levels for an Enterprise Services Application

If a serviced component in one application needs to call a serviced component within a second (server) application, you may need to configure the impersonation level for the client application.

Important: The impersonation level configured for an Enterprise Services application (on the **Security** page of the application's **Properties** dialog box) is the impersonation level used by outgoing calls made by components within the application. It does not affect whether or not serviced components within the application perform impersonation. To impersonate clients within a serviced component, you must use programmatic impersonation techniques, as described in "Flowing the Original Caller," later in this chapter.

To set the application impersonation level declaratively, use the **ApplicationAccessControl** assembly level attribute as shown below.

```
[assembly: ApplicationAccessControl(
            ImpersonationLevel=ImpersonationLevelOption.Identify)]
```

This is equivalent to setting the **Impersonation Level** value on the **Security** page of the application's **Properties** dialog within Component Services.

Programming Security

The Enterprise Services security features are available to .NET components using the **ContextUtil**, **SecurityCallContext**, and **SecurityIdentity** classes.

Programmatic Role-Based Security

For fine grained authorization decisions, you can programmatically test role membership using the **IsCallerInRole** method of the **ContextUtil** class. Prior to calling this method, you should check that component-level access checks are enabled, as shown in the following code fragment. If security is disabled, **IsCallerInRole** always returns true.

```
public void Transfer(string fromAccount, string toAccount, double amount)
{
  // Check that security is enabled
  if (ContextUtil.IsSecurityEnabled)
  {
    // Only Managers are allowed to transfer sums of money in excess of $1000
    if (amount > 1000)
    {
      if (ContextUtil.IsCallerInRole("Manager"))
      {
        // Caller is authorized
      }
      else
      {
        // Caller is unauthorized
      }
    }
  }
}
```

Identifying Callers

The following example shows how to identify all upstream callers from within a serviced component.

```
[ComponentAccessControl]
public class MyServicedComponent : ServicedComponent
{
  public void ShowCallers()
  {
    SecurityCallContext context = SecurityCallContext.CurrentCall;
    SecurityCallers callers = context.Callers;
    foreach(SecurityIdentity id in callers)
    {
      Console.WriteLine(id.AccountName);
    }
  }
}
```

Note: The original caller identity is available via the **SecurityCallContext.OriginalCaller** property.

Choosing a Process Identity

Server activated Enterprise Services applications run within an instance of the Dllhost.exe process. You must configure the account used to run the process in the COM+ catalog by using the Component Services tool.

Note: You cannot specify the run as identity by using a .NET attribute.

Avoid Running as the Interactive User

Do not run server applications using the identity of the interactively logged on user (this is the default setting). There are two main reasons to avoid this:

- The privileges and access rights of the application will vary and will be dependent upon who is currently logged on interactively at the server. If an administrator happens to be logged on, the application will have administrator privileges.

- If the application is launched while a user is interactively logged on and then the user logs off, the server application will be shut down. It will not be able to restart until another user logs on interactively.

The interactive user setting is designed for developers to use at development time, and should not be considered a deployment setting.

Use a Least-Privileged Custom Account

Create a least privileged account to mitigate the threat associated with a process compromise. If a determined attacker manages to compromise the server process, he or she will easily be able to inherit the privileges and access rights granted to the process account. An account configured with minimum privileges restricts the potential damage that can be done.

If you need to access network resources with the process account, the remote computer must be able to authenticate the process account. In this scenario, you have two options:

- You can use a domain account if the two computers are in the same or trusting domains.
- You can use a local account and then create a duplicate account (with the same user name and password) on the remote computer. With this option, you must ensure that the passwords of the two accounts remain synchronized.

   You may be forced to use the duplicated local account approach if the remote computer is located in a separate domain (with no trust relationship), or if the remote computer is behind a firewall (where closed ports do not permit Windows authentication).

Accessing Network Resources

Your serviced components may need to access remote resources. It is important to be able to identify the following:

- The resources the components need to access. For example, files on file shares, databases, other DCOM servers, Active Directory® directory service objects, and so on.
- The identity used to perform the resource access. If your serviced component accesses remote resources, the identity used (which by default is the process identity) must be capable of being authenticated by the remote computer.

Note: For information specific to accessing remote SQL Server databases, see Chapter 12, "Data Access Security."

You can access remote resources from a component within an Enterprise Services application by using any of the following identities:

- The original caller (if you are explicitly impersonating by using **CoImpersonateClient**)
- The current process identity (configured in the COM+ catalog for server applications)
- A specific service account

Using the Original Caller

To use the original caller's identity for remote resource access, you must:

- Programmatically impersonate the original caller by calling **CoImpersonateClient**.
- Be able to delegate the caller's security context from the application server hosting the Enterprise Services application to the remote computer. This assumes that you are using Kerberos authentication between your Enterprise Services application and client application.

Scalability Warning: If you access the data services tier of your application using the original caller's impersonated identity, you severely impact the application's ability to scale, because you prevent database connection pooling from working efficiently; it doesn't work efficiently because the security context of each database connection is tied to many individual callers.

More Information

For more information about impersonating callers, see "Flowing the Original Caller," later in this chapter.

Using the Current Process Identity

If your application is configured to run as a server application, you can use the configured process identity for remote resource access (this is the default case).

If you want to use the server process account for remote resource access, you must either:

- Run the server application using a least-privileged domain account. This assumes that client and server computers are in the same or trusting domains.
- Duplicate the process account using the same username and password on the remote computer.

If ease of administration is your primary concern, you should use a least-privileged domain account.

If your application is configured to run as a library application, the process identity is inherited from the host process (which will often be a Web-based application). For more information about using the ASP.NET process identity for remote resource access, see Chapter 8, "ASP.NET Security."

Using a Specific Service Account

Your Enterprise Services application could access remote resources by using a specifically configured service account (that is, a non-user Windows account). However, this approach is not recommended on Windows 2000 because it relies on you calling the **LogonUser** API. It also presents a credential management problem for the application because the account credentials must be stored securely.

The use of **LogonUser** on Windows 2000 should be avoided, because it forces you to grant the powerful "Act as part of the operating system" privilege to the Enterprise Services process account.

Note: Microsoft Windows .NET Server 2003 will lift this restriction.

Flowing the Original Caller

By default, outgoing calls issued by serviced components (for example, to access local or remote resources) are made using the security context obtained from the host process. For server applications, this is the configured run-as identity. For library applications, this is the identity of the (host) client process (for example, Aspnet_wp.exe when an ASP.NET Web application is the client).

▶ **To flow the original caller's context through an Enterprise Services application**

1. Call **CoImpersonateClient**.

   This creates and attaches a thread impersonation token to the current thread.

2. Perform operation (access local or remote resource).

   As impersonation is enabled, the outgoing call is made using the client's security context (as defined by the impersonation token).

   If local resources are accessed, the caller (client process) must have specified at least Impersonate level impersonation. If remote resources are accessed, the caller must have specified Delegate level impersonation.

   If the caller is an ASP.NET Web application, the default impersonation level for the ASP.NET worker process is Impersonate. Therefore, to flow the original caller to a downstream remote computer, you must change this default to Delegate (on the <**processModel**> element of Machine.config on the client computer).

Note: To use the original caller's security context to access remote resources you must use Kerberos authentication, with accounts configured for delegation. The account used to run the Enterprise Services server application must also be marked in Active Directory as "Trusted for delegation."

3. Cease impersonation by calling **CoRevertToSelf**.

   This removes the impersonation token. Any subsequent call from the current method uses the process security context. If you fail to call **CoRevertToSelf**, it is called implicitly by the runtime when the method ends.

Note: The identity of the original caller automatically flows to an Enterprise Services application and is available using **SecurityCallContext.OriginalCaller**. This can be useful for auditing purposes.

Calling CoImpersonateClient

CoImpersonateClient (and **CoRevertToSelf**) are located within OLE32.dll. You must import their definitions by using the **DllImport** attribute in order to be able to call them through P/Invoke. This is illustrated in the following code fragment.

```
class COMSec
{
  [DllImport("OLE32.DLL", CharSet=CharSet.Auto)]
  public static extern uint CoImpersonateClient();

  [DllImport("OLE32.DLL", CharSet=CharSet.Auto)]
  public static extern uint CoRevertToSelf();
}
. . .
void SomeMethod()
{
  // To flow the original caller's security context and use it to access local
  // or remote resources, start impersonation
  COMSec.CoImpersonateClient();
  // Perform operations as the caller
  // Code here uses the context of the caller - not the context of the process
  . . .
  COMSec.CoRevertToSelf();
  // Code here reverts to using the process context
}
```

More Information

For more information about how to configure a complete Kerberos delegation scenario that shows how to flow the original caller's security context through an ASP.NET Web application, an Enterprise Services application, and onto a database, see the "Flowing the Original Caller" section of Chapter 5, "Intranet Security."

RPC Encryption

To secure the data sent from a client application to a remote serviced component over DCOM, use the RPC Packet Privacy authentication level between client and server. This provides message confidentiality and integrity.

You must configure the authentication level at the client and server.

To configure ASP.NET (where an ASP.NET Web application is the client), set the **comAuthenticationLevel** attribute on the <**processModel**> element in machine.config to **PktPrivacy**.

To configure an Enterprise Services server application, set the application-level authentication level either by using the Component Services tool or the following .NET attribute within the serviced component assembly.

```
[assembly: ApplicationAccessControl(
          Authentication = AuthenticationOption.Privacy)]
```

More Information

- For more information about configuring security (including authentication levels), see "Configuring Security" earlier in this chapter.
- For more information about RPC/DCOM authentication levels, see "Authentication" later in this chapter.
- For more information about authentication-level negotiation, see "Authentication Level Negotiation" later in this chapter.

Building Serviced Components

For a step-by-step walkthrough that shows you how to build a serviced component, see " How To: Use Role-based Security with Enterprise Services" in the Reference section of this book.

DLL Locking Problems

When you rebuild a serviced component, if the DLL is locked:

- Use Component Services to shut down the COM+ server application.
- If you are developing a library application, the application may still be loaded into the Aspnet_wp.exe process. Run **IISReset** from a command prompt or use Task Manager to stop the Aspnet_wp.exe process.
- Use the FileMon.exe tool from www.sysinternals.com to help troubleshoot file locking problems.

Versioning

The default **AssemblyVersion** attribute that is generated by Microsoft Visual Studio® .NET development system when you create a new project is shown below.

```
[assembly: AssemblyVersion("1.0.*")]
```

Each time you rebuild the project, a new assembly version is generated. This also results in the generation of a new class identifier (CLSID) to identify the serviced component classes. If you repeatedly register the assembly with component services using Regsvcs.exe, you will see duplicated components (strictly classes) with different CLSIDs listed beneath the **Components** folder.

While this complies with strict COM versioning semantics and will prevent existing managed and unmanaged clients from breaking, it can be an annoyance during development.

During test and development, consider setting an explicit version by using the assembly level **AssemblyVersion** attribute shown below.

```
[assembly: AssemblyVersion("1.0.0.1")]
```

This setting will prevent a new CLSID being generated with each successive project build. You may also want to fix the interface identifiers (IIDs). If your class implements explicit interfaces, you can fix the IID for a given interface by using the GUID attribute as shown below.

```
[Guid("E1FBF27E-9F11-474d-8DF6-58916F798E9D")]
public interface IMyInterface
{
}
```

▶ **To generate new GUIDs**

1. On the **Tools** menu of Visual Studio .NET, click **Create GUID**.
2. Click **Registry Format**
3. Click **New GUID**.
4. Click **Copy**.
5. Paste the GUID from the clipboard into your source code.

Important: Prior to deploying your serviced component assembly for test and production, remove any fixed GUIDs and revert to an automated assembly versioning mechanism (for example, by using "1.0.*"). Failure to do so increases the likelihood that a new release of your component will break existing clients.

More Information

For more information about versioning for deployment, see Understanding Enterprise Services (COM+) in .NET on MSDN.

QueryInterface Exceptions

If you see a **QueryInterface** call for the **IRoleSecurity** interface failing, this indicates that you have updated an interface definition within your assembly, but have not re-registered the assembly with Component Services using Regsvcs.exe.

Important: Each time you run Regsvcs.exe you will need to reconfigure a server application's run-as identity and will also need to add users to groups again. You can create a simple script to automate this task.

DCOM and Firewalls

Windows 2000 (SP3 or QFE 18.1) or Windows .NET Server 2003 allow you to configure Enterprise Services applications to use a static endpoint. If a firewall separates the client from the server, you only need to open two ports in the firewall. Specifically, you must open port 135 for RPC and a port for your Enterprise Services application.

As an alternative to this approach consider exposing your Enterprise Services application as a Web service. This allows you to activate and call serviced components by using SOAP over port 80. The main issue with this approach is that it doesn't allow you to flow transaction context from client to server. You would need to initiate your transaction at the remote serviced component.

More Information

For more information, see the following Knowledge Base articles:

- Article Q312960, "Cannot Set Fixed Endpoint for a COM+ Application"
- Article Q259011, "SAMPLE: A Simple DCOM Client Server Test Application"
- Article Q248809, "PRB: DCOM Does Not Work over NAT-Based Firewall"
- Article Q250367, "INFO: Configuring Microsoft Distributed Transaction Coordinator (DTC) to Work Through a Firewall"
- Article Q154596, "HOWTO: Configure RPC Dynamic Port Allocation to Work w/ Firewall"

Calling Serviced Components from ASP.NET

This section highlights the main issues you will encounter when an ASP.NET application calls a serviced component.

Caller's Identity

When you call a serviced component from an ASP.NET application, the security identity for the call is obtained from the application's Win32® thread identity. If the Web application is configured to impersonate the caller, this is the caller's identity. Otherwise, this is the ASP.NET process identity (by default, ASPNET).

From an ASP.NET application, you can retrieve the current Win32 thread identity by calling **WindowsIdentity.GetCurrent()**.

From a serviced component, you can retrieve the original caller identity by using **SecurityCallContext.OriginalCaller**.

Use Windows Authentication and Impersonation Within the Web-based Application

To enable meaningful role-based security within your Enterprise Services application, you must use Windows authentication and enable impersonation. This ensures that the serviced components are able to authenticate the original callers and make authorization decisions based on the original caller's identity.

Configure Authentication and Impersonation within Machine.config

DCOM authentication levels are negotiated between client (for example, the Web-based application) and server (the Enterprise Services application). The higher of the two security settings is used.

Configure ASP.NET authentication levels by using the **comAuthenitcation** attribute on the **<processModel>** element of Machine.config.

Impersonation levels are controlled by the client (for example, a Web-based application). The client can determine the degree of impersonation that it is willing to allow the server to use.

Configure ASP.NET impersonation levels (for all outgoing DCOM calls), by using the **comImpersonationLevel** attribute on the **<processModel>** element of Machine.config.

Configuring Interface Proxies

The security settings that apply to individual interface proxies are usually obtained from the default process level security settings. In the case of ASP.NET, default security settings such as the impersonation level and authentication level are configured in Machine.config, as described earlier.

If necessary, you can alter the security settings used by an individual interface proxy. For example, if your ASP.NET application communicates with a serviced component that exposes two interfaces and sensitive data is passed through only one interface, you may choose to use the encryption support provided by the packet privacy authentication level only on the sensitive interface and to use, for example, packet authentication on the other interface. This means that you do not experience the performance hit associated with encryption on both interfaces.

Collectively, the set of security settings that apply to an interface proxy are referred to as the security blanket. COM provides the following functions to allow you to query and manipulate security blanket settings on an individual interface proxy:

- CoQueryProxyBlanket
- CoSetProxyBlanket
- CoCopyProxy

You must use P/Invoke to call these functions from an ASP.NET Web application (the DCOM client), The following code shows how to configure a specific interface to use the Packet Privacy authentication level (which provides encryption). This code can be used from an ASP.NET Web application that communicates with a remote serviced component.

```
// Define a wrapper class for the P/Invoke call to CoSetProxyBlanket
class COMSec
{
  // Constants required for the call to CoSetProxyBlanket
  public const uint RPC_C_AUTHN_DEFAULT          = 0xFFFFFFFF;
  public const uint RPC_C_AUTHZ_DEFAULT          = 0xFFFFFFFF;
  public const uint RPC_C_AUTHN_LEVEL_PKT_PRIVACY = 6;
  public const uint RPC_C_IMP_LEVEL_DEFAULT      = 0;
  public const uint COLE_DEFAULT_AUTHINFO        = 0xFFFFFFFF;
  public const uint COLE_DEFAULT_PRINCIPAL       = 0;
  public const uint EOAC_DEFAULT                 = 0x800;

  // HRESULT  CoSetProxyBlanket( IUnknown * pProxy,
  //                             DWORD dwAuthnSvc,
  //                             DWORD dwAuthzSvc,
  //                             WCHAR * pServerPrincName,
  //                             DWORD dwAuthnLevel,
  //                             DWORD dwImpLevel,
  //                             RPC_AUTH_IDENTITY_HANDLE pAuthInfo,
  //                             DWORD dwCapabilities );
  [DllImport("OLE32.DLL", CharSet=CharSet.Auto)]
  public unsafe static extern uint CoSetProxyBlanket(
                              IntPtr pProxy,
                              uint dwAuthnSvc,
                              uint dwAuthzSvc,
                              IntPtr pServerPrincName,
                              uint dwAuthnLevel,
                              uint dwImpLevel,
                              IntPtr pAuthInfo,
                              uint dwCapababilities);

} // end class COMSec
```

```
// Code to call CoSetProxyBlanket
void CallComponent()
{
  // This is the interface to configure
  Guid IID_ISecureInterface = new Guid("c720ff19-bec1-352c-bb4b-e2de10b858ba");
  IntPtr pISecureInterface;

  // Instantiate the serviced component
  CreditCardComponent comp = new CreditCardComponent();
  // Get its IUnknown pointer
  IntPtr pIUnk = Marshal.GetIUnknownForObject(comp);
  // Get the interface to configure
  Marshal.QueryInterface(pIUnk, ref IID_ISecureInterface,
                         out pISecureInterface);
  try
  {
    // Configure the interface proxy and set packet privacy authentication
    uint hr = COMSec.CoSetProxyBlanket( pISecureInterface,
                                        COMSec.RPC_C_AUTHN_DEFAULT,
                                        COMSec.RPC_C_AUTHZ_DEFAULT,
                                        IntPtr.Zero,
                                        COMSec.RPC_C_AUTHN_LEVEL_PKT_PRIVACY,
                                        COMSec.RPC_C_IMP_LEVEL_DEFAULT,
                                        IntPtr.Zero,
                                        COMSec.EOAC_DEFAULT );
    ISecureInterface secure = (ISecureInterface)comp;
    // The following call will be encrypted as ISecureInterface is configured
    // for packet privacy authentication. Other interfaces use the process
    // level defaults (normally packet authentication).
    secure.ValidateCreditCard("123456789");
  }
  catch (Exception ex)
  {
  }
}
```

More Information

- For more information about configuring an ASP.NET client application to call serviced components, see "Configuring an ASP.NET Client Application," earlier in this chapter.

- For more information about DCOM authentication levels, see "Authentication," later in this chapter.

- For more information about DCOM impersonation levels, see "Impersonation," later in this chapter.

- For more information about using Windows authentication and enabling impersonation within a Web-based application, see Chapter 8, "ASP.NET Security."

Security Concepts

This section provides a brief overview of Enterprise Services security concepts. If you are already experienced with COM+, many of the concepts will be familiar.

For background information on Enterprise Services, see the MSDN article "Understanding Enterprise Services (COM+) in .NET."

The following are summaries of key security concepts that you should understand:

- Security settings for serviced components and Enterprise Services applications are maintained within the COM+ catalog. Most settings can be configured using .NET attributes. All settings can be configured by using the Component Services administration tool or Microsoft Visual Basic® Scripting Edition development system scripts.

- Authorization is provided by Enterprise Services (COM+) roles, which can contain Windows group or user accounts. These are not the same as .NET roles.

  - Role-based security can be applied at the application, interface, class, and method levels.

  - Imperative role checks can be performed programmatically within methods by using the **IsCallerInRole** method of the **ContextUtil** class.

- Effective role-based authorization within an Enterprise Services application relies on a Windows identity being used to call serviced components.

  - This may require you to use Windows authentication coupled with impersonation within an ASP.NET Web application—if the Web application calls serviced components that rely on Enterprise Services (COM+) roles.

  - When you call a serviced component from an ASP.NET Web application or Web service, the identity used for the outgoing DCOM call is determined by the Win32 thread identity as defined by **WindowsIdentity.GetCurrent()**.

- Serviced components can run in server or library applications.

  - Server applications run in separate instances of Dllhost.exe.

  - Library applications run in the client's process address space.

  - Role-based authorization works in a similar fashion for server and library applications, although there are some subtle differences between library and server applications from a security perspective. For details, see "Security for Server and Library Applications" earlier in this chapter.

- Authentication is provided by the underlying services of DCOM and RPC. The client and server's authentication level combined to determine the resulting authentication level used for communication with the serviced component.

- Impersonation is configured within the client application. It determines the impersonation capabilities of the server.

Enterprise Services (COM+) Roles and .NET Roles

Enterprise Services (COM+) roles are used to represent common categories of users who share the same security privileges within an application. While conceptually similar to .NET roles, they are completely independent.

Enterprise Services (COM+) roles contain Windows user and group accounts (unlike .NET roles which can contain arbitrary non-Windows user identities). Because of this, Enterprise Services (COM+) roles are only an effective authorization mechanism for applications that use Windows authentication and impersonation (in order to flow the caller's security context to the Enterprise Services application).

Table 9.1: Comparing Enterprise Services (COM+) roles with .NET roles

Feature	Enterprise Services (COM+) Roles	.NET Roles
Administration	Component Services Administration Tool	Custom
Data Store	COM+ Catalog	Custom data store (for example, SQL Server or Active Directory)

Declarative	Yes
	[SecurityRole("Manager")]
		Yes
		[PrincipalPermission(
		    SecurityAction.Demand,
		    Role="Manager")]

Imperative	Yes ContextUtil.IsCallerInRole()	Yes IPrincipal.IsInRole
Class, Interface, and Method Level Granularity	Yes	Yes
Extensible	No	Yes (using custom IPrincipal implementation)
Available to all .NET components	Only for components that derive from ServicedComponent base class	Yes
Role Membership	Roles contain Windows group or user accounts	When using WindowsPrincipals, roles ARE Windows groups — no extra level of abstraction
Requires explicit Interface implementation	Yes To obtain method level authorization, an interface must be explicitly defined and implemented	No

Authentication

Because Enterprise Services rely on the underlying infrastructure provided by COM+ and DCOM/RPC, the authentication level settings available to Enterprise Services applications are those defined by RPC (and used by DCOM).

Table 9.2: Enterprise Services applications authentication settings

Authentication Level	Description
Default	Choose authentication level using normal negotiation rules
None	No authentication
Connect	Only authenticate credentials when the client initially connects to the server
Call	Authenticate at the start of each remote procedure call
Packet	Authenticate all data received from the client
Packet Integrity	Authenticate all data and verify that none of the transferred data has been modified
Packet Privacy	Authenticate all data and encrypt parameter state for each remote procedure call

Authentication Level Promotion

You should be aware that certain authentication levels are silently promoted. For example:

● If the User Data Protocol (UDP) datagram transport is used, Connect and Call levels are promoted to Packet, because the aforementioned authentication levels only make sense over a connection oriented transport such as TCP.

Note: Windows 2000 defaults to RPC over TCP for DCOM communications.

● For inter-process calls on a single computer, all authentication levels are always promoted to Packet Privacy. However, in a single computer scenario, data is not encrypted for confidentiality (because the data doesn't cross the network).

Authentication Level Negotiation

The authentication level used by Enterprise Services to authenticate a client is determined by two settings:

● **The process level authentication level**. For a server-activated application (running within Dllhost.exe), the authentication level is configured within the COM+ catalog.

- **The client authentication level**. The configured authentication level of the client process that communicates with the serviced component also affects the authentication level that is used.

  The default authentication level for an ASP.NET Web application is defined by the **comAuthenticationLevel** attribute on the <**processModel**> element in Machine.config.

The higher of the two (client and server) authentication level is always chosen. This is illustrated in the Figure 9.4.

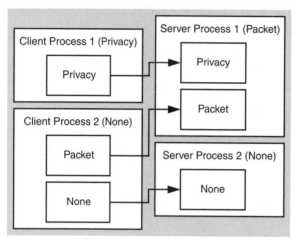

Figure 9.4
Authentication level negotiation

More Information

For information about how to configure authentication levels for an Enterprise Service application, see "Configuring Security" earlier in this chapter.

Impersonation

The impersonation level defined for an Enterprise Services application determines the impersonation level to be used for all outgoing DCOM calls made by serviced components within the application.

Important: It does NOT determine whether or the not serviced components within the application impersonate their callers. By default, serviced components do not impersonate callers. To do so, the service component must call **CoImpersonateClient**, as described in "Flowing the Original Caller" earlier in this chapter.

Impersonation is a client-side setting. It offers a degree of protection to the client as it allows the client to restrict the impersonation capabilities of the server.

Table 9.3: Available impersonation levels

Impersonation Level	Description
Identify	Allows the server to identify the client and perform access checks using the client's access token
Impersonate	Allows the server to access local resources using the client's credentials
Delegate	Allows the server to access remote resources using the client's credentials (this requires Kerberos and specific account configuration)

The default impersonation level used by a Web-based application when it communicates with serviced components (or any component using DCOM) is determined by the **comImpersonationLevel** attribute on the <**processModel**> element in Machine.config.

Cloaking

Cloaking determines precisely how client identity is projected through a COM object proxy to a server during impersonation. There are two forms of cloaking:

- **Dynamic Cloaking**. Enterprise Services server applications use dynamic cloaking (this is not configurable). Cloaking for library applications is determined by the host process, for example the ASP.NET worker process (Aspnet_wp.exe). Web-based applications also use dynamic cloaking—again this is not configurable.

  Dynamic cloaking causes the thread impersonation token to be used to represent the client's identity during impersonation. This means that if you call **CoImpersonateClient** within a serviced component, the client's identity is assumed for subsequent outgoing calls made by the same method, until either **CoRevertToSelf** is called or the method ends (where **CoRevertToSelf** is implicitly called).

- **Static Cloaking**. With static cloaking, the server sees the credentials that are used on the first call from client to server (irrespective of whether or not a thread is impersonating during an outgoing call).

More Information

- For information about how to configure impersonation levels for Enterprise Service applications, see "Configuring Security", earlier in this chapter.
- For more information about cloaking, see the Platform SDK information on "Cloaking" on MSDN.

Summary

This chapter has described how to build secure serviced components within an Enterprise Services application. You have also seen how to configure an ASP.NET Web-based client application that calls serviced components. To summarize:

- Use server activated Enterprise Services applications for increased security. Additional process hops raise the security bar.

- Use least-privileged, local accounts to run server applications.

- Use Packet Privacy level authentication (which must be configured at the server and client) if you need to secure the data sent to and from a serviced component across a network from a client application.

- Enable component-level access checks for a meaningful role-based security implementation.

- Use Windows authentication and enable impersonation in an ASP.NET Web application prior to calling a component within an Enterprise Services application that relies on role-based security.

- Use secured gateway classes as entry points into Enterprise Service applications.

  By reducing the number of gateway classes that provide entry points for clients into your Enterprise Service applications, you reduce the number of classes that need to have roles assigned. Other internal helper classes should have role-based checks enabled but should have no roles assigned to them. This means that external clients will not be able to call them directly, while gateway classes in the same application will have direct access.

- Call **IsSecurityEnabled** immediately prior to checking role membership programmatically.

- Avoid impersonation in the middle tier because this prevents the effective use of database connection pooling and dramatically reduces the scalability of your application.

- Add Windows groups to Enterprise Services (COM+) roles for increased flexibility and easier administration

10

Web Services Security

This chapter describes how to develop and apply authentication, authorization, and secure communication techniques to secure ASP.NET Web services and Web service messages. It describes security from the Web service perspective and shows you how to authenticate and authorize callers and how to flow security context through a Web service. It also explains, from a client-side perspective, how to call Web services with credentials and certificates to support server-side authentication.

Web Service Security Model

Web service security can be applied at three levels:

- Platform/transport level (point-to-point) security
- Application level (custom) security
- Message level (end-to-end) security

Each approach has different strengths and weaknesses, and these are elaborated upon below. The choice of approach is largely dependent upon the characteristics of the architecture and platforms involved in the message exchange.

Note: Note that this chapter focuses on platform and application level security. Message level security is addressed by the Global XML Web Services Architecture (GXA) initiative and specifically the WS-Security specification. At the time of writing, Microsoft has just released a technology preview version of the Web Services Development Kit. This allows you to develop message level security solutions that conform to the WS-Security specification. For more information, see *http://msdn.microsoft.com/webservices/building/wsdk/*.

Platform/Transport Level (Point-to-Point) Security

The transport channel between two endpoints (Web service client and Web service) can be used to provide point-to-point security. This is illustrated in Figure 10.1.

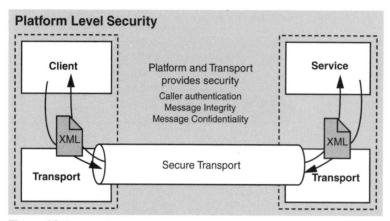

Figure 10.1
Platform/transport level security

When you use platform security, which assumes a tightly-coupled Microsoft® Windows® operating system environment, for example, on corporate intranets:

- The Web server (IIS) provides Basic, Digest, Integrated, and Certificate authentication.
- The ASP.NET Web service inherits some of the ASP.NET authentication and authorization features.
- SSL and/or IPSec may be used to provide message integrity and confidentiality.

When to Use

The transport level security model is simple, well understood, and adequate for many (primarily intranet-based) scenarios, in which the transport mechanisms and endpoint configuration can be tightly controlled.

The main issues with transport level security are:

- Security becomes tightly coupled to, and dependant upon, the underlying platform, transport mechanism, and security service provider (NTLM, Kerberos, and so on).
- Security is applied on a point to point basis, with no provision for multiple hops and routing through intermediate application nodes.

Application Level Security

With this approach, the application takes over security and uses custom security features. For example:

- An application can use a custom SOAP header to pass user credentials to authenticate the user with each Web service request. A common approach is to pass a ticket (or user name or license) in the SOAP header.

- The application has the flexibility to generate its own **IPrincipal** object that contains roles. This might be a custom class or the **GenericPrincipal** class provided by the .NET Framework.

- The application can selectively encrypt what it needs to, although this requires secure key storage and developers must have knowledge of the relevant cryptography APIs.

  An alternative technique is to use SSL to provide confidentiality and integrity and combine it with custom SOAP headers to perform authentication.

When to Use

Use this approach when:

- You want to take advantage of an existing database schema of users and roles that is used within an existing application.

- You want to encrypt parts of a message, rather than the entire data stream.

Message Level (End-to-End) Security

This represents the most flexible and powerful approach and is the one used by the GXA initiative, specifically within the WS-Security specification. Message level security is illustrated in Figure 10.2.

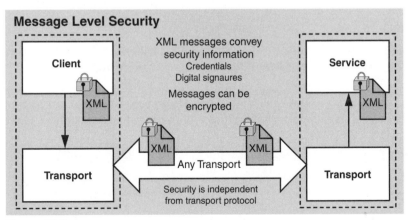

Figure 10.2
Message level security

WS-Security specifications describe enhancements to SOAP messaging that provide message integrity, message confidentiality, and single message authentication.

- Authentication is provided by security tokens, which flow in SOAP headers. No specific type of token is required by WS-Security. The security tokens may include Kerberos tickets, X.509 certificates, or a custom binary token.

- Secure communication is provided by digital signatures to ensure message integrity and XML encryption for message confidentiality.

When to Use

WS-Security can be used to construct a framework for exchanging secure messages in a heterogeneous Web services environment. It is ideally suited to heterogeneous environments and scenarios where you are not in direct control of the configuration of both endpoints and intermediate application nodes.

Message level security:

- Can be independent from the underlying transport.

- Enables a heterogeneous security architecture.

- Provides end-to-end security and accommodates message routing through intermediate application nodes.

- Supports multiple encryption technologies.

- Supports non-repudiation.

The Web Services Development Kit

The Web Services Development Kit provides the necessary APIs to manage security in addition to other services such as routing and message-level referrals. This toolkit conforms to the latest Web service standards such as WS-Security and as a result enables interoperability with other vendors who follow the same specifications.

More Information

- For the latest news about the Web Services Development Kit and WS-Security specifications, see the XML Developer Center page on MSDN at *http:// msdn.microsoft.com/webservices/*.

- For more information about the WS-Specification, see the WS-Security Specification Index Page at *http://msdn.microsoft.com/webservices/default.asp?pull=/library /en-us/dnglobspec/html/wssecurspecindex.asp*.

- For more information about GXA, see the article "Understanding GXA" on MSDN.

- For discussions on this topic, refer to the GXA Interoperability Newsgroup on MSDN.

Platform/Transport Security Architecture

The ASP.NET Web services platform security architecture is shown in Figure 10.3.

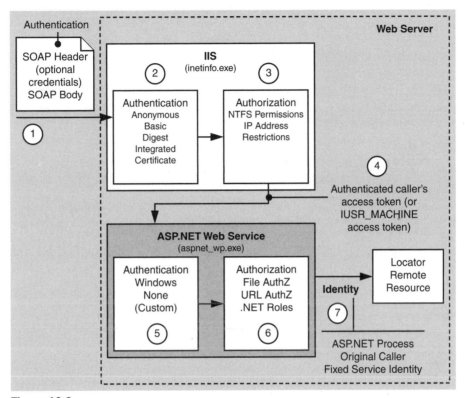

Figure 10.3
Web services security architecture

Figure 10.3 illustrates the authentication and authorization mechanisms provided by ASP.NET Web services. When a client calls a Web service, the following sequence of authentication and authorization events occurs:

1. The SOAP request is received from the network. This may or may not contain authentication credentials depending upon the type of authentication being used.

2. IIS optionally authenticates the caller by using Basic, Digest, Integrated (NTLM or Kerberos), or Certificate authentication. In heterogeneous environments where IIS (Windows) authentication is not possible, IIS is configured for anonymous authentication. In this scenario, the client may be authenticated by using message level attributes such as tickets passed in the SOAP header.

3. IIS can also be configured to accept requests only from client computers with specific IP addresses.

4. IIS passes the authenticated caller's Windows access token to ASP.NET (this may be the anonymous Internet user's access token, if the Web service is configured for anonymous authentication).

5. ASP.NET authenticates the caller. If ASP.NET is configured for Windows authentication, no additional authentication occurs at this point; IIS authenticates the caller.

   If a non-Windows authentication method is being used, the ASP.NET authentication mode is set to None to allow custom authentication.

   > **Note:** Forms and Passport authentication are not currently supported for Web services.

6. ASP.NET authorizes access to the requested Web service (.asmx file) by using URL authorization and File authorization, which uses NTFS permissions associated with the .asmx file to determine whether or not access should be granted to the authenticated caller.

   > **Note:** File authorization is only supported for Windows authentication.

   For fine-grained authorization, .NET roles can also be used (either declaratively or programmatically) to ensure that the caller is authorized to access the requested Web method.

7. Code within the Web service may access local and/or remote resources by using a particular identity. By default, ASP.NET Web services perform no impersonation and, as a result, the configured ASP.NET process account provides the identity. Alternate options include the original caller's identity, or a configured service identity.

Gatekeepers

The gatekeepers within an ASP.NET Web service are:

- IIS
  - If IIS anonymous authentication is disabled IIS only allows requests from authenticated users.
  - IP Address Restrictions

    IIS can be configured to only allow requests from computers with specific IP addresses.
- ASP.NET
  - The File authorization HTTP Module (for Windows authentication only)
  - The URL authorization HTTP Module
- Principal Permission Demands and Explicit Role Checks

More Information

- For more information about the gatekeepers, see "Gatekeepers" in Chapter 8, "ASP.NET Security."

- For more information about configuring security, see "Configuring Security" later in this chapter.

Authentication and Authorization Strategies

This section explains which authorization options (configurable and programmatic) are available for a set of commonly used authentication schemes.

The following authentication schemes are summarized here:

- Windows authentication with impersonation
- Windows authentication without impersonation
- Windows authentication using a fixed identity

Windows Authentication with Impersonation

The following configuration elements show you how to enable Windows (IIS) authentication and impersonation declaratively in Web.config or Machine.config.

Note: You should configure authentication on a per-Web service basis in each Web service's Web.config file.

```
<authentication mode="Windows" />
<identity impersonate="true" />
```

With this configuration, your Web service code impersonates the IIS-authenticated caller. To impersonate the original caller, you must turn off anonymous access in IIS. With anonymous access, the Web service code impersonates the anonymous Internet user account (which by default is IUSR_MACHINE).

Configurable Security

When you use Windows authentication together with impersonation, the following authorization options are available to you:

- **Windows Access Control Lists (ACLs)**
  - **Web service (.asmx) file**. File authorization performs access checks for requested ASP.NET resources (which includes the .asmx Web service file) using the original caller's security context. The original caller must be granted at least read access to the .asmx file.

- **Resources accessed by your Web service**. Windows ACLs on resources accessed by your Web service (files, folders, registry keys, Active Directory® directory service objects and so on) must include an Access Control Entry (ACE) that grants read access to the original caller (because the Web service thread used for resource access is impersonating the caller).

- **URL Authorization.** This is configured in Machine.config and/or Web.config. With Windows authentication, user names take the form DomainName\UserName and roles map one-to-one with Windows groups.

```
<authorization>
  <deny user="DomainName\UserName" />
  <allow roles="DomainName\WindowsGroup" />
</authorization>
```

Programmatic Security

Programmatic security refers to security checks located within your Web service code. The following programmatic security options are available when you use Windows authentication and impersonation:

- **Principal Permission Demands**
  - Imperative (in-line within a method's code)

    ```
    PrincipalPermission permCheck = new PrincipalPermission(
                                null, @"DomainName\WindowsGroup");
    permCheck.Demand();
    ```

  - Declarative (these attributes can precede Web methods or Web classes)

    ```
    // Demand that the caller is a member of a specific role (for Windows
    // authentication this is the same as a Windows group)
    [PrincipalPermission(SecurityAction.Demand,
                     Role=@"DomainName\WindowsGroup")]
    // Demand that the caller is a specific user
    [PrincipalPermission(SecurityAction.Demand,
                     Name=@"DomainName\UserName")]
    ```

- **Explicit Role Checks**. You can perform role checking using the **IPrincipal** interface.

  ```
  IPrincipal.IsInRole(@"DomainName\WindowsGroup");
  ```

When to Use

Use Windows authentication and impersonation when:

- The clients of the Web service can be identified by using Windows accounts, which can be authenticated by the server.

- You need to flow the original caller's security context through the Web service and onto the next tier. For example, a set of serviced components that use Enterprise Services (COM+) roles, or onto a data tier that requires fine-grained (per-user) authorization.

- You need to flow the original caller's security context to the downstream tiers to support operating system level auditing.

Important: Using impersonation can reduce scalability, because it impacts database connection pooling. As an alternative approach, consider using the trusted subsystem model where the Web service authorizes callers and then uses a fixed identity for database access. You can flow the caller's identity at the application level; for example, by using stored procedure parameters.

More Information

- For more information about Windows authentication and impersonation, see Chapter 8, "ASP.NET Security."

- For more information about URL authorization, see "URL Authorization Notes" in Chapter 8, "ASP.NET Security."

Windows Authentication without Impersonation

The following configuration elements show how you enable Windows (IIS) authentication with no impersonation declaratively in Web.config.

```
<authentication mode="Windows" />
<!-- The following setting is equivalent to having no identity element -->
<identity impersonate="false" />
```

Configurable Security

When you use Windows authentication without impersonation, the following authorization options are available to you:

- **Windows ACLs**
  - **Web Service (.asmx) file**. File authorization performs access checks for requested ASP.NET resources (which includes the .asmx Web service file) using the original caller. Impersonation is not required.
  - **Resources accessed by your application**. Windows ACLs on resources accessed by your application (files, folders, registry keys, Active Directory objects) must include an ACE that grants read access to the ASP.NET process identity (the default identity used by the Web service thread when accessing resources).

- **URL Authorization**

  This is configured in Machine.config and Web.config. With Windows authentication, user names take the form DomainName\UserName and roles map one-to-one with Windows groups.

  ```
  <authorization>
    <deny user="DomainName\UserName" />
    <allow roles="DomainName\WindowsGroup" />
  </authorization>
  ```

Programmatic Security

Programmatic security refers to security checks located within your Web service code. The following programmatic security options are available when you use Windows authentication without impersonation:

- **Principal Permission Demands**
  - Imperative

    ```
    PrincipalPermission permCheck = new PrincipalPermission(
                              null, @"DomainName\WindowsGroup");
    permCheck.Demand();
    ```

  - Declarative

    ```
    // Demand that the caller is a member of a specific role (for Windows
    // authentication this is the same as a Windows group)
    [PrincipalPermission(SecurityAction.Demand,
                    Role=@"DomainName\WindowsGroup")]
    // Demand that the caller is a specific user
    [PrincipalPermission(SecurityAction.Demand,
                Name=@"DomainName\UserName")]
    ```

- **Explicit Role Checks**. You can perform role checking using the **IPrincipal** interface.

  ```
  IPrincipal.IsInRole(@"DomainName\WindowsGroup");
  ```

When to Use

Use Windows authentication without impersonation when:

- The clients of the Web service can be identified by using Windows accounts, which can be authenticated by the server.
- You want to use the trusted subsystem model and authorize clients within the Web service and then use a fixed identity to access downstream resources (for example, databases) in order to support connection pooling.

More Information

- For more information about Windows authentication and impersonation, see Chapter 8, "ASP.NET Security."

- For more information about URL authorization, see "URL Authorization Notes" in Chapter 8, "ASP.NET Security."

Windows Authentication Using a Fixed Identity

The **<identity>** element within Web.config supports optional user name and password attributes which allows you to configure a specific fixed identity for your Web service to impersonate. This is shown in the following configuration file fragment.

```
<identity impersonate="true"
          userName="registry:HKLM\SOFTWARE\YourSecureApp\
                    identity\ASPNET_SETREG,userName"
          password="registry:HKLM\SOFTWARE\YourSecureApp\
                    identity\ASPNET_SETREG,password" />
```

This example shows the **<identity>** element where the credentials are encrypted in the registry using the aspnet_setreg.exe utility. The clear text **userName** and **password** attribute values have been replaced with pointers to the secured registry key and named values that contain the encrypted credentials. For details about this utility and to download it, see article Q329290, "HOWTO: Use the ASP.NET Utility to Encrypt Credentials and Session State Connection Strings" in the Microsoft Knowledge Base.

When to Use

Using a fixed impersonated identity is not recommended when using the .NET Framework 1.0 on Windows 2000 servers. This is because you would need to give the ASP.NET process account the powerful "Act as part of the operating system" privilege. This privilege is required by the ASP.NET process because it performs a **LogonUser** call using the credentials that you have provided.

Note: The .NET Framework version 1.1 will provide an enhancement for this scenario on Windows 2000. The logon will be performed by the IIS process, so that ASP.NET does not require the "Act as part of the operating system" privilege.

More Information

- For more information about Windows authentication and impersonation, see Chapter 8, "ASP.NET Security."

- For more information about URL authorization, see "URL Authorization Notes" in Chapter 8, "ASP.NET Security."

Configuring Security

This section shows you the practical steps required to configure security for an ASP.NET Web service. These are summarized in Figure 10.4.

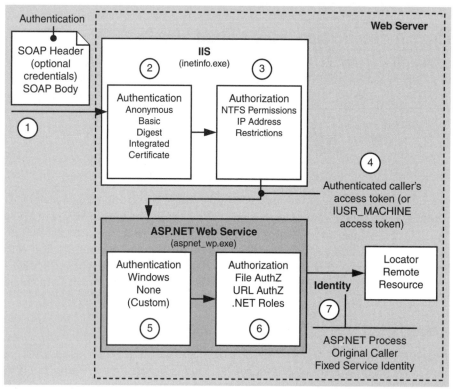

Figure 10.4
Configuring ASP.NET Web service security

Configure IIS Settings

For detailed information about how to configure IIS security settings, see "Configuring Security" in Chapter 8, "ASP.NET Security," because the information is also applicable to ASP.NET Web services.

Configure ASP.NET Settings

Application level configuration settings are maintained in Web.config files, which are located in your Web service's virtual root directory. Configure the following settings:

1. **Configure Authentication**. This should be set on a per-Web service basis (not in Machine.config) in the Web.config file located in the Web service's virtual root directory.

```
<authentication mode="Windows|None" />
```

Note: Web services do not currently support Passport or Forms authentication. For custom and message-level authentication, set the mode to None.

2. **Configure Impersonation and Authorization**. For detailed information, see "Configuring Security" in Chapter 8, "ASP.NET Security."

More Information

For more information about URL authorization, see "URL Authorization Notes" in Chapter 8, "ASP.NET Security."

Secure Resources

You should use the same techniques to secure Web resources as presented in Chapter 8, "ASP.NET Security." In addition, however, for Web services consider removing the HTTP-GET and HTTP-POST protocol from Machine.config on production servers.

Disable HTTP-GET, HTTP-POST

By default, clients can communicate with ASP.NET Web services, using three protocols: HTTP-GET, HTTP-POST, and SOAP over HTTP. You should disable support for both the HTTP-GET and HTTP-POST protocols at the machine level on production machines that do not require them. This is to avoid a potential security breach that could allow a malicious Web page to access an internal Web service running behind a firewall.

Note: Disabling these protocols means that a new client will not be able to test an XML Web service using the **Invoke** button on the Web service test page. Instead, you must create a test client program by adding a reference to the Web service using Microsoft Visual Studio® .NET development system. You may want to leave these protocols enabled on development computers to allow developers to use the test page.

▶ **To disable the HTTP-GET and HTTP-POST protocols for an entire computer**

1. Edit Machine.config.

2. Comment out the lines within the **<webServices>** element that add support for HTTP-GET and HTTP-POST. After doing so, Machine.config should appear as follows.

```
<webServices>
    <protocols>
      <add name="HttpSoap"/>
        <!-- <add name="HttpPost"/> -->
        <!-- <add name="HttpGet"/>  -->
      <add name="Documentation"/>
    </protocols>
</webServices>
```

3. Save Machine.config.

Note: For special cases where you have Web service clients that communicate with a Web service using either HTTP-GET or HTTP-POST, you can add support for those protocols in the application's Web.config file, by creating a **<webServices>** and adding support for these protocols with the **<protocol>** and **<add>** elements, as shown earlier.

More Information

For detailed Information about securing resources, see "Secure Resources" within Chapter 8, "ASP.NET Security."

Secure Communication

Use a combination of SSL and IPSec to secure communication links.

More information

- For information about calling a Web service using SSL, see "How To: Call a Web Service Using SSL" in the Reference section of this book.

- For information about using IPSec between two computers, see "How To: Use IPSec to Provide Secure Communication between Two Servers" in the Reference section of this book.

Passing Credentials for Authentication to Web Services

When you call a Web service, you do so by using a Web service proxy; a local object that exposes the same set of methods as the target Web service.

You can generate a Web service proxy by using the Wsdl.exe command line utility. Alternatively, if you are using Visual Studio .NET you can generate the proxy by adding a Web reference to the project.

Note: If the Web service for which you want to generate a proxy is configured to require client certificates, you must temporarily switch off that requirement while you add the reference, or an error occurs. After you add the reference, you must remember to reconfigure the service to require certificates.

An alternate approach would be to keep an offline Web Services Description Language (WSDL) file available to consumer applications. You must remember to update this if your Web service interface changes.

Specifying Client Credentials for Windows Authentication

If you are using Windows authentication , you must specify the credentials to be used for authentication using the **Credentials** property of the Web service proxy. If you do not explicitly set this property, the Web service is called without any credentials. If Windows authentication is required, this will result in an HTTP status 401, access denied response.

Using DefaultCredentials

Client credentials do not flow implicitly. The Web service consumer must set the credentials and authentication details on the proxy. To flow the security context of the client's Windows security context (either from an impersonating thread token or process token) to a Web service you can set the **Credentials** property of the Web service proxy to **CredentialCache.DefaultCredentials** as shown below.

```
proxy.Credentials = System.Net.CredentialCache.DefaultCredentials;
```

Consider the following points before you use this approach:

- This flows the client credentials only when you use NTLM, Kerberos, or Negotiate authentication.
- If a client-side application (for example, a Windows Forms application) calls the Web service, the credentials are obtained from the user's interactive logon session.
- Server-side applications, such as ASP.NET Web applications, use the process identity, unless impersonation is configured in which case the impersonated caller's identity is used.

Using Specific Credentials

To use a specific set of credentials for authentication when you call a Web service, use the following code.

```
CredentialCache cache = new CredentialCache();
cache.Add( new Uri(proxy.Url), // Web service URL
           "Negotiate",        // Kerberos or NTLM
           new NetworkCredential("username", "password", "domainname") );
proxy.Credentials = cache;
```

In the above example, the requested Negotiate authentication type results in either Kerberos or NTLM authentication.

Request a Specific Authentication Type

You should request a specific authentication type as illustrated above. Avoid direct use of the **NetworkCredential** class as shown in the following code.

```
proxy.Credentials = new
                    NetworkCredential("username", "password", "domainname");
```

This should be avoided in production code because you have no control over the authentication mechanism used by the Web service and as a result you have no control over how the credentials are used.

For example, you may expect a Kerberos or NTLM authentication challenge from the server but instead you may receive a Basic challenge. In this case, the supplied user name and password will be sent to the server in clear text form.

Set the PreAuthenticate Property

The proxy's **PreAuthenticate** property can be set to true or false. Set it to true to supply specific authentication credentials to cause a **WWW-authenticate** HTTP header to be passed with the Web request. This saves the Web server denying access on the request, and performing authentication on the subsequent retry request.

Note: Pre-authentication only applies after the Web service successfully authenticates the first time. Pre-authentication has no impact on the first Web request.

```
private void ConfigureProxy( WebClientProtocol proxy,
                             string domain, string username,
                             string password )
{
  // To improve performance, force pre-authentication
  proxy.PreAuthenticate = true;
  // Set the credentials
  CredentialCache cache = new CredentialCache();
```

```
    cache.Add( new Uri(proxy.Url),
            "Negotiate",
            new NetworkCredential(username, password, domain) );
  proxy.Credentials = cache;
  proxy.ConnectionGroupName = username;
}
```

Using the ConnectionGroupName Property

Notice that the above code sets the **ConnectionGroupName** property of the Web service proxy. This is only required if the security context used to connect to the Web service varies from one request to the next as described below.

If you have an ASP.NET Web application that connects to a Web service and flows the security context of the original caller (by using **DefaultCredentials** or by setting explicit credentials, as shown above), you should set the **ConnectionGroupName** property of the Web service proxy within the Web application. This is to prevent a new, unauthenticated client from reusing an old, authenticated TCP connection to the Web service that is associated with a previous client's authentication credentials. Connection reuse can occur as a result of HTTP KeepAlives and authentication persistence which is enabled for performance reasons within IIS.

Set the **ConnectionGroupName** property to an identifier (such as the caller's user name) that distinguishes one caller from the next as shown in the previous code fragment.

Note: If the original caller's security context does not flow through the Web application and onto the Web service, and instead the Web application connects to the Web service using a fixed identity (such as the Web application's ASP.NET process identity), you do not need to set the **ConnectionGroupName** property. In this scenario, the connection security context remains constant from one caller to the next.

Calling Web Services from Non-Windows Clients

There are a number of authentication approaches that work for cross-browser scenarios. These include:

- **Certificate Authentication**. Using cross platform X.509 certificates.
- **Basic Authentication**. For an example of how to use Basic authentication against a custom data store (without requiring Active Directory), see *http://www.rassoc.com/gregr/weblog/stories/2002/06/26/webServicesSecurityHttpBasicAuthenticationWithoutActiveDirectory.html*.
- **GXA Message Level Approaches**. Use the Web Services Development Toolkit to implement GXA (WS-Security) solutions.
- **Custom Approaches**. For example, flow credentials in SOAP headers.

Proxy Server Authentication

Proxy server authentication is not supported by the Visual Studio .NET **Add Web Reference** dialog box (although it will be supported with the next version of Visual Studio .NET). As a result you might receive an HTTP status 407: "Proxy Authentication Required" response when you attempt to add a Web reference.

Note: You may not see this error when you view the .asmx file from a browser, because the browser automatically sends credentials.

To work around this issue, you can use the Wsdl.exe command line utility (instead of the **Add Web Reference** dialog) as shown below.

```
wsdl.exe /proxy:http://<YourProxy> /pu:<YourName> /pp:<YourPassword> /
pd:<YourDomain> http://www.YouWebServer.com/YourWebService/YourService.asmx
```

If you need to programmatically set the proxy server authentication information, use the following code.

```
YourWebServiceProxy.Proxy.Credentials = CredentialsCache.DefaultCredentials;
```

Flowing the Original Caller

This section describes how you can flow the original caller's security context through an ASP.NET Web application and onto a Web service located on a remote application server. You may need to do this in order to support per-user authorization within the Web service or within subsequent downstream subsystems (for example, databases, where you want to authorize original callers to individual database objects).

In Figure 10.5, the security context of the original caller (Alice) flows through the front-end Web server that hosts an ASP.NET Web application, onto the remote object, hosted by ASP.NET on a remote application server and finally through to a backend database server.

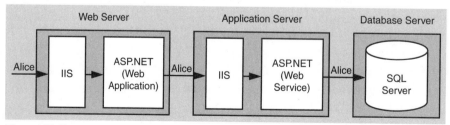

Figure 10.5
Flowing the original caller's security context

In order to flow credentials to a Web service, the Web service client (the ASP.NET Web application in this scenario) must configure the Web service proxy and explicitly set the proxy's **Credentials** property, as described in "Passing Credentials for Authentication to Web Services" earlier in this chapter.

There are two ways to flow the caller's context.

- **Pass default credentials and use Kerberos authentication (and delegation).** This approach requires that you impersonate within the ASP.NET Web application and configure the remote object proxy with **DefaultCredentials** obtained from the impersonated caller's security context.

- **Pass explicit credentials and use Basic or Forms authentication.** This approach does not require impersonation within the ASP.NET Web application. Instead, you programmatically configure the Web service proxy with explicit credentials obtained from either server variables (with Basic authentication) or HTML form fields (with Forms authentication) that are available to the Web application. With Basic or Forms authentication, the user name and password are available to the server in clear text.

Default Credentials with Kerberos Delegation

To use Kerberos delegation, all computers (servers and clients) must be running Windows 2000 or later. Additionally, client accounts that are to be delegated must be stored in Active Directory and must not be marked as "Sensitive and cannot be delegated."

The following tables show the configuration steps required on the Web server, and application server.

Configuring the Web Server

Configure IIS Step	More Information
Disable Anonymous access for your Web application's virtual root directory	
Enable Windows Integrated Authentication for the Web application's virtual root	Kerberos authentication will be negotiated assuming clients and server are running Windows 2000 or later. **Note**: If you are using Internet Explorer 6 on Windows 2000, it defaults to NTLM authentication instead of the required Kerberos authentication. To enable Kerberos delegation, see article Q299838, "Unable to Negotiate Kerberos Authentication after upgrading to Internet Explorer 6," in the Microsoft Knowledge Base.

Configure ASP .NET Step	More Information
Configure your ASP.NET Web application to use Windows authentication	Edit Web.config in your Web application's virtual directory Set the **\<authentication\>** element to: `<authentication mode="Windows" />`
Configure your ASP.NET Web application for impersonation	Edit Web.config in your Web application's virtual directory Set the **\<identity\>** element to: `<identity impersonate="true" />`

Configure the Web Service Proxy Step	More Information
Set the credentials property of the Web service proxy to **DefaultCredentials**.	See "Using DefaultCredentials" earlier in this chapter for a code sample.

Configuring the Remote Application Server

Configure IIS Step	More Information
Disable Anonymous access for your Web service's virtual root directory Enable Windows Integrated Authentication for the Web application's virtual root	

Configure ASP.NET (Web Service Host) Step	More Information
Configure ASP.NET to use Windows authentication	Edit Web.config in the Web service's virtual directory. Set the **\<authentication\>** element to: `<authentication mode="Windows" />`

Configure ASP.NET (Web Service Host)	
Step	**More Information**
Configure ASP.NET for impersonation	Edit Web.config in the Web service's virtual directory. Set the **<identity>** element to: `<identity impersonate="true" />` **Note**: This step is only required if you want to flow the original caller's security context through the Web service and onto the next downstream, subsystem (for example, a database). With impersonation enabled here, resource access (local and remote) uses the impersonated original caller's security context. If your requirement is simply to allow per-user authorization checks in the Web service, you do not need to impersonate here.

More Information

For more information about configuring Kerberos delegation, see "How To: Implement Kerberos Delegation for Windows 2000" in the Reference section of this book.

Explicit Credentials with Basic or Forms Authentication

As an alternative to Kerberos delegation, you can use Basic or Forms authentication at the Web application to capture the client's credentials and then use Basic (or Integrated Windows) authentication to the Web service.

With this approach, the client's clear text credentials are available to the Web application. These can be passed to the Web service through the Web service proxy. For this, you must write code in the Web application to retrieve the client's credentials and configure the proxy.

Basic Authentication

With Basic authentication, the original caller's credentials are available to the Web application in server variables. The following code shows how to retrieve them and configure the Web service proxy.

```
// Retrieve client's credentials (available with Basic authentication)
string pwd = Request.ServerVariables["AUTH_PASSWORD"];
string uid = Request.ServerVariables["AUTH_USER"];
// Associate the credentials with the Web service proxy
// To improve performance, force preauthentication
proxy.PreAuthenticate = true;
// Set the credentials
CredentialCache cache = new CredentialCache();
cache.Add( new Uri(proxy.Url),
           "Basic",
           new NetworkCredential(uid, pwd, domain) );
proxy.Credentials = cache;
```

Forms Authentication

With Forms authentication, the original caller's credentials are available to the Web application in form fields (rather than server variables). In this case, use the following code.

```
// Retrieve client's credentials from the logon form
string pwd = txtPassword.Text;
string uid = txtUid.Text;
// Associate the credentials with the Web service proxy
// To improve performance, force preauthentication
proxy.PreAuthenticate = true;
// Set the credentials
CredentialCache cache = new CredentialCache();
cache.Add( new Uri(proxy.Url),
           "Basic",
           new NetworkCredential(uid, pwd, domain) );
proxy.Credentials = cache;
```

The following tables show the configuration steps required on the Web server, and application server.

Configuring the Web Server

Configure IIS Step	More Information
To use Basic authentication, disable Anonymous access for your Web application's virtual root directory and select Basic authentication - or -	Both Basic and Forms authentication should be used in conjunction with SSL to protect the clear text credentials sent over the network. If you use Basic authentication, SSL should be used for all pages (not just the initial logon page), as Basic credentials are transmitted with every request.
To use Forms authentication, enable anonymous access	Similarly, SSL should be used for all pages if you use Forms authentication, to protect the clear text credentials on the initial log on and to protect the authentication ticket passed on subsequent requests.

Configure ASP.NET Step	More Information

If you use Basic authentication, configure your ASP.NET Web application to use Windows authentication
 	
- or -
 	
If you use Forms authentication, configure your ASP.NET Web application to use Forms authentication
	Edit Web.config in your Web application's virtual directory Set the <**authentication**> element to:
	
	`<authentication mode="Windows" />`
	
	- or -
	
	Edit Web.config in your Web application's virtual directory Set the <**authentication**> element to:
	
	`<authentication mode="Forms" />`

Disable impersonation within the ASP.NET Web application	Edit Web.config in your Web application's virtual directory. Set the <**identity**> element to: `<identity impersonate="false" />` **Note**: This is equivalent to having no <**identity**> element. Impersonation is not required, as the user's credentials will be passed explicitly to the Web service through the proxy.

Configure the Web Service Proxy Step	More Information
Write code to capture and explicitly set the credentials on the Web Service proxy	Refer to the code fragments shown earlier in the Basic Authentication and Forms Authentication sections.

Configuring the Application Server

Configure IIS Step	More Information
Disable Anonymous access for your application's virtual root directory Enable Basic authentication	 **Note:** Basic authentication at the (Web service) application server, allows the Web service to flow the original caller's security context to the database (as the caller's user name and password are available in clear text and can be used to respond to network authentication challenges from the database server). If you don't need to flow the original caller's security context beyond the Web service, consider configuring IIS at the application server to use Windows Integrated authentication, as this provides tighter security — credentials are not passed across the network and are not available to the Web service.

Configure ASP.NET (Web Service) Step	More Information
Configure ASP.NET to use Windows authentication	Edit Web.config in the Web service's virtual directory. Set the **<authentication>** element to: `<authentication mode="Windows" />`
Configure your ASP.NET Web service for impersonation	Edit Web.config in the Web service's virtual directory. Set the **<identity>** element to: `<identity impersonate="true" />` **Note**: This step is only required if you want to flow the original caller's security context through the Web service and onto the next downstream, subsystem (for example, a database). With impersonation enabled here, resource access (local and remote) uses the impersonated original caller's security context. If your requirement is simply to allow per-user authorization checks in the Web service, you do not need to impersonate here.

Trusted Subsystem

The trusted subsystem model provides an alternative (and simpler to implement) approach to flowing the original caller's security context. In this model a trust boundary exists between the Web service and Web application. The Web service trusts the Web application to properly authenticate and authorize callers, prior to letting requests proceed to the Web service. No authentication of the original callers occurs at the Web service. The Web service authenticates the fixed trusted identity used by the Web application to communicate with the Web service. In most cases, this is the process identity of the ASP.NET worker process.

The trusted subsystem model is shown in Figure 10.6.

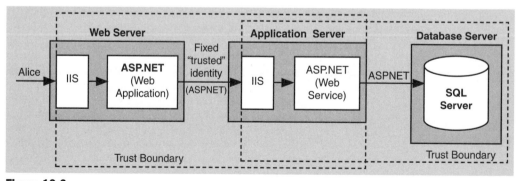

Figure 10.6

The trusted subsystem model

Flowing the Caller's Identity

If you use the trusted subsystem model, you may still need to flow the original caller's identity (name, not security context), for example, for auditing purposes at the database.

You can flow the identity at the application level by using method and stored procedure parameters and trusted query parameters (as shown in the following example) can be used to retrieve user-specific data from the database.

```
SELECT x,y,z FROM SomeTable WHERE UserName = "Alice"
```

Configuration Steps

The following tables show the configuration steps required on the Web server, and application server.

Configuring the Web Server

Configure IIS Step	More Information
Configure IIS authentication	The Web application can use any form of authentication to authenticate the original callers.

Configure ASP.NET Step	More Information

Configure authentication and make sure impersonation is disabled	Edit Web.config in your Web application's virtual directory. Set the <**authentication**> element to "Windows", "Forms" or "Passport."
	
	  `<authentication mode="Windows|Forms|Passport" />`
	
	Set the <**identity**> element to:
	
	  `<identity impersonate="false" />`
	
	(OR remove the <**identity**> element)

Reset the password of the ASPNET account used to run ASP.NET OR create a least privileged domain account to run ASP.NET and specify account details on the <**processModel**> element within Web.config	For more information about how to access network resources (including Web services) from ASP.NET and about choosing and configuring a process account for ASP.NET, see "Accessing Network Resources" and "Process Identity for ASP.NET" in Chapter 8, "ASP.NET Security."

Configure Web Service Proxy Step	More Information
Configure the Web service proxy to use default credentials for all calls to the Web service	Use the following line of code: `proxy.Credentials = DefaultCredentials;`

Configuring the Application Server

Configure IIS Step	More Information
Disable Anonymous access for your Web service's virtual root directory Enable Windows Integrated authentication	

Configure ASP.NET Step	More Information
Configure ASP.NET to use Windows authentication	Edit Web.config in the Web service's virtual directory. Set the <**authentication**> element to: `<authentication mode="Windows" />`
Disable impersonation	Edit Web.config in the application's virtual directory. Set the <**identity**> element to: `<identity impersonate="false" />`

Accessing System Resources

For details about accessing system resources (for example the event log and the registry) from ASP.NET Web services, see "Accessing System Resources" within Chapter 8, "ASP.NET Security." The approaches and restrictions discussed in Chapter 8 also apply to ASP.NET Web services.

Accessing Network Resources

When you access network resources from a Web service, you need to consider the identity that is used to respond to network authentication challenges from the remote computer. You have three options:

- The process identity (determined by the account used to run the ASP.NET worker process)
- A service identity (for example, one created by calling **LogonUser**)
- The original caller identity (with the Web service configured for impersonation)

For details about the relative merits of each of these approaches, together with configuration details, see "Accessing Network Resources" in Chapter 8, "ASP.NET Security."

Accessing COM Objects

The **AspCompat** directive (used by Web applications when they call apartment threaded COM objects) is not available to Web services. This means that when you call apartment model objects from Web services, a thread switch occurs. This results in a slight performance hit, and if your Web service is impersonating, your impersonation token will be lost when calling the COM component. This typically results in an Access Denied exception.

More Information

- For more information about access denied exceptions when calling apartment threaded COM objects, see article Q325791,"PRB: Access Denied Error Message Occurs When Impersonating in ASP.NET and Calling STA COM Components," in the Microsoft Knowledge Base.
- For more information about accessing COM objects and using the AspCompat attribute, see "Accessing COM Objects" within Chapter 8, "ASP.NET Security."
- For more information about calling apartment threaded COM objects from Web services, see article Q303375, "INFO: XML Web Services and Apartment Objects," in the Microsoft Knowledge Base.

Using Client Certificates with Web Services

This section describes techniques for using X.509 client certificates for Web service authentication.

You can use client certificate authentication within a Web service to authenticate:

- Other Web services.
- Applications that communicate directly with the Web service (for example, server-based or client-side desktop applications).

Authenticating Web Browser Clients with Certificates

A Web service cannot use client certificates to authenticate callers if they interact with an intermediate Web application, because it is not possible to forward the original caller's certificate through the Web application and onto the Web service. While the Web application can authenticate its clients with certificates, the same certificates cannot then be used by the Web service for authentication.

The reason that this server-to-server scenario fails is that the Web application does not have access to the client's certificate (specifically its private key) in its certificate store. This problem is illustrated in Figure 10.7.

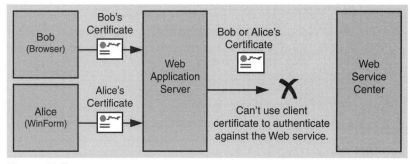

Figure 10.7
Web service client certificate authentication

Using the Trusted Subsystem Model

To address this restriction, and to support certificate authentication at the Web service, you must use a trusted-subsystem model. With this approach, the Web service authenticates the Web application using the Web application's certificate (and not the original caller's certificate). The Web service must trust the Web application to authenticate its users and to perform the necessary authorization to ensure that only authorized callers are able to access the data and functionality exposed by the Web service.

This approach is shown in Figure 10.8.

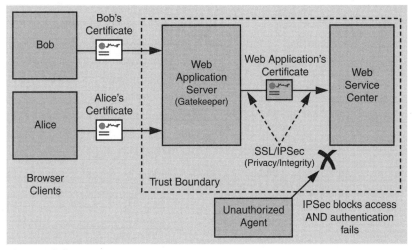

Figure 10.8
The Web service authenticates the trusted Web application

If the authorization logic within the Web service requires multiple roles, the Web application can send different certificates based upon the role membership of the caller. For example, one certificate may be used for members of an Administrators group (who are allowed to update data within a back-end database) and another certificate may be used for all other users (who are authorized only for read operations).

Note: In scenarios such as these, a local certificate server (accessible only by the two servers) can be used to manage all the Web application certificates.

In this scenario:

- The Web application authenticates its users by using client certificates.
- The Web application acts as a gatekeeper and authorizes its users and controls access to the Web service.
- The Web application calls the Web service and passes a different certificate that represents the application (or possibly a range of certificates based on the role membership of the caller).
- The Web service authenticates the Web application and it trusts the application to perform the necessary client authorization.
- IPSec is used between the Web application server and Web service server to provide additional access control. Unauthorized access attempts from other computers are prevented by IPSec. Certificate authentication at the Web service server also prevents unauthorized access.

Solution Implementation

To use certificate authentication at the Web service in this scenario, use a separate process to call the Web service and pass the certificate. You cannot manipulate the certificates directly from the ASP.NET Web application because it does not have a loaded user profile and associated certificate store. The separate process must be configured to run using an account that has an associated user profile (and certificate store). You have two main options:

- You can use an Enterprise Services server application
- You can use a Windows service.

Figure 10.9 illustrates this scenario with an Enterprise Services server application.

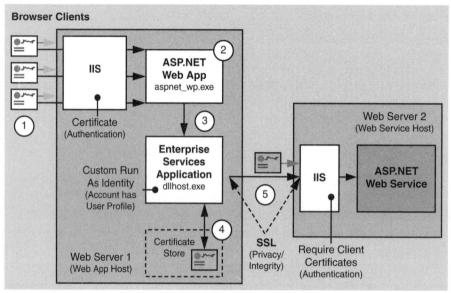

Figure 10.9
Client certificate authentication with Web services

The following summarizes the sequence of events illustrated by Figure 10.9:

1. The original caller is authenticated by the Web application using client certificates.

2. The Web application is the gatekeeper and is responsible for authorizing access to specific areas of functionality (including those that involve interaction with the Web service).

3. The Web application calls a serviced component running in an out-of-process Enterprise Services application.

4. The account used to run the Enterprise Services application has an associated user profile. The component accesses a client certificate from its certificate store, which is used by the Web service to authenticate the Web application.

5. The serviced component calls the Web service, passing the client certificate on each method request. The Web service authenticates the Web application using this certificate and trusts the Web application to correctly authorize original callers.

Why Use an Additional Process?

An additional process is required (rather than using the Aspnet_wp.exe Web process to contact the Web service) due to the fact that a user profile containing a certificate store is required.

A Web application that runs using the ASPNET account does not have access to any certificates on the Web server. This is because certificate stores are maintained within user profiles associated with interactive user accounts. User profiles are only created for interactive accounts when you physically log on using the account. The ASPNET account is not intended to be an interactive user account and is configured with the "Deny interactive logon" privilege for added security.

Important: Do not reconfigure the ASPNET account to remove this privilege and turn the account into an interactive logon account. Use a separate process with a configured service account to access certificates, as described earlier in this chapter.

More Information

- For more information about how to implement this approach, see "How To: Call a Web Service Using Client Certificates from ASPNET" in the Reference section of this book.

- For more information about configuring IPSec, see "How To: Use IPSec to Provide Secure Communication between Two Servers" in the Reference section of this book.

Secure Communication

Secure communication is concerned with guaranteeing the integrity and confidentiality of Web service messages as they flow from application to application across the network. There are two approaches to this problem; transport level options and message level options.

Transport Level Options

Transport level options include:

- SSL
- IPSec

These options may be appropriate if the following conditions are met:

- You are sending a message directly from your application to a Web service and the message will not be routed through intermediate systems.
- You can control the configuration of both endpoints involved in the message transfer.

Message Level Options

Message level approaches can be used to guarantee the confidentiality and integrity of messages as they pass through an arbitrary number of intermediate systems. Messages can be signed to provide integrity. For confidentiality, you can choose between encrypting the entire message or part of a message.

Use a message level approach if the following conditions are met:

- You are sending a message to a Web service and the message is likely to be forwarded to other Web services or may be routed through intermediate systems.
- You do not control the configuration of both endpoints; for example, because you are sending messages from one company to another.

More Information

- The Web Service Development Toolkit will provide message encryption functionality in accordance with the WS-Security specification.
- For more information about SSL and IPSec, see Chapter 4, "Secure Communication."

Summary

This chapter has focused on platform/transport level (point-to-point) Web service security provided by the underlying services of ASP.NET, IIS, and the operating system. While platform level security provides secure solutions for tightly-coupled intranet scenarios, it is not suited to heterogeneous scenarios. For this, message level security provided by the GXA WS-Security specification is required. Use the Web Services Development Kit to build message level Web service security solutions.

For tightly-coupled Windows domain environments:

- If you want to flow the original caller's identity from an ASP.NET Web application to a remote Web service, the ASP.NET Web application should use Kerberos authentication (with accounts configured for delegation), Basic authentication, or Forms authentication.

  - With Kerberos authentication, enable impersonation with the Web application and configure the **Credentials** property of the Web service proxy using **DefaultCredentials**.

  - With Basic or Forms authentication, capture the caller's credentials and set the **Credentials** property of the Web service proxy by adding a new **CredentialCache** object.

For Web-service to Web-service scenarios:

- Use Basic or Kerberos authentication and set credentials in the client proxy.

- Use an out of process Enterprise Services application or a Windows service to manipulate X.509 certificates from Web applications.

- As far as possible, use system level authorization checks such as File and URL authorization.

- For granular authorization (for example, at the Web method level) use .NET roles (declaratively and imperatively).

- Authorize non-Windows users by using .NET roles (based on a **GenericPrincipal** object that contains roles).

- Disable HTTP-GET and HTTP-POST protocols on product servers.

- Use transport level security if you are not worried about passing messages securely through intermediary systems.

- Use transport level security if SSL performance is acceptable.

- Use WS-Security and the Web Services Development Kit to develop message-level solutions.

11

.NET Remoting Security

The .NET Framework provides a remoting infrastructure that allows clients to communicate with objects, hosted in remote application domains and processes, or on remote computers. This chapter shows you how to implement secure .NET Remoting solutions.

.NET Remoting Architecture

Figure 11.1 on the next page shows the basic .NET Remoting architecture when a remote object is hosted within ASP.NET. An ASP.NET host, coupled with the HTTP channel for communication, is the recommended approach if security is the key concern, because it allows the remote object to utilize the underlying security services provided by ASP.NET and IIS.

For more information about the range of possible host and channel types, together with comparison information, see "Choosing a Host Process" later in this chapter.

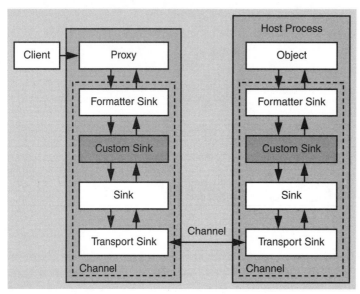

Figure 11.1
The .NET remoting architecture

The client communicates with an in-process proxy object. Credentials for authentication (for example, user names, passwords, certificates, and so on) can be set through the remote object proxy. The method call proceeds through a chain of sinks (you can implement your own custom sinks, for example, to perform data encryption) and onto a transport sink that is responsible for sending the data across the network. At the server side, the call passes through the same pipeline after which the call is dispatched to the object.

Note: The term *proxy* used throughout this chapter refers to the client-side, in-process proxy object through which clients communicate with the remote object. Do not confuse this with the term *proxy server*.

Remoting Sinks

.NET Remoting uses transport channels sinks, custom channel sinks, and formatter channel sinks when a client invokes a method call on a remote object.

Transport Channel Sinks

Transport channel sinks pass method calls across the network between the client and the server. .NET supplies the **HttpChannel** and the **TcpChannel** classes, although the architecture is fully extensible and you can plug in your own custom implementations.

- **HttpChannel**. This channel is designed to be used when you host a remote object in ASP.NET. This channel uses the HTTP protocol to send messages between the client and the server.
- **TcpChannel**. This channel is designed to be used when you host a remote object in a Microsoft® Windows® operating system service or other executable. This channel uses TCP sockets to send messages between the client and the server.
- **Custom channels**. A custom transport channel can use any underlying transport protocol to send messages between the client and server. For example, a custom channel may use named pipes or mail slots.

Comparing Transport Channel Sinks

The following table provides a comparison of the two main transport channel sinks.

Table 11.1: Comparison of TcpChannel and HttpChannel

Feature	TCP Channel	HTTP Channel	Comments
Authentication	No	Yes	The HTTP channel uses the authentication features provided by IIS and ASP.NET, although Passport and Forms authentication is not supported.
Authorization	No	Yes	The HTTP channel supports the authorization features provided by IIS and ASP.NET. These include NTFS permissions, URL authorization and File authorization.
Secure Communication	Yes	Yes	Use IPSec with the TCP channel. Use SSL and/or IPSec with the HTTP channel.

Custom Sinks

Custom channels sinks can be used at different locations within the channel sink pipeline to modify the messages sent between the client and the server. A channel sink that provides encryption and decryption is an example of a custom channel sink.

Formatter Sinks

Formatter sinks take method calls and serialize them into a stream capable of being sent across the network. .NET supplies two formatter sinks:

- **Binary Formatter**. This uses the **BinaryFormatter** class to package method calls into a serialized binary stream, which is subsequently posted (using an HTTP POST) to send the data to the server. The binary formatter sets the content-type in the HTTP request to "application/octet-stream."

The binary formatter offers superior performance in comparison to the SOAP formatter.

- **SOAP Formatter**. This uses the **SoapFormatter** class to package method calls into a SOAP message. The content type is set to "text/xml" in the HTTP request and is posted to the server with an HTTP POST.

Anatomy of a Request When Hosting in ASP.NET

Remote object endpoints are addressed by URLs that end with the .rem or .soap file name extension, for example http://someserver/vDir/remoteobject.soap. When a request for a remote object (with the extension .rem or .soap), is received by IIS, it is mapped (within IIS) to the ASP.NET ISAPI extension (Aspnet_isapi.dll). The ISAPI extension forwards the request to an application domain within the ASP.NET worker process (Aspnet_wp.exe). The sequence of events is shown in Figure 11.2.

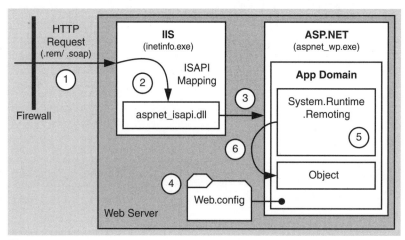

Figure 11.2
Server-side processing

Figure 11.2 shows the following sequence of events:

1. A .soap or .rem request is received over HTTP and is mapped to a specific virtual directory on the Web server.

2. IIS checks the .soap/.rem mapping and maps the file extension to the ASP.NET ISAPI extension, Aspnet_isapi.dll.

3. The ISAPI extension transfers the request to an application domain inside the ASP.NET worker process (Aspnet_wp.exe). If this is the first request directed at this application, a new application domain is created.

4. The **HttpRemotingHandlerFactory** handler is invoked and the remoting infrastructure reads the **<system.runtime.remoting>** section in the Web.config that controls the server-side object configuration (for example, single-call or singleton parameters) and authorization parameters (from the **<authorization>** element).

5. The remoting infrastructure locates the assembly that contains the remote object and instantiates it.

6. The remoting infrastructure reads the HTTP headers and the data stream, and then invokes the method on the remote object.

Note: During this process, ASP.NET calls the normal sequence of event handlers. You can optionally implement one or more of these in Global.asax. For example, **BeginRequest**, **AuthenticationRequest**, **AuthorizeRequest**, and so on. By the time the request reaches the remote object method, the **IPrincipal** object that represents the authenticated user is stored in **HttpContext.User** (and **Thread.CurrentPrincipal**) and is available for authorization. For example, by using principal permission demands and programmatic role checks.

ASP.NET and the HTTP Channel

Remoting does not have its own security model. Authentication and authorization between the client (proxy) and server (remote object) is performed by the channel and host process. You can use the following combination of hosts and channels:

- **A custom executable and the TCP Channel**. This combination does not provide any inbuilt security features.

- **ASP.NET and the HTTP Channel**. This combination provides authentication and authorization through the underlying ASP.NET and IIS security features.

Objects hosted within ASP.NET benefit from the underlying security features of ASP.NET and IIS. These include:

- **Authentication Features**. Windows authentication is configured within Web.config:

```
<authentication mode="Windows"/>
```

The settings in IIS control what type of HTTP authentication is used.

Common HTTP headers are used to authenticate requests. You can supply credentials for the client by configuring the remote object proxy or you can use default credentials.

You cannot use Forms or Passport authentication because the channel does not provide a way to allow the client to access cookies, which is a requirement for both of these authentication mechanisms. Also, Forms and Passport require a redirect to a logon page that requires client interaction. Remote, server side objects are designed for non-interactive use.

- **Authorization Features**. Clients are authorized using standard ASP.NET authorization techniques.

    Configurable authorization options include:
    - URL authorization.
    - File authorization (this requires specific configuration, as described in Using File Authorization later in this chapter).

    Programmatic authorization options include:
    - Principal permission demands (declarative and imperative).
    - Explicit role checks using **IPrincipal.IsInRole**.
- **Secure Communication Features**. SSL (and/or IPSec) should be used to secure the transport of data between the client and server.

More Information

- For more information about the authentication and authorization features provided by ASP.NET and IIS, see Chapter 8, "ASP.NET Security."
- For information about how to host an object in ASP.NET/IIS, see article Q312107, "HOW TO: Host a Remote Object in Microsoft Internet Information Services," in the Microsoft Knowledge Base.

.NET Remoting Gatekeepers

The authorization points (or gatekeepers) available to a remote object hosted by ASP.NET are:

- **IIS**. With anonymous authentication turned off, IIS only permits requests from users that it can authenticate either in its domain or in a trusted domain. IIS also provides IP address and DNS filtering.
- **ASP.NET**
    - **UrlAuthorizationModule**. You can configure **<authorization>** elements within your application's Web.config to control which users and groups of users should have access to the application. Authorization is based on the **IPrincipal** object stored in **HttpContext.User**.
    - **FileAuthorizationModule**. The **FileAuthorizationModule** is available to remote components, although this requires specific configuration, as described in "Using File Authorization" later in this chapter.

Note: Impersonation is not required for File authorization to work.

The **FileAuthorizationModule** class only performs access checks against the requested file or URI (for example .rem and .soap), and not for files accessed by code within the remote object.

- **Principal Permission Demands and Explicit Role Checks**. In addition to the IIS and ASP.NET configurable gatekeepers, you can also use principal permission demands (declaratively or imperatively) as an additional fine-grained access control mechanism. Principal permission checks allow you to control access to classes, methods, or individual code blocks based on the identity and group membership of individual users, as defined by the **IPrincipal** object attached to the current thread.

Note: Principal permission checks used to demand role membership are different from calling **IPrincipal.IsInRole** to test role membership. The former results in an exception if the caller is not a member of the specified role, while the latter simply returns a Boolean value to confirm role membership.

With Windows authentication, ASP.NET automatically attaches a **WindowsPrincipal** object that represents the authenticated user to the current Web request (using **HttpContext.User**).

Authentication

When you use remoting in conjunction with an ASP.NET Web application client, authentication occurs within the Web application and at the remote object host. The available authentication options for the remote object host depend on the type of host.

Hosting in ASP.NET

When objects are hosted in ASP.NET the HTTP channel is used to communicate method calls between the client-side proxy and the server. The HTTP channel uses the HTTP protocol to authenticate the remote object proxy to the server.

The following list shows the range of authentication options available when you host inside ASP.NET:

- **IIS Authentication Options**. Anonymous, Basic, Digest, Windows Integrated and Certificate.
- **ASP.NET Authentication Options**. Windows authentication or None (for custom authentication implementations).

> **Note:** Forms and Passport authentication cannot be used directly by .NET Remoting. Calls to remote objects are designed to be non-interactive. If the client of the remote object is a .NET Web application, the Web application can use Forms and Passport authentication and pass credentials explicitly to the remote object. This type of scenario is discussed further in the "Flowing the Original Caller" section later in this chapter.

Hosting in a Windows Service

When objects are hosted in a Windows service, the TCP channel is used to communicate method calls between the client and server. This uses raw socket-based communications. Because there is no authentication provided with sockets, there is no way for the server to authenticate the client.

In this scenario, the remote object must use custom authentication.

Custom Authentication

For simple custom authentication, the remote object can expose a **Login** method which accepts a user name and password. The credentials can be validated against a store, a list of roles retrieved, and a token sent back to the client to use on subsequent requests. When the token is retrieved at the server it is used to create an **IPrincipal** object (with roles) which is stored in **Thread.CurrentPrincipal**, where it is used for authorization purposes.

Other examples of custom authentication include creating a custom transport channel sink that uses an inter-process communication channel that provides authentication, such as named pipes, or creating a channel sink that performs authentication using the Windows Security Service Provider Interface (SSPI).

More Information

- For information about how to host an object in a Windows service, see "How To: Host a Remote Object in a Windows Service" in the Reference section of this book.
- For more information about sinks and sink chains, search for see the section of the .NET Framework on "Sinks and Sink Chains" in the MSDN Library.
- For more information about how to create a custom authentication solution that uses SSPI, see the MSDN article ".NET Remoting Security Solution, Part 1: Microsoft.Samples.Security.SSPI Assembly" at *http://msdn.microsoft.com/library /en-us/dndotnet/html/remsspi.asp*.

> **Note:** The implementation in this article is a sample and not a product tested and supported by Microsoft.

Authorization

When objects are hosted by ASP.NET and the HTTP channel is used for communication, the client can be authenticated and authorization can be controlled by the following mechanisms:

- URL authorization
- File authorization
- Principal permission demands (declarative and imperative)
- **IPrincipal.IsInRole** checks in code

When objects are hosted in a Windows service, there is no authentication provided by the TCP channel. As a result, you must perform custom authentication and then perform authorization by creating an **IPrincipal** object and storing it in **Thread.CurrentPrincipal**.

You can then annotate your remote object's methods with declarative principal permission demand checks, like the one shown below.

```
[PrincipalPermission(SecurityAction.Demand,
                     Role="Manager")]
void SomeMethod()
{
}
```

Within your object's method code, imperative principal permission demands and explicit role checks using **IPrincipal.IsInRole** can also be used.

Using File Authorization

You may want to use built-in Windows access control to secure the remote object as a securable Windows resource. Without File authorization (using Windows ACLs), you only have URL authorization.

To use the **FileAuthorizationModule** to authorize access to remote object endpoints (identified with .rem or .soap URLs), you must create a physical file with the .rem or .soap extension within your application's virtual directory.

Note: The .rem and .soap extensions are used by IIS to map requests for object endpoints to the ASP.NET ISAPI extension (aspnet_isapi.dll). They do not usually exist as physical files.

► **To configure File authorization for .NET Remoting**

1. Create a file with the same name as the objectUri (for example, RemoteMath.rem) in the root of the application's virtual directory.

2. Add the following line to the top of the file and save the file.

```
<%@ webservice class="YourNamespace.YourClass" ... %>
```

3. Add an appropriately configured ACL to the file using Windows Explorer.

> **Note:** You can obtain the objectUri from the web.config file used to configure the remote object on the server. Look for the <**wellknown**> element, as shown in the following example.
>
> ```
> <wellknown mode="SingleCall" objectUri="RemoteMath.rem"
> type="RemotingObjects.RemoteMath, RemotingObjects, Version=1.0.000.000
> Culture=neutral, PublicKeyToken=4b5ae668c251b606"/>
> ```

More Information

- For more information about these authorization mechanisms, see Chapter 8, "ASP.NET Security."

- For more information about principal permission demands, see Chapter 8, "ASP.NET Security."

Authentication and Authorization Strategies

In many applications that use .NET Remoting, the remote objects are used to provide business functionality within the application's middle tier and this functionality is called by ASP.NET Web applications. This arrangement is shown in Figure 11.3.

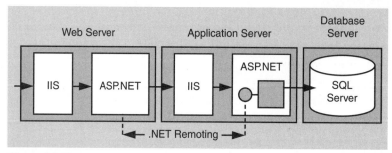

Figure 11.3
Remote objects called by an ASP.NET Web application

In this scenario, the IIS and ASP.NET gatekeepers available to the Web application can be used to secure access to the client-side proxy, and the IIS and ASP.NET gatekeepers available to the ASP.NET host on the remote application server are available to secure access to the remote object.

There are essentially two authentication and authorization strategies for remote objects that are accessed by .NET Web applications.

- You can authenticate and authorize callers at the Web server and then flow the caller's security context to the remote object by using impersonation. This is the impersonation/delegation model.

  With this approach you use an IIS authentication mechanism that allows you to delegate the caller's security context, such as Kerberos, Basic, or Forms authentication (the latter two allow the Web application to access the caller's credentials) and explicitly flow credentials to the remote object using the remote object's proxy.

  The ASP.NET configurable and programmatic gatekeepers (including URL authorization, File authorization, principal permission demands, and .NET roles) are available to authorize individual callers within the remote object.

- You can authenticate and authorize callers at the Web server and then use a trusted identity to communicate with the remote object. This is the trusted subsystem model.

  This model relies on the Web application to authenticate and properly authorize callers before invoking the remote object. Any requests received by the remote object from the trusted identity projected from the Web application are allowed to proceed.

More Information

- For more information about the impersonation/delegation and trusted subsystem models, see "Resource Access Models" in Chapter 3, "Authentication and Authorization Design."

- For more information about using the original caller model with remoting, see "Flowing the Original Caller" later in this chapter.

- For more information about using the trusted subsystem model with remoting, see "Trusted Subsystem" later in this chapter.

Accessing System Resources

For details about accessing system resources (for example, the event log and the registry) from a remote object hosted by ASP.NET, see "Accessing System Resources" in Chapter 8, "ASP.NET Security." The approaches and restrictions discussed in Chapter 8 also apply to remote objects hosted by ASP.NET.

Accessing Network Resources

When you access network resources from a remote object, you need to consider the identity that is used to respond to network authentication challenges from the remote computer. You have three options:

- **The Process Identity (this is the default).** If you host within ASP.NET, the identity used to run the ASP.NET worker process and defined by the <**processModel**> element in Machine.config determines the security context used for resource access.

  If you host within a Windows service, the identity used to run the service process (configured with the Services MMC snap-in) determines the security context used for resource access.

- **A Fixed Service Identity.** For example, one created by calling **LogonUser**.

Note: Don't confuse this service identity with the identity used to run a Windows service. A fixed service identity refers to a Windows user account created specifically for the purposes of accessing resources from an application.

- **The Original Caller Identity.** With ASP.NET configured for impersonation, or programmatic impersonation used within a Windows service.

For details about the relative merits of each of these approaches, together with configuration details, see "Accessing Network Resources" in Chapter 8, "ASP.NET Security."

Passing Credentials for Authentication to Remote Objects

When a client process calls a remote object, it does so by using a proxy. This is a local object that exposes the same set of methods as the target object.

Specifying Client Credentials

If the remote object is hosted within ASP.NET and is configured for Windows authentication, you must specify the credentials to be used for authentication using the credentials property of the channel. If you do not explicitly set credentials, the remote object is called without any credentials. If Windows authentication is required, this will result in an HTTP status 401, which is an access denied response.

Using DefaultCredentials

If you want to use the credentials of the process that hosts the remote object proxy (or the current thread token, if the thread that calls the proxy is impersonating), you should set the credentials property of the channel to the **DefaultCredentials** maintained by the process credential cache.

You can either specify the use of **DefaultCredentials** in a configuration file or set the credentials programmatically.

Explicit Configuration

Within the client application configuration file (Web.config, if the client application is an ASP.NET Web application) set the **useDefaultCredentials** attribute on the **<channel>** element to **true** in order to specify that the proxy should use **DefaultCredentials** when it communicates with the remote object.

```
<channel ref="http" useDefaultCredentials="true" />
```

Programmatic Configuration

For programmatic configuration, use the following code to establish the use of **DefaultCredentials** programmatically.

```
IDictionary channelProperties;
channelProperties = ChannelServices.GetChannelSinkProperties(proxy);
channelProperties ["credentials"] = CredentialCache.DefaultCredentials;
```

Using Specific Credentials

To use a specific set of credentials for authentication when you call a remote object, disable the use of default credentials within the configuration file, by using the following setting.

```
<channel ref="http" useDefaultCredentials="false" />
```

Note: Programmatic settings always override the settings in the configuration file.

Then, use the following code to configure the proxy to use specific credentials.

```
IDictionary channelProperties =
                        ChannelServices.GetChannelSinkProperties(proxy);
NetworkCredential credentials;
credentials = new NetworkCredential("username", "password", "domain");
ObjRef objectReference = RemotingServices.Marshal(proxy);
Uri objectUri = new Uri(objectReference.URI);
CredentialCache credCache = new CredentialCache();
// Substitute "authenticationType" with "Negotiate", "Basic", "Digest",
// "Kerberos" or "NTLM"
credCache.Add(objectUri, "authenticationType", credentials);
channelProperties["credentials"] = credCache;
channelProperties["preauthenticate"] = true;
```

Request a Specific Authentication Type

You should request a specific authentication type by using the **CredentialCache.Add** method, as illustrated above. Avoid direct use of the **NetworkCredential** class as shown in the following code.

```
IDictionary providerData = ChannelServices.GetChannelSinkProperties(yourProxy);
providerData["credentials"] = new NetworkCredential(uid, pwd);
```

This should be avoided in production code because you have no control over the authentication mechanism used by the remote object host and as a result you have no control over how the credentials are used.

For example, you may expect a Kerberos or NTLM authentication challenge from the server but instead you may receive a Basic challenge. In this case, the supplied user name and password will be sent to the server in clear text form.

Set the preauthenticate Property

The proxy's **preauthenticate** property can be set to true or false. Set it to true (as shown in the above code) to supply specific authentication credentials to cause a **WWW-Authenticate** HTTP header to be passed with the initial request. This stops the Web server denying access on the initial request, and performing authentication on the subsequent request.

Using the connectiongroupname Property

If you have an ASP.NET Web application that connects to a remote component (hosted by ASP.NET) and flows the security context of the original caller (by using **DefaultCredentials** and impersonation or by setting explicit credentials, as shown above), you should set the **connectiongroupname** property of the channel within the Web application. This is to prevent a new, unauthenticated client from reusing an old, authenticated connection to the remote component that is associated with a previous client's authentication credentials. Connection reuse can occur as a result of HTTP KeepAlives and authentication persistence which is enabled for performance reasons within IIS.

Set the **connectiongroupname** property to an identifier (such as the caller's user name) that distinguishes one caller from the next.

```
channelProperties["connectiongroupname"] = userName;
```

Note: You do not need to set the **connectiongroupname** property if the original caller's security context does not flow through the Web application and onto the remote component but connects to the remote component using a fixed identity (such as the Web application's ASP.NET process identity). In this scenario, the connection security context remains constant from one caller to the next.

The next version of the .NET Framework will support connection pooling based on the SID of the thread that calls the proxy object, which will help to address the problem described above, if the Web application is impersonating the caller. Pooling will be supported for .NET Remoting clients and not for Web services clients.

Flowing the Original Caller

This section describes how you can flow the original caller's security context through an ASP.NET Web application and onto a remote component hosted by ASP.NET on a remote application server. You may need to do this in order to support per-user authorization within the remote object or within subsequent downstream subsystems (for example databases).

In Figure 11.4, the security context of the original caller (Bob) flows through the front-end Web server that hosts an ASP.NET Web application, onto the remote object, hosted by ASP.NET on a remote application server, and finally through to a back-end database server.

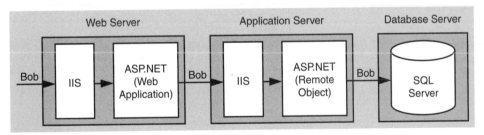

Figure 11.4
Flowing the original caller's security context

In order to flow credentials to a remote object, the remote object client (the ASP.NET Web application in this scenario) must configure the object's proxy and explicitly set the proxy's **credentials** property, as described in "Passing Credentials for Authentication to Remote Objects" earlier in this chapter.

Note: IPrincipal objects do not flow across .NET Remoting boundaries.

There are two ways to flow the caller's context:

- **Pass default credentials and use Kerberos authentication (and delegation).** This approach requires that you impersonate within the ASP.NET Web application and configure the remote object proxy with **DefaultCredentials** obtained from the impersonated caller's security context.

- **Pass explicit credentials and use Basic or Forms authentication.** This approach does not require impersonation within the ASP.NET Web application. Instead, you programmatically configure the remote object proxy with explicit credentials obtained from either, server variables (with Basic authentication), or HTML form fields (with Forms authentication) that are available to the Web application. With Basic or Forms authentication, the username and password are available to the server in clear text.

Default Credentials with Kerberos Delegation

To use Kerberos delegation, all computers (servers and clients) must be running Windows 2000 or later. Additionally, client accounts that are to be delegated must be stored in Active Directory® directory service and must not be marked as "Sensitive and cannot be delegated."

The following tables show the configuration steps required on the Web server and application server.

Configuring the Web Server

Configure IIS Step	More Information
Disable Anonymous access for your Web application's virtual root directory	
Enable Windows Integrated Authentication for the Web application's virtual root	Kerberos authentication will be negotiated assuming clients and server are running Windows 2000 or above. **Note**: If you are using Microsoft Internet Explorer 6 on Windows 2000, it defaults to NTLM authentication instead of the required Kerberos authentication. To enable Kerberos delegation, see article Q299838, "Unable to Negotiate Kerberos Authentication after upgrading to Internet Explorer 6," in the Microsoft Knowledge Base.

Configure ASP.NET Step	More Information
Configure your ASP.NET Web application to use Windows authentication	Edit Web.config in your Web application's virtual directory. Set the <**authentication**> element to: `<authentication mode="Windows" />`
Configure your ASP.NET Web application for impersonation	Edit Web.config in your Web application's virtual directory. Set the <**identity**> element to: `<identity impersonate="true" />`

Configure Remoting (Client Side Proxy) Step	More Information

Configure the remote object proxy to use default credentials for all calls to the remote object	Add the following entry to Web.config:
	
	`<channel ref="http"`
	`        useDefaultCredentials="true" />`
	
	Credentials will be obtained from the Web application's thread impersonation token.

Configuring the Remote Application Server

Configure IIS Step	More Information
Disable Anonymous access for your Web application's virtual root directory Enable Windows Integrated Authentication for the Web application's virtual root	

Configure ASP.NET (Remote Object Host)	
Step	**More Information**
Configure ASP.NET to use Windows authentication	Edit Web.config in the application's virtual directory. Set the **<authentication>** element to: `<authentication mode="Windows" />`
Configure ASP.NET for impersonation	Edit Web.config in the application's virtual directory. Set the **<identity>** element to: `<identity impersonate="true" />` **Note**: This step is only required if you want to flow the original caller's security context through the remote object and onto the next, downstream subsystem (for example, database). With impersonation enabled here, resource access (local and remote) uses the impersonated original caller's security context. If your requirement is simply to allow per-user authorization checks in the remote object, you do not need to impersonate here.

More Information

For more information about Kerberos delegation, see "How To: Implement Kerberos Delegation for Windows 2000" in the Reference section of this book.

Explicit Credentials with Basic or Forms Authentication

As an alternative to Kerberos delegation, you can use Basic or Forms authentication at the Web application to capture the client's credentials and then use Basic (or Integrated Windows) authentication to the remote object.

With this approach, the client's clear text credentials are available to the Web application. These can be passed to the remote object through the remote object proxy. For this, you must include code in the Web application to retrieve the client's credentials and configure the remote object proxy.

Basic Authentication

With Basic authentication, the original caller's credentials are available to the Web application in server variables. The following code shows how to retrieve them and configure the remote object proxy.

```
// Retrieve client's credentials (available with Basic authentication)
string pwd = Request.ServerVariables["AUTH_PASSWORD"];
string uid = Request.ServerVariables["AUTH_USER"];
// Associate the credentials with the remote object proxy
IDictionary channelProperties =
```

```
                         ChannelServices.GetChannelSinkProperties(proxy);
NetworkCredential credentials;
credentials = new NetworkCredential(uid, pwd);
ObjRef objectReference = RemotingServices.Marshal(proxy);
Uri objectUri = new Uri(objectReference.URI);
CredentialCache credCache = new CredentialCache();
credCache.Add(objectUri, "Basic", credentials);
channelProperties["credentials"] = credCache;
channelProperties["preauthenticate"] = true;
```

Note: The **NetworkCredential** constructor shown in the above code is supplied with the user ID
and password. To avoid hard coding the domain name, a default domain can be configured at
the Web server within IIS when you configure Basic authentication.

Forms Authentication

With Forms authentication, the original caller's credentials are available to the Web
application in form fields (rather than server variables). In this case, use the following code.

```
// Retrieve client's credentials from the logon form
string pwd = txtPassword.Text;
string uid = txtUid.Text;
// Associate the credentials with the remote object proxy
IDictionary channelProperties =
                         ChannelServices.GetChannelSinkProperties(proxy);
NetworkCredential credentials;
credentials = new NetworkCredential(uid, pwd);
ObjRef objectReference = RemotingServices.Marshal(proxy);
Uri objectUri = new Uri(objectReference.URI);
CredentialCache credCache = new CredentialCache();
credCache.Add(objectUri, "Basic", credentials);
channelProperties["credentials"] = credCache;
channelProperties["preauthenticate"] = true;
```

The following tables show the configuration steps required on the Web server and
application server.

Configuring the Web Server

Configure IIS Step	More Information
To use Basic authentication, disable Anonymous access for your Web application's virtual root directory and select Basic authentication - or - To use Forms authentication, enable anonymous access	Both Basic and Forms authentication should be used in conjunction with SSL to protect the clear text credentials sent over the network. If you use Basic authentication, SSL should be used for all pages (not just the initial logon page) because Basic credentials are transmitted with every request. Similarly, SSL should be used for all pages if you use Forms authentication to protect the clear text credentials on the initial logon and to protect the authentication ticket passed on subsequent requests.

Configure ASP.NET Step	More Information

If you use Basic authentication, configure your ASP.NET Web application to use Windows authentication
 	
- or -
 	
If you use Forms authentication, configure your ASP.NET Web application to use Forms authentication
	Edit Web.config in your Web application's virtual directory. Set the <**authentication**> element to:
	
	`<authentication mode="Windows" />`
	
	- or -
	
	Edit Web.config in your Web application's virtual directory. Set the <**authentication**> element to:
	
	`<authentication mode="Forms" />`

Disable impersonation within the ASP.NET Web application	Edit Web.config in your Web application's virtual directory. Set the <**identity**> element to: `<identity impersonate="false" />` **Note**: This is equivalent to having no <**identity**> element. Impersonation is not required because the user's credentials will be passed explicitly to the remote object through the remote object proxy.

Configure Remoting (Client Side Proxy) Step	More Information

Configure the remoting proxy to not use default credentials for all calls to the remote object	Add the following entry to Web.config:
	
	`<channel ref="http"`
	`        useDefaultCredentials="false" />`
	
	You do not want default credentials to be used (because the Web application is configured not to impersonate; this would result in the security context of the ASP.NET process identity being used).

Write code to capture and explicitly set the credentials on the remote object proxy	Refer to the code fragments shown earlier.

Configuring the Application Server

Configure IIS Step	More Information
Disable Anonymous access for your application's virtual root directory	
Enable Basic authentication	**Note:** Basic authentication at the application server (remote object), allows the remote object to flow the original caller's security context to the database (because the caller's user name and password are available in clear text and can be used to respond to network authentication challenges from the database server). If you don't need to flow the original caller's security context beyond the remote object, consider configuring IIS at the application server to use Windows Integrated authentication because this provides tighter security — credentials are not passed across the network and are not available to the application.

Configure ASP.NET (Remote Object Host)	
Step	More Information
Configure ASP.NET to use Windows authentication	Edit Web.config in the application's virtual directory. Set the <**authentication**> element to: `<authentication mode="Windows" />`
Configure ASP.NET for impersonation	Edit Web.config in the application's virtual directory. Set the <**identity**> element to: `<identity impersonate="true" />` **Note**: This step is only required if you want to flow the original caller's security context through the remote object and onto the next, downstream subsystem (for example, database). With impersonation enabled here, resource access (local and remote) uses the impersonated original caller's security context. If your requirement is simply to allow per-user authorization checks in the remote object, you do not need to impersonate here.

Trusted Subsystem

The trusted subsystem model provides an alternative (and simpler to implement) approach to flowing the original caller's security context. In this model, a trust boundary exists between the remote object host and Web application. The remote object trusts the Web application to properly authenticate and authorize callers, prior to letting requests proceed to the remote object. No authentication of the original caller occurs within the remote object host. The remote object host authenticates the fixed, trusted identity used by the Web application to communicate with the remote object. In most cases, this is the process identity of the ASP.NET Web application.

The trusted subsystem model is shown in Figure 11.5. This diagram also shows two possible configurations. The first uses the ASP.NET host and the HTTP channel, while the second uses a Windows service host and the TCP channel.

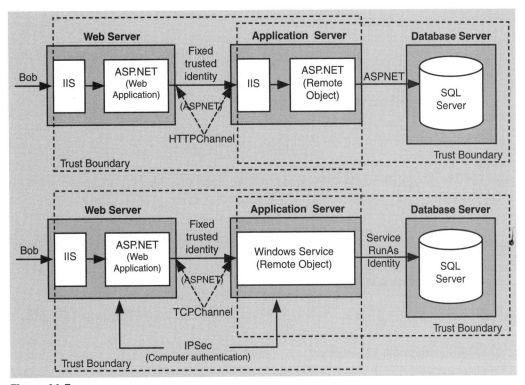

Figure 11.5
The trusted subsystem model

Flowing the Caller's Identity

If you use the trusted subsystem model, you may still need to flow the original caller's identity (name, not security context), for example, for auditing purposes at the database.

You can flow the identity at the application level by using method and stored procedure parameters and trusted query parameters (as shown in the following example) can be used to retrieve user-specific data from the database.

```
SELECT x,y,z FROM SomeTable WHERE UserName = "Bob"
```

Choosing a Host

The trusted subsystem model means that the remote object host does not authenticate the original callers. However, it must still authenticate (and authorize) its immediate client (the ASP.NET Web application in this scenario), to prevent unauthorized applications issuing requests to the remote object.

If you host within ASP.NET and use the HTTP channel, you can use Windows Integrated authentication to authenticate the ASP.NET Web application process identity.

If you host within a Windows service, you can use the TCP channel which offers superior performance but no authentication capabilities. In this scenario, you can use IPSec between the Web server and application server. An IPSec policy can be established that only allows the Web server to communicate with the application server.

Configuration Steps

The following tables show the configuration steps required on the Web server and application server.

Configuring the Web Server

Configure IIS Step	More Information
Configure IIS authentication	The Web application can use any form of authentication to authenticate the original callers.

Configure ASP.NET Step	More Information

Configure authentication and make sure impersonation is disabled	Edit Web.config in your Web application's virtual directory. Set the **<authentication>** element to "Windows", "Forms" or "Passport."
	
	 `<authentication mode="Windows|Forms|Passport" />`
	
	 Set the **<identity>** element to:
	
	 `<identity impersonate="false" />`
	
	 (OR remove the **<identity>** element)

Configure ASP.NET	
Step	**More Information**
Reset the password of the ASPNET account used to run ASPNET OR create a least privileged domain account to run ASPNET and specify account details on the <**processModel**>	For more information about how to access network resources (including remote objects) from ASPNET and about choosing and configuring a process account for ASPNET, see "Accessing Network Resources" and "Process Identity for ASPNET" in Chapter 8, "ASPNET Security."

Configure Remoting (Client Side Proxy	
Step	**More Information**

Configure the remoting proxy to use default credentials for all calls to the remote object	Add the following entry to Web.config:
	
	`<channel ref="http"`
	`            useDefaultCredentials="true" />`
	
	Because the Web application is not impersonating, using default credentials results in the use of the ASPNET process identity for all calls to the remote object.

Configuring the Application Server

The following steps apply if you are using an ASP.NET host.

Configure IIS	
Step	**More Information**
Disable Anonymous access for your application's virtual root directory Enable Windows Integrated authentication	

Configure ASP.NET (Remote Object Host)	
Step	**More Information**
Configure ASPNET to use Windows authentication	Edit Web.config in the application's virtual directory. Set the <**authentication**> element to: `<authentication mode="Windows" />`
Disable impersonation	Edit Web.config in the application's virtual directory. Set the <**identity**> element to: `<identity impersonate="false" />`

Using a Windows Service Host

If you are using a Windows service host process, you must create a Windows account to run the service. This security context provided by this account will be used by the remote object for all local and remote resource access.

To access a remote Microsoft SQL Server™ database (using Windows authentication), you can use a least privileged domain account, or use a least privileged local account and then create a duplicated account (with the same user name and password) on the database server.

Secure Communication

Secure communication is related to guaranteeing the integrity and confidentiality of messages as they flow across the network. You can use a platform-based approach to secure communication and use SSL or IPSec, or you can use a message-level approach and develop a custom encryption sink to encrypt the entire message, or selected parts of a message.

Platform Level Options

The two platform-level options to consider for securing the data passed between a client and remote component are:

- SSL
- IPSec

If you host remote objects in ASP.NET, you can use SSL to secure the communication channel between client and server. This requires a server authentication certificate on the computer that hosts the remote object.

If you host remote objects in a Windows service, you can use IPSec between the client and host (server) computers, or develop a custom encryption sink.

Message Level Options

Due to the extensible nature of the .NET Remoting architecture, you can develop your own custom sinks and plug them into the processing pipeline. To provide secure communication, you can develop a custom sink that encrypts and decrypts the message data sent to and from the remote object.

The advantage of this approach is that it allows you to selectively encrypt parts of a message. This is in contrast to the platform-level approaches that encrypt all the data sent between client and server.

More Information

For more information about SSL and IPSec, see Chapter 4, "Secure Communication"

Choosing a Host Process

Objects that are to be accessed remotely must run in a host executable. The host listens for incoming requests and dispatches calls to objects. The type of host selected influences the message transport mechanism called a channel. The type of channel that you select influences the authentication, authorization, secure communication, and performance characteristics of your solution.

The HTTP channel provides better security options, but the TCP channel provides superior performance.

You have the following main options for hosting remote objects:

- Host in ASP.NET
- Host in a Windows Service
- Host in a Console Application

Recommendation

To take advantage of the security infrastructure provided by ASP.NET and IIS, it is recommended from a security standpoint to host remote objects in ASP.NET. This requires clients to communicate with the remote objects over the HTTP channel. ASP.NET and IIS authentication, authorization, and secure communication features are available to remote objects that are hosted in ASP.NET.

If performance (and not security) is the primary concern, consider hosting remote objects in Windows services.

Hosting in ASP.NET

When you host a remote object in ASP.NET:

- The object is accessed using the HTTP protocol.
- It has an endpoint that is accessible by a URL.
- It exists in an application domain inside the Aspnet_wp.exe worker process.
- It inherits the security features offered by IIS and ASP.NET.

Advantages

If you host remote objects in IIS, you benefit from the following advantages:

- Authentication, authorization, and secure communication features provided by IIS and ASP.NET are immediately available.
- You can use the auditing features of IIS.
- The ASP.NET worker process is always running.

- You have a high degree of control over the hosting executable through the <processModel> element in Machine.config. You can control thread management, fault tolerance, memory management, and so on.
- You can create a Web services façade layer in front of the remote object.

Disadvantages

If you use ASP.NET to host remote objects, you should be aware of the following disadvantages:

- It requires the use of the HTTP channel which is slower than the TCP channel.
- User profiles are not loaded by ASP.NET. Various encryption techniques (including DPAPI) may require user profiles.
- If the object is being accessed from code running in an ASP.NET Web application, you may have to use Basic authentication.

Hosting in a Windows Service

When you host a remote object in a Windows service, the remote object lives in an application domain contained within the service process. You cannot use the HTTP channel and must use the TCP channel. The TCP channel supports the following security features:

- **Authentication Features**

  You must provide a custom authentication solution. Options include:

  - **Using the underlying authentication services of the SSPI**. You can create a channel sink that uses the Windows SSPI credential and context management APIs to authenticate the caller and optionally impersonate the caller. The channel-sink sits on top of the TCP channel. The SSPI in conjunction with the TCP channel allows the client and server to exchange authentication information. After authentication the client and server can send messages ensuring confidentiality and integrity.

  - **Using an underlying transport that supports authentication, for example, named pipes**. The named pipe channel uses named pipes as the transport mechanism. This provides authentication of the caller and also introduces Windows ACL-based security on the pipe and also impersonation of the caller.

- **Authorization Features**

  Authorization is possible only if you implement a custom authentication solution.

  - If you are able to impersonate the user (for example, by using an underlying named pipe transport), you can use **WindowsPrincipal.IsInRole**.

- If you are able to create an **IPrincipal** object to represent the authenticated client, you can use .NET roles (through principal permission demands and explicit role checking using **IPrincipal.IsInRole**)
- **Secure Communication Features**

  You have two options:

  - Use IPSec to secure the transport of data between the client and server.
  - Create a custom channel sink that performs asymmetric encryption. This option is discussed later in this chapter.

Advantages

If you host remote objects in Windows services, you benefit from the following advantages:

- High degree of activation control over the host process
- Inherits the benefits of Windows service architecture
- No need to introduce IIS on your application's middle tier
- User profiles are automatically loaded
- Performance is good as clients communicate over the TCP channel using binary encoded data

Disadvantages

If you use a Windows service to host remote objects, you should be aware of the following disadvantages:

- You must provide custom authentication and authorization solutions.
- You must provide secure communication solutions.
- You must provide auditing solutions.

Hosting in a Console Application

When you host a remote object in a console application, the remote object lives in an application domain contained within the console application process. You cannot use the HTTP channel and must use the TCP channel.

This approach is not recommended for production solutions.

Advantages

There are very few advantages to this approach, although it does mean that IIS is not required on the middle tier. However, this approach is only recommended for development and testing and not for production environments.

Disadvantages

If you host remote objects in a custom executable, you should be aware of the following disadvantages:

- The host must be manually started and runs under the interactive logon session (which is not recommended).
- There is no fault tolerance.
- You must provide custom authentication and authorization.
- There is no auditing capability.

Remoting vs. Web Services

.NET offers many different techniques to allow clients to communicate with remote objects including the use of Web services.

If you need interoperability between heterogeneous systems, a Web services approach that uses open standards such as SOAP, XML, and HTTP is the right choice. On the other hand, if you are creating server to server intranet-based solutions, remoting offers the following features:

- Rich object fidelity because any .NET type (including custom types created using Microsoft C#® development tool and Microsoft Visual Basic® .NET development system) can be remoted.

  This includes classes, class hierarchies, interfaces, fields, properties, methods and delegates, datasets, hash tables, and so on.
- Objects may be marshaled by value and by reference.
- Object lifetime management is lease-based.
- High performance, particularly with the TCP channel and binary formatter.
- It allows you to construct load balanced middle tiers, using network load balancing.

Table 11.2: The major differences between remoting and Web services

Remoting	Web Services
State full or stateless, lease-based object lifetime management	All method calls are stateless
No need for IIS (Although hosting in IIS/ASP.NET is recommended for security)	Must have IIS installed on the server
All managed types are supported	Limited data types are supported. For more information about the types supported by ASP.NET Web services, see the ".NET Framework Developer's Guide" on MSDN.

Remoting	Web Services
Objects can be passed by reference or by value	Objects cannot be passed
Contains an extensible architecture not limited to HTTP or TCP transports	Limited to XML over HTTP
Can plug custom processing sinks into the message processing pipeline	No ability to modify messages
SOAP implementation is limited and can only use RPC encoding	SOAP implementation can use RPC or document encoding and can fully interoperate with other Web service platforms. For more information, see the "Message Formatting and Encoding" section of the "Distributed Application Communication" article on MSDN.
Tightly coupled	Loosely coupled

Summary

.NET Remoting does not provide its own security model. However, by hosting remote objects in ASP.NET and by using the HTTP channel for communication, remote objects can benefit from the underlying security services provided by IIS and ASP.NET. In comparison, the TCP channel and a custom host executable offers improved performance, but this combination provides no built-in security.

- If you want to authenticate the client, use the HTTP channel, host in ASP.NET, and disable Anonymous access in IIS.

- Use the TCP channel for better performance and if you don't care about authenticating the client.

- Use IPSec to secure the communication channel between client and server if you use the TCP channel. Use SSL to secure the HTTP channel.

- If you need to make trusted calls to a remote resource, host the component in Windows service and not a console application.

- **IPrincipal** objects are not passed across .NET Remoting boundaries. You could consider implementing your own **IPrincipal** class that can be serialized. If you do so, be aware that it would be relatively easy for a rogue client to spoof an **IPrincipal** object and send it to your remote object. Also, be careful of **IlogicalThreadAffinitive** if you implement your own **IPrincipal** class for remoting.

- Don't expose remote objects to the Internet. Use Web services for this scenario.

  .NET Remoting should be used on the intranet only. Objects should be accessed from Web applications internally. Even if an object is hosted in ASP.NET, don't expose them to Internet clients, as clients would need to be .NET clients.

12

Data Access Security

This chapter covers key data access security issues and solutions. Some relate to the use of SQL Server while others apply to any data store. Read this chapter to help you:

- Choose between Microsoft® Windows® operating system authentication and SQL authentication when connecting to SQL Server™.
- Store connection strings securely.
- Decide whether to flow the original caller's security context through to the database.
- Take advantage of connection pooling.
- Protect against SQL injection attacks.
- Store credentials securely within a database.

The chapter also presents various trade offs that relate to the use of roles, for example, roles in the database versus role logic applied in the middle tier. Finally, a set of core recommendations for data access are presented.

Introducing Data Access Security

Figure 12.1 on the next page shows key security issues associated with data access.

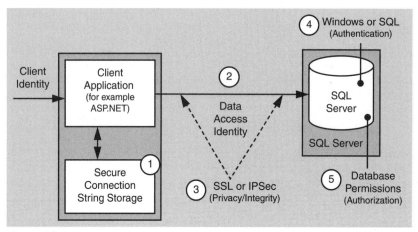

Figure 12.1
Key data access security issues

The key issues shown in Figure 12.1 and discussed throughout the remainder of this chapter are summarized below:

1. **Storing database connection strings securely**. This is particularly significant if your application uses SQL authentication to connect to SQL Server or connects to non-Microsoft databases that require explicit logon credentials. In these cases, connection strings include clear text usernames and passwords.

2. **Using an appropriate identity or identities to access the database**. Data access may be performed by using the process identity of the calling process, one or more service identities, or the original caller's identity (with impersonation/delegation). The choice is determined by your data access model—trusted subsystem or impersonation/delegation.

3. **Securing data that flows across the network**. For example, securing login credentials and sensitive data passed to and from SQL Server.

Note: Login credentials are only exposed on the network if you use SQL authentication, not Windows authentication.

SQL Server 2000 supports SSL, with server certificates. IPSec can also be used to encrypt traffic between the client computer (for example, a Web or application server) and database server.

4. **Authenticating callers at the database**. SQL Server supports Windows authentication (using NTLM or Kerberos) and SQL authentication (using SQL Server's built-in authentication mechanism).

5. **Authorizing callers at the database**. Permissions are associated with individual database objects. Permissions can be associated with users, groups, or roles.

SQL Server Gatekeepers

Figure 12.2 highlights the key gatekeepers for SQL server data access.

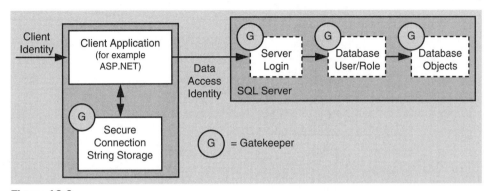

Figure 12.2
SQL Server gatekeepers

The key gatekeepers are:

- The chosen data store used to maintain the database connection string.
- The SQL Server login (as determined by the server name specified in the connection string).
- The database user (the user context within the database to which the SQL Server login is mapped) and associated database roles.
- Permissions attached to individual database objects.

  Permissions may be assigned to users, groups, or roles.

Trusted Subsystem vs. Impersonation/Delegation

Granularity of access to the database is a key factor to consider. You must consider whether you need user-level authorization at the database, which requires the impersonation/delegation model, or whether you can use application role logic within the middle tier of your application to authorize users. This implies the trusted subsystem model.

If your database requires user-level authorization, you need to impersonate the original caller. While this impersonation/delegation model is supported, you are encouraged to use the trusted subsystem model, where the original caller is checked at the IIS/ASP.NET gate, mapped to a role, and then authorized based on role membership. System resources for the application are then authorized at the application or role level using service accounts, or using the application's process identity (such as the ASPNET account).

Figure 12.3 shows the two models.

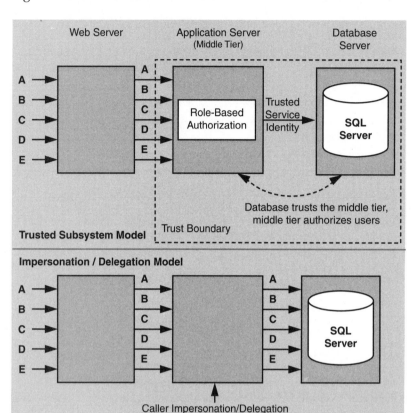

Figure 12.3
The trusted sub-system and impersonation/delegation models for database access

There are a number of key factors that you should consider when connecting to SQL Server for data access. These are summarized below and elaborated upon in subsequent sections:

- **What type of authentication should you use**? Windows authentication offers improved security, but firewalls and non-trusting domain issues may force you to use SQL authentication. If so, you should ensure that your application's use of SQL authentication is as secure as possible, as discussed in the "SQL Authentication" section later in this chapter.

- **Single user role versus multiple user roles**. Does your application need to access SQL using a single account with a fixed set of permissions within the database, or are multiple (role-based) accounts required depending on the user of the application?

- **Caller identity**. Does the database need to receive the identity of the original caller through the call context either to perform authorization or to perform auditing, or can you use one or more trusted connections and pass the original caller identity at the application level?

  For the operating system to flow the original caller's identity, it requires impersonation/delegation in the middle tier. This dramatically reduces the effectiveness of connection pooling. Connection pooling is still enabled, but it results in many small pools (for each separate security context), with little if any reuse of connections.

- **Are you sending sensitive data to and from the database server?** While Windows authentication means that you do not pass user credentials over the network to the database server, if your application's data is sensitive (for example, employee details or payroll data), then this should be secured using IPSec or SSL.

Authentication

This section discusses how you should authenticate clients to SQL Server and how you choose an identity to use for database access within client applications, prior to connecting to SQL Server.

Windows Authentication

Windows authentication is more secure than SQL authentication for the following reasons:

- Credentials are managed for you and the credentials are not transmitted over the network.

- You avoid embedding user names and passwords in connection strings.

- Logon security improves through password expiration periods, minimum lengths, and account lockout after multiple invalid logon requests. This mitigates the threat from dictionary attacks.

Use Windows authentication in the following scenarios:

- You have used the trusted subsystem model and you connect to SQL Server using a single fixed identity. If you are connecting from ASP.NET, this assumes that the Web application is not configured for impersonation.

  In this scenario, use the ASP.NET process identity or a serviced component identity (obtained from the account used to run an Enterprise Services server application).

- You are intentionally delegating the original caller's security context by using delegation (and are prepared to sacrifice application scalability by foregoing database connection pooling).

Consider the following key points when you use Windows authentication to connect to SQL Server:

- Use the principle of least privilege for the ASP.NET process account. Avoid giving the ASP.NET process account the "Act as part of the operating system" privilege to enable **LogonUser** API calls.
- Determine which code requires additional privileges, and place it within serviced components that run in out-of-process Enterprise Services applications.

More Information

For more information about accessing network resources from ASP.NET and choosing and configuring an appropriate account to run ASP.NET, see Chapter 8, "ASP.NET Security."

Using Windows Authentication

You have the following options when you use Windows authentication to connect to SQL Server from an ASP.NET application (or Web service, or remote component hosted by ASP.NET):

- Use the ASP.NET process identity.
- Use fixed identities within ASP.NET.
- Use serviced components.
- Use the **LogonUser** API and impersonating a specific identity.
- Use the original caller's identity.
- Use the anonymous Internet User account.

Recommendation

The recommendation is to configure the local ASP.NET process identity by changing the password to a known value on the Web server and create a mirrored account on the database server by creating a local user with the same name and password. Further details for this and the other approaches are presented below.

Using the ASP.NET Process Identity

If you connect to SQL Server directly from an ASP.NET application (or Web service, or remote component hosted by ASP.NET), use the ASP.NET process identity. This is a common approach and the application defines the trust boundary, that is, the database trusts the ASP.NET account to access database objects.

You have three options:

- Use mirrored ASPNET local accounts.
- Use mirrored, custom local accounts.
- Use a custom domain account.

Use Mirrored ASPNET Local Accounts

This is the simplest approach and is the one generally used when you own the target database (and can control the administration of local database-server accounts). With this option, you use the ASPNET least-privileged, local account to run ASP.NET and then create a duplicated account on the database server.

Note: This approach has the added advantages that it works across non-trusting domains and through firewalls. The firewall may not open sufficient ports to support Windows authentication.

Use Mirrored, Custom Local Accounts

This approach is the same as the previous approach except that you don't use the default ASPNET account. This means two things:

- You will need to create a custom local account with appropriate permissions and privileges.

  For more information, see "How To: Create a Custom Account to Run ASP.NET" in the Reference section of this book.

- You are no longer using the default account created by the .NET Framework installation process. Your company may have a policy not to use default installation accounts. This can potentially raise the security bar of your application.

  For more information, see the Sans Top 20, "G2—Accounts with No Passwords or Weak Passwords" (*http://www.sans.org/top20.htm*).

Use a Custom Domain Account

This approach is similar to the previous one except that you use a least-privileged domain account instead of a local account. This approach assumes that client and server computers are in the same or trusting domains. The main benefit is that credentials are not shared across machines; the machines simply give access to the domain account. Also, administration is easier with domain accounts.

Implementing Mirrored ASPNET Process Identity

In order to use mirrored accounts to connect from ASP.NET to a database, you need to perform the following actions:

- Use User Manager on the Web server to reset the ASPNET account's password to a known strong password value.

Important: If you change the ASPNET password to a known value, the password in the Local Security Authority (LSA) on the local computer will no longer match the account password stored in the Windows Security Account Manager (SAM) database. If you need to revert to the AutoGenerate default, you must do the following:

Run Aspnet_regiis.exe to reset ASPNET to its default configuration. For more information, see article Q306005, "HOWTO: Repair IIS Mapping After You Remove and Reinstall IIS," in the Microsoft Knowledge Base. When you do this, you get a new account and a new Windows Security Identifier (SID). The permissions for this account are set to their default values. As a result, you need to explicitly reapply permissions and privileges that you had originally set for the old ASPNET account.

- Explicitly set the password in Machine.config. Use the aspnet_setreg.exe utility to encrypt the <**processModel**> credentials in a secured registry key. For details, see article Q329290, "HOWTO: Use the ASP.NET Utility to Encrypt Credentials and Session State Connection Strings" in the Microsoft Knowledge Base.

```
<processModel
        userName="registry:HKLM\SOFTWARE\YourSecureApp\
                processModel\ASPNET_SETREG,userName"
        password="registry:HKLM\SOFTWARE\YourSecureApp\
                processModel\ASPNET_SETREG,password" . . . />
```

You should protect machine.config from unauthorized access by using Windows ACLs. For example, restrict Machine.config from the IIS anonymous Internet user account.

- Create a mirrored account (with the same name and password) on the database server.

- Within the SQL database, create a server login for the local ASPNET account and then map the login to a database user within the required database. Then create a database user role, add the database user to the role, and configure the appropriate database permissions for the role.

For more information, see "Creating a least privileged database account" later in this chapter.

Connecting to SQL Server Using Windows Authentication

To connect to SQL Server using Windows authentication:

- Within the client application, use a connection string that contains either "Trusted Connection=Yes", or "Integrated Security=SSPI". The two strings are equivalent and both result in Windows authentication (assuming that your SQL Server is configured for Windows authentication). For example:

```
SqlConnection conn = new SqlConnection(
        "server=YourServer; database=YourDatabase;" +
        "Trusted_Connection=Yes;");
```

```
- or -

SqlConnection conn = new SqlConnection(
        "server=YourServer; database=YourDatabase;" +
        "Integrated Security=SSPI;");
```

> **Note:** The identity of the client making the request (that is, the client authenticated by SQL Server) is determined by the client's thread impersonation token (if the thread is currently impersonating) or the client's current process token.

Using Fixed Identities within ASP.NET

With this approach, you configure your ASP.NET application to impersonate a specified, fixed identity, by using the **<identity>** element in Web.config. The following example shows the **<identity>** element where the credentials are encrypted in the registry using aspnet_setreg.exe as discussed in Chapter 8, "ASP.NET Security".

```
<identity
    impersonate="true"
    userName="registry:HKLM\SOFTWARE\YourSecureApp\
            identity\ASPNET_SETREG,userName"
    password="registry:HKLM\SOFTWARE\YourSecureApp\
            identity\ASPNET_SETREG,password" />
```

This becomes the default identity that is used when you connect to network resources, including databases.

Using a fixed impersonated identity is not recommended when using the .NET Framework 1.0 on Windows 2000 servers. This is because you would need to give the ASP.NET process account the powerful "Act as part of the operating system" privilege. This privilege is required by the ASP.NET process because it performs a **LogonUser** call using the credentials that you have provided.

> **Note:** Microsoft Windows .NET Server 2003 does not require the "Act as Part of the operating system" privilege to make **LogonUser** calls.
>
> Also, the .NET Framework version 1.1 will provide an enhancement for this scenario on Windows 2000. The logon will be performed by the IIS process, so that ASP.NET does not require the "Act as part of the operating system" privilege.

For more information about this strong privilege, see the Security Briefs column in the August 99 copy of Microsoft Systems Journal (*http://msdn.microsoft.com/library /default.asp?url=/library/en-us/dnmsj99/html/security0899.asp*).

The .NET Framework version 1.1 will provide an enhancement for this scenario on Windows 2000. The logon will be performed by the IIS process, so that ASP.NET does not require the "Act as part of the operating system" privilege.

Using Serviced Components

You can develop a serviced component specifically to contain data access code. With serviced components, you can access the database by either hosting your component in an Enterprise Services (COM+) server application running under a specific identity, or you can write code that uses the **LogonUser** API to perform impersonation.

Using out of process serviced components raises the security bar because process hops make an attacker's job more difficult, particularly if the processes run with different identities. The other advantage is that you can isolate code that requires more privilege from the rest of the application.

Calling LogonUser and Impersonating a Specific Windows Identity

You should not call **LogonUser** directly from ASP.NET. In Windows 2000, this approach requires you to give the ASP.NET process identity "Act as part of the operating system".

A preferred approach is to call **LogonUser** outside of the ASP.NET process using a serviced component in an Enterprise Services server application, as discussed above.

Using the Original Caller's Identity

For this approach to work, you need to use Kerberos delegation and impersonate the caller to the database, either directly from ASP.NET or from a serviced component.

From ASP.NET add the following to your application's Web.config.

```
<identity impersonate="true" />
```

From a serviced component, call **CoImpersonateClient**. For more information about using **CoImpersonateClient**, see Chapter 9, "Enterprise Services Security".

Using the Anonymous Internet User Account

As a variation of the previous approach, for scenarios where your application uses Forms or Passport authentication (which implies IIS anonymous authentication), you can enable impersonation within your application's web.config in order to use the anonymous Internet user account for database access.

```
<identity impersonate="true" />
```

With IIS configured for anonymous authentication, this configuration results in your Web application's code running using the anonymous Internet user's impersonation token. In a Web hosting environment, this has the advantage of allowing you to separately audit and track database access from multiple Web applications.

More Information

- For more information and implementation details about using the original caller's identity, see "Flowing the Original Caller to the Database" in Chapter 5, "Intranet Security."

- For more information about how to configure IIS to use anonymous user account refer to Chapter 8, "ASP.NET Security."

When Can't You Use Windows Authentication?

Certain application scenarios may prevent the use of Windows authentication. For example:

- Your database client and database server are separated by a firewall which prevents Windows authentication.

- Your application needs to connect to one or more databases using multiple identities.

- You are connecting to databases other than SQL Server.

- You don't have a secure way within ASP.NET to run code as a specific Windows user. Either you can't (or won't) forward the original caller's security context, and/or you want to use a dedicated service account rather than grant logons to end users.

In these scenarios, you will have to use SQL authentication (or the database's native authentication mechanism), and you must:

- Protect database user credentials on the application server.
- Protect database user credentials while in transit from the server to the database.

If you do use SQL authentication, there are various ways in which you can make SQL authentication more secure. These are highlighted in the next section.

SQL Authentication

If your application needs to use SQL authentication, you need to consider the following key points:

- Use a least-privileged account to connect to SQL.
- Credentials are passed over the wire so they must be secured.
- The SQL connection string (which contains credentials) must be secured.

Connection String Types

If you connect to a SQL Server database using credentials (user name and password) then your connection string looks like this:

```
Using the SQL Server .NET Data Provider:
SqlConnection conn = new SqlConnection(
        "server=YourServer; uid=YourUserName; pwd=YourStrongPwd;" +
        "database=YourDatabase");

Using the OLE DB .NET Data Provider:
OleDbConnection conn = new OleDbConnection(
        "Provider=SQLOLEDB; Data Source=YourServer;" +
        "uid=YourUserName; pwd=YourStrongPwd; Initial Catalog=YourDatabase");
```

If you need to connect to a specific instance of SQL Server (a feature available only in SQL Server 2000 or later) installed on the same computer then your connection string looks like this:

```
Using the SQL Server .NET Data Provider:
SqlConnection conn = new SqlConnection(
        "server=YourServer\Instance; uid=YourUserName; pwd=YourStrongPwd;" +
        "database=YourDatabase");
```

If you are connecting to an Oracle database by using explicit credentials (user name and password) then your connection string looks like this:

```
OleDbConnection conn = new OleDbConnection(
        "Provider=MSDAORA; Data Source=YourDatabaseAlias;" +
        "User ID=YourUserName; Password=YourStrongPwd;");
```

More Information

For more information about using Universal Data Link (UDL) files for your connection, see article Q308426, "HOW TO: Use Data Link Files with the OleDbConnection Object in Visual C# .NET," in the Microsoft Knowledge Base.

Choosing a SQL Account for Your Connections

Don't use the built-in **sa** account or any account that is a member of the SQL Server **sysadmin** fixed server role or **db_owner** fixed database role for data access. Members of **sysadmin** can perform any activity in SQL Server. Members of **db_owner** have unrestricted permissions in the database. Instead, use least-privileged accounts with a strong password.

Avoid the following connection string:

```
SqlConnectionString = "Server=YourServer\Instance;
                       Database=YourDatabase; uid=sa; pwd=;"
```

Use least privileged accounts with a strong password, for example:

```
SqlConnectionString= "Server=YourServer\Instance;
                      Database=YourDatabase;
                      uid=YourStrongAccount;
                      pwd=YourStrongPassword;"
```

Note that this does not address the issue of storing credentials in plain text in your Web.config files. All you've done so far is limit the scope of damage possible in the event of a compromise, by using a least-privileged account. To further raise the security bar, you should encrypt the credentials.

Note: If you selected a case-sensitive sort order when you installed SQL Server, your login ID is also case-sensitive.

Passing Credentials over the Network

When you connect to SQL Server with SQL authentication, the user name and password are sent across the network in clear text. This can represent a significant security concern. For more information about how to secure the channel between an application or Web server and database server, see "Secure Communication" later in this chapter.

Securing SQL Connection Strings

User names and passwords should not be stored in clear text in configuration files. For details about how to store connection strings securely, see "Storing Database Connection Strings" later in this chapter.

Authenticating Against Non-SQL Server Databases

The typical issues you may encounter when connecting to non-SQL databases are similar to scenarios where you need to use SQL authentication. You may need to supply explicit credentials if the target resources do not support Windows authentication. To secure this type of scenario, you must store the connection string securely and you must also secure the communication over the network (to prevent interception of credentials).

Authorization

SQL Server provides a number of role-based approaches for authorization. These revolve around the following thee types of roles supported by SQL Server:

- **User-defined Database Roles**. These are used to group together users who have the same security privileges within the database. You create SQL Server logins and then map these to specific database users. You then add the database users to database roles and establish permissions on individual database objects (stored procedures, tables, views, and so on) using the roles.

- **Application Roles**. These are similar to user database roles in that they are used when establishing object permissions. However, unlike user database roles, they do not contain users or groups. Instead, they must are activated by an application using a built-in stored procedure. Once active, the permissions granted to the role determine the data access capabilities of the application.

  Application roles allow database administrators to grant selected applications access to specified database objects. This is in contrast to granting permissions to users.

- **Fixed Database Roles**. SQL Server also provides fixed server roles such as **db_datareader** and **db_datawriter**. These built-in roles are present in all databases and can be used to quickly give a user read specific (and other commonly used) sets of permissions within the database.

For more information about these various role types (and also fixed server roles which are similar to fixed database roles but apply at the server level instead of the database level), see SQL Server Books Online (*http://www.microsoft.com/sql/techinfo/productdoc/2000/books.asp*).

Using Multiple Database Roles

If your application has multiple categories of users, and the users within each category require the same permissions within the database, your application requires multiple roles. Each role requires a different set of permissions within the database. For example, members of an Internet User role may require read-only permissions to the majority of tables within a database, while members of an Administrator or Operator role may require read/write permissions.

In this scenario, you can use multiple user-defined SQL Server database roles. These are used to assign permissions to database objects for the groups of users who share the same permissions in the database. With this approach, you must:

- Create multiple service accounts to use for database access.
- Create a SQL Server login for each account.

- Create database users to grant the login access to the database.
- Add each database user to a user-defined database role.
- Establish the necessary database permissions for each role within the database.
- Authorize users within your application (ASP.NET Web application, Web service, or middle tier component) and then use application logic within your data access layer to determine which account to connect to the database with. This is based on the role-membership of the caller.

  Declaratively, you can configure individual methods to allow only those users that belong to a set of roles. You then add imperative role-checks within method code to determine precise role membership, which determines the connection to use.

Figure 12.4 illustrates this approach.

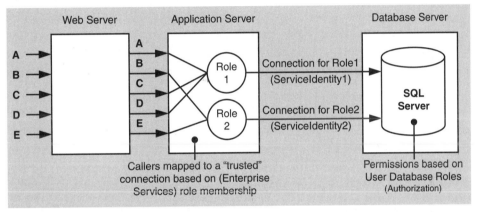

Figure 12.4
Connecting to SQL Server using multiple SQL user database roles

To use the preferred Windows authentication for this scenario, you develop code (using the **LogonUser** API) in an out of process serviced component to impersonate one of a set of Windows identities.

With SQL authentication, you use a different connection string (containing different user names and passwords) depending upon role-based logic within your application.

Secure Communication

In most application scenarios you need to secure the communication link between your application server and database. You need to be able to guarantee:

- **Message Confidentiality**. The data must be encrypted to ensure that it remains private.
- **Message Integrity**. The data must be signed to ensure that it remains unaltered.

In some scenarios, all of the data passed between application server and database server must be secured, while in other scenarios, selected items of data sent over specific connections must be secured. For example:

- In an intranet Human Resources application, some of the employee details passed between client and the database server are sensitive.

- In Internet scenarios, such as secure banking applications, all of the data passed between the application server and database server must be secured.

- If you are using SQL authentication, you should also secure the communication link to ensure that user names and passwords can not be compromised with network monitoring software.

The Options

You have two options for securing the network link between an application server and database server:

- IPSec
- SSL (Using a server certificate on the SQL Server computer)

> **Note:** You must be running SQL Server 2000 to support the use of SSL. Earlier versions do not support it. The client must have the SQL Server 2000 client libraries installed.

Choosing an Approach

Whether or not you should use IPSec or SSL depends on a number of primarily environmental factors, such as firewall considerations, operating system and database versions, and so on.

> **Note:** IPSec is not intended as a replacement for application-level security. Today it is used as a defense in depth mechanism, or to secure insecure applications without changing them, and to secure non-TLS (for example, SSL) protocols from network-wire attacks.

More Information

- For more information about configuring IPSec, see "How To: Use IPSec to Provide Secure Communication between Two Servers" in the Reference section of this book.

- For more information about configuring SSL, see "How To: Use SSL to Secure Communication with SQL Server 2000" in the Reference section of this book.

- For more information about SSL and IPSec in general, see Chapter 4, "Secure Communication."

Connecting with Least Privilege

Connecting to the database with least privilege means that the connection you establish only has the minimum privileges that you need within the database. Simply put, you don't connect to your database using the **sa** account, members of the **sysadmin** role or members of the **db_owner** role. Ideally, if the current user is not authorized to add or update records, then the corresponding account used for their connection (which may be aggregated to an identity that represents a particular role) cannot add or update records in the database.

When you connect to SQL Server, your approach needs to support the necessary granularity that your database authorization requires. You need to consider what the database trusts. It can trust:

- The application.
- Application defined roles.
- The original caller.

The Database Trusts the Application

Consider a finance application that you authorize to use your database. The finance application is responsible for managing user authentication and authorizing access. In this case, you can manage your connections through a single trusted account (which corresponds to either a SQL login or a Windows account mapped to a SQL login). If you're using Windows authentication, this would typically mean allowing the process identity of the calling application (such as the ASP.NET worker process, or an Enterprise Services server application identity) to access the database.

From an authorization standpoint, this approach is very coarse-grained, because the connection runs as an identity that has access to all database objects and resources needed by the application. The benefits of this approach are that you can use connection pooling and you simplify administration because you are authorizing a single account. The downside is that all of your users run with the same connection privileges.

The Database Trusts Different Roles

You can use pools of separate, connections to the database that correspond to the roles defined by your application, for example, one connection that is for tellers, another for managers, and so on.

These connections may or may not use Windows authentication. The advantage of Windows authentication is that it handles credential management and doesn't send the credentials over the network. However, while Windows authentication is possible at the process or application level, there are additional challenges presented by the fact you need multiple identities (one per role).

Applications that use the **LogonUser** API to create a thread level Windows access token to establish security context are faced with credential management issues because the application has to securely store the account user name and password. Such applications also face privilege issues because the powerful "Act as part of the operating system" privilege must be granted to the process account.

Applications that use SQL Authentication also face credential management issues and in addition require a secure communication channel to the database to protect the credentials.

The Database Trusts the Original Caller

In this case, you need to flow the original caller through multiple tiers to the database. This means that your clients need network credentials to be able to hop from one computer to the next. This requires Kerberos delegation.

Although this solution provides a fine-grained level of authorization within the database, because you know the identity of the original caller and can establish per user permissions on database objects, it impacts application performance and scalability. Connection pooling, although still enabled, becomes ineffective.

Creating a Least Privilege Database Account

The following steps are provided as a simple example to show you how to create a least privilege database account. While most database administrators are already familiar with these steps, many developers may not be and resort to using the **sa** account to force their applications to work.

This can create difficulties when moving from a development environment, to a test environment, and then to a production environment because the application moves from an environment that's wide open into a more tightly controlled setting, which prevents the application from functioning correctly.

You start by creating a SQL login for either a SQL account or a Windows user or group account. You then grant the login access to a database by creating a database user, add the database user to a user-defined database role and assign permissions to the role.

▶ **To set up a data access account for SQL**

1. Create a new Windows user account and add the account to a Windows group. If you are managing multiple users, you would use a group. If you are dealing with a single application account (such as a duplicated ASP.NET process account), you may choose not to add the account to a Windows group.

2. Create a SQL Server login for the user/group.

   a. Start **Enterprise Manager**, locate your database server, and then expand the **Security** folder.

   b. Right-click **Logins**, and then click **New Login**.

   c. Enter the Windows account name into the **Name** field, and then click **OK** to close the **SQL Server Login Properties** dialog box.

3. Create a new database user in the database of interest to grant the login access to the database.

   a. Use **Enterprise Manager** and expand the **Databases** folder, and then expand the required database for which the login requires access.

   b. Right-click **Users**, and then click **New Database User**.

   c. Select the previously created Login name.

   d. Enter a user name.

4. Create a new database role to which permissions will be assigned.

   a. Right-click **Roles** beneath the **Databases** folder, and then click **New Database Role**.

   b. Enter a role name.

   c. Click **Add**, to add the database user to the role.

   d. Configure permissions as discussed below.

5. Grant the database user **Select** permissions on the tables that need to be accessed and **Execute** permissions on any relevant stored procedures.

> **Note:** If the stored procedure and the table are owned by the same person, and access the table only through the stored procedure (and do not need to access the table directly), it is sufficient to grant execute permissions on the stored procedure alone. This is because of the concept of ownership chaining. For more information, see SQL Server Books online.

6. If you want the user account to have access to all the views and tables in the database, add them to the **db_datareader** fixed database role.

> **Note:** A **public** role exists in each database to which every other database user and role belongs and cannot be removed. You should revoke or deny permissions on this role, so that authorization is determined purely by the permissions associated with the user-defined database role.

Storing Database Connection Strings Securely

There are a number of possible locations and approaches for storing database connection strings, each with varying degrees of security and configuration flexibility.

The Options

The following list represents the main options for storing connection strings:

- Encrypted with DPAPI
- Clear text in Web.config or Machine.config
- UDL files
- Custom text files
- Registry
- COM+ catalog

Using DPAPI

Windows 2000 and later operating systems provide the Win32® Data Protection API (DPAPI) for encrypting and decrypting data. DPAPI is part of the Cryptography API (Crypto API) and is implemented in Crypt32.dll. It consists of two methods—**CryptProtectData** and **CryptUnprotectData**.

DPAPI is particularly useful in that it can eliminate the key management problem exposed to applications that use cryptography. While encryption ensures the data is secure, you must take additional steps to ensure the security of the key. DPAPI uses the password of the user account associated with the code that calls the DPAPI functions in order to derive the encryption key. As a result the operating system and not the application, manages the key.

Why Not LSA?

Many applications use the Local Security Authority (LSA) to store secrets. DPAPI has the following advantages over the LSA approach:

- To use the LSA, a process requires administrative privileges. This is a security concern because it greatly increases the potential damage that can be done by an attacker who manages to compromise the process.
- The LSA provides only a limited number of slots for secret storage, many of which are already used by the system.

Machine Store vs. User Store

DPAPI can work with either the machine store or user store (which requires a loaded user profile). DPAPI defaults to the user store, although you can specify that the machine store be used by passing the CRYPTPROTECT_LOCAL_MACHINE flag to the DPAPI functions.

The user profile approach affords an additional layer of security because it limits who can access the secret. Only the user who encrypts the data can decrypt the data. However, use of the user profile requires additional development effort when DPAPI is used from an ASP.NET Web application because you need to take explicit steps to load and unload a user profile. ASP.NET does not automatically load a user profile.

The machine store approach is easier to develop because it does not require user profile management. However, unless an additional entropy parameter is used, it is less secure because any user on the computer can decrypt data. Entropy is a random value designed to make deciphering the secret more difficult. The problem with using an additional entropy parameter is that this must be securely stored by the application, which presents another key management issue.

Note: If you use DPAPI with the machine store, the encrypted string is specific to a given computer and therefore you must generate the encrypted data on every computer. Do not copy the encrypted data across computers in a farm or cluster.

If you use DPAPI with the user store, you can decrypt the data on any computer with a roaming user profile.

DPAPI Implementation Solutions

This section presents two implementation solutions that show you how to use DPAPI from an ASP.NET Web application to secure a connection string or a secret of any type. The implementation solutions described in this section are:

- **Using DPAPI from Enterprise Services**. This solution allows you to use DPAPI with the user store.
- **Using DPAPI Directly from ASP.NET**. This solution allows you to use DPAPI with the machine store, which makes the solution easier to develop as DPAPI can be called directly from an ASP.NET Web application.

Using DPAPI from Enterprise Services

An ASP.NET Web application can't call DPAPI and use the user store because this requires a loaded user profile. The ASPNET account usually used to run Web applications is a non-interactive account and as such does not have a user profile. Furthermore, if the ASP.NET application is impersonating, the Web application thread runs as the currently authenticated user, which can vary from one request to the next.

This presents the following issues for an ASP.NET Web application that wants to use DPAPI:

- Calls to DPAPI from an ASP.NET application running under the default ASPNET account will fail. This is because the ASPNET account does not have a user profile, as it is not used for interactive logons.

- If an ASP.NET Web application is configured to impersonate its callers, the ASP.NET application thread has an associated thread impersonation token. The logon session associated with this impersonation token is a network logon session (used on the server to represent the caller). Network logon sessions do not result in user profiles being loaded.

To overcome this issue, you can create a serviced component (within an out-of-process Enterprise Services (COM+) server application) to call DPAPI. You can ensure that the account used to run the component has a user profile and you can use a Win32 service to automatically load the profile.

Note: It is possible to avoid the use of a Win32 service by placing calls to Win32 profile management functions (**LoadUserProfile** and **UnloadUserProfile**) within the serviced component.

There are two drawbacks to this approach. First, calls to these APIs on a per-request basis would severely impact performance. Second, these APIs require that the calling code have administrative privileges on the local computer, which defeats the principle of least privilege for the Enterprise Services process account.

Figure 12.5 shows the Enterprise Services DPAPI solution.

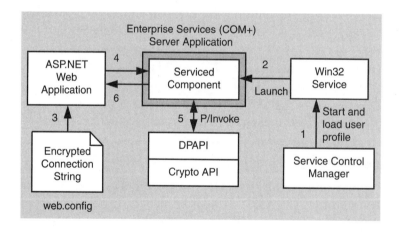

Figure 12.5
The ASP.NET Web application uses a COM+ server application to interact with DPAPI

In Figure 12.5, the runtime sequence of events is as follows:

1. The Windows service control manager starts the Win32 service and automatically loads the user profile associated with the account under which the service runs. The same Windows account is used to run the Enterprise Services application.

2. The Win32 service calls a launch method on the serviced component that starts the Enterprise Services application and loads the serviced component.

3. The Web application retrieves the encrypted string from the Web.config file.

   You can store the encrypted string by using an **<appSettings>** element within Web.config as shown below. This element supports arbitrary key-value pairs.

```
<configuration>
 <appSettings>
  <add key="SqlConnString"
       value="AQAAANCMnd8BFdERjHoAwE/C1+sBAAAABcqc/xCHxki3" />
 </appSettings>
</configuration>
```

   You can retrieve the encrypted string with the following line of code:

```
string connString = ConfigurationSettings.AppSettings["SqlConnString"];
```

> **Note:** You can use Web.config or Machine.config to store encrypted connection strings. Machine.config is preferred as it is in a system directory outside of a virtual directory. This is discussed further in the next section, "Using Web.config and Machine.config."

4. The application calls a method on the serviced component to decrypt the connection string.

5. The serviced component interacts with DPAPI using P/Invoke to call the Win32 DPAPI functions.

6. The decrypted string is returned to the Web application.

> **Note:** To store encrypted connection strings in the Web.config file in the first place, write a utility application that takes the connection strings and calls the serviced component's **EncryptData** method to obtain the encrypted string. It is essential that you run the utility application while logged on with the same account that you use to run the Enterprise Services server application.

Using DPAPI Directly from ASP.NET

If you use the machine store and call the DPAPI functions with the CRYPTPROTECT_LOCAL_MACHINE flag you can call the DPAPI functions directly from an ASP.NET Web application because you don't need a user profile.

However, because you are using the machine store, any Windows account that can log on to the computer has access to the secret. A mitigating approach is to add entropy but this requires additional key management.

As alternatives to using entropy with the machine store, consider the following options:

- Use Windows ACLs to restrict access to the encrypted data (whether the data is stored in the file system or registry).
- Consider hard-coding the entropy parameter into your application to avoid the key management issue.

More Information

- For more information about creating a DPAPI library for use with .NET Web applications, see "How To: Create a DPAPI Library" in the Reference section of this book.
- For a detailed implementation walkthrough that shows you how to use DPAPI directly from ASP.NET, see "How To: Use DPAPI (Machine Store) from ASP.NET" in the Reference section of this book.
- For a detailed implementation walkthrough that shows you how to use DPAPI from Enterprise Services, see "How To: Use DPAPI (User Store) from ASP.NET with Enterprise Services" in the Reference section of this book.
- For more information about Windows Data Protection with DPAPI, see the MSDN article, "Windows Data Protection."

Using Web.config and Machine.config

Storing plain text passwords in Web.config is not recommended. By default, the **HttpForbiddenHandler** protects the file from being downloading and viewed by malicious users. However, users who have access directly to the folders that contain the configuration files can still see the user name and password.

Machine.config is considered a more secure storage location than Web.config because it is located in a system directory (with ACLs) outside of a Web application's virtual directory. For more information about securing Machine.config, see Chapter 8, "ASP.NET Security."

Using UDL Files

The OLE DB .NET Data Provider supports UDL file names in its connection string. To reference a UDL file, use "File Name=name.udl" within the connection string.

Important: This option is only available if you use the OLE DB .NET Data Provider to connect to the database. The SQL Server .NET Data Provider does not use UDL files.

It is not recommended to store UDL files in a virtual directory along with other application files. You should store them outside the Web application's virtual directory hierarchy and then secure the file or the folder containing the file with Windows ACLs. You should also consider storing UDL files on a separate logical volume from the operating system to protect against possible file canonicalization and directory traversal bugs.

ACL Granularity

UDL files (or indeed any text file) offer added granularity when you apply ACLs in comparison to Machine.config. The default ACLs associated with Machine.config grant access to a wide variety of local and remote users. For example, Machine.config has the following default ACLs:

```
MachineName\ASPNET:R
BUILTIN\Users:R
BUILTIN\Power Users:C
BUILTIN\Administrators:F
NT AUTHORITY\SYSTEM:F
```

By contrast, you can lock down your own application's UDL file much further. For example, you can restrict access to Administrators, the System account, and the ASP.NET process account (which requires read access) as shown below.

```
BUILTIN\Administrators:F
MachineName\ASPNET:R
NT AUTHORITY\SYSTEM:F
```

Note: Because UDL files can be modified externally to any ADO.NET client application, connection strings that contain references to UDL files are parsed every time the connection is opened. This can impact performance and it is therefore recommended, for best performance, that you use a static connection string that does not include a UDL file.

▶ **To create a new UDL file**

1. Use Windows Explorer and navigate to the folder in which you want to create the UDL file.

2. Right-click within the folder, point to **New,** and then click **Text Document**.

3. Supply a file name with a .udl file extension.

4. Double-click the new file to display the **UDL Properties** dialog box.

More Information

For more information about using UDL files from Microsoft C#® development tool programs, see article Q308426, "HOW TO: Use Data Link Files with OleDbConnection Object in VC#," in the Microsoft Knowledge Base.

Using Custom Text Files

Many applications use custom text files to store connection strings. If you do adopt this approach consider the following recommendations:

- Store custom files outside of your application's virtual directory hierarchy.
- Consider storing files on a separate logical volume from the operating system to protect against possible file canonicalization and directory traversal bugs.
- Protect the file with a restricted ACL that grants read access to your application's process account.
- Avoid storing the connection string in clear text in the file. Instead, consider using DPAPI to store an encrypted string.

Using the Registry

You can use a custom key in the Windows registry to store the connection string. This information stored can either be stored in the HKEY_LOCAL_MACHINE (HKLM) or HKEY_CURRENT_USER (HKCU) registry hive. For process identities, such as the ASPNET account, that do not have user profiles, the information must be stored in HKLM in order to allow ASP.NET code to retrieve it.

If you do use this approach, you should:

- Use ACLs to protect the registry key using Regedt32.exe.
- Encrypt the data prior to storage.

More Information

For more information about encrypting data for storage in the registry, see "How To: Store an Encrypted Connection String in the Registry" in the Reference section of this book.

Using the COM+ Catalog

If your Web application includes serviced components, you can store connection strings in the COM+ catalog as constructor strings. These are easily administered (by using the Component Services tool) and are easily retrieved by component code. Enterprise Services calls an object's **Construct** method immediately after instantiating the object, and passes the configured construction string.

The COM+ catalog doesn't provide a high degree of security, because the information is not encrypted; however, it raises the security bar in comparison to configuration files because of the additional process hop.

To prevent access to the catalog through the Component Services tool, include only the desired list of users in the **Administrator** and **Reader** roles in the **System** application.

The following example shows how to retrieve an object constructor string from a serviced component.

```
[ConstructionEnabled(Default="Default Connection String")]
public class YourClass : ServicedComponent
{
  private string _ConnectionString;
  override protected void Construct(string s)
  {
    _ConnectionString = s;
  }
}
```

For added security, you can add code to encrypt the construction string prior to storage and decrypt it within the serviced component.

More Information

- For more information on using connection strings, see article Q271284, "HOWTO: Access COM+ Object Constructor String in a VB Component," in the Microsoft Knowledge Base.

- For a complete code sample provided by the .NET Framework SDK, see the object constructor sample located in \Program Files\Microsoft Visual Studio .NET\FrameworkSDK\Samples\Technologies\ComponentServices\ObjectConstruction.

Authenticating Users against a Database

If you are building an application that needs to validate user credentials against a database store, consider the following points:

- Store one-way password hashes with a random salt value.
- Avoid SQL injection when validating user credentials.

Store One-way Password Hashes (with Salt)

Web applications that use Forms authentication often need to store user credentials including passwords in a database. For security reasons, you should not store passwords (clear text or encrypted) in the database.

You should avoid storing encrypted passwords because it raises key management issues—you can secure the password with encryption, but you then have to consider how to store the encryption key. If the key becomes compromised, an attacker can decrypt all the passwords within your data store.

The preferred approach is to:

- **Store a one way hash of the password**. Re-compute the hash when the password needs to be validated.
- **Combine the password hash with a salt value (a cryptographically strong random number)**. By combining the salt with the password hash, you mitigate the threat associated with dictionary attacks.

Creating a Salt Value

The following code shows how to generate a salt value by using random number generation functionality provided by the **RNGCryptoServiceProvider** class within the **System.Security.Cryptography** namespace.

```
public static string CreateSalt(int size)
{
  RNGCryptoServiceProvider rng = new RNGCryptoServiceProvider();
  byte[] buff = new byte[size];
  rng.GetBytes(buff);
  return Convert.ToBase64String(buff);
}
```

Creating a Hash Value (with Salt)

The following code fragment shows how to generate a hash value from a supplied password and salt value.

```
public static string CreatePasswordHash(string pwd, string salt)
{
  string saltAndPwd = string.Concat(pwd, salt);
  string hashedPwd =
        FormsAuthentication.HashPasswordForStoringInConfigFile(
                                      saltAndPwd, "SHA1");
  return hashedPwd;
}
```

More Information

For the full implementation details of this approach, see "How To: Use Forms Authentication with SQL Server 2000" in the Reference section of this book.

SQL Injection Attacks

If you're using Forms authentication against a SQL database, you should take the precautions discussed in this section to avoid SQL injection attacks. SQL injection is the act of passing additional (malicious) SQL code into an application which is typically appended to the legitimate SQL code contained within the application. All SQL databases are susceptible to SQL injection to varying degrees, but the focus in this chapter is on SQL Server.

You should pay particular attention to the potential for SQL injection attacks when you process user input that forms part of a SQL command. If your authentication scheme is based on validating users against a SQL database, for example, if you're using Forms authentication against SQL Server, then you must guard against SQL injection attacks.

If you build SQL strings using unfiltered input, your application may be subject to malicious user input (remember, never trust user input). The risk is that when you insert user input into a string that becomes an executable statement, a malicious user can append SQL commands to your intended SQL statements by using escape characters.

The code fragments in the following sections use the Pubs database that is supplied with SQL Server to illustrate examples of SQL injection.

The Problem

Your application may be susceptible to SQL injection attacks when you incorporate user input or other unknown data into database queries. For example, both of the following code fragments are susceptible to attack.

- You build SQL statements with unfiltered user input.

```
SqlDataAdapter myCommand = new SqlDataAdapter(
        "SELECT au_lname, au_fname FROM authors WHERE au_id = '" +
        Login.Text + "'", myConnection);
```

- You call a stored procedure by building a single string that incorporates unfiltered user input.

```
SqlDataAdapter myCommand = new SqlDataAdapter("LoginStoredProcedure '" +
                            Login.Text + "'", myConnection);
```

Anatomy of a SQL Script Injection Attack

When you accept unfiltered user input values (as shown above) in your application, a malicious user can use escape characters to append their own commands.

Consider a SQL query that expects the user's input to be in the form of a Social Security Number, such as 172-32-xxxx, which results in a query like this:

```
SELECT au_lname, au_fname FROM authors WHERE au_id = '172-32-xxxx'
```

A malicious user can enter the following text into your application's input field (for example a text box control).

```
' ; INSERT INTO jobs (job_desc, min_lvl, max_lvl) VALUES ('Important Job', 25,
100)  -
```

In this example, an INSERT statement is injected (but any statement that is permitted for the account that's used to connect to SQL Server could be executed). The code can be especially damaging if the account is a member of the **sysadmin** role (this allows shell commands using **xp_cmdshell**) and SQL Server is running under a domain account with access to other network resources.

The command above results in the following combined SQL string:

```
SELECT au_lname, au_fname FROM authors WHERE au_id = '';INSERT INTO jobs
(job_desc, min_lvl, max_lvl) VALUES ('Important Job', 25, 100)  -
```

In this case, the ' (single quotation mark) character that starts the rogue input terminates the current string literal in your SQL statement. It closes the current statement only if the following parsed token doesn't make sense as a continuation of the current statement, but does make sense as the start of a new statement.

```
SELECT au_lname, au_fname FROM authors WHERE au_id = ' '
```

The ; (semicolon) character tells SQL that you're starting a new statement, which is then followed by the malicious SQL code:

```
; INSERT INTO jobs (job_desc, min_lvl, max_lvl) VALUES ('Important Job', 25, 100)
```

Note: The semicolon is not necessarily required to separate SQL statements. This is vendor/ implementation dependent, but SQL Server does not require them. For example, SQL Server will parse the following as two separate statements:

```
SELECT * FROM MyTable DELETE FROM MyTable
```

Finally, the — (double dash) sequence of characters is a SQL comment that tells SQL to ignore the rest of the text, which in this case, ignores the closing ' (single quote) character (which would otherwise cause a SQL parser error).

The full text that SQL executes as a result of the statement shown above is:

```
SELECT au_lname, au_fname FROM authors WHERE au_id = '' ; INSERT INTO jobs
(job_desc, min_lvl, max_lvl) VALUES ('Important Job', 25, 100) -'
```

The Solution

The following approaches can be used to call SQL safely from your application.

- Use the **Parameters** collection when building your SQL statements.

```
SqlDataAdapter myCommand = new SqlDataAdapter(
        "SELECT au_lname, au_fname FROM Authors WHERE au_id= @au_id",
        myConnection);

SqlParameter parm = myCommand.SelectCommand.Parameters.Add(
                                        "@au_id",
                                        SqlDbType.VarChar, 11);

parm.Value= Login.Text;
```

- Use the **Parameters** collection when you call a stored procedure.

```
// AuthorLogin is a stored procedure that accepts a parameter named Login
SqlDataAdapter myCommand = new SqlDataAdapter("AuthorLogin", myConnection);
myCommand.SelectCommand.CommandType = CommandType.StoredProcedure;
SqlParameter parm = myCommand.SelectCommand.Parameters.Add(
                                "@LoginId", SqlDbType.VarChar,11);
parm.Value=Login.Text;
```

If you use the **Parameters** collection, no matter what a malicious user includes as input, the input is treated as a literal. An additional benefit of using the **Parameters** collection is that you can enforce type and length checks. Values outside of the range trigger an exception. This is a healthy example of defense in depth.

- Filter user input for SQL characters. The following method shows how to ensure that any string literal used in a simple SQL comparison statement (equal to, less than, greater than) is safe. It does this by ensuring that any apostrophe used in the string is escaped with an additional apostrophe. Within a SQL string literal, two consecutive apostrophes are treated as an instance of the apostrophe character within the string rather than as delimiters.

```
private string SafeSqlLiteral(string inputSQL)
{
   return inputSQL.Replace("'", "''");
}
...
string safeSQL = SafeSqlLiteral(Login.Text);
SqlDataAdapter myCommand = new SqlDataAdapter(
        "SELECT au_lname, au_fname FROM authors WHERE au_id = '" +
        safeSQL + "'", myConnection);
```

Additional Best Practices

The following are some additional measures you can take to limit the chance of exploit, as well as limit the scope of potential damage:

- Prevent invalid input at the gate (the front-end application) by limiting the size and type of input. By limiting the size and type of input, you significantly reduce the potential for damage. For example, if your database lookup field is eleven characters long and comprised entirely of numeric characters, enforce it.

- Run SQL code with a least privileged account. This significantly reduces the potential damage that can be done.

    For example, if a user were to inject SQL to DROP a table from the database, but the SQL connection used an account that didn't have appropriate permissions, the SQL code would fail. This is another reason not to use the **sa** account or members of **sysadmin** or **db_owner** for your application's SQL connections.

- When an exception occurs in your SQL code, do not expose the SQL errors raised by the database to the end user. Log error information and show only user-friendly information. This prevents exposing unnecessary detail that could help an attacker.

Protecting Pattern Matching Statements

If input is to be used within string literals in a 'LIKE' clause, characters other than apostrophe also take on special meaning for pattern matching.

For example, in a LIKE clause the % character means "match zero or more characters." In order to treat such characters in the input as literal characters without special meaning, they also need to be escaped. If they are not handled specially, the query can return incorrect results; a non-escaped pattern matching character at or near the beginning of the string could also defeat indexing.

For SQL Server, the following method should be used to ensure valid input:

```
private string SafeSqlLikeClauseLiteral(string inputSQL)
{
  // Make the following replacements:
  // '   becomes   ''
  // [   becomes   [[]
  // %   becomes   [%]
  // _   becomes   [_]

  string s = inputSQL;
  s = inputSQL.Replace("'", "''");
  s = s.Replace("[", "[[]");
  s = s.Replace("%", "[%]");
  s = s.Replace("_", "[_]");
  return s;
}
```

Auditing

Auditing of logons is not on by default within SQL Server. You can configure this either through SQL Server Enterprise Manager or in the registry. The dialog box in Figure 12.6 shows auditing enabled for both the success and failure of user logons.

Log entries are written to SQL log files which are by default located in C:\Program Files\Microsoft SQL Server\MSSQL\LOG. You can use any text reader, such as Notepad, to view them.

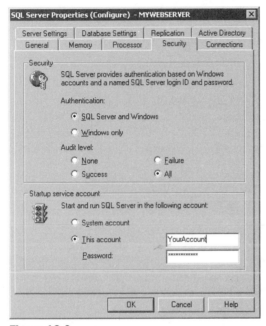

Figure 12.6
SQL Server Properties dialog with Audit level settings

You can also enable SQL Server auditing in the registry. To enable SQL Server auditing, create the following **AuditLevel** key within the registry and set its value to one of the REG_DWORD values specified below.

```
HKEY_LOCAL_MACHINE\SOFTWARE\Microsoft\MSSQLServer\AuditLevel
```

You can choose from one of the following values, which allow you to capture the level of detail you want:

3—captures both success and failed login attempts

2—captures only failed login attempts

1—captures only success login attempts

0—captures no logins

It is recommended that you turn on failed login auditing because this is a way to determine if someone is attempting a brute attack into SQL Server. The performance impacts of logging failed audit attempts are minimal unless you are being attacked, in which case you need to know anyway.

You can also script against SQL Database Management Objects (DMO). The following code fragment shows some sample VBScript code.

```
Sub SetAuditLevel(Server As String, NewAuditLevel As SQLDMO_AUDIT_TYPE)
    Dim objServer As New SQLServer2
    objServer.LoginSecure = True       'Use integrated security
    objServer.Connect Server           'Connect to the target SQL Server
    'Set the audit level
    objServer.IntegratedSecurity.AuditLevel = NewAuditLevel
    Set objServer = Nothing
End Sub
```

From SQL Server Books online, the members of the enumerated type, SQLDMO_AUDIT_TYPE are:

```
SQLDMOAudit_All       3  Log all authentication attempts regardless of success
                         or failure
SQLDMOAudit_Failure   2  Log failed authentication
SQLDMOAudit_Success   1  Log successful authentication
SQLDMOAudit_None      0  Do not log authentication attempts
```

Process Identity for SQL Server

Run SQL Server using a least privileged local account. When you install SQL Server, you have the option of running the SQL Server service using the local SYSTEM account, or a specified account.

Don't use the SYSTEM account or an administrator account. Instead, use a least privileged local account. You do not need to grant this account any specific privileges, as the installation process (or SQL Server Enterprise Manager, if you are reconfiguring the SQL Service after installation) grants the specified account the necessary privileges.

If SQL Server needs to access remote computers for example for network backup and restores or replication, you will need to use a least privileged domain account or create a duplicate local account on the remote server with the same user name and password. Password synchronization can be scripted. The duplicated account approach is required if you need to access servers in other domains that don't have trust relationships.

Summary

The following is a summary that highlights the recommendation for data access in your .NET Web applications:

- Use Windows authentication to SQL Server when possible.
- Use accounts with least privilege in the database.
- Use least privileged, local accounts for running ASP.NET/Enterprise Services when connecting to SQL Server.
- Use user-defined database roles in the database for authorization.
- If you are using SQL authentication, take the following steps to improve security:
  - Use custom accounts with strong passwords.
  - Limit the permissions of each account within SQL Server using database roles.
  - Add ACLs to any files used to store connection strings.
  - Encrypt connection strings.
  - Consider DPAPI for credential storage.
- When you use Forms authentication against SQL, take precautions to avoid SQL injection attacks.
- Don't store user passwords in databases for user validation. Instead, store password hashes with a salt instead of clear text or encrypted passwords.
- Protect sensitive data sent over the network to and from SQL Server.
  - Windows authentication protects credentials, but not application data.
  - Use IPSec or SSL.

13

Troubleshooting Security Issues

This chapter presents a process for troubleshooting and provides a range of techniques and tools that can be used to help diagnose security related problems.

Process for Troubleshooting

The following approach has proven to be helpful for resolving security and security context related issues.

1. Start by describing the problem very clearly. Make sure you know precisely what is supposed to happen, what is actually happening, and most importantly, the detailed steps required to reproduce the problem.

2. Isolate the problem as accurately as you can. Try to determine at which stage during the processing of a request the problem occurs. Is it a client or server related issue? Does it appear to be a configuration or code related error? Try to isolate the problem by stripping away application layers. For example, consider building a simple console-based test client application to take the place of more complex client applications.

3. Analyze error messages and stack traces (if they are available). Start by consulting the Windows event and security logs.

4. Check the Microsoft Knowledge Base to see if the problem has been documented as a Knowledge Base article.

5. Many security related problems relate to the identity used to run code; these are not always the identities you imagine are running the code. Use the code samples presented in the "Determining Identity" subsection of the "ASP.NET" section in this chapter to retrieve and diagnose identity information. If the identities appear incorrect, check the configuration settings in web.config and machine.config and also check the IIS authentication settings for your

application's virtual directory. Factors that can affect identity within an ASP.NET Web application include:

- The **<processModel>** element in machine.config used to determine the process identity of the ASP.NET worker process (aspnet_wp.exe).
- Authentication settings in IIS.
- Authentication settings in web.config.
- Impersonation settings in web.config.

6. Even if it appears that the correct settings are being used and displayed, you may want to explicitly configure a web.config file for your application (in the application's virtual directory) to make sure it is not inheriting settings from a higher level application (perhaps from a web.config in a higher-level virtual directory) or from machine.config.

7. Use some of the troubleshooting tools listed in the "Troubleshooting Tools" section later in this chapter to capture additional diagnostics.

8. Attempt to reproduce the problem on another computer. This can help isolate environmental related problems and can indicate whether or not the problem is in your application's code or configuration.

9. If your application is having problems accessing a remote resource, you may be running into impersonation/delegation related problems. Identify the security context being used for the remote resource access, and if you are using Windows authentication, verify that the account providing the context (for example, a process account), should be able to be authenticated by the remote computer.

10. Search newsgroups to see if the problem has already been reported. If not, post the problem to the newsgroup to see if anyone within the development community can provide assistance.

    The online newsgroup for ASP.NET is located at: *http://communities.microsoft.com /newsgroups/default.asp?icp=mscom&slcid=US&newsgroup=microsoft.public.dotnet .framework.aspnet*

11. Call the Microsoft Support Center. For details, see the Microsoft Knowledge Base.

Searching for Implementation Solutions

If you have a specific issue and need to understand the best way to tackle the problem, use the following approach.

- Search in Chapters 5, 6, and 7of this book for your scenario or a similar scenarios.
- Consult the MSDN library documentation and samples.
- Refer to one of the many ASP.NET information Web sites, such as:

- www.asp.net
- www.gotdotnet.com
- www.asptoday.com
- Search the Microsoft Knowledge Base for an appropriate How To article.
- Post questions to newsgroups.
- Call the Microsoft Support Center.

Troubleshooting Authentication Issues

The first step when troubleshooting authentication issues is to distinguish between IIS and ASP.NET authentication failure messages.

- If you are receiving an IIS error message you will not see an ASP.NET error code. Check the IIS authentication settings for your application's virtual directory.

  Create a simple HTML test page to remove ASP.NET from the solution.

- If you are receiving an ASP.NET error message, review the ASP.NET authentication settings within your application's web.config file.

IIS Authentication Issues

Because the authentication process starts with IIS, make sure IIS is configured correctly.

- Make sure a user is being authenticated. Consider enabling just Basic authentication and manually log in to ensure you know what principal is being authenticated. Log in with a user name of the form "domain\username".
- Restart IIS to ensure log on sessions aren't being cached. (Run IISReset.exe to restart IIS).
- Close your browser between successive tests to ensure the browser isn't caching credentials.
- If you are using Integrated Windows authentication, check browser settings as described below.
  - Click **Tools** from the **Internet Options** menu and then click the **Advanced** tab. Select **Enable Integrated Windows Authentication (requires restart)**. Then restart the browser.
  - Click **Tools** from the **Internet Options** menu, and then click the **Security** tab. Select the appropriate Web content zone and click **Custom Level**. Within **User Authentication** ensure the Logon setting is set correctly for your application. You may want to select **Prompt for user name and password** to ensure that for each test you are providing explicit credentials and that nothing is being cached.

- If the browser prompts you for credentials this could mean you are currently logged into a domain that the server doesn't recognize (for example, you may be logged in as administrator on the local machine).

- When you browse to an application on your local computer, your interactive logon token is used, as you are interactively logged onto the Web server.

- Test with a simple Web page that displays security context information. A sample page is provided later in this chapter.

  If this fails, enable auditing on the requested file and check the Security event log. You must also enable auditing using Group Policy (through either the Local Security Policy tool, or the Domain Security Policy tool). Examine the log for invalid usernames or invalid object access attempts.

  - If your Web application is having problems accessing a remote resource, enable auditing on the remote resource.

  - An invalid username and/or password usually means that the account used to run ASP.NET on your Web server is failing to be correctly authenticated at the remote computer. If you are attempting to access remote resources with the default ASPNET local account, check that you have duplicated the account (and password) on the remote computer.

  - If you see an error message that indicates that the login has failed for NT AUTHORITY\ANONYMOUS this indicates that the identity on Web server does not have any network credentials and is attempting to access the remote computer.

    Identify which account is being used by the Web application for remote resource access and confirm that it has network credentials. If the Web application is impersonating, this requires either Kerberos delegation (with suitably configured accounts) or Basic authentication at the Web server.

Using Windows Authentication

If the <**authentication**> element in your application's web.config is configured for Windows authentication, use the following code in your Web application to check whether anonymous access is being used (and the authenticated user is the anonymous Internet user account [IUSR_MACHINE]).

```
WindowsIdentity winId = HttpContext.Current.User.Identity as WindowsIdentity;
if (null != winId)
{
   Response.Write(winId.IsAnonymous.ToString());
}
```

Using Forms Authentication

Make sure that the cookie name specified in the **<forms>** element is being retrieved in the global.asax event handler correctly (**Application_AuthenticateRequest**). Also, make sure the cookie is being created. If the client is continuously sent back to the login page (specified by the **loginUrl** attribute on the **<forms>** element) this indicates that the cookie is not being created for some reason or an authenticated identity is not being placed into the context (**HttpContext.User**)

Kerberos Troubleshooting

Use the following tools to help troubleshoot Kerberos related authentication and delegation issues.

- **Kerbtray.exe**. This utility can be used to view the Kerberos tickets in the cache on the current computer. It is part of the Windows 2000 Resource Kit and can be downloaded from *http://www.microsoft.com/downloads/search.asp. Search for "Kerbtray.exe".*

- **Klist.exe**. This is a command line tool similar to Kerbtray, but it also allows you to view and delete Kerberos tickets. Once again, it is part of the Windows 2000 Resource Kit and can be downloaded from *http://www.microsoft.com/downloads /search.asp.* Search for "Klist.exe"

- **Setspn.exe**. This is a command-line tool that allows you to manage the Service Principal Names (SPN) directory property for an Active Directory service account. SPNs are used to locate a target principal name for running a service.

  It is part of the Windows 2000 Resource Kit and can be downloaded from *http://www.microsoft.com/downloads/search.asp.* Search for "setspn.exe".

Troubleshooting Authorization Issues

Check Windows ACLs

If your application is having problems accessing a file or registry key (or any securable Windows object protected with ACLs), check the ACLs to ensure that the Web application identity has at least read access.

Check Identity

Also make sure you know which identity is being used for resource access by the ASP.NET Web application. This is likely to be:

- The ASP.NET process identity (as configured on the **<processModel>** element in web.config.

This defaults to the local ASPNET account specified with the username "machine" and password "AutoGenerate".

- The authenticated caller's identity (if impersonation is enabled within web.config) as shown below.

```
<identity impersonate="true" />
```

If you have not disabled anonymous access in IIS, this will be IUSR_MACHINE.

- A specified impersonation identity as shown below.

```
<identity impersonate="true"
         userName="registry:HKLM\SOFTWARE\YourSecureApp\
                   identity\ASPNET_SETREG,userName"
         password="registry:HKLM\SOFTWARE\YourSecureApp\
                   identity\ASPNET_SETREG,password" />
```

This example shows the <identity> element where the credentials are encrypted in the registry using the aspnet_setreg.exe utility. The clear text userName and password attribute values have been replaced with pointers to the secured registry key and named values that contain the encrypted credentials. For details about this utility and to download it, see article Q329290, "HOWTO: Use the ASP.NET Utility to Encrypt Credentials and Session State Connection Strings" in the Microsoft Knowledge Base.

More Information

For more information about the identity used to run ASP.NET and the identity used to access local and network resources, see Chapter 8, "ASP.NET Security".

Check the <authorization> Element

Confirm that the **<allow>** and **<deny>** elements are configured correctly.

- If you have **<deny users="?" />** and you are using Forms authentication and/or IIS anonymous authentication, you must explicitly place an **IPrincipal** object into **HttpContext.User** or you will receive an access denied 401 response.
- Make sure the authenticated user is in the roles specified in <**allow**> and <**deny**> elements.

ASP.NET

Enable Tracing

ASP.NET provides quick and simple tracing to show the execution of events within a page and the values of common variables. This can be a very effective diagnostic aid. Use the page level **Trace** directive to turn on tracing, as shown below

```
<%@ Page language="c#" Codebehind="WebForm1.aspx.cs" AutoEventWireup="false"
Inherits="Test.WebForm1" Trace="true" %>
```

More Information

For more information on the new tracing feature in ASP.NET see the Knowledge Base article Q306731, "INFO: New Tracing Feature in ASP.NET".

Configuration Settings

Most application settings should be placed in web.config. The following list shows main security related settings that can be placed in web.config.

```
<authentication>
<authorization>
<trust>
<identity>
```

The following setting which controls the identity used to run the ASP.NET worker process (aspnet_wp.exe) must be located in machine.config.

```
<processModel>
```

Configuration settings for an application are always retrieved from the application's web.config file first and these override any equivalent settings within machine.config. If you want a particular setting to be applied to your application, explicitly configure the setting in the application's web.config file.

The main (and often only) web.config file for a particular application lives in its virtual directory root. Subdirectories can also contain web.config files. Settings in these files override the settings from web.config files in parent directories.

Determining Identity

Many security and access denied problems relate to the identity used for resource access. The following code samples presented in this section can be used to help determine identity in Web pages, COM objects, and Web services.

For more information about .NET identity variables, see "ASP.NET Identity Matrix" in the Reference section of this book.

Determining Identity in a Web Page

The following script can be used to gather security context related information and indicates the identity being used to run a Web page.

To use this code, copy and paste it to create a file with an .aspx file extension. Copy the file to an IIS virtual directory and view the page from a browser.

```
<%@ Page language="c#" AutoEventWireup="true" %>
<%@ Import Namespace="System.Threading" %>
<%@ Import Namespace="System.Security.Principal" %>
<HTML>
  <HEAD>
    <title>WhoAmI</title>
  </HEAD>
  <body>
    <form id="WhoAmI" method="post" runat="server">
      <TABLE id=contextTable border=1>
        <TR>
          <TD align=middle colSpan=3 rowSpan="">
                HttpContext.Current.User.Identity</TD>
        </TR>
        <TR>
          <TD><b>Name</b></TD>
          <TD><asp:Label ID="contextName" Runat=server /></TD>
        </TR>
        <TR>
          <TD><b>IsAuthenticated</b></TD>
          <TD><asp:Label ID="contextIsAuth" Runat=server /></TD>
        </TR>
        <TR>
          <TD><b>AuthenticationType</b></TD>
          <TD><asp:Label ID="contextAuthType" Runat=server /></TD>
        </TR>
      </TABLE>
      <br><br>

      <TABLE id=windowsIdentityTable border=1>
        <TR>
          <TD align=middle colSpan=3 rowSpan="">WindowsIdentity.GetCurrent()</TD>
        </TR>
        <TR>
```

```
            <TD><b>Name</b></TD>
              <TD><asp:Label ID="windowsName" Runat=server /></TD>
          </TR>
          <TR>
            <TD><b>IsAuthenticated</b></TD>
              <TD><asp:Label ID="windowsIsAuth" Runat=server /></TD>
          </TR>
          <TR>
            <TD><b>AuthenticationType</b></TD>
              <TD><asp:Label ID="windowsAuthType" Runat=server /></TD>
          </TR>
        </TABLE>
        <br><br>

        <TABLE id=threadIdentityTable border=1>
          <TR>
            <TD align=middle colSpan=3
                  rowSpan="">Thread.CurrentPrincipal.Identity</TD>
          </TR>
          <TR>
            <TD><b>Name</b></TD>
              <TD><asp:Label ID="threadName" Runat=server /></TD>
          </TR>
          <TR>
            <TD><b>IsAuthenticated</b></TD>
              <TD><asp:Label ID="threadIsAuthenticated" Runat=server /></TD>
          </TR>
          <TR>
            <TD><b>AuthenticationType</b></TD>
              <TD><asp:Label ID="threadAuthenticationType" Runat=server /></TD>
          </TR>
        </TABLE>
      </form>
  </body>
</HTML>
<script runat=server>
  void Page_Load(Object sender, EventArgs e)
  {
    IIdentity id = HttpContext.Current.User.Identity;
    if(null != id)
    {
      contextName.Text = id.Name;
      contextIsAuth.Text = id.IsAuthenticated.ToString();
      contextAuthType.Text = id.AuthenticationType;
    }
    id = Thread.CurrentPrincipal.Identity;
    if(null != id)
    {
      threadName.Text = id.Name;
      threadIsAuthenticated.Text = id.IsAuthenticated.ToString();
      threadAuthenticationType.Text = id.AuthenticationType;
    }
    id = WindowsIdentity.GetCurrent();
    windowsName.Text = id.Name;
```

```
    windowsIsAuth.Text = id.IsAuthenticated.ToString();
    windowsAuthType.Text = id.AuthenticationType;
  }
</script>
```

Determining Identity in a Web service

The following code can be used within a Web service to obtain identity information.

```
[WebMethod]
public string GetDotNetThreadIdentity()
{
  return Thread.CurrentPrincipal.Identity.Name;
}
[WebMethod]
public string GetWindowsThreadIdentity()
{
  return WindowsIdentity.GetCurrent().Name;
}
[WebMethod]
public string GetUserIdentity()
{
  return User.Identity.Name;
}
[WebMethod]
public string GetHttpContextUserIdentity()
{
  return HttpContext.Current.User.Identity.Name;
}
```

More Information

- For a list of all ASP.NET security related Knowledge Base articles, go to *http://support.microsoft.com*, click "Advanced Search and Help" and search under ASP.NET security.

- For a list of security related articles that deal with frequently seen error messages, use the following search keywords:

  prb kbsecurity kbaspnet

Determining Identity in a Visual Basic 6 COM Object

The following method can be used to return the identity of a Visual Basic 6 COM object. You can call Visual Basic 6.0 COM objects directly from ASP.NET applications through COM interop. The following method can be helpful when you need to troubleshoot access denied errors from your component when it attempts to access resources.

```
Private Declare Function GetUserName Lib "advapi32.dll" _
      Alias "GetUserNameA" (ByVal lpBuffer As String, nSize As Long) As Long
```

```
Public Function WhoAmI()
    Dim sBuff    As String
    Dim lConst   As Long
    Dim lRet     As Long
    Dim sName    As String

    lConst = 199
    sBuff = Space$(200)
    lRet = GetUserName(sBuff, lConst)
    WhoAmI = Trim$(Left$(sBuff, lConst))
End Function
```

.NET Remoting

If a remote object is hosted in ASP.NET, and is configured for Windows authentication, you must specify the credentials to be used for authentication through the credentials property of the channel. If you do not explicitly set credentials, the remote object is called without any credentials. If Windows authentication is required, this will result in an HTTP status 401, access denied response.

To use the credentials associated with the current thread impersonation token (if the client thread is impersonating), or the process token (with no impersonation), use default credentials. This can be configured in the client-side configuration file using the following setting:

```
<channel ref="http" useDefaultCredentials="true" />
```

If an ASP.NET Web application calls a remote component and the Web application is configured for impersonation, the Web application must be using Kerberos or Basic authentication. All other authentication types can not be used in delegation scenarios.

If the Web application is not configured for impersonation, the process identity of the ASP.NET worker process is used. This is specified on the <**processModel**> element of machine.config and defaults to the local ASPNET account.

Note: Ensure the process in running under an account that can be authenticated by the remote computer.

More Information

For more information about setting client-side credentials when calling remote components, see Chapter 11, ".NET Remoting Security."

SSL

To troubleshoot SSL related problems:

- Confirm whether you can telnet to port 443 on the IP addresses of the client and server computer. If you cannot, this usually signifies that the sspifilt.dll is not loaded, or is the wrong version, or perhaps conflicts with other ISAPI extensions.

- Examine the certificate. If you can telnet to 443, check the certificates attribute using the browser's **View Certificate** dialog box. Check the certificates effective and expiration dates, whether the common name is correct, and also what the Authority Information Access (AIA) or Certificate Revocation List (CRL) distribution point is.

  Confirm that you can browse directory to those AIA/CRL points successfully.

- If you are using a custom client application (and not a Web browser) to access an SSL-enabled Web site that requires client certificates, check that the client certificate is located in the correct store that the client application accesses.

  When you use a browser, the certificate must be in the interactive user's user store. Services or custom applications may load the client certificate from the machine store or a store associated with a service account's profile. Use the Services MMC snap-in (available when Certificate Services is installed), from the Administrative Tools program group to examine the contents of certificate stores.

More Information

See the following SSL related Knowledge Base articles.

- Q257591, "Description of the Secure Sockets Layer (SSL) Handshake"
- Q257586, "Description of the Client Authentication Process During the SSL Handshake"
- Q257587, "Description of the Server Authentication Process During the SSL Handshake"
- Q301429, "HOWTO: Install Client Certificate on IIS Server for ServerXMLHTTP Request Object"
- Q295070, "SSL (https) Connection Slow with One Certificate but Faster with Others"

IPSec

The following articles in the Knowledge Base provide steps for troubleshooting IPSec issues.

- Q259335, "Basic L2TP/IPSec Troubleshooting in Windows"
- Q257225, "Basic IPSec Troubleshooting in Windows 2000"

Auditing and Logging

Windows Security Logs

Consult the Windows event and security logs early on in the problem diagnostic process.

More Information

For more information on how to enable auditing and monitoring events, see the Knowledge Base and article Q300958, "HOW TO: Monitor for Unauthorized User Access in Windows 2000".

SQL Server Auditing

By default, logon auditing is disabled. You can configure this either through SQL Server Enterprise Manager or by changing the registry.

SQL Server log files are by default located in the following directory. They are text-based and can be read with any text editor such as Notepad.

    C:\Program Files\Microsoft SQL Server\MSSQL\LOG

▶ **To enable logon auditing with Enterprise Manager**

1. Start Enterprise Manager.
2. Select the required SQL Server in the left hand tree control, right-click and then click **Properties**.
3. Click the **Security** tab.
4. Select the relevant Audit level – **Failure**, **Success** or **All**.

▶ **To enable logon auditing using a registry setting**

Create the following **AuditLevel** key within the registry and set its value to one of the REG_DWORD values specified below.

    HKEY_LOCAL_MACHINE\SOFTWARE\Microsoft\MSSQLServer\AuditLevel

Set the value of this key to one of the following numeric values, which allow you to capture the relevant level of detail.

3—captures both success and failed login attempts

2—captures only failed login attempts

1—captures only success login attempts

0—captures no logins

It is recommended that you turn on failed login auditing as this is a way to determine if someone is attempting a brute force attack into SQL Server. The performance impacts of logging failed audit attempts are minimal unless you are being attacked, in which case you need to know anyway.

You can also set audit levels by using script against the SQL Server DMO (Database Management Objects), as shown in the following code fragment.

```
Sub SetAuditLevel(Server As String, NewAuditLevel As SQLDMO_AUDIT_TYPE)
    Dim objServer As New SQLServer2
    objServer.LoginSecure = True   'Use integrated security
    objServer.Connect Server        'Connect to the target SQL Server
    'Set the audit level
    objServer.IntegratedSecurity.AuditLevel = NewAuditLevel
    Set objServer = Nothing
End Sub
```

From SQL Server Books online, the members of the enumerated type, SQLDMO_AUDIT_TYPE are:

```
SQLDMOAudit_All      3 Log all authentication attempts - success or failure
SQLDMOAudit_Failure  2 Log failed authentication
SQLDMOAudit_None     0 Do not log authentication attempts
SQLDMOAudit_Success  1 Log successful authentication
```

Sample Log Entries

The following list shows some sample log entries for successful and failed entries in the SQL Server logs.

Successful login using Integrated Windows authentication:

```
2002-07-06 22:54:32.42 logon      Login succeeded for user 'SOMEDOMAIN\Bob'.
Connection: Trusted.
```

Successful login using SQL standard authentication:

```
2002-07-06 23:13:57.04 logon      Login succeeded for user 'SOMEDOMAIN\Bob'.
Connection: Non-Trusted.
```

Failed Login:

```
2002-07-06 23:21:15.35 logon      Login failed for user 'SOMEDOMAIN\BadGuy'.
```

IIS Logging

IIS logging can be set to different formats. If you use W3C Extended Logging, then you can take advantage of some additional information. For example, you can turn on Time Taken to log how long a page takes to be served. This can be helpful for isolating slow pages on your production Web site. You can also enable URI Query which will log Query String parameters, which can be helpful for troubleshooting GET operations against your Web pages. The figure below shows the Extended Properties dialog box for IIS logging.

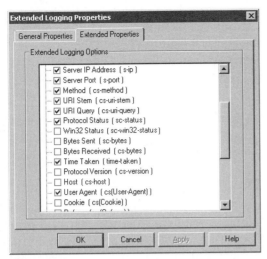

Figure 13.1
IIS extended logging properties

Troubleshooting Tools

The list of tools presented in this section can prove invaluable and will help you diagnose both security and non-security related problems.

File Monitor (FileMon.exe)

This tool allows you to monitor files and folders for access attempts. It is extremely useful to deal with file access permission issues. It is available from www.sysinternals.com.

More Information

For more information see the Knowledge Base article Q286198, "HOWTO: Track 'Permission Denied' Errors on DLL Files".

Fusion Log Viewer (Fuslogvw.exe)

Fusion Log Viewer is provided with the .NET Framework SDK. It is a utility that can be used to track down problems with Fusion binding (see the .NET Framework documentation for more information).

To create Fusion logs for ASP.NET, you need to provide a log path in the registry and you need to enable the log failures option through the Fusion Log Viewer utility.

To provide a log path for your log files, use regedit.exe and add a directory location, such as e:\MyLogs, to the following registry key:

[HKLM\Software\Microsoft\Fusion\LogPath]

ISQL.exe

ISQL can be used to test SQL from a command prompt. This can be helpful when you want to efficiently test different logins for different users. You run ISQL by typing isql.exe at a command prompt on a computer with SQL Server installed.

Connecting Using SQL Authentication

You can pass a user name by using the –U switch and you can optionally specify the password with the –P switch. If you don't specify a password, ISQL will prompt you for one. The following command, issued from a Windows command prompt, results in a password prompt. The advantage of this approach (rather than using the –P switch) is that the password doesn't appear on screen.

C:\ >isql -S YourServer -d pubs -U YourUser

Password:

Connecting Using Windows Authentication

You can use the –E switch to use a trusted connection which uses the security context of the current interactively logged on user.

C:\ >isql -S YourServer -d pubs -E

Running a Simple Query

Once you are logged in, you can run a simple query, such as the one shown below.

1> use pubs

2> SELECT au_lname, au_fname FROM authors

3> go

To quit ISQL, type **quit** at the command prompt.

Windows Task Manager

Windows Task Manager on Windows XP and Windows .NET Server allows you to display the identity being used to run a process.

▶ **To view the identity under which a process is running**

1. Start **Task Manager**.
2. Click the **Processes** tab.
3. From the **View** menu, click **Select Columns**.

4. Select **User Name**, and click **OK**.

The user name (process identity) is now displayed.

Network Monitor (NetMon.exe)

NetMon is used to capture and monitor network traffic.

More Information

See the following Knowledge Base articles:

- Q243270, "HOW TO: Install Network Monitor in Windows 2000"
- Q148942, "HOW TO: Capture Network Traffic with Network Monitor"
- Q252876, "HOW TO: View HTTP Data Frames Using Network Monitor"
- Q294818, "Frequently Asked Questions About Network Monitor"

There are a couple of additional tools to capture the network trace when the client and the server are on the same machine (this can't be done with Netmon):

- **tcptrace.exe**. Available from www.pocketsoap.com. This is particularly useful for Web services since you can set it up to record and show traffic while your application runs. You can switch to Basic authentication and use tcptrace to see what credentials are being sent to the Web service.
- **packetmon.exe**. Available from www.analogx.com. This is a cut down version of Network Monitor, but much easier to configure.

Registry Monitor (regmon.exe)

This tool allows you to monitor registry access. It can be used to show read accesses and updates either from all processes or from a specified set of processes. This tool is very useful when you need to troubleshoot registry permission issues. It is available from www.sysinternals.com.

WFetch.exe

This tool is useful for troubleshooting connectivity issues between IIS and Web clients. In this scenario, you may need to view data that is not displayed in the Web browser, such as the HTTP headers that are included in the request and response packets.

More Information

For more information about this tool and the download, see the Knowledge Base article Q284285, "How to Use Wfetch.exe to Troubleshoot HTTP Connections".

Visual Studio .NET Tools

The Microsoft .NET Framework SDK security tools can be found at *http://msdn.microsoft.com/library/default.asp?url=/library/en-us/cptools/html/cpconnetframeworktools.asp*

More Information

See the following Knowledge Base articles:

- Q316365, "INFO: ROADMAP for How to Use the .NET Performance Counters"
- Q308626, "INFO: Roadmap for Debugging in .NET Framework and Visual Studio"
- Q317297, "INFO: Roadmap for Debugging Hangs, Memory Leaks in VB .NET"

WebServiceStudio

This tool can be used as a generic client to test the functionality of your Web service. It captures and displays the SOAP response and request packets.

You can download the tool from *http://www.gotdotnet.com/team/tools/web_svc/default.aspx*

Windows 2000 Resource Kit

Available from *http://www.microsoft.com/windows2000/techinfo/reskit/default.asp*

For a complete tools list, see *http://www.microsoft.com/windows2000/techinfo/reskit/tools/default.asp*

Index of How Tos

Building Secure ASP.NET Applications includes a series of How Tos that provide step-by-step instructions to help you learn and implement various key procedures used to develop secure solutions. This index lists the How Tos that are included.

ASP.NET

How To: Create a Custom Account to Run ASP.NET

How To: Use Forms Authentication with Active Directory

How To: Use Forms Authentication with SQL Server 2000

How To: Create GenericPrincipal Objects with Forms Authentication

Authentication and Authorization

How To: Implement Kerberos Delegation for Windows 2000

How To: Implement IPrincipal

Cryptography

How To: Create a DPAPI Library

How To: Use DPAPI (Machine Store) from ASP.NET

How To: Use DPAPI (User Store) from ASP.NET with Enterprise Services

How To: Create an Encryption Library

How To: Store an Encrypted Connection String in the Registry

Enterprise Services Security

How To: Use Role-based Security with Enterprise Services

Web Services Security

How To: Call a Web Service Using Client Certificates from ASP.NET

How To: Call a Web Service Using SSL

Remoting Security

How To: Host a Remote Object in a Windows Service

Secure Communication

How To: Set Up SSL on a Web Server

How To: Set Up Client Certificates

How To: Use IPSec to Secure Communication Between Two Servers

How To: Use SSL to Secure Communication with SQL Server 2000

How To:
Create a Custom Account
to Run ASP.NET

This How To describes how to create a least privileged local account to run the ASP.NET worker process (aspnet_wp.exe) or for impersonated identities in virtual directories. Although the procedures in this How To create a local account, the same concepts apply to a domain account.

ASP.NET Worker Process Identity

The default account for running ASP.NET, created at installation time, is a least privileged local account and is specified in machine.config as follows:

```
<processModel enable="true" userName="machine" password="AutoGenerate" />
```

This account is identified as ASPNET under Local Users and Groups, and has a strong password secured in the Local System Authority (LSA).

When you need to access network resources, such as a database, using the ASP.NET process identity, you can do one of the following:

- Use a domain account.
- Use "mirrored" local accounts (that is, accounts with matching usernames and passwords on two computers). You need to use this approach when the computers are in separate domains with no trust relationship or when the computers are separated by a firewall and you cannot open the ports required for NTLM or Kerberos authentication.

The simplest approach is to change the ASPNET account's password to a known value on the Web server and then create an account named ASPNET with the same password on the target computer. On the Web server, you must first change the ASPNET account password in Local Users and Groups and then replace the credentials on the <**processModel**> element in machine.config. You should not store encrypted passwords in the registry. For more details, see Chapter 8, "ASP.NET Security."

```
<processModel enable="true"
        userName="registry:HKLM\SOFTWARE\YourSecureApp\processModel\
                ASPNET_SETREG,userName"
        password="registry:HKLM\SOFTWARE\YourSecureApp\processModel\
                ASPNET_SETREG,password" . . ./>
```

You can use the steps presented in this How To to create a least privileged local account.

Impersonating Fixed Identities

You can set fixed identities for specific virtual directories by using the following setting in web.config. Use aspnet_setreg.exe to store encrypted credentials in the registry.

```
<identity impersonate="true"
        userName="registry:HKLM\SOFTWARE\YourSecureApp\
                identity\ASPNET_SETREG,userName"
        password="registry:HKLM\SOFTWARE\YourSecureApp\
                identity\ASPNET_SETREG,password" />
```

This approach is typically used when you have multiple Web sites on the same Web server that need to run under different identities; for example, in application hosting scenarios.

This How To describes how to create a least privileged local account. If administration is your primary concern, you can use a least privileged, constrained domain account with a strong password.

Notes

When considering the account used to run ASP.NET, remember the following:

- ASP.NET does not impersonate by default. As a result, any resource access performed by your Web application uses the ASP.NET process identity. In this event, Windows resources must have an access control list (ACL) that grants access to the ASP.NET process account.

- If you enable impersonation, your application accesses resources using the original caller's security context, or the anonymous Internet user account (by default IUSR_MACHINE), if IIS is configured for anonymous authentication. In this event, resources must have ACLs based on the original caller identity (or IUSR_MACHINE).

- Always adhere to the principle of least privilege when creating a custom account—give the minimum set of required privileges and permissions only.

- Avoid running ASP.NET using the SYSTEM account.

- Avoid granting the account the "Act as part of the operating system" privilege.

Summary

This How To includes the following procedures:

1. Create a New Local Account
2. Assign Minimum Privileges
3. Assign NTFS Permissions
4. Configure ASP.NET to Run Using the New Account

1. Create a New Local Account

This procedure creates a new local account. By default, it will be added to the local **Users** group.

► **To create a new local account**

1. Create a local account (for example, "CustomASPNET").

   Make sure you use a strong password for the account. Strong password should include at least seven characters, and use a mixture of uppercase and lowercase letters, numbers, and other characters such as *, ?, or $.

2. Clear the **User must change password at next logon** option.
3. Select the **Password never expires** option.

2. Assign Minimum Privileges

This procedure assigns the minimum set of privileges necessary to run ASP.NET.

► **To assign minimum privileges**

1. From the **Administrative Tools** programs group, start the **Local Security Policy** tool.
2. Expand **Local Policies**, and then select **User Rights Assignment**.

   A list of privileges is displayed in the right pane.

3. Assign the following privileges to the new account:
   - Access this computer from the network
   - Log on as a batch job
   - Log on as a service
   - Deny logon locally
   - Deny logon through Terminal Services

   Note: To assign a privilege to an account, double-click the privilege, and then click **Add** to select the required account.

4. Close the tool.

3. Assign NTFS Permissions

This procedure grants the custom ASP.NET account required NTFS permissions within the local file system.

Note: The steps in this procedure apply to the file system on the Web server (and not on a remote computer, where you may be duplicating the account, for network authentication purposes).

▶ **To assign NTFS permissions**

1. Start Windows Explorer and assign the appropriate permissions to the folders specified in Table 1.

   The fixed impersonation account referred to in Table 1 refers to the account that can be optionally configured using the **<identity>** element in web.config as shown below.

   ```
   userName="registry:HKLM\SOFTWARE\YourSecureApp\
           identity\ASPNET_SETREG,userName"
   password="registry:HKLM\SOFTWARE\YourSecureApp\
           identity\ASPNET_SETREG,password" />
   ```

In this example, aspnet_setreg.exe has been used to store the custom account credentials in encrypted format in the registry.

Table 1: Required NTFS permissions

Location	Required Permission	Account	Comments
Temporary ASP.NET Files: C:\WINNT\Microsoft.NET\ Framework\<version>\ Temporary ASP.NET Files	Full Control	Process and fixed impersonation accounts	This is the ASP.NET dynamic compilation location. Application code is generated in a discrete directory for each application beneath this folder. The tempdir attribute on the <compilation> element can be used to change this default location.
Temporary Folder: C:\WINNT\temp	Read/Write/ Delete	Process	Location used by Web services to generate serialization proxies. Note that the **Delete** permission is set using the **Advanced** button on the **Security** page of the Windows Explorer folder properties dialog box.

Location	Required Permission	Account	Comments
Application Virtual Directory: C:\inetpub\wwwroot\webapp1	Read	Process	The location of your Web application files (that is, your application's virtual root directory). By default, the Users group has the appropriate access rights.
Installation (%installroot) Hierarchy: (C:\WINNT\Microsoft.Net\Framework\v1.0.3705)	Read	Process and fixed impersonation accounts	ASP.NET must be able to access .NET Framework assemblies. By default, the Users group has the appropriate access rights.
Global Assembly Cache: C:\WINNT\assembly	Read	Process and fixed impersonation accounts	This is the global assembly cache. You cannot directly use Windows Explorer to edit ACLs for this folder. Instead, use a command Windows and run the following command: cacls %windir%\assembly /e /t /p domain\useraccount:R Alternatively, prior to using Windows Explorer, unregister shfusion.dll with the following command: regsvr32 –u shfusion.dll After setting permissions with Windows Explorer, re-register shfusion.dll with the following command: regsvr32 shfusion.dll
Web site root: C:\inetpub\wwwroot or the path that the default Web site points to	Read	Process	ASP.NET reads configuration files and monitors for file changes in this folder.
System Root: C:\WINNT\system32	Read	Process	For system DLLs loaded by the Framework.
Application Folder Hierarchy C:\ C:\inetpub C:\inetpub\wwwroot\ C:\inetpub\wwwroot\ mywebapp1	List Folder/ Read	Process	For file change notifications and the C# compiler (for file canonicalization reasons), the process account needs list folder and read data permissions to the application folder hierarchy. That is all parent folders all the way back to the root.

4. Configure ASP.NET to Run Using the New Account

This procedure edits machine.config to configure ASP.NET to run using the new account.

▶ **To configure ASP.NET to run using the new account**

1. At a command prompt, run aspnet_setreg.exe to add an encrypted version of your custom account's user name and password to the registry. For details about this utility and to download it, see article Q329290, "HOWTO: Use the ASP.NET Utility to Encrypt Credentials and Session State Connection Strings" in the Microsoft Knowledge Base.

   ```
   aspnet_setreg -k:SOFTWARE\YourSecureApp\processModel
                 -u:"CustomASPNET" -p:"YourStrongPassword"
   ```

2. Open machine.config using Visual Studio.NET or Notepad. Machine.config is located in the following folder:

   ```
   C:\WINNT\Microsoft.NET\Framework\v1.0.3705\CONFIG
   ```

3. Locate the <processModel> element and set the userName and password attributes to contain the following strings which point to the encrypted credential details.

   ```
   Default:
   <processModel userName="machine" password="AutoGenerate" . . ./>
   Becomes:
   <processModel
     userName="registry:HKLM\SOFTWARE\YourSecureApp\processModel\
               ASPNET_SETREG,userName"
     password="registry:HKLM\SOFTWARE\YourSecureApp\processmodel\
               ASPNET_SETREG,password" . . . />
   ```

4. Save the changes to machine.config

How To:
Use Forms Authentication
with Active Directory

ASP.NET Forms authentication allows users to identify themselves by entering credentials (a user name and password) into a Web Form. Upon receipt of these credentials, the Web application can authenticate the user by checking the user name and password combination against a data source.

This How To describes how to authenticate users against the Microsoft® Active Directory® directory service by using the Lightweight Directory Access Protocol (LDAP). It also describes how to retrieve a list of security groups and distribution lists that the user belongs to, to store this information in a **GenericPrincipal** object, and to store this into the **HttpContext.Current.User** property that flows with the request through the ASP.NET Web application. This can subsequently be used for .NET role-based authorization.

Requirements

The following items describe the recommended hardware, software, network infrastructure, skills and knowledge, and service packs you will need.

- Microsoft Windows® 2000 operating system
- Microsoft Visual Studio® .NET development system

The procedures in this How To also require that you have knowledge of the Microsoft Visual C#™ development tool.

Summary

This How To includes the following procedures:

1. Create a Web Application with a Logon Page
2. Configure the Web Application for Forms Authentication
3. Develop LDAP Authentication Code to Look Up the User in Active Directory
4. Develop LDAP Group Retrieval Code to Look Up the User's Group Membership
5. Authenticate the User and Create a Forms Authentication Ticket
6. Implement an Authentication Request Handler to Construct a **GenericPrincipal** Object
7. Test the Application

1. Create a Web Application with a Logon Page

This procedure creates a simple C# Web application that contains a logon page that allows a user to enter a user name and password and a default page that displays the identity name and group membership information associated with the current Web request.

▶ **To create a Web application with a logon page**

1. Start Visual Studio .NET and create a new C# ASP.NET Web Application called **FormsAuthAD**.

2. Use Solution Explorer to rename WebForm1.aspx to Logon.aspx.

3. Add a new assembly reference to System.DirectoryServices.dll. This provides access to the **System.DirectoryServices** namespace that contains managed types to help with Active Directory querying and manipulation.

4. Add the controls listed in Table 1 to Logon.aspx to create a simple logon form.

Table 1: Logon.aspx controls

Control Type	Text	ID
Label	Domain Name:	-
Label	User Name:	-
Label	Password	-
Text Box	-	txtDomainName
Text Box	-	txtUserName
Text Box	-	txtPassword
Button	Log On	btnLogon
Label		lblError

5. Set the **TextMode** property of txtPassword to **Password**.

6. In Solution Explorer, right-click **FormsAuthAd**, point to **Add**, and then click **Add Web Form**.

7. In the **Name** field, type **default.aspx**, and then click **Open**.

8. In Solution Explorer, right-click **default.aspx**, and then click **Set As Start Page**.

9. Double-click **default.aspx** to display the page load event handler.

10. Add the following code to the event handler to display the identity name associated with the current Web request.

```
Response.Write( HttpContext.Current.User.Identity.Name );
```

2. Configure the Web Application for Forms Authentication

This procedure edits the application's Web.config file to configure the application for Forms authentication.

▶ **To configure the Web application for forms authentication**

1. Use Solution Explorer to open Web.config.

2. Locate the **<authentication>** element and change the **mode** attribute to **Forms**.

3. Add the following **<forms>** element as a child of the authentication element and set the **loginUrl**, **name**, **timeout**, and **path** attributes as shown in the following.

```
<authentication mode="Forms">
  <forms loginUrl="logon.aspx" name="adAuthCookie" timeout="60" path="/">
  </forms>
</authentication>
```

4. Add the following **<authorization>** element beneath the **<authentication>** element. This will allow only authenticated users to access the application. The previously establish **loginUrl** attribute of the **<authentication>** element will redirect unauthenticated requests to the logon.aspx page.

```
<authorization>
  <deny users="?" />
  <allow users="*" />
</authorization>
```

5. Save Web.config.

6. Start the IIS Microsoft Management Console (MMC) snap-in.

7. Right-click the application's virtual directory, and then click **Properties**.

8. Click the **Directory Security** tab, and then click the **Edit** button in the **Anonymous access and authentication control** group.

9. Select the **Anonymous access** check box and clear the **Allow IIS to control password** check box.

10. Because the default anonymous account IUSR_MACHINE does not have permission to access Active Directory, create a new least privileged account and enter the account details in the **Authentication Methods** dialog box.

11. Click **OK**, and then click **OK** again to close the **Properties** dialog box.

12. Return to Visual Studio .NET and add an **<identity>** element beneath the **<authorization>** element in Web.config and set the impersonate attribute to **true**. This causes ASP.NET to impersonate the anonymous account specified earlier.

```
<identity impersonate="true" />
```

As a result of this configuration, all requests to the application will run under the security context of the configured anonymous account. The user will provide credentials through the Web form to authenticate against Active Directory, but the account used to access Active Directory will be the configured anonymous account.

3. Develop LDAP Authentication Code to Look Up the User in Active Directory

This procedure adds a new helper class to the Web application to encapsulate the LDAP code. The class will initially provide an **IsAuthenticated** method to validate a supplied domain, user name, and password against an Active Directory user object.

▶ **To develop LDAP authentication code to look up the user in Active Directory**

1. Add a new C# class file called LdapAuthentication.cs.

2. Add a reference to the System.DirectoryServices.dll assembly.

3. Add the following **using** statements to the top of LdapAuthentication.cs.

```
using System.Text;
using System.Collections;
using System.DirectoryServices;
```

4. Rename the existing namespace as **FormsAuthAD**.

5. Add two private strings to the **LdapAuthentication** class; one to hold the LDAP path to Active Directory and the other to hold a filter attribute used for searching Active Directory.

```
private string _path;
private string _filterAttribute;
```

6. Add a public constructor that can be used to initialize the Active Directory path.

```
public LdapAuthentication(string path)
{
  _path = path;
}
```

7. Add the following **IsAuthenticated** method that accepts a domain name, user name and password as parameters and returns **bool** to indicate whether or not the user with a matching password exists within Active Directory. The method initially attempts to bind to Active Directory using the supplied credentials. If this is successful, the method uses the **DirectorySearcher** managed class to search

for the specified user object. If located, the **_path** member is updated to point to the user object and the **_filterAttribute** member is updated with the common name attribute of the user object.

```
public bool IsAuthenticated(string domain, string username, string pwd)
{
  string domainAndUsername = domain + @"\" + username;
  DirectoryEntry entry = new DirectoryEntry( _path,
                                             domainAndUsername, pwd);

  try
  {
    // Bind to the native AdsObject to force authentication.
    Object obj = entry.NativeObject;
    DirectorySearcher search = new DirectorySearcher(entry);
    search.Filter = "(SAMAccountName=" + username + ")";
    search.PropertiesToLoad.Add("cn");
    SearchResult result = search.FindOne();
    if(null == result)
    {
      return false;
    }
    // Update the new path to the user in the directory
    _path = result.Path;
    _filterAttribute = (String)result.Properties["cn"][0];
  }
  catch (Exception ex)
  {
    throw new Exception("Error authenticating user. " + ex.Message);
  }
  return true;
}
```

4. Develop LDAP Group Retrieval Code to Look Up the User's Group Membership

This procedure extends the **LdapAuthentication** class to provide a **GetGroups** method which will retrieve the list of groups that the current user is a member of. The **GetGroups** method will return the group list as a pipe separated string, as in the following.

```
"Group1|Group2|Group3|"
```

► **To develop LDAP group retrieval code to look up the user's group membership**

1. Add the following implementation of the **GetGroups** method to the
   LdapAuthentication class.

```
public string GetGroups()
{
  DirectorySearcher search = new DirectorySearcher(_path);
  search.Filter = "(cn=" + _filterAttribute + ")";
  search.PropertiesToLoad.Add("memberOf");
  StringBuilder groupNames = new StringBuilder();
  try
  {
    SearchResult result = search.FindOne();
    int propertyCount = result.Properties["memberOf"].Count;
    String dn;
    int equalsIndex, commaIndex;

    for( int propertyCounter = 0; propertyCounter < propertyCount;
         propertyCounter++)
    {
      dn = (String)result.Properties["memberOf"][propertyCounter];

      equalsIndex = dn.IndexOf("=", 1);
      commaIndex = dn.IndexOf(",", 1);
      if (-1 == equalsIndex)
      {
        return null;
      }
      groupNames.Append(dn.Substring((equalsIndex + 1),
                        (commaIndex - equalsIndex) - 1));
      groupNames.Append("|");
    }
  }
  catch(Exception ex)
  {
    throw new Exception("Error obtaining group names. " + ex.Message);
  }
  return groupNames.ToString();
}
```

5. Authenticate the User and Create a Forms Authentication Ticket

This procedure implements the **btnLogon_Click** event handler to authenticate users.
For authenticated users, you will then create a Forms authentication ticket that
contains the user's group list. You will then redirect the user to the original page that
they requested (before being redirected to the logon page).

▶ **To authenticate the user and create a forms authentication ticket**

1. Return to the Logon.aspx form and double-click the **Log On** button to create an empty **btnLogon_Click** event handler.

2. At the top of the file add the following **using** statement beneath the existing **using** statements. This provides access to the **FormsAuthentication** methods.

```
using System.Web.Security;
```

3. Add code to create a new instance of the **LdapAuthentication** class initialized to point to your LDAP Active Directory, as shown in the following code. Remember to change the path to point to your Active Directory server.

```
// Path to you LDAP directory server.
// Contact your network administrator to obtain a valid path.
string adPath = "LDAP://yourCompanyName.com/DC=yourCompanyName,DC=com";
LdapAuthentication adAuth = new LdapAuthentication(adPath);
```

4. Add the code that follows to perform the following steps:

   a. Authenticate the caller against Active Directory.

   b. Retrieve the list of groups that the user is a member of.

   c. Create a **FormsAuthenticationTicket** that contains the group list.

   d. Encrypt the ticket.

   e. Create a new cookie that contains the encrypted ticket.

   f. Add the cookie to the list of cookies returned to the user's browser.

```
try
{
  if(true == adAuth.IsAuthenticated(txtDomainName.Text,
                                    txtUserName.Text,
                                    txtPassword.Text))
  {
    // Retrieve the user's groups
    string groups = adAuth.GetGroups();
    // Create the authetication ticket
    FormsAuthenticationTicket authTicket =
        new FormsAuthenticationTicket(1,  // version
                                      txtUserName.Text,
                                      DateTime.Now,
                                      DateTime.Now.AddMinutes(60),
                                      false, groups);
    // Now encrypt the ticket.
    string encryptedTicket = FormsAuthentication.Encrypt(authTicket);
    // Create a cookie and add the encrypted ticket to the
    // cookie as data.
    HttpCookie authCookie =
                new HttpCookie(FormsAuthentication.FormsCookieName,
                               encryptedTicket);
```

```
            // Add the cookie to the outgoing cookies collection.
            Response.Cookies.Add(authCookie);

            // Redirect the user to the originally requested page
            Response.Redirect(
                    FormsAuthentication.GetRedirectUrl(txtUserName.Text,
                                                       false));
    }
    else
    {
        lblError.Text =
            "Authentication failed, check username and password.";
    }
}
catch(Exception ex)
{
    lblError.Text = "Error authenticating. " + ex.Message;
}
```

6. Implement an Authentication Request Handler to Construct a GenericPrincipal Object

This procedure implements the **Application_AuthenticateRequest** event handler within global.asax and creates a **GenericPrincipal** object for the currently authenticated user. This will contain the list of groups that the user is a member of, retrieved from the **FormsAuthenticationTicket** contained in the authentication cookie. Finally, you will associate the **GenericPrincipal** object with the current **HttpContext** object that is created for each Web request.

▶ **To implement an authentication request handler to construct a GenericPricipal object**

1. Use Solution Explorer to open global.asax.cs.

2. Add the following **using** statements to the top of the file.

```
using System.Web.Security;
using System.Security.Principal;
```

3. Locate the **Application_AuthenticateRequest** event handler and add the following code to obtain the cookie that contains the encrypted **FormsAuthenticationTicket**, from the cookie collection passed with the request.

```
// Extract the forms authentication cookie
string cookieName = FormsAuthentication.FormsCookieName;
HttpCookie authCookie = Context.Request.Cookies[cookieName];

if(null == authCookie)
{
```

```
   // There is no authentication cookie.
   return;
}
```

4. Add the following code to extract and decrypt the **FormsAuthenticationTicket** from the cookie.

```
FormsAuthenticationTicket authTicket = null;
try
{
   authTicket = FormsAuthentication.Decrypt(authCookie.Value);
}
catch(Exception ex)
{
   // Log exception details (omitted for simplicity)
   return;
}

if (null == authTicket)
{
   // Cookie failed to decrypt.
   return;
}
```

5. Add the following code to parse out the pipe separate list of group names attached to the ticket when the user was originally authenticated.

```
// When the ticket was created, the UserData property was assigned a
// pipe delimited string of group names.
String[] groups = authTicket.UserData.Split(new char[]{'|'});
```

6. Add the following code to create a **GenericIdentity** object with the user name obtained from the ticket name and a **GenericPrincipal** object that contains this identity together with the user's group list.

```
// Create an Identity object
GenericIdentity id = new GenericIdentity(authTicket.Name,
                                   "LdapAuthentication");

// This principal will flow throughout the request.
GenericPrincipal principal = new GenericPrincipal(id, groups);
// Attach the new principal object to the current HttpContext object
Context.User = principal;
```

7. Test the Application

This procedure uses the Web application to request the default.aspx page. You will be redirected to the logon page for authentication. Upon successful authentication, your browser will be redirected to the originally requested default.aspx page. This will extract and display the list of groups that the authenticated user belongs to from the **GenericPrincipal** object that has been associated with the current request by the authentication process.

▶ **To test the application**

1. On the **Build** menu, click **Build Solution**.

2. In Solution Explorer, right-click default.aspx, and then click **View in Browser**.

3. Enter a valid domain name, user name, and password and then click **Log On**.

4. If you are successfully authenticated, you should be redirected back to default.aspx. The code on this page should display the user name of the authenticated user.

   To see the list of groups the authenticated user is a member of, add the following code at the end of the **Application_AuthenticateRequest** event handler in the global.aspx.cs file.

   ```
   Response.Write("Groups: " + authTicket.UserData + "<br>");
   ```

How To:
Use Forms Authentication
with SQL Server 2000

Web applications that use Forms authentication often store user credentials (user names and passwords) together with associated role or group lists in Microsoft® SQL Server™ 2000.

This How To describes how to securely look up user names and validate passwords against SQL Server 2000. There are two key concepts for storing user credentials securely:

- **Storing password digests**. For security reasons, passwords should not be stored in clear text in the database. This How To describes how to create and store a one-way hash of a user's password rather than the password itself. This approach is preferred to storing an encrypted version of the user's password in order to avoid the key management issues associated with encryption techniques.

    For added security and to mitigate the threat associated with dictionary attacks, the approach described in this How To combines a salt (a cryptographically generated random number) with the password, prior to creating the password hash.

Important: The one drawback of not storing passwords in the database is that if a user forgets a password, it cannot be recovered. As a result, your application should use password hints and store them alongside the password digest within the database.

- **Validating user input**. Where user input is passed to SQL commands, for example as string literals in comparison or pattern matching statements, great care should be taken to validate the input, to ensure that the resulting commands do not contain syntax errors and also to ensure that a hacker cannot cause your application to run arbitrary SQL commands. Validating the supplied user name during a logon process is particularly vital as your application's security model is entirely dependent on being able to correctly and securely authenticate users.

    For more information about validating user input for SQL commands and for validation functions, see "SQL Injection Attacks" in Chapter 12, "Data Access Security."

Requirements

The following items describe the recommended hardware, software, network infrastructure, skills and knowledge, and service packs you will need.

- Microsoft Windows® 2000 operating system
- Microsoft Visual Studio® .NET development system
- Microsoft SQL Server 2000

The procedures in this How To also require that you have knowledge of Web development with the Microsoft Visual C#™ development tool.

Summary

This How To includes the following procedures:

1. Create a Web Application with a Logon Page
2. Configure the Web Application for Forms Authentication
3. Develop Functions to Generate a Hash and Salt value
4. Create a User Account Database
5. Use ADO.NET to Store Account Details in the Database
6. Authenticate User Credentials against the Database
7. Test the Application

1. Create a Web Application with a Logon Page

This procedure creates a simple C# Web application that contains a logon page that allows a user to enter a username and password.

▶ **To create a Web application with a logon page**

1. Start Visual Studio .NET and create a new C# ASP.NET Web application called **FormsAuthSQL**.
2. Use Solution Explorer to rename WebForm1.aspx to Logon.aspx
3. Add the controls listed in Table 1 to Logon.aspx to create a simple logon form.

Table 1: Logon.aspx controls

Control Type	Text	ID
Label	User Name:	-
Label	Password	-
Text Box	-	txtUserName
Text Box	-	txtPassword
Button	Register	btnRegister
Button	Logon	btnLogon
Label	-	lblMessage

Your Web page should resemble the one illustrated in Figure 1.

Figure 1
Logon page Web form

4. Set the **TextMode** property of the **txtPassword** to **Password**.

2. Configure the Web Application for Forms Authentication

This procedure edits the application's Web.config file to configure the application for Forms authentication.

▶ **To configure the Web application for Forms authentication**

1. Use Solution Explorer to open Web.config.
2. Locate the **<authentication>** element and change the **mode** attribute to **Forms**.
3. Add the following **<forms>** element as a child of the **<authentication>** element and set the **loginUrl**, **name**, **timeout**, and **path** attributes as follows.

```
<authentication mode="Forms">
  <forms loginUrl="logon.aspx" name="sqlAuthCookie" timeout="60" path="/">
  </forms>
</authentication>
```

4. Add the following **<authorization>** element beneath the **<authentication>** element. This will allow only authenticated users to access the application. The previously established **loginUrl** attribute of the **<authentication>** element will redirect unauthenticated requests to the logon.aspx page.

```
<authorization>
  <deny users="?" />
  <allow users="*" />
</authorization>
```

3. Develop Functions to Generate a Hash and Salt value

This procedure adds two utility methods to your Web application; one to generate a random salt value, and one to create a hash based on a supplied password and salt value.

▶ **To develop functions to generate a hash and salt value**

1. Open Logon.aspx.cs and add the following **using** statements to the top of the file beneath the existing **using** statements.

```
using System.Security.Cryptography;
using System.Web.Security;
```

2. Add the following static method to the **WebForm1** class to generate a random salt value and return it as a Base 64 encoded string.

```
private static string CreateSalt(int size)
{
  // Generate a cryptographic random number using the cryptographic
  // service provider
  RNGCryptoServiceProvider rng = new RNGCryptoServiceProvider();
  byte[] buff = new byte[size];
  rng.GetBytes(buff);
  // Return a Base64 string representation of the random number
  return Convert.ToBase64String(buff);
}
```

3. Add the following static method to generate a hash value based on a supplied password and salt value.

```
private static string CreatePasswordHash(string pwd, string salt)
{
  string saltAndPwd = String.Concat(pwd, salt);
  string hashedPwd =
        FormsAuthentication.HashPasswordForStoringInConfigFile(
                                    saltAndPwd, "SHA1");
  return hashedPwd;
}
```

4. Create a User Account Database

This procedure creates a new user account database in SQL Server that contains a single users table and a stored procedure used to query the user database.

► **To create a user account database**

1. On the **Microsoft SQL Server programs** menu, click **Query Analyzer**, and then connect to your local SQL Server.

2. Enter the following SQL script. Note that you must replace "LocalMachine" with your own computer name towards the end of the script.

```
USE master
GO
-- create a database for the security information
IF EXISTS (SELECT * FROM   master..sysdatabases WHERE  name = 'UserAccounts')
   DROP DATABASE UserAccounts
GO
CREATE DATABASE UserAccounts
GO
USE UserAccounts
GO
CREATE TABLE [Users] (
  [UserName] [varchar] (255) NOT NULL ,
  [PasswordHash] [varchar] (40) NOT NULL ,
  [salt] [varchar] (10) NOT NULL,
  CONSTRAINT [PK_Users] PRIMARY KEY  CLUSTERED
  (
    [UserName]
  )  ON [PRIMARY]
) ON [PRIMARY]
GO
-- create stored procedure to register user details
CREATE PROCEDURE RegisterUser
@userName varchar(255),
@passwordHash varchar(40),
@salt varchar(10)
AS
INSERT INTO Users VALUES(@userName, @passwordHash, @salt)
GO
-- create stored procedure to retrieve user details
CREATE PROCEDURE LookupUser
@userName varchar(255)
AS
SELECT PasswordHash, salt
FROM Users
WHERE UserName = @userName
GO
-- Add a login for the local ASPNET account
-- In the following statements, replace LocalMachine with your
-- local machine name
```

```
exec sp_grantlogin [LocalMachine\ASPNET]
-- Add a database login for the UserAccounts database for the ASPNET account
exec sp_grantdbaccess [LocalMachine\ASPNET]
-- Grant execute permissions to the LookupUser and RegisterUser stored procs
grant execute on LookupUser to [LocalMachine\ASPNET]
grant execute on RegisterUser to [LocalMachine\ASPNET]
```

3. Run the query to create the **UserAccounts** database.

4. Exit Query Manager.

5. Use ADO.NET to Store Account Details in the Database

This procedure modifies the Web application code to store the supplied user name, generated password hash and salt value in the database.

▶ **To use ADO.NET to store account details in the database**

1. Return to Visual Studio .NET and double-click the **Register** button on the Web form to create a button click event handler.

2. Add the following code to the method.

```
string salt = CreateSalt(5);
string passwordHash = CreatePasswordHash(txtPassword.Text,salt);
try
{
   StoreAccountDetails( txtUserName.Text, passwordHash, salt);
}
catch(Exception ex)
{
   lblMessage.Text = ex.Message;
}
```

3. Add the following **using** statement at the top of the file, beneath the existing **using** statements.

```
using System.Data.SqlClient;
```

4. Add the **StoreAccountDetails** utility method using the following code. This code uses ADO.NET to connect to the **UserAccounts** database and stores the supplied username, password hash and salt value in the **Users** table.

```
private void StoreAccountDetails( string userName,
                                  string passwordHash,
                                  string salt )
{
```

```
// See "How To Use DPAPI (Machine Store) from ASP.NET" for information
// about securely storing connection strings.
SqlConnection conn = new SqlConnection( "Server=(local);" +
                                        "Integrated Security=SSPI;" +
                                        "database=UserAccounts");

SqlCommand cmd = new SqlCommand("RegisterUser", conn );
cmd.CommandType = CommandType.StoredProcedure;
SqlParameter sqlParam = null;

sqlParam = cmd.Parameters.Add("@userName", SqlDbType.VarChar, 255);
sqlParam.Value = userName;

sqlParam = cmd.Parameters.Add("@passwordHash ", SqlDbType.VarChar, 40);
sqlParam.Value = passwordHash;

sqlParam = cmd.Parameters.Add("@salt", SqlDbType.VarChar, 10);
sqlParam.Value = salt;

try
{
  conn.Open();
  cmd.ExecuteNonQuery();
}
catch( Exception ex )
{
  // Code to check for primary key violation (duplicate account name)
  // or other database errors omitted for clarity
  throw new Exception("Exception adding account. " + ex.Message);
}
finally
{
  conn.Close();
}
}
```

6. Authenticate User Credentials Against the Database

This procedure develops ADO.NET code to look up the supplied user name in the database and validate the supplied password, by matching password hashes.

Note: In many Forms authentication scenarios where you are using .NET role-based authorization, you may also retrieve the roles that the user belongs to from the database at this point. These can subsequently be used to generate a **GenericPrincipal** object that can be associated with authenticated Web requests, for .NET authorization purposes.

For more information about constructing a Forms authentication ticket incorporating a user's role details, see "How To: Use Forms Authentication with GenericPrincipal Objects" in the Reference section of this book.

▶ **To authenticate user credentials against the database**

1. Return to the Logon.aspx.cs and add the **VerifyPassword** private helper method as shown in the following code.

```csharp
private bool VerifyPassword(string suppliedUserName,
                           string suppliedPassword )
{
  bool passwordMatch = false;
  // Get the salt and pwd from the database based on the user name.
  // See "How To: Use DPAPI (Machine Store) from ASP.NET," "How To: Use DPAPI
  // (User Store) from Enterprise Services," and "How To: Create a DPAPI
  // Library" for more information about how to use DPAPI to securely store
  // connection strings.
  SqlConnection conn = new SqlConnection( "Server=(local);" +
                                          "Integrated Security=SSPI;" +
                                          "database=UserAccounts");
  SqlCommand cmd = new SqlCommand( "LookupUser", conn );
  cmd.CommandType = CommandType.StoredProcedure;

  SqlParameter sqlParam = cmd.Parameters.Add("@userName",
                                             SqlDbType.VarChar, 255);
  sqlParam.Value = suppliedUserName;
  try
  {
    conn.Open();
    SqlDataReader reader = cmd.ExecuteReader();
    reader.Read(); // Advance to the one and only row
    // Return output parameters from returned data stream
    string dbPasswordHash = reader.GetString(0);
    string salt = reader.GetString(1);
    reader.Close();
    // Now take the salt and the password entered by the user
    // and concatenate them together.
    string passwordAndSalt = String.Concat(suppliedPassword, salt);
    // Now hash them
    string hashedPasswordAndSalt =
              FormsAuthentication.HashPasswordForStoringInConfigFile(
                                           passwordAndSalt, "SHA1");
    // Now verify them.
    passwordMatch = hashedPasswordAndSalt.Equals(dbPasswordHash);
  }
  catch (Exception ex)
  {
    throw new Exception("Execption verifying password. " + ex.Message);
  }
  finally
  {
    conn.Close();
  }
  return passwordMatch;
}
```

7. Test the Application

This procedure tests the application. You will register a user, which results in the user name, password hash and salt value being added to the **Users** table in the **UserAccounts** database. You will then log on the same user to ensure the correct operation of the password verification routines.

▶ **To test the application**

1. Return to the Logon form and double-click the **Logon** button to create a button click event handler.

2. Add the following code to the **Logon** button click event handler to call the **VerifyPassword** method and display a message based on whether or not the supplied user name and password are valid.

```
bool passwordVerified = false;
try
{
    passwordVerified = VerifyPassword(txtUserName.Text,txtPassword.Text);
}
catch(Exception ex)
{
  lblMessage.Text = ex.Message;
  return;
}
if (passwordVerified == true )
{
  // The user is authenticated
  // At this point, an authentication ticket is normally created
  // This can subsequently be used to generate a GenericPrincipal
  // object for .NET authorization purposes
  // For details, see "How To: Use Forms authentication with GenericPrincipal
  // objects
  lblMessage.Text = "Logon successful: User is authenticated";
}
else
{
  lblMessage.Text = "Invalid username or password";
}
```

3. On the **Build** menu, click **Build Solution**.

4. In Solution Explorer, right-click logon.aspx, and then click **View in Browser**.

5. Enter a user name and password, and then click **Register**.

6. Use SQL Server Enterprise Manager to view the contents of the **Users** table. You should see a new row for the new user name together with a generated password hash.

7. Return to the Logon Web page, re-enter the password, and then click **Logon**. You should see the message "Logon successful: User is authenticated."

8. Now enter an invalid password (leaving the user name the same). You should see the message "Invalid username or password."

9. Close Internet Explorer.

Additional Resources

For more information, see the following:

- "How To: Use DPAPI (Machine Store) from ASP.NET"
- "How To: Use Forms Authentication with GenericPrincipal Objects"
- "SQL Injection Attacks" in Chapter 12, "Data Access Security"

How To:
Create GenericPrincipal Objects with Forms Authentication

Applications that use Forms authentication will often want to use the **GenericPrincipal** class (in conjunction with the **FormsIdentity** class), to create a non-Windows specific authorization scheme, independent of a Windows domain.

For example, an application may:

- Use Forms authentication to obtain user credentials (user name and password).
- Validate the supplied credentials against a data store; for example, a database or Microsoft® Active Directory® directory service.
- Create **GenericPrincipal** and **FormsIdentity** objects based on values retrieved from the data store. These may include a user's role membership details.
- Use these objects to make authorization decisions.

This How To describes how to create a Forms-based Web application that authenticates users and creates a custom Forms authentication ticket that contains user and role information. It also shows you how to map this information into **GenericPrincipal** and **FormsIdentity** objects and associate the new objects with the HTTP Web request context, allowing them to be used for authorization logic within your application.

This How To focuses on the construction of the **GenericPrincipal** and **FormsIdentity** objects together with the processing of the forms authentication ticket. For details about how to authenticate users against Active Directory and SQL Server 2000, see the following related How Tos in the Reference section of this book:

- "How to Use Forms Authentication with Active Directory"
- "How to Use Forms Authentication with SQL Server 2000"

Requirements

The following items describe the recommended hardware, software, network infrastructure, skills and knowledge, and service packs you will need.

- Microsoft SQL Server™ 2000
- Microsoft Visual Studio® .NET development system

The procedures in this article also require that you have knowledge of ASP.NET Web development with the Microsoft Visual C#™ development tool.

Summary

This How To includes the following procedures:

1. Create a Web Application with a Logon Page
2. Configure the Web Application for Forms Authentication
3. Generate an Authentication Ticket for Authenticated Users
4. Construct **GenericPrincipal** and **FormsIdentity** Objects
5. Test the Application

1. Create a Web Application with a Logon Page

This procedure creates a new ASP.NET Web application. The application will contain two pages; a default page that only authenticated users are allowed to access, and a logon page used to collect user credentials.

▶ **To create a Web application with a logon page**

1. Start Visual Studio .NET and create a new C# ASP.NET Web Application called **GenericPrincipalApp**.
2. Rename WebForm1.aspx to Logon.aspx.
3. Add the following controls to Logon.aspx to create a logon form.

Table 1: Logon.aspx controls

Control Type	Text	ID
Label	User Name:	-
Label	Password	-
Text Box	-	txtUserName
Text Box	-	txtPassword
Button	Logon	btnLogon

4. Set the **TextMode** property of the password Text Box control to **Password**.

5. In Solution Explorer, right-click **GenericPrincipalApp**, point to **Add**, and then click **Add Web Form**.

6. Enter **default.aspx** as the new form's name, and then click **Open**.

2. Configure the Web Application for Forms Authentication

► **To edit the application's Web.config file to configure the application for Forms authentication**

1. Use Solution Explorer to open Web.config.

2. Locate the <**authentication**> element and change the **mode** attribute to **Forms**.

3. Add the following <**forms**> element as a child of the <**authentication**> element and set the **loginUrl**, **name**, **timeout**, and **path** attributes as follows:

```
<authentication mode="Forms">
  <forms loginUrl="logon.aspx" name="AuthCookie" timeout="60" path="/">
  </forms>
</authentication>
```

4. Add the following <**authorization**> element beneath the <**authentication**> element. This allows only authenticated users to access the application. The previously established **loginUrl** attribute of the <**authentication**> element redirects unauthenticated requests to the Logon.aspx page.

```
<authorization>
  <deny users="?" />
  <allow users="*" />
</authorization>
```

3. Generate an Authentication Ticket for Authenticated Users

This procedure writes code to generate an authentication ticket for authenticated users. The authentication ticket is a type of cookie used by the ASP.NET **FormsAuthenticationModule**.

The authentication code typically involves looking up the supplied user name and password against either a custom database or against Active Directory.

For information about performing these lookups, see the following How To articles in the Reference section of this book:

● "How To: Use Forms Authentication with Active Directory"

● "How To: Use Forms Authentication with SQL Server 2000"

▶ **To generate an authentication ticket for authenticated users**

1. Open the Logon.aspx.cs file and the following **using** statement to the top of the file beneath the existing **using** statements:

```
using System.Web.Security;
```

2. Add the following private helper method to the WebForm1 class called **IsAuthenticated,** which is used to validate user names and passwords to authenticate users. This code assumes that all user name and password combinations are valid.

```
private bool IsAuthenticated( string username, string password )
{
  // Lookup code omitted for clarity
  // This code would typically validate the user name and password
  // combination against a SQL database or Active Directory
  // Simulate an authenticated user
  return true;
}
```

3. Add the following private helper method called **GetRoles,** which is used to obtain the set of roles that the user belongs to.

```
private string GetRoles( string username, string password )
{
  // Lookup code omitted for clarity
  // This code would typically look up the role list from a database table.
  // If the user was being authenticated against Active Directory, the
  // Security groups and/or distribution lists that the user belongs to may be
  // used instead

  // This GetRoles method returns a pipe delimited string containing roles
  // rather than returning an array, because the string format is convenient
  // for storing in the authentication ticket / cookie, as user data
  return "Senior Manager|Manager|Employee";
}
```

4. Display the Logon.aspx form in Designer mode and double-click the **Logon** button to create a click event handler.

5. Add a call to the **IsAuthenticated** method, supplying the user name and password captured through the logon form. Assign the return value to a variable of type **bool,** which indicates whether or not the user is authenticated.

```
bool isAuthenticated = IsAuthenticated( txtUserName.Text,
                                        txtPassword.Text );
```

6. If the user is authenticated, add a call to the **GetRoles** method to obtain the user's role list.

```
if (isAuthenticated == true )
{
  string roles = GetRoles( txtUserName.Text, txtPassword.Text );
```

7. Create a new forms authentication ticket that contains the user name, an expiration time, and the list of roles that the user belongs to. Note that the user data property of the authentication ticket is used to store the user's role list. Also note that the following code creates a non-persistent ticket, although whether or not the ticket / cookie is persistent is dependent upon your application scenario.

```
// Create the authentication ticket
FormsAuthenticationTicket authTicket = new
     FormsAuthenticationTicket(1,                          // version
                          txtUserName.Text,                // user name
                          DateTime.Now,                    // creation
                          DateTime.Now.AddMinutes(60),// Expiration
                          false,                           // Persistent
                          roles );                         // User data
```

8. Add code to create an encrypted string representation of the ticket and store it as data within an **HttpCookie** object.

```
// Now encrypt the ticket.
string encryptedTicket = FormsAuthentication.Encrypt(authTicket);
// Create a cookie and add the encrypted ticket to the
// cookie as data.
HttpCookie authCookie =
          new HttpCookie(FormsAuthentication.FormsCookieName,
                         encryptedTicket);
```

9. Add the cookie to the cookies collection returned to the user's browser.

```
// Add the cookie to the outgoing cookies collection.
Response.Cookies.Add(authCookie);
```

10. Redirect the user to the originally requested page

```
// Redirect the user to the originally requested page
Response.Redirect( FormsAuthentication.GetRedirectUrl(
                                      txtUserName.Text,
                                      false ));
}
```

4. Construct GenericPrincipal and FormsIdentity Objects

This procedure implements an application authentication event handler and constructs **GenericPrincipal** and **FormsIdentity** objects based on information contained within the authentication ticket.

▶ **To construct GenericPrincipal and FormsIdentity objects**

1. From Solution Explorer, open global.asax.

2. Switch to code view and add the following **using** statements to the top of the file:

```
using System.Web.Security;
using System.Security.Principal;
```

3. Locate the **Application_AuthenticateRequest** event handler and add the following code to obtain the forms authentication cookie from the cookie collection passed with the request.

```
// Extract the forms authentication cookie
string cookieName = FormsAuthentication.FormsCookieName;
HttpCookie authCookie = Context.Request.Cookies[cookieName];

if(null == authCookie)
{
  // There is no authentication cookie.
  return;
}
```

4. Add the following code to extract and decrypt the authentication ticket from the forms authentication cookie.

```
FormsAuthenticationTicket authTicket = null;
try
{
  authTicket = FormsAuthentication.Decrypt(authCookie.Value);
}
catch(Exception ex)
{
  // Log exception details (omitted for simplicity)
  return;
}

if (null == authTicket)
{
  // Cookie failed to decrypt.
  return;
}
```

5. Add the following code to parse out the pipe separate list of role names attached to the ticket when the user was originally authenticated.

```
// When the ticket was created, the UserData property was assigned a
// pipe delimited string of role names.
string[] roles = authTicket.UserData.Split(new char[]{'|'});
```

6. Add the following code to create a **FormsIdentity** object with the user name obtained from the ticket name and a **GenericPrincipal** object that contains this identity together with the user's role list.

```
// Create an Identity object
FormsIdentity id = new FormsIdentity( authTicket );

// This principal will flow throughout the request.
GenericPrincipal principal = new GenericPrincipal(id, roles);
// Attach the new principal object to the current HttpContext object
Context.User = principal;
```

5. Test the Application

This procedure adds code to the default.aspx page to display information from the **GenericPrincipal** object attached to the current **HttpContext** object, to confirm that the object has been correctly constructed and assigned to the current Web request. You will then build and test the application.

► **To test the application**

1. In Solution Explorer, double-click default.aspx.
2. Double-click the default.aspx Web form to display the page load event handler.
3. Scroll to the top of the file and add the following **using** statement beneath the existing **using** statements.

```
using System.Security.Principal;
```

4. Return to the page load event handler and add the following code to display the identity name attached to the **GenericPrincipal** associated with the current Web request.

```
IPrincipal p = HttpContext.Current.User;
Response.Write( "Authenticated Identity is: " +
                p.Identity.Name );
Response.Write( "<p>" );
```

5. Add the following code to test role membership for the current authenticated identity.

```
if ( p.IsInRole("Senior Manager") )
  Response.Write( "User is in Senior Manager role<p>" );
else
  Response.Write( "User is not in Senior Manager role<p>" );

if ( p.IsInRole("Manager") )
  Response.Write( "User is in Manager role<p>" );
else
  Response.Write( "User is not in Manager role<p>" );

if ( p.IsInRole("Employee") )
  Response.Write( "User is in Employee role<p>" );
else
  Response.Write( "User is not in Employee role<p>" );

if ( p.IsInRole("Sales") )
  Response.Write( "User is in Sales role<p>" );
else
  Response.Write( "User is not in Sales role<p>" );
```

6. In Solution Explorer, right-click default.aspx, and then click **Set As Start Page**.

7. On the **Build** menu, click **Build Solution**. Eliminate any build errors.

8. Press **Ctrl+F5** to run the application. Because default.aspx is configured as the start up page, this is the initially requested page.

9. When you are redirected to the logon page (because you do not initially have an authentication ticket), enter a user name and password (any will do), and then click **Logon**.

10. Confirm that you are redirected to default.aspx and that the user identity and the correct role details are displayed. The user should be a member of the Senior Manager, Manager, and Employee role, but not a member of the Sales role.

Additional Resources

For more information, see the following related How Tos in the Reference section of this book:

- "How To: Use Forms Authentication with Active Directory"
- "How To: Use Forms Authentication with SQL Server 2000"

How To:
Implement Kerberos Delegation
for Windows 2000

By default, the Microsoft® Windows® 2000 operating system uses the Kerberos protocol for authentication. This How To describes how to configure Kerberos delegation, a powerful feature that allows a server, while impersonating a client, to access remote resources on behalf of the client.

Important: Delegation is a very powerful feature and is unconstrained on Windows 2000. It should be used with caution. Computers that are configured to support delegation should be under controlled access to prevent misuse of this feature.

Windows .NET Server will support a constrained delegation feature.

When a server impersonates a client, Kerberos authentication generates a delegate-level token (capable of being used to respond to network authentication challenges from remote computers) if the following conditions are met:

1. The client account that is being impersonated is not marked as sensitive and cannot be delegated in Microsoft Active Directory® directory service.

2. The server process account (the user account under which the server process is running, or the computer account if the process is running under the local SYSTEM account) is marked as trusted for delegation in Active Directory.

Notes

- For Kerberos delegation to be successful, all computers (clients and servers) must be part of a single Active Directory forest.

- If you impersonate within serviced components and want to flow the callers context through an Enterprise Services application, the application server that hosts Enterprise Services must have Hotfix Rollup 18.1 or greater.

  For more information, see INFO: Availability of Windows 2000 Post-Service Pack 2 COM+ Hotfix Rollup Package 18.1.

Requirements

The following items describe the recommended hardware, software, network infra-structure, skills and knowledge and service packs you will need: Windows 2000 Server with Active Directory.

Summary

This How To includes the following procedures:

1. Confirm that the Client Account is Configured for Delegation
2. Confirm that the Server Process Account is Trusted for Delegation

1. Confirm that the Client Account is Configured for Delegation

This procedure ensures that the client account is capable of being delegated.

▶ **To confirm that the client account is configured for delegation**

1. Log onto the domain controller using an administrator account.
2. On the taskbar, click the **Start** button, point to **Programs**, point to **Administrative Tools,** and then click **Active Directory Users and Computers**.
3. Under your domain, click the **Users** folder.
4. Right-click the user account that is to be delegated, and then click **Properties**.
5. Click the **Account** tab.
6. Within the **Account options** list, make sure **Account is sensitive and cannot be delegated** is not selected.
7. Click **OK** to close the **Properties** dialog box.

2. Confirm that the Server Process Account is Trusted for Delegation

This procedure ensures that the account used to run the server process (the process that performs impersonation) is allowed to delegate client accounts. You must configure the user account under which the server process runs, or if the process runs under the local SYSTEM account, you must configure the computer account. Perform the appropriate procedure that follows, depending on if your server process runs under a Windows account or a local SYSTEM account.

▶ **To confirm that the server process account is trusted for delegation if the server process runs under a Windows user account**

1. Within the **Users** folder of **Active Directory Users and Computers**, right-click the user account that is used to run the server process that will impersonate the client, and then click **Properties**.

2. Click the **Account** tab.

3. Within the **Account options** list, click **Account is trusted for delegation**.

▶ **To confirm that the server process account is trusted for delegation if the server process runs under the local SYSTEM account**

1. Right-click the **Computers** folder within **Active Directory Users and Computers**, and then click **Properties**.

2. Right-click the server computer (where the process that impersonates the client will be running), and then click **Properties**.

3. On the **General** page, click **Trust computer for delegation**.

References

- For a list of the files that are affected by the Windows 2000 Post-Service Pack 2 (SP2) COM+ hotfix package 18.1, see article Q313582, "INFO: Availability of Windows 2000 Post-Service Pack 2 COM+ Hotfix Rollup Package 18.1," in the Microsoft Knowledge Base.

- To see how to configure a complete delegation scenario, involving ASP.NET, Enterprise Services and SQL Server, see "Flowing the Original Caller to the Database" in Chapter 5, "Intranet Security."

How To:
Implement IPrincipal

The .NET Framework provides the **WindowsPrincipal** and **GenericPrincipal** classes, which provide basic role-checking functionality for Windows and non-Windows authentication mechanisms respectively. Both classes implement the **IPrincipal** interface. To be used for authorization, ASP.NET requires that these objects are stored in **HttpContext.User**. For Windows-based applications, they must be stored in **Thread.CurrentPrincipal**.

The functionality offered by these classes is sufficient for most application scenarios. Applications can explicitly call the **IPrincipal.IsInRole** method to perform programmatic role checks. The **Demand** method of the **PrincipalPermission** class, when used to demand that a caller belong to a particular role (either declaratively or imperatively) also results in a call to **IPrincipal.IsInRole**.

In some circumstances, you might need to develop your own principal implementations by creating a class that implements the **IPrincipal** interface. Any class that implements **IPrincipal** can be used for .NET authorization.

Reasons for implementing your own **IPrincipal** class include:

- You want extended role checking functionality. You might want methods that allow you to check whether a particular user is a member of multiple roles. For example:

```
CustomPrincipal.IsInAllRoles( "Role1", "Role2", "Role3" )
CustomPrincipal.IsInAnyRole( "Role1", "Role2", "Role3" )
```

- You want to implement an extra method or property that returns a list of roles in an array. For example:

```
string[] roles = CustomPrincipal.Roles;
```

- You want your application to enforce role hierarchy logic. For example, a Senior Manager may be considered higher up in the hierarchy than a Manager. This could be tested using methods like the following.

```
CustomPrincipal.IsInHigherRole("Manager");
CustomPrincipal.IsInLowerRole("Manager");
```

- You want to implement lazy initialization of the role lists. For example, you could dynamically load the role list only when a role check is requested.

This How To describes how to implement a custom **IPrincipal** class and use it for role-based authorization in an ASP.NET application that uses Forms authentication.

Requirements

The following items describe the recommended hardware, software, network infrastructure, skills and knowledge, and service packs you will need:

- Microsoft® Visual Studio® .NET development system

The procedures in this article also require that you have knowledge of ASP.NET Web development with the Microsoft Visual C#™ development tool.

Summary

This How To includes the following procedures:

1. Create a Simple Web Application
2. Configure the Web Application for Forms Authentication
3. Generate an Authentication Ticket for Authenticated Users
4. Create a Class that Implements and Extends **IPrincipal**
5. Create the **CustomPrincipal** Object
6. Test the Application

1. Create a Simple Web Application

This procedure creates a new ASP.NET Web application. The application will contain two pages, a default page that only authenticated users are allowed to access and a logon page used to collect user credentials.

▶ **To create a simple Web application**

1. Start Visual Studio .NET and create a new C# ASP.NET Web Application called **CustomPrincipalApp**.
2. Rename WebForm1.aspx to Logon.aspx.
3. Add the controls listed in Table 1 to Logon.aspx to create a logon form.

Table 1: Logon.aspx controls

Control Type	Text	ID
Label	User Name:	-
Label	Password	-
Text Box	-	txtUserName
Text Box	-	txtPassword
Button	Logon	btnLogon

4. Set the **TextMode** property of the password Text Box control to **Password**.

5. In **Solution Explorer**, right-click **CustomPrincipalApp**, point to **Add**, and then click **Add Web Form**.

6. Enter **default.aspx** as the new form's name, and then click **Open**.

2. Configure the Web Application for Forms Authentication

▶ **To edit the application's Web.config file to configure the application for Forms authentication**

1. Use **Solution Explorer** to open **Web.config**.

2. Locate the **<authentication>** element and change the **mode** attribute to **Forms**.

3. Add the following **<forms>** element as a child of the **<authentication>** element and set the **loginUrl**, **name**, **timeout**, and **path** attributes as follows:

```
<authentication mode="Forms">
  <forms loginUrl="logon.aspx" name="AuthCookie" timeout="60" path="/">
  </forms>
</authentication>
```

4. Add the following **<authorization>** element beneath the **<authentication>** element. This allows only authenticated users to access the application. The previously established **loginUrl** attribute of the **<authentication>** element redirects unauthenticated requests to the Logon.aspx page.

```
<authorization>
  <deny users="?" />
  <allow users="*" />
</authorization>
```

3. Generate an Authentication Ticket for Authenticated Users

This procedure writes code to generate an authentication ticket for authenticated users. The authentication ticket is a type of cookie used by the ASP.NET **FormsAuthenticationModule**.

The authentication code typically involves looking up the supplied user name and password against either a custom database or against Microsoft Active Directory® directory service.

For information about performing these lookups, see the following How To articles in the Reference section of this book:

- "How To: Use Forms Authentication with Active Directory"
- "How To: Use Forms Authentication with SQL Server 2000"

▶ **To generate an authentication ticket for authenticated users**

1. Open the Logon.aspx.cs file and the following **using** statement to the top of the file beneath the existing **using** statements.

```
using System.Web.Security;
```

2. Add the following private helper method to the WebForm1 class called **IsAuthenticated**, which is used to validate user names and passwords to authenticate users. This code assumes that all user name and password combinations are valid.

```
private bool IsAuthenticated( string username, string password )
{
  // Lookup code omitted for clarity
  // This code would typically validate the user name and password
  // combination against a SQL database or Active Directory
  // Simulate an authenticated user
  return true;
}
```

3. Add the following private helper method called **GetRoles**, which is used to obtain the set of roles that the user belongs to.

```
private string GetRoles( string username, string password )
{
  // Lookup code omitted for clarity
  // This code would typically look up the role list from a database table.
  // If the user was being authenticated against Active Directory, the
  // Security groups and/or distribution lists that the user belongs to may be
  // used instead

  // This GetRoles method returns a pipe delimited string containing roles
```

```
   // rather than returning an array, because the string format is convenient
   // for storing in the authentication ticket / cookie, as user data
   return "Senior Manager|Manager|Employee";
}
```

4. Display the Logon.aspx form in Designer mode, and then double-click the **Logon** button to create a click event handler.

5. Add a call to the **IsAuthenticated** method, supplying the user name and password captured through the logon form. Assign the return value to a variable of type **bool**, which indicates whether or not the user is authenticated.

```
bool isAuthenticated = IsAuthenticated( txtUserName.Text,
                                        txtPassword.Text );
```

6. If the user is authenticated, add a call to the **GetRoles** method to obtain the user's role list.

```
if (isAuthenticated == true )
{
   string roles = GetRoles( txtUserName.Text, txtPassword.Text );
```

7. Create a new forms authentication ticket that contains the user name, an expiration time, and the list of roles that the user belongs to. Note that the user data property of the authentication ticket is used to store the user's role list. Also note that the following code creates a non-persistent ticket, although whether or not the ticket / cookie is persistent is dependent upon your application scenario.

```
// Create the authentication ticket
FormsAuthenticationTicket authTicket = new
    FormsAuthenticationTicket(1,                          // version
                       txtUserName.Text,                  // user name
                       DateTime.Now,                      // creation
                       DateTime.Now.AddMinutes(60),// Expiration
                       false,                             // Persistent
                       roles );                           // User data
```

8. Add code to create an encrypted string representation of the ticket and store it as data within an **HttpCookie** object.

```
// Now encrypt the ticket.
string encryptedTicket = FormsAuthentication.Encrypt(authTicket);
// Create a cookie and add the encrypted ticket to the
// cookie as data.
HttpCookie authCookie =
            new HttpCookie(FormsAuthentication.FormsCookieName,
                       encryptedTicket);
```

9. Add the cookie to the cookies collection returned to the user's browser.

```
// Add the cookie to the outgoing cookies collection.
Response.Cookies.Add(authCookie);
```

10. Redirect the user to the originally requested page.

```
// Redirect the user to the originally requested page
Response.Redirect( FormsAuthentication.GetRedirectUrl(
                                       txtUserName.Text,
                                       false ));
}
```

4. Create a Class that Implements and Extends IPrincipal

This procedure creates a class that implements the **IPrincipal** interface. It also adds additional methods and properties to the class to provide additional role-based authorization functionality.

▶ **To create a class that implements and extends IPrincipal**

1. Add a new class called **CustomPrincipal** to the current project.

2. Add the following **using** statement to the top of CustomPrincipal.cs.

```
using System.Security.Principal;
```

3. Derive the **CustomPrincipal** class from the **IPrincipal** interface.

```
public class CustomPrincipal : IPrincipal
```

4. Add the following private member variables to the class to maintain the **IIdentity** object associated with the current principal and the principal's role list.

```
private IIdentity _identity;
private string [] _roles;
```

5. Modify the class' default constructor to accept an **IIdentity** object and array of roles. Use the supplied values to initialize the private member variables as shown below.

```
public CustomPrincipal(IIdentity identity, string [] roles)
{
  _identity = identity;
  _roles = new string[roles.Length];
  roles.CopyTo(_roles, 0);
  Array.Sort(_roles);
}
```

6. Implement the **IsInRole** method and **Identity** property defined by the **IPrincipal** interface as shown below.

```
// IPrincipal Implementation
public bool IsInRole(string role)
{
  return Array.BinarySearch( _roles, role ) >= 0 ? true : false;
}
public IIdentity Identity
{
  get
  {
    return _identity;
  }
}
```

7. Add the following two public methods which provide extended role-based checking functionality.

```
// Checks whether a principal is in all of the specified set of roles
public bool IsInAllRoles( params string [] roles )
{
  foreach (string searchrole in roles )
  {
    if (Array.BinarySearch(_roles, searchrole) < 0 )
      return false;
  }
  return true;
}
// Checks whether a principal is in any of the specified set of roles
public bool IsInAnyRoles( params string [] roles )
{
  foreach (string searchrole in roles )
  {
    if (Array.BinarySearch(_roles, searchrole ) > 0 )
      return true;
  }
  return false;
}
```

5. Create the CustomPrincipal Object

This procedure implements an application authentication event handler and constructs a **CustomPrincipal** object to represent the authenticated user based on information contained within the authentication ticket.

▶ **To construct the CustomPrincipal object**

1. From **Solution Explorer**, open **global.asax**.

2. Switch to code view, and then add the following **using** statements to the top of the file.

```
using System.Web.Security;
using System.Security.Principal;
```

3. Locate the **Application_AuthenticateRequest** event handler and add the following code to obtain the forms authentication cookie from the cookie collection passed with the request.

```
// Extract the forms authentication cookie
string cookieName = FormsAuthentication.FormsCookieName;
HttpCookie authCookie = Context.Request.Cookies[cookieName];

if(null == authCookie)
{
  // There is no authentication cookie.
  return;
}
```

4. Add the following code to extract and decrypt the authentication ticket from the forms authentication cookie.

```
FormsAuthenticationTicket authTicket = null;
try
{
  authTicket = FormsAuthentication.Decrypt(authCookie.Value);
}
catch(Exception ex)
{
  // Log exception details (omitted for simplicity)
  return;
}

if (null == authTicket)
{
  // Cookie failed to decrypt.
  return;
}
```

5. Add the following code to parse out the pipe separate list of role names attached to the ticket when the user was originally authenticated.

```
// When the ticket was created, the UserData property was assigned a
// pipe delimited string of role names.
string[] roles = authTicket.UserData.Split('|');
```

6. Add the following code to create a **FormsIdentity** object with the user name obtained from the ticket name and a **CustomPrincipal** object that contains this identity together with the user's role list.

```
// Create an Identity object
FormsIdentity id = new FormsIdentity( authTicket );

// This principal will flow throughout the request.
CustomPrincipal principal = new CustomPrincipal(id, roles);
// Attach the new principal object to the current HttpContext object
Context.User = principal;
```

5. Test the Application

This procedure adds code to the default.aspx page to display information from the **CustomPrincipal** object attached to the current **HttpContext** object, to confirm that the object has been correctly constructed and assigned to the current Web request. It also tests the role-based functionality supported by the new class.

▶ **To test the application**

1. In **Solution Explorer**, double-click **default.aspx**.
2. Double-click the default.aspx Web form to display the page load event handler.
3. Scroll to the top of the file and add the following **using** statement beneath the existing **using** statements.

```
using System.Security.Principal;
```

4. Return to the page load event handler and add the following code to display the identity name attached to the **CustomPrincipal** associated with the current Web request.

```
CustomPrincipal cp = HttpContext.Current.User as CustomPrincipal;
Response.Write( "Authenticated Identity is: " +
                cp.Identity.Name );
Response.Write( "<p>" );
```

5. Add the following code to test role membership for the current authenticated identity, using the standard **IsInRole** method and the additional **IsInAnyRoles** and **IsInAllRoles** methods supported by the **CustomPrincipal** class.

```
if ( cp.IsInRole("Senior Manager") )
{
  Response.Write( cp.Identity.Name + " is in the " + "Senior Manager Role" );
  Response.Write( "<p>" );
}
```

```
if ( cp.IsInAnyRoles("Senior Manager", "Manager", "Employee", "Sales") )
{
  Response.Write( cp.Identity.Name + " is in one of the specified roles");
  Response.Write( "<p>" );
}
if ( cp.IsInAllRoles("Senior Manager", "Manager", "Employee", "Sales") )
{
  Response.Write( cp.Identity.Name + " is in ALL of the specified roles" );
  Response.Write( "<p>" );
}
else
{
  Response.Write( cp.Identity.Name +
                    " is not in ALL of the specified roles" );
  Response.Write("<p>");
}

if ( cp.IsInRole("Sales") )
  Response.Write( "User is in Sales role<p>" );
else
  Response.Write( "User is not in Sales role<p>" );
```

6. In **Solution Explorer**, right-click **default.aspx**, and then click **Set As Start Page**.

7. On the **Build** menu, click **Build Solution**.

8. Press **CTRL+F5** to run the application. Because default.aspx is configured as the start up page, this is the initially requested page.

9. When you are redirected to the logon page (because you do not initially have an authentication ticket), enter a user name and password (any will do), and then click **Logon**.

10. Confirm that you are redirected to default.aspx and that the user identity and the correct role details are displayed. The user is a member of the Senior Manager, Manager and Employee roles, but not a member of the Sales role.

Additional Resources

For more information about Forms based authentication, see the following How Tos in the Reference section of this book:

- "How To: Create GenericPrincipal Objects with Forms Authentication"
- "How To: Use Forms Authentication with Active Directory"
- "How To: Use Forms Authentication with SQL Server 2000"

How To:
Create a DPAPI Library

Web applications often need to store security sensitive data, such as database connection strings and service account credentials in application configuration files. For security reasons, this type of information should never be stored in plain text and should always be encrypted prior to storage.

This How To describes how to create a managed class library that encapsulates calls to the Data Protection API (DPAPI) to encrypt and decrypt data. This library can then be used from other managed applications such as ASP.NET Web applications, Web services and Enterprise Services applications.

For related How To articles that use the DPAPI library created in this article, see the following articles in the Reference section of this book:

- "How To: Use DPAPI (Machine Store) from ASP.NET"
- "How To: Use DPAPI (User Store) from ASP.NET with Enterprise Services"

Notes

- Microsoft® Windows® 2000 operating system and later operating systems provide the Win32® Data Protection API (DPAPI) for encrypting and decrypting data.

- DPAPI is part of the Cryptography API (Crypto API) and is implemented in crypt32.dll. It consists of two methods, **CryptProtectData** and **CryptUnprotectData**.

- DPAPI is particularly useful in that it can eliminate the key management problem exposed to applications that use cryptography. While encryption ensures the data is secure, you must take additional steps to ensure the security of the key. DPAPI uses the password of the user account associated with the code that calls the DPAPI functions in order to derive the encryption key. As a result, the operating system (and not the application) manages the key.

- DPAPI can work with either the machine store or user store (which requires a loaded user profile). DPAPI defaults to the user store, although you can specify that the machine store be used by passing the CRYPTPROTECT_LOCAL_MACHINE flag to the DPAPI functions.

- The user profile approach affords an additional layer of security because it limits who can access the secret. Only the user who encrypts the data can decrypt the data. However, use of the user profile requires additional development effort when DPAPI is used from an ASP.NET Web application because you need to take explicit steps to load and unload a user profile (ASP.NET does not automatically load a user profile).

- The machine store approach is easier to develop because it does not require user profile management. However, unless an additional entropy parameter is used, it is less secure because any user on the computer can decrypt data. (Entropy is a random value designed to make deciphering the secret more difficult). The problem with using an additional entropy parameter is that this must be securely stored by the application, which presents another key management issue.

> **Note:** If you use DPAPI with the machine store, the encrypted string is specific to a given computer and therefore you must generate the encrypted data on every computer. Do not copy the encrypted data across computers in a farm or cluster.
>
> If you use DPAPI with the user store, you can decrypt the data on any computer with a roaming user profile.

Requirements

The following items describe the recommended hardware, software, network infrastructure, skills and knowledge, and service packs you will need:

- Microsoft Windows 2000
- Microsoft Visual Studio® .NET development system

The procedures in this How To also require that you have knowledge of the Microsoft Visual C#™ development tool.

Summary

This How To includes the following procedures:

1. Create a C# Class Library
2. Strong Name the Assembly (Optional)

1. Create a C# Class Library

This procedure creates a C# class library that exposes Encrypt and Decrypt methods. It encapsulates calls to the Win32 DPAPI functions.

► **To create a C# class library**

1. Start Visual Studio .NET and create a new Visual C# Class Library project called **DataProtection**.

2. Use Solution Explorer to rename class1.cs as DataProtection.cs.

3. Within DataProtection.cs, rename **class1** as **DataProtector** and rename the default constructor accordingly.

4. In Solution Explorer, right-click **DataProtection**, and then click **Properties**.

5. Click the **Configuration Properties** folder and set **Allow unsafe code blocks** to **True**.

6. Click **OK** to close the **Properties** dialog box.

7. Add the following **using** statements to the top of DataProtection.cs beneath the existing **using** statement.

```
using System.Text;
using System.Runtime.InteropServices;
```

8. Add the following **DllImport** statements to the top of the **DataProtector** class to allow the Win32 DPAPI functions together with the **FormatMessage** utility function to be called through P/Invoke.

```
[DllImport("Crypt32.dll", SetLastError=true,
          CharSet=System.Runtime.InteropServices.CharSet.Auto)]
private static extern bool CryptProtectData(
                              ref DATA_BLOB pDataIn,
                              String szDataDescr,
                              ref DATA_BLOB pOptionalEntropy,
                              IntPtr pvReserved,
                              ref CRYPTPROTECT_PROMPTSTRUCT pPromptStruct,
                              int dwFlags,
                              ref DATA_BLOB pDataOut);
[DllImport("Crypt32.dll", SetLastError=true,
          CharSet=System.Runtime.InteropServices.CharSet.Auto)]
private static extern bool CryptUnprotectData(
                              ref DATA_BLOB pDataIn,
                              String szDataDescr,
                              ref DATA_BLOB pOptionalEntropy,
                              IntPtr pvReserved,
                              ref CRYPTPROTECT_PROMPTSTRUCT pPromptStruct,
                              int dwFlags,
                              ref DATA_BLOB pDataOut);
[DllImport("kernel32.dll",
          CharSet=System.Runtime.InteropServices.CharSet.Auto)]
private unsafe static extern int FormatMessage(int dwFlags,
                                        ref IntPtr lpSource,
                                        int dwMessageId,
                                        int dwLanguageId,
                                        ref String lpBuffer, int nSize,
                                        IntPtr *Arguments);
```

9. Add the following structure definitions and constants used by the DPAPI functions.

```
[StructLayout(LayoutKind.Sequential, CharSet=CharSet.Unicode)]
internal struct DATA_BLOB
{
  public int cbData;
  public IntPtr pbData;
}

[StructLayout(LayoutKind.Sequential, CharSet=CharSet.Unicode)]
internal struct CRYPTPROTECT_PROMPTSTRUCT
{
  public int cbSize;
  public int dwPromptFlags;
  public IntPtr hwndApp;
  public String szPrompt;
}
static private IntPtr NullPtr = ((IntPtr)((int)(0)));
private const int CRYPTPROTECT_UI_FORBIDDEN = 0x1;
private const int CRYPTPROTECT_LOCAL_MACHINE = 0x4;
```

10. Add a public enumerated type called **Store** to the class. This is used to indicate whether DPAPI should be used in conjunction with the machine or user stores.

```
public enum Store {USE_MACHINE_STORE = 1, USE_USER_STORE};
```

11. Add a private member variable of type **Store** to the class.

```
private Store store;
```

12. Replace the class' default constructor with the following constructor that accepts a **Store** parameter and places the supplied value in the **store** private member variable.

```
public DataProtector(Store tempStore)
{
  store = tempStore;
}
```

13. Add the following public **Encrypt** method to the class.

```
public byte[] Encrypt(byte[] plainText, byte[] optionalEntropy)
{
  bool retVal = false;

  DATA_BLOB plainTextBlob = new DATA_BLOB();
  DATA_BLOB cipherTextBlob = new DATA_BLOB();
  DATA_BLOB entropyBlob = new DATA_BLOB();
```

```
CRYPTPROTECT_PROMPTSTRUCT prompt = new CRYPTPROTECT_PROMPTSTRUCT();
InitPromptstruct(ref prompt);

int dwFlags;
try
{
  try
  {
    int bytesSize = plainText.Length;
    plainTextBlob.pbData = Marshal.AllocHGlobal(bytesSize);
    if(IntPtr.Zero == plainTextBlob.pbData)
    {
      throw new Exception("Unable to allocate plaintext buffer.");
    }
    plainTextBlob.cbData = bytesSize;
    Marshal.Copy(plainText, 0, plainTextBlob.pbData, bytesSize);
  }
  catch(Exception ex)
  {
    throw new Exception("Exception marshalling data. " + ex.Message);
  }
  if(Store.USE_MACHINE_STORE == store)
  {//Using the machine store, should be providing entropy.
    dwFlags = CRYPTPROTECT_LOCAL_MACHINE|CRYPTPROTECT_UI_FORBIDDEN;
    //Check to see if the entropy is null
    if(null == optionalEntropy)
    {//Allocate something
      optionalEntropy = new byte[0];
    }
    try
    {
      int bytesSize = optionalEntropy.Length;
      entropyBlob.pbData = Marshal.AllocHGlobal(optionalEntropy.Length);;
      if(IntPtr.Zero == entropyBlob.pbData)
      {
        throw new Exception("Unable to allocate entropy data buffer.");
      }
      Marshal.Copy(optionalEntropy, 0, entropyBlob.pbData, bytesSize);
      entropyBlob.cbData = bytesSize;
    }
    catch(Exception ex)
    {
      throw new Exception("Exception entropy marshalling data. " +
                          ex.Message);
    }
  }
  else
  {//Using the user store
    dwFlags = CRYPTPROTECT_UI_FORBIDDEN;
  }
  retVal = CryptProtectData(ref plainTextBlob, "", ref entropyBlob,
                            IntPtr.Zero, ref prompt, dwFlags,
                            ref cipherTextBlob);
```

```
      if(false == retVal)
      {
        throw new Exception("Encryption failed. " +
                         GetErrorMessage(Marshal.GetLastWin32Error()));
      }
    }
    catch(Exception ex)
    {
      throw new Exception("Exception encrypting. " + ex.Message);
    }
    byte[] cipherText = new byte[cipherTextBlob.cbData];
    Marshal.Copy(cipherTextBlob.pbData, cipherText, 0, cipherTextBlob.cbData);
    return cipherText;
  }
```

14. Add the following public **Decrypt** method to the class.

```
public byte[] Decrypt(byte[] cipherText, byte[] optionalEntropy)
{
  bool retVal = false;
  DATA_BLOB plainTextBlob = new DATA_BLOB();
  DATA_BLOB cipherBlob = new DATA_BLOB();
  CRYPTPROTECT_PROMPTSTRUCT prompt = new CRYPTPROTECT_PROMPTSTRUCT();
  InitPromptstruct(ref prompt);
  try
  {
    try
    {
      int cipherTextSize = cipherText.Length;
      cipherBlob.pbData = Marshal.AllocHGlobal(cipherTextSize);
      if(IntPtr.Zero == cipherBlob.pbData)
      {
        throw new Exception("Unable to allocate cipherText buffer.");
      }
      cipherBlob.cbData = cipherTextSize;
      Marshal.Copy(cipherText, 0, cipherBlob.pbData, cipherBlob.cbData);
    }
    catch(Exception ex)
    {
      throw new Exception("Exception marshalling data. " + ex.Message);
    }
    DATA_BLOB entropyBlob = new DATA_BLOB();
    int dwFlags;
    if(Store.USE_MACHINE_STORE == store)
    {//Using the machine store, should be providing entropy.
      dwFlags = CRYPTPROTECT_LOCAL_MACHINE|CRYPTPROTECT_UI_FORBIDDEN;
      //Check to see if the entropy is null
      if(null == optionalEntropy)
      {//Allocate something
        optionalEntropy = new byte[0];
      }
      try
      {
```

```
        int bytesSize = optionalEntropy.Length;
        entropyBlob.pbData = Marshal.AllocHGlobal(bytesSize);
        if(IntPtr.Zero == entropyBlob.pbData)
        {
          throw new Exception("Unable to allocate entropy buffer.");
        }
        entropyBlob.cbData = bytesSize;
        Marshal.Copy(optionalEntropy, 0, entropyBlob.pbData, bytesSize);
      }
      catch(Exception ex)
      {
        throw new Exception("Exception entropy marshalling data. " +
                            ex.Message);
      }
    }
    else
    {//Using the user store
      dwFlags = CRYPTPROTECT_UI_FORBIDDEN;
    }
    retVal = CryptUnprotectData(ref cipherBlob, null, ref entropyBlob,
                               IntPtr.Zero, ref prompt, dwFlags,
                               ref plainTextBlob);
    if(false == retVal)
    {
      throw new Exception("Decryption failed. " +
                          GetErrorMessage(Marshal.GetLastWin32Error()));
    }
    //Free the blob and entropy.
    if(IntPtr.Zero != cipherBlob.pbData)
    {
      Marshal.FreeHGlobal(cipherBlob.pbData);
    }
    if(IntPtr.Zero != entropyBlob.pbData)
    {
      Marshal.FreeHGlobal(entropyBlob.pbData);
    }
  }
  catch(Exception ex)
  {
    throw new Exception("Exception decrypting. " + ex.Message);
  }
  byte[] plainText = new byte[plainTextBlob.cbData];
  Marshal.Copy(plainTextBlob.pbData, plainText, 0, plainTextBlob.cbData);
  return plainText;
}
```

15. Add the following private helper methods to the class.

```
private void InitPromptstruct(ref CRYPTPROTECT_PROMPTSTRUCT ps)
{
  ps.cbSize = Marshal.SizeOf(typeof(CRYPTPROTECT_PROMPTSTRUCT));
  ps.dwPromptFlags = 0;
```

```
    ps.hwndApp = NullPtr;
    ps.szPrompt = null;
}

private unsafe static String GetErrorMessage(int errorCode)
{
  int FORMAT_MESSAGE_ALLOCATE_BUFFER = 0x00000100;
  int FORMAT_MESSAGE_IGNORE_INSERTS = 0x00000200;
  int FORMAT_MESSAGE_FROM_SYSTEM   = 0x00001000;
  int messageSize = 255;
  String lpMsgBuf = "";
  int dwFlags = FORMAT_MESSAGE_ALLOCATE_BUFFER | FORMAT_MESSAGE_FROM_SYSTEM |
                FORMAT_MESSAGE_IGNORE_INSERTS;
  IntPtr ptrlpSource = new IntPtr();
  IntPtr prtArguments = new IntPtr();
  int retVal = FormatMessage(dwFlags, ref ptrlpSource, errorCode, 0,
                            ref lpMsgBuf, messageSize, &prtArguments);
  if(0 == retVal)
  {
    throw new Exception("Failed to format message for error code " +
                        errorCode + ". ");
  }
  return lpMsgBuf;
}
```

16. On the **Build** menu, click **Build Solution**.

2. Strong Name the Assembly (Optional)

If the managed DPAPI class library is to be called by an Enterprise Services application (which must be strong named), then the DPAPI class library must also be strong named. This procedure creates a strong name for the class library.

If the managed DPAPI class library is to be called directly from an ASP.NET Web application (which is not strong named), you can skip this procedure.

▶ **To strong name the assembly**

1. Open a command window and change directory to the **DataProtection** project folder.

2. Use the sn.exe utility to generate a key pair used to sign the assembly.

   ```
   sn -k dataprotection.snk
   ```

3. Return to Visual Studio .NET and open Assemblyinfo.cs.

4. Locate the **AssemblyKeyFile** attribute and add a path to the key file within the project folder.

```
[assembly: AssemblyKeyFile(@"..\..\dataprotection.snk")]
```

5. On the **Build** menu, click **Build Solution**.

References

For more information, see the following related How Tos:

- "How To: Use DPAPI (Machine Store) from ASP.NET" in the Reference section of this book
- "How To: Use DPAPI (User Store) from ASP.NET with Enterprise Services" in the Reference section of this book

How To:
Use DPAPI (Machine Store)
from ASP.NET

Web applications often need to store security-sensitive data, such as database connection strings and service account credentials in application configuration files. For security reasons, this type of information should never is stored in plain text and should always be encrypted prior to storage.

This How To describes how to use DPAPI from ASP.NET. This includes ASP.NET Web applications, Web services, and .NET Remoting components that are hosted in ASP.NET.

The code in this How To references DPAPI through a managed class library, the creation of which is described in "How To: Create a DPAPI Library" in the Reference section of this book.

Notes

- DPAPI can work with either the machine store or user store (which requires a loaded user profile). DPAPI defaults to the user store, although you can specify that the machine store be used by passing the CRYPTPROTECT_LOCAL_MACHINE flag to the DPAPI functions.

- The user profile approach affords an additional layer of security because it limits who can access the secret. Only the user who encrypts the data can decrypt the data. However, use of the user profile requires additional development effort when DPAPI is used from an ASP.NET Web application because you need to take explicit steps to load and unload a user profile (ASP.NET does not automatically load a user profile).

- The machine store approach (adopted in this How To) is easier to develop because it does not require user profile management. However, unless an additional entropy parameter is used, it is less secure because any user on the computer can decrypt data. (Entropy is a random value designed to make deciphering the secret more difficult.) The problem with using an additional entropy parameter is that this must be securely stored by the application, which presents another key management issue.

Note: If you use DPAPI with the machine store, the encrypted string is specific to a given computer and therefore you must generate the encrypted data on every computer. Do not copy the encrypted data across computers in a farm or cluster.

- For a related article that shows how to use DPAPI with the user store from an ASP.NET Web application (by using a serviced component within an Enterprise Services application), see "How To: Use DPAPI (User Store) from ASP.NET with Enterprise Services" within the Reference section of this book.

Requirements

The following items describe the recommended hardware, software, network infrastructure, skills and knowledge, and service packs you will need.

- Microsoft® Windows® 2000 operating system
- Microsoft Visual Studio® .NET development system

The procedures in this How To also require that you have knowledge of building ASP.NET Web applications with Microsoft Visual C#™ development tool.

Before working through this How To, you must perform the steps described in "How To: Create a DPAPI Library" in order to create the DPAPI managed class library used by code in this How To.

Summary

This How To includes the following steps:

1. Create an ASP.NET Client Web Application
2. Test the Application
3. Modify the Web Application to Read an Encrypted Connection String from Web.Config

1. Create an ASP.NET Client Web Application

This procedure creates an ASP.NET client Web application that will call the DPAPI class library to encrypt and decrypt data stored within the Web.config file.

▶ **To create an ASP.NET client Web application**

1. Start Visual Studio .NET and create a new C# ASP.NET Web application called **DPAPIClientWeb**.
2. Add a reference to the DataProtector.dll assembly, previously created in "How To: Create a DPAPI Library."

3. Open WebForm1.aspx.cs and add the following using statements to the top of the file beneath the existing using statements.

```
using System.Text;
using DataProtection;
```

4. Add the controls listed in Table 1 to WebForm1.aspx.

Table 1: WebForm1.aspx controls

Control Type	Text	ID
Button	Encrypt	btnEncrypt
Button	Decrypt	btnDecrypt
TextBox		txtDataToEncrypt
TextBox		txtEncryptedData
TextBox		txtDecryptedData
Label		lblError
Label	Data To Encrypt	
Label	Encrypted Data	
Label	Decrypted Data	

Your Web form should look similar to Figure 1.

Figure 1
DPAPIClientWeb Web Form

5. Double-click the **Encrypt** button to create a button click event handler.

```
DataProtector dp = new DataProtector( DataProtector.Store.USE_MACHINE_STORE );
try
{
  byte[] dataToEncrypt = Encoding.ASCII.GetBytes(txtDataToEncrypt.Text);
  // Not passing optional entropy in this example
  // Could pass random value (stored by the application) for added security
```

```
        // when using DPAPI with the machine store.
        txtEncryptedData.Text =
                    Convert.ToBase64String(dp.Encrypt(dataToEncrypt,null));
    }
    catch(Exception ex)
    {
      lblError.ForeColor = Color.Red;
      lblError.Text = "Exception.<br>" + ex.Message;
      return;
    }
    lblError.Text = "";
```

6. Return to the Web form and double-click the **Decrypt** button. Add the following code to the button click event handler.

```
    DataProtector dp = new DataProtector(DataProtector.Store.USE_MACHINE_STORE);
    try
    {
      byte[] dataToDecrypt = Convert.FromBase64String(txtEncryptedData.Text);
      // Optional entropy parameter is null.
      // If entropy was used within the Encrypt method, the same entropy parameter
      // must be supplied here
      txtDecryptedData.Text =
                    Encoding.ASCII.GetString(dp.Decrypt(dataToDecrypt,null));
    }
    catch(Exception ex)
    {
      lblError.ForeColor = Color.Red;
      lblError.Text = "Exception.<br>" + ex.Message;
      return;
    }
    lblError.Text = "";
```

7. On the **Build** menu, click **Build Solution**.

2. Test the Application

This procedure tests the Web application to confirm that data is successfully encrypted and decrypted.

▶ **To test the application**

1. Press **Ctrl+F5** to run the Web application.

2. Enter a string in the **Data to Encrypt** text box and click **Encrypt**.

   Confirm that encrypted data (in Base64 encoded format) is displayed in the **Encrypted Data** text box.

3. Click the **Decrypt** button.

   Confirm that the encrypted data is successfully decrypted and displayed in the **Decrypted Data** text box.

3. Modify the Web Application to Read an Encrypted Connection String from Web.Config

This procedure takes an encrypted database connection string and places the encrypted cipher text into the application's Web.config file within an **<appSettings>** element. You will then add code to read and decrypt this string from the configuration file.

▶ **To modify the Web application to read an encrypted connection string from Web.config**

1. Return to Visual Studio .NET and display the WebForm1.aspx in Designer mode.

2. Add another button to the form. Set its **Text** property to **Decrypt string from config file** and its **ID** property to **btnDecryptConfig**.

3. Double-click the button to create a button click event handler.

4. Add the following **using** statement to the top of the file beneath the existing **using** statements.

```
using System.Configuration;
```

5. Return to the **btnDecryptConfig_Click** event handler and add the following code to retrieve a database connection string from the **<appSettings>** section of the Web.config file.

```
DataProtector dp = new DataProtector(DataProtector.Store.USE_MACHINE_STORE);
try
{
  string appSettingValue =
           ConfigurationSettings.AppSettings["connectionString"];
  byte[] dataToDecrypt = Convert.FromBase64String(appSettingValue);
  string connStr = Encoding.ASCII.GetString(
                             dp.Decrypt(dataToDecrypt,null));
  txtDecryptedData.Text = connStr;
}
catch(Exception ex)
{
  lblError.ForeColor = Color.Red;
  lblError.Text = "Exception.<br>" + ex.Message;
  return;
}
lblError.Text = "";
```

6. On the **Build** menu, click **Build Solution** to rebuild the projects.

7. Right-click **WebForm1.aspx**, and then click **View in Browser**.

8. Enter a database connection string such as the one that follows into the **Data to Encrypt** field.

```
server=(local);Integrated Security=SSPI; database=Northwind
```

9. Click the **Encrypt** button.

10. Select the encrypted cipher text and copy it to the clipboard.

11. Switch to Visual Studio .NET, open Web.config and add the following
    <**appSettings**> element outside of the <**system.web**> element. Assign the
    encrypted connection string currently on the clipboard to the **value** attribute.

    ```
    <appSettings>
        <add key="connectionString" value="encrypted connection string" />
    </appSettings>
    ```

12. Save Web.config.

13. Click the **Decrypt string from config file** button and confirm that the encrypted
    database connection string is successfully read from the Web.config file and that
    the decrypted connection string is successfully displayed in the **Decrypted data**
    field.

References

For more information, see the following related How Tos in the Reference section of
this book:

- "How To: Create a DPAPI Library" in the Reference section of this book.
- "How To: Use DPAPI (User Store) from ASP.NET with Enterprise Services" in the
  Reference section of this book.

How To:
Use DPAPI (User Store) from ASP.NET with Enterprise Services

Web applications often need to store security-sensitive data, such as database connection strings and service account credentials in application configuration files. For security reasons, this type of information should never is stored in plain text and should always be encrypted prior to storage.

This How To describes how to use Data Protection API (DPAPI) from an ASP.NET application with Enterprise Services.

Notes

- DPAPI can work with either the machine store or user store (which requires a loaded user profile). DPAPI defaults to the user store, although you can specify that the machine store be used by passing the CRYPTPROTECT_LOCAL_MACHINE flag to the DPAPI functions.

- The user profile approach (adopted by this How To) affords an additional layer of security because it limits who can access the secret. Only the user who encrypts the data can decrypt the data. However, use of the user profile requires additional development effort when DPAPI is used from an ASP.NET Web application because you need to take explicit steps to load and unload a user profile (ASP.NET does not automatically load a user profile).

- For a related article that shows how to use DPAPI with the machine store (directly) from an ASP.NET Web application (without requiring an Enterprise Services application), see "How To: Use DPAPI (Machine Store) from ASP.NET" within the Reference section of this book.

The approach described in this How To uses a .NET serviced component running in an Enterprise Services (COM+) server application to perform the DPAPI processing for the reasons outlined in the following section, "Why Use Enterprise Services?" It also uses a Windows service for the reasons in the "Why use a Windows Service?" section. The solution configuration is shown in Figure 1 on the next page.

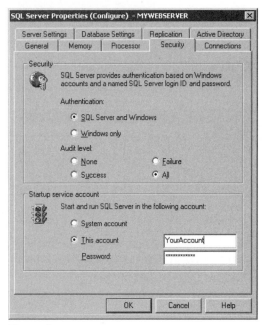

Figure 1
ASP.NET Web application uses a serviced component in an Enterprise Services server application to interact with DPAPI

In Figure1, the sequence of events is as follows:

1. The Windows service control manager starts the Win32 service and automatically loads the user profile associated with the account under which the service runs. The same Windows account is used to run the Enterprise Services application.

2. The Win32 service calls a launch method on the serviced component, which starts the Enterprise Services application and loads the serviced component.

3. The Web application retrieves the encrypted string from the Web.config file.

4. The application calls a method on the serviced component to decrypt the connection string.

5. The serviced component interacts with DPAPI using P/Invoke to call the Win32 DPAPI functions.

6. The decrypted string is returned to the Web application.

Why Use Enterprise Services?

DPAPI requires a Windows account password in order to derive an encryption key. The account that DPAPI uses is obtained either from the current thread token (if the thread that calls DPAPI is currently impersonating), or the process token. Furthermore, using DPAPI with the user store requires that the user profile associated with the account is loaded. This presents the following issues for an ASP.NET Web application that wants to use DPAPI with the user store:

- Calls to DPAPI from an ASP.NET application running under the default ASPNET account will fail. This is because the ASPNET account does not have a loaded user profile.

- If an ASP.NET Web application is configured to impersonate its callers, the ASP.NET application thread has an associated thread impersonation token. The logon session associated with this impersonation token is a network logon session (used on the server to represent the caller). Network logon sessions do not result in user profiles being loaded and it would also not be possible to derive an encryption key from the password because the server does not have the impersonated user's password (unless the application uses Basic authentication).

To overcome these limitations, you can use a serviced component within an Enterprise Services server application (with a fixed process identity) to provide encryption and decryption services using DPAPI.

Why Use a Windows Service?

A Windows service is used in this solution in order to ensure that a user profile is automatically loaded. When the Windows Service Control Manager (SCM) starts a service, the SCM also loads the profile of the account the service is configured to run as.

The service is then used to load the serviced component, which causes the Enterprise Services server application (in an instance of Dllhost.exe) to start.

Due to the fact that the Windows service and the serviced component are configured to both run using the same least privileged account, the serviced component has access to the loaded user profile and as a result can call DPAPI functions to encrypt and decrypt data.

If the service component is not launched from a Windows service (and the service is taken out of the picture) the user profile will not automatically be loaded. While there is a Win32 API that can be called to load a user profile (**LoadUserProfile**), it requires the calling code to be part of the **Administrators** group, which would defeat the principle of running with least privilege.

The service must be running whenever the **Encrypt** and **Decrypt** methods of the serviced component are called. When Windows services are stopped, the configured profile is automatically unloaded. At this point, the DPAPI methods within the serviced component would cease to work.

Requirements

The following items describe the recommended hardware, software, network infrastructure, skills and knowledge, and service packs you will need:

- Microsoft® SQL Server™ 2000 or Microsoft Windows® XP operating system
- Microsoft Visual Studio® .NET development system

The procedures in this article also require that you have knowledge of ASP.NET Web development with Microsoft Visual C#™ development tool.

Summary

This How To includes the following procedures:

1. Create a Serviced Component that Provides **Encrypt** and **Decrypt** Methods
2. Call the Managed DPAPI Class Library
3. Create a Dummy Class Used to Launch the Serviced Component
4. Create a Windows Account to Run the Enterprise Services Application and Windows Service
5. Configure, Strong Name, and Register the Serviced Component
6. Create a Windows Service Application to Launch the Serviced Component
7. Install and Start the Windows Service
8. Write a Web Application to Test the Encryption and Decryption Routines
9. Modify the Web Application to Read an Encrypted Connection String from an Application Configuration File

1. Create a Serviced Component that Provides Encrypt and Decrypt Methods

This procedure creates a serviced component that exposes **Encrypt** and **Decrypt** methods. In a later procedure, these will be called by an ASP.NET Web application when it requires encryption services.

▶ **To create a serviced component that provides Encrypt and Decrypt methods**

1. Start Visual Studio .NET and create a new C# class library project called **DPAPIComp**.
2. Use Solution Explorer to rename Class1.cs as DataProtectorComp.cs.
3. Within DataProtectorComp.cs, rename Class1 as DataProtectorComp and rename the default constructor accordingly.
4. Add an assembly reference to the System.EnterpriseServices.dll assembly.

5. Add the following **using** statements to the top of DataProtectorComp.cs.

```
using System.EnterpriseServices;
using System.Security.Principal;
using System.Runtime.InteropServices;
```

6. Derive the **DataProtectorComp** class from the **ServicedComponent** class.

```
public class DataProtectorComp : ServicedComponent
```

7. Add the following two empty public methods to the **DataProtectorComp** class.

```
public byte[] Encrypt(byte[] plainText)
{}
public byte[] Decrypt(byte[] cipherText)
{}
```

2. Call the Managed DPAPI Class Library

This procedure calls the managed DPAPI class library to encrypt and decrypt data. This class library encapsulates the calls to the Win32 DPAPI functions. If you have not yet created this class library, refer to "How To: Create a DPAPI Library" in the Reference section of this book.

▶ **To call the managed DPAPI class library**

1. Add a file reference to the DataProtection.dll assembly.

2. Add the following **using** statement beneath the existing **using** statements in DataProtectorComp.cs.

```
using DataProtection;
```

3. Add the following code to the **Encrypt** method to encrypt the supplied data.

```
DataProtector dp = new DataProtector( DataProtector.Store.USE_USER_STORE );
byte[] cipherText = null;
try
{
   cipherText = dp.Encrypt(plainText, null);
}
catch(Exception ex)
{
   throw new Exception("Exception encrypting. " + ex.Message);
}
return cipherText;
```

4. Add the following code to the **Decrypt** method to decrypt the supplied cipher text.

```
DataProtector dp = new DataProtector( DataProtector.Store.USE_USER_STORE );
byte[] plainText = null;

try
{
   plainText = dp.Decrypt(cipherText,null);
}
catch(Exception ex)
{
   throw new Exception("Exception decrypting. " + ex.Message);
}
return plainText;
```

3. Create a Dummy Class that will Launch the Serviced Component

This procedure creates a dummy class that exposes a single **Launch** method. This will be called from the Windows service to start the Enterprise Services application that hosts the serviced component.

▶ **To create a dummy class that will launch the serviced component**

1. Add a new C# class to the project and name it Launcher.cs.

2. Add the following method to the class. This method will be called by the service when the service starts.

```
public bool Launch()
{
   return true;
}
```

3. On the **Build** menu, click **Build Solution**.

4. Create a Windows Account to Run the Enterprise Services Application and Windows Service

This procedure creates a Windows account that you will use to run the Enterprise Services application that hosts the **DataProtectorComp** serviced component and the Windows service. It also results in the creation of a user profile for the new account. This is required by DPAPI when it uses the user store.

▶ **To create a Windows account to run the Enterprise Services application and Windows service**

1. Create a new local user account called **DPAPIAccount**. Enter a password, clear the **User must change password at next logon** check box, and then select the **Password never expires** check box.

2. Use the **Local Security Policy** tool in the **Administrative Tools** programs group to give the account the **Log on locally** and **Log on as a batch job** privileges.

▶ **To create a user profile for the new account**

1. Log off Windows.

2. Log back on using the new **DPAPIAccount**.

   This results in the creation of a user profile for this account.

3. Log off Windows and log back on as your normal developer account.

5. Configure, Strong Name, and Register the Serviced Component

This procedure signs the serviced component assembly to give it a strong name. This is a mandatory requirement for assemblies containing serviced components. You will then add assembly level attributes to the serviced component assembly used to configure the serviced component within the COM+ catalog. After that, you will use the Regsvcs.exe utility to register the serviced component and create a host COM+ server application. Finally, you will set the COM+ application's "run as" identity to the service account created in the previous procedure.

▶ **To configure, strong name, and register the serviced component**

1. Open a command window and change directory to the **DPAPIComp** project folder.

2. Use the sn.exe utility to generate a key pair used to sign the assembly.

```
sn -k dpapicomp.snk
```

3. Return to Visual Studio .NET and open Assemblyinfo.cs.

4. Locate the **AssemblyKeyFile** attribute and add a path to the key file within the project folder.

```
[assembly: AssemblyKeyFile(@"..\..\dpapicomp.snk")]
```

5. Add the following **using** statement to the top of the file.

```
using System.EnterpriseServices;
```

6. Add the following assembly level attributes to configure the COM+ application as a server application, and to specify the application's name.

```
[assembly: ApplicationActivation(ActivationOption.Server)]
[assembly: ApplicationName("DPAPI Helper Application")]
```

7. On the **Build** menu, click **Build Solution** to build the serviced component project.

8. Open a command window and go to the project output directory that contains the DPAPIComp.dll file.

9. Use regsvcs.exe to register the serviced component and create the COM+ application.

```
regsvcs DPAPIComp.dll
```

10. Start the Component Services Microsoft Management Console (MMC) snap-in.

11. Expand the **Component Services, Computers, My Computer,** and **COM+ Applications** folders.

12. Locate and right-click **DPAPI Helper Application**, and then click **Properties**.

13. Click the **Activation** tab and confirm that the application type is set to **Server application**.

14. Click the **Identity** tab, and then click the **This user** radio button.

15. Enter **DPAPIAccount** as the user, enter the appropriate password, and then click **OK** to close the **Properties** dialog box.

6. Create a Windows Service Application that will Launch the Serviced Component

This procedure creates a simple Windows service application that will launch the serviced component when it starts. This ensures that the profile of the configured account is loaded and that the serviced component is available to encrypt and decrypt data.

▶ **To create a Windows service application that will launch the serviced component**

1. Start a new instance of Visual Studio .NET and create a new C# Windows service project called **DPAPIService**.

2. Use Solution Explorer to rename Service1.cs as DPAPIService.cs.

3. Within DPAPIService.cs, rename **Service1** as **DPAPIService** and rename the default constructor accordingly.

4. Within DPAPIService.cs, locate the **InitializedComponent** method and change the service name to **DPAPIService**.

5. Set a reference to the System.EnterpriseServices.dll and System.Configuration.Install.dll assemblies.

6. Set a file reference to the **DPAPIComp** assembly.

7. Add the following **using** statement to the top of DPAPIService.cs beneath the existing **using** statements.

```
using DPAPIComp;
```

8. Locate the **Main** method and replace the following code

```
ServicesToRun = new System.ServiceProcess.ServiceBase[]{new Service1()};
```

with the following line.

```
ServicesToRun = new System.ServiceProcess.ServiceBase[]{new DPAPIService()};
```

9. Locate the **OnStart** method and add the following code, which will launch the **DPAPIComp** component whenever the service starts.

```
Launcher launchComponent = new Launcher();
launchComponent.Launch();
```

10. Add a new C# class file to the project and name it **DPAPIServiceInstaller**.

11. Add the following **using** statements to the top of **DPAPIServiceInstaller** beneath the existing **using** statement.

```
using System.ComponentModel;
using System.ServiceProcess;
using System.Configuration.Install;
```

12. Derive the **DPAPIServiceInstaller** class from the **Installer** class.
```
public class DPAPIServiceInstaller : Installer
```

13. Add the **RunInstaller** attribute at the class level as follows.

```
[RunInstaller(true)]
public class DPAPIServiceInstaller : Installer
```

14. Add the following two private member variables to the **DPAPIServiceInstaller** class. The objects will be used when installing the service.

```
private ServiceInstaller dpApiInstaller;
private ServiceProcessInstaller dpApiProcessInstaller;
```

15. Add the following code to the constructor of the **DPAPIServiceInstaller** class.

```
dpApiInstaller = new ServiceInstaller();
dpApiInstaller.StartType = System.ServiceProcess.ServiceStartMode.Manual;
dpApiInstaller.ServiceName = "DPAPIService";
dpApiInstaller.DisplayName = "DPAPI Service";
Installers.Add (dpApiInstaller);
dpApiProcessInstaller = new ServiceProcessInstaller();
dpApiProcessInstaller.Account = ServiceAccount.User;
Installers.Add (dpApiProcessInstaller);
```

16. On the **Build** menu, click **Build Solution**.

7. Install and Start the Windows Service Application

This procedure installs the Windows service using the installutil.exe utility and then starts the service.

► **To install and start the Windows service application**

1. Open a command window and change directory to the Bin\Debug directory beneath the **DPAPIService** project folder.

2. Run the installutil.exe utility to install the service.

```
Installutil.exe DPAPIService.exe
```

3. In the **Set Service Login** dialog box, enter the user name and password of the account created earlier in Procedure 4, "Create a Windows Account to Run the Enterprise Services Application and Windows Service," and then click **OK**.

   The user name must be of the form "authority\username."

   View the output from the installutil.exe utility and confirm that the service is installed correctly.

4. Start the **Services** MMC snap-in from the **Administrative Tools** program group.

5. Start the DPAPI service.

8. Write a Web Application to Test the Encryption and Decryption Routines

This procedure develops a simple Web application that you will use to test the encryption and decryption routines. Later, you will also use it to decrypt encrypted data maintained within the Web.config file.

▶ **To write a Web application to test the encryption and decryption routines**

1. Add a new C# Web application project called **DPAPIWeb** to the existing **DPAPIComp** solution.

2. Add an assembly reference to System.EnterpriseServices and add a project reference to the **DPAPIComp** project.

3. Open WebForm1.aspx in Design mode and create a form similar to the one shown in Figure 2. Use the IDs listed in Table 1 for the individual controls.

Table 1: WebForm1.aspx control IDs

Control	ID
Data To Encrypt Text Box	txtDataToEncrypt
Encrypted Data	txtEncryptedData
Decrypted Data	txtDecryptedData
Encrypt Button	btnEncrypt
Decrypt Button	btnDecrypt
Error Label	lblError

Figure 2
DPAPIWeb Web Form

4. Double-click the **Encrypt** button to display the button click event handler.

5. Add the following **using** statements to the top of the file beneath the existing **using** statements.

```
using System.Text;
using DPAPIComp;
```

6. Return to the **Encrypt** button click event handler and add the following code to call the **DataProtectorComp** serviced component to encrypt the data entered via the Web form.

```
DataProtectorComp dp = new DataProtectorComp();
try
{
  byte[] dataToEncrypt = Encoding.ASCII.GetBytes(txtDataToEncrypt.Text);
  txtEncryptedData.Text = Convert.ToBase64String(
                                    dp.Encrypt(dataToEncrypt));
}
catch(Exception ex)
{
  lblError.ForeColor = Color.Red;
  lblError.Text = "Exception.<br>" + ex.Message;
  return;
}
lblError.Text = "";
```

7. Display the Web form again and double-click the **Decrypt** button to create a button click event handler.

8. Add the following code to call the **DataProtectorComp** services component to decrypt the previous encrypted data contained within the **txtEncryptedData** field.

```
DataProtectorComp dp = new DataProtectorComp();
try
{
  byte[] dataToDecrypt = Convert.FromBase64String(txtEncryptedData.Text);
  txtDecryptedData.Text = Encoding.ASCII.GetString(
                                    dp.Decrypt(dataToDecrypt));
}
catch(Exception ex)
{
  lblError.ForeColor = Color.Red;
  lblError.Text = "Exception.<br>" + ex.Message;
  return;
}
lblError.Text = "";
```

9. On the **Build** menu, click **Build Solution**.

10. Right-click **WebForm1.aspx**, and then click **View in Browser**.

11. Enter a text string into the **Data to Encrypt** field.

12. Click the **Encrypt** button. This results in a call to the **DataProtector** serviced component within the COM+ application. The encrypted data should be displayed in the **Encrypted Data** field.

13. Click the **Decrypt** button and confirm that the original text string is displayed in the **Decrypted Data** field.

14. Close the browser window.

Note: If an access denied error message appears that indicates that the component's ProgID cannot be read from HKEY_CLASSES_ROOT, you probably need to re-run Regsvcs.exe to reregister the serviced component.

This error message appears if you have recompiled the serviced component assembly but not reregistered the assembly. Because the assembly version changes on each build (due to the default "1.0.*" assembly version attribute), a new CLSID is generated on each successive build. The error is due to the fact that ASP.NET cannot access this CLSID in the registry as it doesn't exist yet. Rerun Regsvcs.exe and restart the Web application to resolve the problem.

---

9. Modify the Web Application to Read an Encrypted Connection String from an Application Configuration File

This procedure takes an encrypted database connection string and places the encrypted cipher text into the application's Web.config file within an **<appSettings>** element. You will then add code to read and decrypt this string from the configuration file.

▶ **To modify the Web application to read an encrypted connection string from an application configuration file**

1. Return to Visual Studio .NET and display the WebForm1.aspx in Designer mode.

2. Add another button to the form. Set its **Text** property to **Decrypt string from config file** and its **ID** property to **btnDecryptConfig**,

3. Double-click the button to create a button click event handler.

4. Add the following **using** statement to the top of the file beneath the existing **using** statements.

```
using System.Configuration;
```

5. Return to the **btnDecryptConfig_Click** event handler and add the following code to retrieve a database connection string from the **<appSettings>** section of the Web.config file.

```
DataProtectorComp dec = new DataProtectorComp();
try
{
  string appSettingValue =
          ConfigurationSettings.AppSettings["connectionString"];
  byte[] dataToDecrypt = Convert.FromBase64String(appSettingValue);
  string connStr = Encoding.ASCII.GetString(
                          dec.Decrypt(dataToDecrypt));
```

```
    txtDecryptedData.Text = connStr;
}
catch(Exception ex)
{
  lblError.ForeColor = Color.Red;
  lblError.Text = "Exception.<br>" + ex.Message;
  return;
}
lblError.Text = "";
```

6. On the **Build** menu, click **Build Solution** to rebuild the projects.

7. Right-click **WebForm1.aspx**, and then click **View in Browser**.

8. In the **Data to Encrypt** field, enter a database connection string such as the one that follows.

   ```
   server=(local);Integrated Security=SSPI; database=Northwind
   ```

9. Click the **Encrypt** button.

10. Select the encrypted cipher text and copy it to the clipboard.

11. Switch to Visual Studio .NET, open Web.config and add the following **<appSettings>** element outside of the **<system.web>** element. Assign the encrypted connection string currently on the clipboard to the **value** attribute.

    ```
    <appSettings>
        <add key="connectionString" value="encrypted connection string" />
    </appSettings>
    ```

12. Save Web.config.

13. Click the **Decrypt string from config file** button and confirm that the encrypted database connection string is successfully read from the Web.config file and that the decrypted connection string is successfully displayed in the **Decrypted data** field.

References

- "Windows Data Protection" on MSDN (*http://msdn.microsoft.com/library /default.asp?url=/library/en-us/dnsecure/html/windataprotection-dpapi.asp*)
- "How To: Create a DPAPI Library" in the Reference section of this book.
- "How To: Use DPAPI (Machine Store) from ASP.NET" in the Reference section of this book.

How To: Create an Encryption Library

This How To describes how to create a generic encryption library that can be used to encrypt and decrypt data using the following algorithms:

- DES (Digital Encryption Standard)
- Triple DES
- Rijndael
- RC2

For an example application that uses the class library created in this How To, see "How To: Store Encrypted Connection Strings in the Registry" in the Reference section of this book.

Requirements

The following items describe the recommended hardware, software, network infrastructure, skills and knowledge, and service packs you will need.

- Microsoft® Windows® 2000 operating system
- Microsoft Visual Studio® .NET development system

The procedures in this article also require that you have knowledge of the Microsoft Visual C#™ development tool.

Summary

This How To includes the following procedures:

1. Create a C# Class Library
2. Create a Console Test Application

1. Create a C# Class Library

This procedure creates a C# class library, which will provide encryption and decryption functionality.

▶ **To create a C# class library**

1. Start Visual Studio .NET and create a new C# Class Library project called **Encryption**.

2. Use Solution Explorer to rename class1.cs as EncryptTransformer.cs.

3. In EncryptTransformer.cs, rename **Class1** as **EncryptTransformer**.

4. Change the scope of the class from **public** to **internal**.

```
internal class EncryptTransformer
```

5. Add the following **using** statement at the top of the file.

```
using System.Security.Cryptography;
```

6. Add the following enumerated type within the **Encryption** namespace.

```
public enum EncryptionAlgorithm {Des = 1, Rc2, Rijndael, TripleDes};
```

7. Add the following private member variables to the **EncryptTransformer** class.

```
private EncryptionAlgorithm algorithmID;
private byte[] initVec;
private byte[] encKey;
```

8. Replace the default constructor with the following constructor.

```
internal EncryptTransformer(EncryptionAlgorithm algId)
{
  //Save the algorithm being used.
  algorithmID = algId;
}
```

9. Add the following method to the class.

```
internal ICryptoTransform GetCryptoServiceProvider(byte[] bytesKey)
{
  // Pick the provider.
  switch (algorithmID)
  {
    case EncryptionAlgorithm.Des:
    {
      DES des = new DESCryptoServiceProvider();
      des.Mode = CipherMode.CBC;
```

```
    // See if a key was provided
    if (null == bytesKey)
    {
      encKey = des.Key;
    }
    else
    {
      des.Key = bytesKey;
      encKey = des.Key;
    }
    // See if the client provided an initialization vector
    if (null == initVec)
    { // Have the algorithm create one
      initVec = des.IV;
    }
    else
    { //No, give it to the algorithm
      des.IV = initVec;
    }
    return des.CreateEncryptor();
}
case EncryptionAlgorithm.TripleDes:
{
  TripleDES des3 = new TripleDESCryptoServiceProvider();
  des3.Mode = CipherMode.CBC;
  // See if a key was provided
  if (null == bytesKey)
  {
    encKey = des3.Key;
  }
  else
  {
    des3.Key = bytesKey;
    encKey = des3.Key;
  }
  // See if the client provided an IV
  if (null == initVec)
  { //Yes, have the alg create one
    initVec = des3.IV;
  }
  else
  { //No, give it to the alg.
    des3.IV = initVec;
  }
  return des3.CreateEncryptor();
}
case EncryptionAlgorithm.Rc2:
{
  RC2 rc2 = new RC2CryptoServiceProvider();
  rc2.Mode = CipherMode.CBC;
  // Test to see if a key was provided
  if (null == bytesKey)
  {
```

```
        encKey = rc2.Key;
      }
      else
      {
        rc2.Key = bytesKey;
        encKey = rc2.Key;
      }
      // See if the client provided an IV
      if (null == initVec)
      { //Yes, have the alg create one
        initVec = rc2.IV;
      }
      else
      { //No, give it to the alg.
        rc2.IV = initVec;
      }
      return rc2.CreateEncryptor();
    }
    case EncryptionAlgorithm.Rijndael:
    {
      Rijndael rijndael = new RijndaelManaged();
      rijndael.Mode = CipherMode.CBC;
      // Test to see if a key was provided
      if(null == bytesKey)
      {
        encKey = rijndael.Key;
      }
      else
      {
        rijndael.Key = bytesKey;
        encKey = rijndael.Key;
      }
      // See if the client provided an IV
      if(null == initVec)
      { //Yes, have the alg create one
        initVec = rijndael.IV;
      }
      else
      { //No, give it to the alg.
        rijndael.IV = initVec;
      }
      return rijndael.CreateEncryptor();
    }
    default:
    {
      throw new CryptographicException("Algorithm ID '" + algorithmID +
                                "' not supported.");
    }
  }
}
```

10. Add the following properties to the class.

```
internal byte[] IV
{
  get{return initVec;}
  set{initVec = value;}
}
internal byte[] Key
{
  get{return encKey;}
}
```

11. Add a new class called **DecryptTransformer** to the project.

12. Add the following **using** statement at the top of the DecryptTransformer.cs file.

```
using System.Security.Cryptography;
```

13. Change the class scope from **public** to **internal**.

14. Replace the default constructor with the following constructor.

```
internal DecryptTransformer(EncryptionAlgorithm deCryptId)
{
  algorithmID = deCryptId;
}
```

15. Add the following private variables to the class.

```
private EncryptionAlgorithm algorithmID;
private byte[] initVec;
```

16. Add the following method to the class.

```
internal ICryptoTransform GetCryptoServiceProvider(byte[] bytesKey)
{
  // Pick the provider.
  switch (algorithmID)
  {
    case EncryptionAlgorithm.Des:
    {
      DES des = new DESCryptoServiceProvider();
      des.Mode = CipherMode.CBC;
      des.Key = bytesKey;
      des.IV = initVec;
      return des.CreateDecryptor();
    }
    case EncryptionAlgorithm.TripleDes:
    {
      TripleDES des3 = new TripleDESCryptoServiceProvider();
      des3.Mode = CipherMode.CBC;
      return des3.CreateDecryptor(bytesKey, initVec);
    }
```

```
      case EncryptionAlgorithm.Rc2:
      {
        RC2 rc2 = new RC2CryptoServiceProvider();
        rc2.Mode = CipherMode.CBC;
        return rc2.CreateDecryptor(bytesKey, initVec);
      }
      case EncryptionAlgorithm.Rijndael:
      {
        Rijndael rijndael = new RijndaelManaged();
        rijndael.Mode = CipherMode.CBC;
        return rijndael.CreateDecryptor(bytesKey, initVec);
      }
      default:
      {
        throw new CryptographicException("Algorithm ID '" + algorithmID +
                                   "' not supported.");
      }
    }
  }
} //end GetCryptoServiceProvider
```

17. Add the following property to the class.

```
internal byte[] IV
{
  set{initVec = value;}
}
```

18. Add a new class called **Encryptor** to the project.

19. Add the following **using** statements at the top of Encryptor.cs.

```
using System.Security.Cryptography;
using System.IO;
```

20. Replace the default constructor with the following constructor.

```
public Encryptor(EncryptionAlgorithm algId)
{
  transformer = new EncryptTransformer(algId);
}
```

21. Add the following private member variables to the class.

```
private EncryptTransformer transformer;
private byte[] initVec;
private byte[] encKey;
```

22. Add the following **Encrypt** method to the class.

```
public byte[] Encrypt(byte[] bytesData, byte[] bytesKey)
{
```

```
//Set up the stream that will hold the encrypted data.
MemoryStream memStreamEncryptedData = new MemoryStream();

transformer.IV = initVec;
ICryptoTransform transform = transformer.GetCryptoServiceProvider(bytesKey);
CryptoStream encStream = new CryptoStream(memStreamEncryptedData,
                                          transform,
                                          CryptoStreamMode.Write);
try
{
   //Encrypt the data, write it to the memory stream.
   encStream.Write(bytesData, 0, bytesData.Length);
}
catch(Exception ex)
{
   throw new Exception("Error while writing encrypted data to the stream: \n"
                       + ex.Message);
}
//Set the IV and key for the client to retrieve
encKey = transformer.Key;
initVec = transformer.IV;
encStream.FlushFinalBlock();
encStream.Close();

//Send the data back.
return memStreamEncryptedData.ToArray();
}//end Encrypt
```

23. Add the following properties to the class.

```
public byte[] IV
{
   get{return initVec;}
   set{initVec = value;}
}

public byte[] Key
{
   get{return encKey;}
}
```

24. Add a new class called **Decryptor** to the project.

25. Add the following **using** statements at the top of Decryptor.cs

```
using System.Security.Cryptography;
using System.IO;
```

26. Replace the default constructor with the following constructor.

```
public Decryptor(EncryptionAlgorithm algId)
{
   transformer = new DecryptTransformer(algId);
}
```

27. Add the following private member variables to the class.

```
private DecryptTransformer transformer;
private byte[] initVec;
```

28. Add the following **Decrypt** method to the class.

```
public byte[] Decrypt(byte[] bytesData, byte[] bytesKey)
{
   //Set up the memory stream for the decrypted data.
   MemoryStream memStreamDecryptedData = new MemoryStream();

   //Pass in the initialization vector.
   transformer.IV = initVec;
   ICryptoTransform transform = transformer.GetCryptoServiceProvider(bytesKey);
   CryptoStream decStream = new CryptoStream(memStreamDecryptedData,
                                        transform,
                                        CryptoStreamMode.Write);
   try
   {
      decStream.Write(bytesData, 0, bytesData.Length);
   }
   catch(Exception ex)
   {
      throw new Exception("Error while writing encrypted data to the stream: \n"
                        + ex.Message);
   }
   decStream.FlushFinalBlock();
   decStream.Close();
   // Send the data back.
   return memStreamDecryptedData.ToArray();
} //end Decrypt
```

29. Add the following property to the class.

```
public byte[] IV
{
   set{initVec = value;}
}
```

30. On the **Build** menu, click **Build Solution**.

2. Create a Console Test Application

This procedure creates a simple console test application to test the encryption and decryption functionality.

► **To create a console test application**

1. Add a new C# Console application called **EncryptionTester** to the current solution.

2. In Solution Explorer, right-click the **EncryptionTester** project, and then click **Set as StartUp Project**.

3. Use Solution Explorer to rename class1.cs as EncryptionTest.cs.

4. In EncryptionTest.cs, rename **Class1** as **EncryptionTest**.

5. Add a project reference to the **Encryption** project.

6. Add the following **using** statements at the top of EncryptionTest.cs.

```
using System.Text;
using Encryption;
```

7. Add the following code to the **Main** method.

```
// Set the required algorithm
EncryptionAlgorithm algorithm = EncryptionAlgorithm.Des;

// Init variables.
byte[] IV = null;
byte[] cipherText = null;
byte[] key = null;

try
{ //Try to encrypt.
  //Create the encryptor.
  Encryptor enc = new Encryptor(EncryptionAlgorithm.Des);
  byte[] plainText = Encoding.ASCII.GetBytes("Test String");

  if ((EncryptionAlgorithm.TripleDes == algorithm) ||
      (EncryptionAlgorithm.Rijndael == algorithm))
  { //3Des only work with a 16 or 24 byte key.
    key = Encoding.ASCII.GetBytes("password12345678");
    if (EncryptionAlgorithm.Rijndael == algorithm)
    { // Must be 16 bytes for Rijndael.
      IV = Encoding.ASCII.GetBytes("init vec is big.");
    }
    else
    {
      IV = Encoding.ASCII.GetBytes("init vec");
    }
  }
  else
```

```
    { //Des only works with an 8 byte key. The others uses variable length keys.
      //Set the key to null to have a new one generated.
      key = Encoding.ASCII.GetBytes("password");
      IV = Encoding.ASCII.GetBytes("init vec");
    }
    // Uncomment the next lines to have the key or IV generated for you.
    // key = null;
    // IV = null;

    enc.IV = IV;

    // Perform the encryption.
    cipherText = enc.Encrypt(plainText, key);
    // Retrieve the intialization vector and key. You will need it
    // for decryption.
    IV = enc.IV;
    key = enc.Key;

    // Look at your cipher text and initialization vector.
    Console.WriteLine("            Cipher text: " +
                  Convert.ToBase64String(cipherText));
    Console.WriteLine("Initialization vector: " + Convert.ToBase64String(IV));
    Console.WriteLine("                    Key: " + Convert.ToBase64String(key));
}
catch(Exception ex)
{
    Console.WriteLine("Exception encrypting. " + ex.Message);
    return;
}
try
{ //Try to decrypt.
    //Set up your decryption, give it the algorithm and initialization vector.
    Decryptor dec = new Decryptor(algorithm);
    dec.IV = IV;
    // Go ahead and decrypt.
    byte[] plainText = dec.Decrypt(cipherText, key);
    // Look at your plain text.
    Console.WriteLine("            Plain text: " +
                  Encoding.ASCII.GetString(plainText));
}
catch(Exception ex)
{
    Console.WriteLine("Exception decrypting. " + ex.Message);
    return;
}
```

8. On the **Build** menu, click **Build Solution**.

9. Run the test application to verify the operation of the **Encryptor** and **Decryptor** classes.

References

For more information, see "How To: Store an Encrypted Connection String in the Registry" in the Reference section of this book.

How To:
Store an Encrypted Connection String in the Registry

The registry represents one possible location for an application to store database connection strings. Although individual registry keys can be secured with Windows access control lists (ACLs), for added security you should store encrypted connection strings.

This How To describes how to store an encrypted database connection string in the registry and retrieve it from an ASP.NET Web application. It uses the generic encryption and decryption managed class library created in "How to: Create an Encryption Library," which can be found in Reference section of this book.

If you have not already created the encryption class library assembly, do so before continuing with the current How To.

For more information about other locations and ways of securely storing database connection strings, see "Storing Database Connection Strings Securely" in Chapter 12, "Data Access Security."

Notes

- The connection string, initialization vector and key used for encryption will be stored in the registry as named values beneath the following registry key.

  HKEY_LOCAL_MACHINE\Software\TestApplication

- The initialization vector and key must be stored in order to allow the connection string to be decrypted.

Requirements

The following items describe the recommended hardware, software, network infrastructure, skills and knowledge, and service packs you will need.

- Microsoft® Windows® 2000 operating system
- Microsoft Visual Studio® .NET development system

The procedures in this article also require that you have knowledge of the Microsoft Visual C#™ development tool.

Summary

This How To includes the following procedures:

1. Store the Encrypted Data in the Registry
2. Create an ASP.NET Web Application

1. Store the Encrypted Data in the Registry

This procedure creates a Windows application that will be used to encrypt a sample database string and store it in the registry.

▶ **To store the encrypted data in the registry**

1. Start Visual Studio .NET and create a new C# Windows project called **EncryptionTestApp**.

2. Add an assembly reference to the Encryption.dll assembly.

   To create this assembly, you must perform the steps described in "How To: Create an Encryption Library" in the Reference section of this book.

3. Add the following **using** statements to the top of Form1.cs beneath the existing **using** statements.

   ```
   using Encryption;
   using System.Text;
   using Microsoft.Win32;
   ```

4. Add the controls in Table 1 to Form1 and arrange them as illustrated in Figure 1.

Table 1: EncryptionTestApp controls

Control	Text	ID
Label	Connection String:	
TextBox		txtConnectionString
Label	Key:	
TextBox		txtKey
Label	Initialization Vector:	
TextBox		txtInitializationVector
Label	Encrypted String	
TextBox		txtEncryptedString
Label	Decrypted String	
TextBox		txtDecryptedString

Control	Text	ID
Button	Encrypt	btnEncrypt
Button	Decrypt	btnDecrypt
Button	Write Registry Data	btnWriteRegistryData

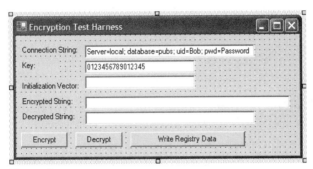

Figure 1
Encryption Test Harness dialog box

5. Set the **Text** property of **txtConnectionString** to

   ```
   "Server=local; database=pubs; uid=Bob; pwd=Password"
   ```

6. Set the **Text** property of **txtKey** to

   ```
   "0123456789012345"
   ```

   The key length is 16 bytes to suite the Triple DES encryption algorithm.

7. Set the **Text** property of **Form1** to

   ```
   "Encryption Test Harness"
   ```

8. Double-click the **Encrypt** button to create a button click event handler and add the following code to the event handler.

   ```
   try
   {
     // Create the encryptor object, specifying 3DES as the
     // encryption algorithm
     Encryptor enc = new Encryptor(EncryptionAlgorithm.TripleDes);
     // Get the connection string as a byte array
     byte[] plainText = Encoding.ASCII.GetBytes(txtConnectionString.Text);
     byte[] key = Encoding.ASCII.GetBytes(txtKey.Text);
   ```

```
    // Perform the encryption
    byte[] cipherText = enc.Encrypt(plainText, key);
    // Store the intialization vector, as this will be required
    // for decryption
    txtInitializationVector.Text = Encoding.ASCII.GetString(enc.IV);

    // Display the encrypted string
    txtEncryptedString.Text = Convert.ToBase64String(cipherText);
}
catch(Exception ex)
{
    MessageBox.Show("Exception encrypting: " + ex.Message,
                    "Encryption Test  Harness");
}
```

9. Return to Form1 in Designer mode and double-click the **Decrypt** button to create a button click event handler.

10. Add the following code to the **Decrypt** button event handler.

```
try
{
    // Set up the Decryptor object
    Decryptor dec = new Decryptor(EncryptionAlgorithm.TripleDes);

    // Set the Initialization Vector
    dec.IV = Encoding.ASCII.GetBytes(txtInitializationVector.Text);

    byte[] key = Encoding.ASCII.GetBytes(txtKey.Text);
    // Perform the decryption
    byte[] plainText =  dec.Decrypt(Convert.FromBase64String(
                                    txtEncryptedString.Text),
                                    key);

    // Display the decrypted string.
    txtDecryptedString.Text = Encoding.ASCII.GetString(plainText);
}
catch(Exception ex)
{
    MessageBox.Show("Exception decrypting. " + ex.Message,
                    "Encryption Test Harness");
}
```

11. Return to Form1 in Designer mode and double-click the **Write Registry Data** button to create a button click event handler.

12. Add the following code to the event handler.

```
// Create registry key and named values
RegistryKey rk = Registry.LocalMachine.OpenSubKey("Software",true);
rk = rk.CreateSubKey("TestApplication");
```

```
// Write encrypted string, initialization vector and key to the registry
rk.SetValue("connectionString",txtEncryptedString.Text);
rk.SetValue("initVector",Convert.ToBase64String(
            Encoding.ASCII.GetBytes(txtInitializationVector.Text)));
rk.SetValue("key",Convert.ToBase64String(Encoding.ASCII.GetBytes(
                                  txtKey.Text)));
MessageBox.Show("The data has been successfully written to the registry");
```

13. Run the application, and then click **Encrypt**.

    The encrypted connection string is displayed in the **Encrypted String** field.

14. Click **Decrypt**.

    The original string is displayed in the **Decrypted String** field.

15. Click **Write Registry Data**.

16. In the message box, click **OK**.

17. Run regedit.exe and view the contents of the following key.

    ```
    HKLM\Software\TestApplication
    ```

    Confirm that encoded values are present for the **connectionString**, **initVector** and **key** named values.

18. Close regedit and the test harness application.

2. Create an ASP.NET Web Application

This procedure develops a simple ASP.NET Web application that will retrieve the encrypted connection string from the registry and decrypt it.

▶ **To create an ASP.NET application**

1. Create a new Visual C# ASP.NET Web Application called **EncryptionWebApp**.

2. Add an assembly reference to the Encryption.dll assembly.

   To create this assembly, you must perform the steps described in "How To: Create an Encryption Library" in the Reference section of this book.

3. Open Webform1.aspx.cs and add the following **using** statements at the top of the file beneath the existing **using** statements.

   ```
   using Encryption;
   using System.Text;
   using Microsoft.Win32;
   ```

4. Add the controls listed in Table 2 to WebForm1.aspx.

Table 2: WebForm1.aspx controls

Control	Text	ID
Label		lblEncryptedString
Label		lblDecryptedString
Button	Get Connection String	btnGetConnectionString

5. Double-click the **Get Connection String** button to create a button click event handler.

6. Add the following code to the event handler.

```
RegistryKey rk = Registry.LocalMachine.OpenSubKey(
                              @"Software\TestApplication",false);
lblEncryptedString.Text = (string)rk.GetValue("connectionString");

string initVector = (string)rk.GetValue("initVector");
string strKey = (string)rk.GetValue("key");

Decryptor dec = new Decryptor(EncryptionAlgorithm.TripleDes );
dec.IV = Convert.FromBase64String(initVector);

// Decrypt the string
byte[] plainText = dec.Decrypt(Convert.FromBase64String(
                        lblEncryptedString.Text),
                        Convert.FromBase64String(strKey));

lblDecryptedString.Text = Encoding.ASCII.GetString(plainText);
```

7. On the **Build** menu, click **Build Solution**.

8. Right-click **Webform1.aspx** in Solution Explorer, and then click **View in Browser**.

9. Click **Get Connection String**.

The encrypted and decrypted connection strings are displayed on the Web form.

References

For more information, see "How To: Create an Encryption Library" in the Reference section of this book.

How To:
Use Role-based Security
with Enterprise Services

This How To describes how to create a simple serviced component that uses Enterprise Services (ES) roles for authorization.

Notes

- ES roles are not the same as .NET roles.
- ES roles can contain Windows group or Windows user accounts.
- ES roles are maintained in the COM+ catalog.
- ES roles can be applied at the (ES) application, interface, class or method levels.
- ES roles can be partially configured declaratively by using .NET attributes in the serviced component's assembly.
- Windows group and user accounts must be added by an administrator at deployment time.
- Administrators can use the Component Services administration tool, or script.
- To effectively use Enterprise Services role-based security from an ASP.NET Web application, the Web application must use Windows authentication and impersonate callers prior to calling the serviced components.

Requirements

The following items describe the recommended hardware, software, network infrastructure, skills and knowledge, and service packs you will need.

- Microsoft® Visual Studio® .NET development system

The procedures in this article also require that you have knowledge of ASP.NET Web development with the Microsoft Visual C#™ development tool.

Summary

This How To includes the following procedures:

1. Create a C# Class Library Application to Host the Serviced Component
2. Create the Serviced Component
3. Configure the Serviced Component
4. Generate a Strong Name for the Assembly
5. Build the Assembly and Add it to the Global Assembly Cache
6. Manually Register the Serviced Component
7. Examine the Configured Application
8. Create a Test Client Application

1. Create a C# Class Library Application to Host the Serviced Component

This procedure creates a new C# class library application that contains the serviced component.

▶ **To create a C# class library application to host the serviced component**

1. Start Visual Studio .NET and create a new C# class library application called **ServicedCom**.
2. Rename the default class file Class1.cs to SimpleComponent.cs.
3. Double-click SimpleComponent.cs to open it and rename the **Class1** type as **SimpleComponent**. Also update the name of the class' default constructor.

2. Create the Serviced Component

This procedure derives the **SimpleComponent** class from the **EnterpriseServices.ServicedComponent** class to turn this type into a serviced component. You will then create an interface and implement it within the **SimpleComponent** class. To use interface and method level security, you must define and implement interfaces.

▶ **To create the serviced component**

1. Add a reference to the System.EnterpriseServices assembly.
2. Add the following **using** statement to the top of the SimpleComponent.cs file beneath the existing **using** statements.

```
using System.EnterpriseServices;
```

3. Derive the **SimpleComponent** class from **ServicedComponent**.

```
public class SimpleComponent : ServicedComponent
```

4. Add the following interface definition within the **ServicedCom** namespace.

```
public interface ISomeInterface
{
   int Add( int operand1, int operand2 );
}
```

5. Derive **SimpleComponent** from this interface.

```
public class SimpleComponent : ServicedComponent, ISomeInterface
```

6. Implement the interface within the **SimpleComponent** class as follows.

```
public int Add( int operand1, int operand2 )
{
    return operand1 + operand2;
}
```

3. Configure the Serviced Component

This procedure configures the serviced component for method-level role-based security.

► **To configure the serviced component**

1. Add the following attributes directly above the **SimpleComponent** class. The **ComponentAccessControl** attribute enables component-level access checks and the **SecureMethod** attribute enables method level access checks.

```
[ComponentAccessControl]
[SecureMethod]
public class SimpleComponent : ServicedComponent, ISomeInterface
```

2. Add the following attribute above the **Add** method to create the **Manager** role and associate it with the method.

```
[SecurityRole("Manager")]
public int Add( int operand1, int operand2 )
{
   return operand1 + operand2;
}
```

3. Open assemblyinfo.cs and add the following **using** statement to the top of the file below the existing **using** statements.

```
using System.EnterpriseServices;
```

4. Move to the bottom of the file and add the following attributes. These are used to configure the Enterprise Services application used to host the serviced component.

```
// Configure the application as a server (out-of-process) application
[assembly: ApplicationActivation(ActivationOption.Server)]
// For meaningful role-based security, enable access checking at the process
// and component levels by using the following .NET attribute.
[assembly: ApplicationAccessControl(AccessChecksLevel=
                        AccessChecksLevelOption.ApplicationComponent)]
// Set the name and description for the application
[assembly: ApplicationName("SimpleRoles")]
[assembly: Description("Simple application to show ES Roles")]
// Add some additional roles
[assembly:SecurityRole("Employee")]
[assembly:SecurityRole("Senior Manager")]
```

4. Generate a Strong Name for the Assembly

Assemblies that host serviced components must be strong named. This procedure generates a public-private key pair used to strong name the assembly.

▶ **To generate a strong name for the assembly**

1. Open a command window and go to the current project directory.

2. Use the sn.exe utility to generate a key file that contains a public-private key pair.

```
sn.exe -k SimpleComponent.snk
```

3. In Visual Studio, open assemblyinfo.cs.

4. Locate the [**AssemblyKeyFile**] attribute and modify it to reference the key file in the project directory as follows.

```
[assembly: AssemblyKeyFile(@"..\..\SimpleComponent.snk")]
```

5. Build the Assembly and Add it to the Global Assembly Cache

This procedure builds the assembly that contains the serviced component and then adds it to the global assembly cache. Serviced components should generally be registered in the global assembly cache because they are system level resources. Serviced components hosted in COM+ server applications require installation in the global assembly cache, while library applications do not (although it is recommended).

▶ **To build the assembly and add it to the global assembly cache**

1. On the **Build** menu, click **Build Solution**.

2. Return to the command window and run the following command to add the assembly to the global assembly cache.

```
gacutil -i bin\debug\ServicedCom.dll
```

6. Manually Register the Serviced Component

Serviced components can either be manually registered with the Regsvcs.exe tool, or they can be automatically registered using "lazy" registration. With "lazy" registration, the component is registered (and the hosting COM+ application created and configured using the assembly's meta data) the first time an instance of the serviced component is instantiated.

To avoid the one time performance hit associated with this approach, this procedure manually registers the serviced component.

▶ **To manually register the serviced component**

1. Return to the command window.

2. Run regsvcs.exe to register the component.

```
regsvcs bin\debug\ServicedCom.dll
```

7. Examine the Configured Application

This procedure uses the Component Services tool and examines the catalog settings created as a result of the .NET attributes used earlier.

▶ **To examine the configured application**

1. From the **Administrative Tools** program group, start Component Services.

2. Expand **Component Services**, **Computers**, **My Computer**, and **COM+ Applications**.

3. Right-click **SimpleRoles**, and then click **Properties**.

4. Click the **Security** tab and make sure that **Enforce access checks for this application** is selected and that the security level is set to perform access checks at the process and component level. This configuration is a result of the .NET attributes used earlier.

5. Click **OK** to close the **Properties** dialog box.

6. Expand the **SimpleRoles** application, and then expand the **Components** folder and the **ServicedCom.SimpleComponent** class.

7. Navigate to the **Add** method beneath the **ISomeInterface** method in the Interfaces folder.

8. Right-click **Add**, and then click **Properties**.

9. Click the **Security** tab and notice that the **Manager** role is associated with the method.

10. Click **OK** to close the **Properties** dialog box.

11. Expand the **Roles** folder beneath the **SimpleRoles** application. Notice the roles that you created earlier with .NET attributes. Also notice the **Marshaler** role. This is created as a direct result of the [**SecureMethod**] attribute added earlier, and is required for method level security.

8. Create a Test Client Application

This procedure creates a Windows Forms-based test client application to instantiate and call the serviced component.

▶ **To create a test client application**

1. Add a new C# Windows-based application called **TestClient** to the current solution.

2. Add a new project reference to the **ServicedCom** project.

   a. In Solution Explorer, right-click **References**, and then click **Add Reference**.

   b. Click the **Projects** tab.

   c. Select **ServicedCom**, click **Select**, and then click **OK**.

3. Add a reference to **System.EnterpriseServices**.

4. Add a button to the application's main form.

5. Double-click the button to create a button click event handler.

6. Add the following **using** statement to the top of the form1.cs beneath the existing **using** statements.

```
using ServicedCom;
```

7. Return to the button click event handler and add the following code to instantiate and call the serviced component.

```
SimpleComponent comp = new SimpleComponent();
MessageBox.Show( "Result is: " + comp.Add(1, 2));
```

8. On the **Build** menu, click **Build Solution**.

9. In Solution Explorer, right-click the **TestClient** project, and then click **Set as StartUp Project**.

10. Press **Ctrl+F5** to run the **TestClient** application.

    You should see that an unhandled exception is generated.

11. Click the **Details** button on the message box to view the exception details.

    You will see that a **System.UnauthorizedAccessException** has been generated. This is because your interactive logon account used to run the **TestClient** application is not a member of the **Manager** role, which is required to call the **Add** on the serviced component.

12. Click **Quit** to stop the application.

13. Return to Component Services and add your current (interactive) account to the **Manager** role and the **Marshaler** role.

Note: The Enterprise Services infrastructure uses a number of system-level interfaces that are exposed by all serviced components. These include **IManagedObject**, **IDisposable**, and **IServiceComponentInfo**. If access checks are enabled at the interface or method levels, the Enterprise Services infrastructure is denied access to these interfaces.

As a result, Enterprise Services creates a special role called **Marshaler** and associates the role with these interfaces. At deployment time, application administrators need to add all users to the **Marshaler** role who needs to access any methods or interface of the class. You could automate this in two different ways:

1. Write a script that uses the Component Services object model to copy all users from other roles to the Marshaler role.

2. Write a script which assigns all other roles to these three special interfaces and delete the Marshaler role.

---

14. Close the **SimpleRoles** application to enable the changes to take effect. To do this, right-click the application name, and then click **Shut down**.

15. Return to Visual Studio .NET and press **Ctrl+F5** to run the **TestClient** application again.

16. Click the form's button and confirm that the method is successfully called.

How To:
Call a Web Service Using
Client Certificates from ASP.NET

Web services often need to be able to authenticate their callers (other applications) in order to perform authorization. Client certificates provide an excellent authentication mechanism for Web services. When you use client certificates, your application also benefits from the creation of a secure channel (using Secure Sockets Layer [SSL]) between the client application and Web service. This allows you to securely send confidential information to and from the Web service. SSL ensures message integrity and confidentiality.

This How To describes how to call a Web service that is configured to require client certificates.

Note: The information in this How To also applies to remote components hosted by ASP.NET and IIS.

Why Use a Serviced Component?

The solution presented in this How To uses a serviced component configured to run in an Enterprise Services server application, using a custom service account. The ASP.NET Web application calls the serviced component, which makes the call to the Web service (passing a client certificate). This solution configuration is illustrated in Figure 1 on the next page.

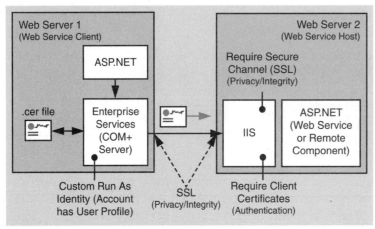

Figure 1
ASP.NET calls a serviced component to invoke the Web service

This arrangement is to ensure that the system has access to a user profile when communicating with the Web service. This is required for the initial SSL handshake.

Note: The ASPNET account used to run Web applications has the "Deny interactive logon" privilege, which prevents you from logging on interactively with this account. As a result, this account does not have a user profile.

Do not grant the ASPNET account (or any account used to run Web applications) the interactive logon capability. Always follow the principle of least privilege when configuring accounts to run Web applications and grant them as few privileges as possible. For more information, see "How To: Create a Custom Account to Run ASP.NET" in the Reference section of this book.

Why is a User Profile Required?

When you make a request to a Web service that requires client certificates, there is an SSL handshake that takes place between the client and server. A few of the components exchanged are the server certificate, client certificate, and a "pre-master secret" which is generated by the client. This secret is used later in the protocol to generate a "master secret."

In order for the server to verify that the presenter of the certificate is indeed the holder of the private key, the client must encrypt the pre-master secret with the private key and send the encrypted pre-master secret to the server. In order for the system to access the client's private key to sign the pre-master secret it must access the private key from the key store of the client. The key store is located in the client's profile which must be loaded.

Requirements

The following items describe the recommended hardware, software, network infrastructure, skills and knowledge, and service packs you will need.

- Microsoft® Windows® 2000 operating system
- Microsoft Visual Studio® .NET development system
- Access to a Certificate Authority (CA) to generate new certificates
- A Web server with an installed server certificate

   For more information about installing Web server certificates, see "How To: Setup SSL on a Web Server".

The procedures in this How To also require that you have knowledge of the Microsoft Visual C#™ development tool.

Summary

This How To includes the following procedures:

1. Create a Simple Web Service
2. Configure the Web Service Virtual Directory to Require Client Certificates
3. Create a Custom Account for Running a Serviced Component
4. Request a Client Certificate for the Custom Account
5. Test the Client Certificate using a Browser
6. Export the Client Certificate to a File
7. Develop the Serviced Component Used to Call the Web Service
8. Configure and Install the Serviced Component
9. Develop a Web Application to Call the Serviced Component

Note: In this How To, the Web service computer (this hosts the Web service) is named "WSServer" and the Web service client computer (this hosts the client ASP.NET Web application and serviced component) is named "WSClient."

---

1. Create a Simple Web Service

▶ **To create a simple Web service on the Web service host computer**

1. Start Visual Studio .NET and create a new C# ASP.NET Web Service application called **SecureMath**.

2. Rename service1.asmx as math.asmx.

3. Open math.asmx.cs and rename the **Service1** class as **math**.

4. Add the following Web method to the **math** class.

```
[WebMethod]
public long Add(long operand1, long operand2)
{
    return (operand1 + operand2);
}
```

5. On the **Build** menu, click **Build Solution** to create the Web service.

2. Configure the Web Service Virtual Directory to Require Client Certificates

This procedure uses Internet Information Services to configure your Web service's virtual directory for SSL and to require certificates.

This procedure assumes that you have a valid certificate installed on your Web server. For more information about installing Web server certificates, see "How To Setup SSL on a Web Server" in the Reference section of this book.

▶ **To configure the Web service virtual directory to require client certificates**

1. Start Internet Information Services on the Web service host computer.

2. Navigate to the **SecureMath** virtual directory.

3. Right-click **SecureMath**, and then click **Properties**.

4. Click the **Directory Security** tab.

5. Under **Secure communications**, click **Edit**.

   If **Edit** is unavailable, it is most likely that you haven't installed a Web server certificate.

6. Select the **Require secure channel (SSL)** check box.

7. Select the **Require client certificates** option.

8. Click **OK**, and then click **OK** again.

9. In the Inheritance Overrides dialog box, click **Select All**, and then click **OK** to close the **SecureMath** properties dialog box.

   This applies the new security settings to all subdirectories beneath the virtual directory root.

3. Create a Custom Account for Running the Serviced Component

This procedure creates a new user account on the Web service client computer that you will use to run the serviced component that calls the Web service.

▶ **To create a custom account for running the serviced component**

1. Create a new user account with a strong password on the client computer. Clear the **User must change password at next logon** check box, and then select the **Password never expires** option.

2. Add the account to the **Administrators** group.

   The account used to load a user profile must be an administrator on the local computer.

4. Request a Client Certificate for the Custom Account

In this procedure, you will log on to the client computer using the new custom account. You will then issue a request for a certificate. This procedure assumes that you are using Microsoft Certificate Services. If you are not using Microsoft Certificate Services to create new certificates, issue a request to your preferred CA for a client certificate and install the certificate, while logged on using the custom account.

This procedure also assumes that Microsoft Certificate Services is configured to automatically issue certificates in response to certificate requests. It can also be configured for pending requests, which require an administrator to explicitly issue the certificate.

▶ **To check the Microsoft Certificate Services setting**

1. On the Microsoft Certificate Services computer, click **Certification Authority** in the **Administrative Tools** programs group.

2. Expand **Certification Authority (Local)**, right-click the certification authority, and click **Properties**.

3. Click the **Policy Module** tab, and then click **Configure**.

4. Check the default action.

The following procedure assumes that **Always issue the certificate** is selected.

▶ **To request a client certificate for the custom account**

1. Log off the client computer and log back on using the custom account.

   This forces the creation of a user profile for the custom account.

2. Browse to the CA in order to request a client certificate. For example, if your CA is located on the CAServer computer, browse to the following location.

   ```
   http://caserver/certsrv
   ```

3. Click **Request a certificate**, and then click **Next**.

4. Ensure User Certificate is selected, and then click **Next**.

5. Click **Submit**.

   A request is generated and sent to the CA for processing.

6. After the certificate is issued and you receive a response from the CA server, click **Install this certificate**.

7. Ensure that the issuing CA's certificate is installed as a trusted root certificate authority on the local computer.

   To confirm this, perform the following steps:

   a. On the taskbar, click the **Start** button, and then click **Run**.

   b. Type **mmc**, and then click **OK**.

   c. On the **File** menu, click **Add/Remove Snap-in**.

   d. Click **Add**.

   e. Click **Certificates**, and then click **Add**.

   f. Click **Computer account**, and then click **Next**.

   g. Click **Local Computer: (the computer this console is running on)**, and then click **Finish**.

   h. Click **Close**, and then click **OK**.

   i. In the left pane of the MMC snap-in, expand **Certificates (Local Computer)**.

   j. Expand **Trusted Root Certification Authorities**, and then click **Certificates**.

   k. Confirm that your CA's certificate is listed.

   If the CA's certificate isn't listed, perform the following steps:

   a. Browse to *http://caserver/certsrv*.

   b. Click **Retrieve the CA certificate or certificate revocation list**, and then click **Next**.

   c. Click **Install this CA certification path**.

5. Test the Client Certificate Using a Browser

In this procedure, you will browse to the Web service in order to confirm that there are no problems with either the server or client certificates.

▶ **To test the client certificate using a browser**

1. Use Internet Explorer and navigate to *https://server/SecureMath/Math.asmx*.

   Make sure that you specify "https" because the site is configured to require SSL.

2. A **Client Authentication** dialog box should appear. Select your client certificate, and then click **OK**.

3. Confirm that the Web service test page is displayed successfully within your browser.

   If you see the dialog box illustrated in Figure 2, you need to install the certificate authority's certificate into the **Trusted Root Certification Authorities** store, as described in the previous procedure.

Figure 2
Security Alert dialog box

6. Export the Client Certificate to a File

This procedure exports the client certificate to a file. This is subsequently retrieved by the serviced component, when it needs to pass the certificate to the Web service.

▶ **To export the client certificate to a file**

1. Within Internet Explorer, click **Internet Options** on the **Tools** menu.

2. Click the **Content** tab.

3. Click **Certificates**.

4. Click the client certificate, and then click **Export**.

5. Click **Next** to move past the welcome dialog box of the Certificate Export Wizard.

6. Confirm that **No, do not export the private key** is selected, and then click **Next**.

7. Make sure that **DER encoded binary X.509 (.CER)** is selected, and then click **Next**.

   You must use this format, because the .NET Framework does not support Base-64 or PKCS #7 formats.

8. Enter an export file name. Note the location of the .cer export file, because you will require this again in a subsequent procedure.

9. Click **Next,** and then click **Finish** to export the certificate.

10. Close Internet Explorer.

11. Log off the computer and log back on using your regular development account.

7. Develop the Serviced Component Used to Call the Web Service

This procedure creates a new C# Class Library application and creates the serviced component used to call the Web service. This procedure assumes that you are working on the client computer.

▶ **To develop the serviced component used to call the Web service**

1. Start Visual Studio.NET and create a new C# Class Library project called **WebServiceRequestor**.

2. Add a Web reference to the **SecureMath** Web service.

> **Important:** You must temporarily reconfigure your Web service's virtual directory to not require client certificates (although still require SSL), prior to adding the Web reference. After you successfully add the Web reference, change the virtual directory configuration back to require client certificates.
>
> In practice, if a site requires client certificates, the publisher of the service makes the WSDL available as a separate offline file, which the consumers (of the service) can use to create the proxy.

In the **Add Web Reference** dialog box, be sure to specify **https** when specifying the Web service location. Failure to do so results in an error because the Web service virtual directory is configured to require SSL.

3. Add a reference to the System.EnterpriseServices assembly.

4. Rename class1.cs as ProfileManager.cs.

5. Add the following class definition to ProfileManager.cs (replacing the skeleton class1 class). The **ProfileManager** class uses P/Invoke to call the **LoadUserProfile** and **UnloadUserProfile** Win32 APIs.

```
internal class ProfileManager
{
    [DllImport("Userenv.dll", SetLastError=true,
               CharSet=System.Runtime.InteropServices.CharSet.Auto)]
    internal static extern bool LoadUserProfile(IntPtr hToken,
                                        ref PROFILEINFO lpProfileInfo);

    [DllImport("Userenv.dll", SetLastError=true,
               CharSet=System.Runtime.InteropServices.CharSet.Auto)]
    internal static extern bool  UnloadUserProfile(IntPtr hToken,
                                        IntPtr hProfile);

    [StructLayout(LayoutKind.Sequential, CharSet=CharSet.Ansi)]
    public struct PROFILEINFO
    {
        public int dwSize;
        public int dwFlags;
        public String lpUserName;
        public String lpProfilePath;
        public String lpDefaultPath;
        public String lpServerName;
        public String lpPolicyPath;
        public IntPtr hProfile;
    }
}
```

6. Add a second class file called MathServiceComponent.cs to the project.

7. Add the following **using** statements to MathServiceComponent.cs below the existing **using** statement.

```
using System.Net;
using System.Web.Services;
using System.Security.Principal;
using System.EnterpriseServices;
using System.Runtime.InteropServices;
using System.Security.Cryptography.X509Certificates;
using WebServiceRequestor.WebReference1;
```

8. Add the following class definition, which provides a public **CallMathWebService** method. You will call this method in a later procedure from a client ASP.NET Web application.

> **Note:** In the following code, replace the account name used to load the user profile with the name of the custom account you created in Step 3, "Create a Custom Account for Running the Serviced Component."

```
// This class calls the web service that requires a certificate.
public class MathServiceComponent : ServicedComponent
{
    [DllImport("advapi32.dll", CharSet=CharSet.Auto, SetLastError=true)]
    private extern static bool DuplicateToken(IntPtr ExistingTokenHandle,
                                     int SECURITY_IMPERSONATION_LEVEL,
                                     ref IntPtr DuplicateTokenHandle);

    [DllImport("kernel32.dll", CharSet=CharSet.Auto)]
    private extern static bool CloseHandle(IntPtr handle);

    // Calls the Web service that requires client certificates
    // certFilepath points to the .cer file to use
    // url is the Web service url
    // operand1 and operand2 are the parameters to pass to the Web service
    public long CallMathWebService(String certFilepath,
                                     String url, int operand1, int operand2)
    {
        bool retVal = false;
        // Need to duplicate the token. LoadUserProfile needs a token with
        // TOKEN_IMPERSONATE and TOKEN_DUPLICATE.
        const int SecurityImpersonation = 2;
        IntPtr dupeTokenHandle = DupeToken(WindowsIdentity.GetCurrent().Token,
                                     SecurityImpersonation);
        if(IntPtr.Zero == dupeTokenHandle)
        {
            throw new Exception("Unable to duplicate token.");
        }
        // Load the profile.
        ProfileManager.PROFILEINFO profile = new ProfileManager.PROFILEINFO();
        profile.dwSize = 32;
        //TODO: Replace with custom account name created in step 3.
        profile.lpUserName = @"machinename\customaccountname";
        retVal = ProfileManager.LoadUserProfile(dupeTokenHandle, ref profile);
        if(false == retVal)
        {
            throw new Exception("Error loading user profile. " +
                                Marshal.GetLastWin32Error());
        }
        // Instantiate the Web service proxy
        math mathservice = new math();
        mathservice.Url = url;
        String certPath = certFilepath;
        mathservice.ClientCertificates.Add(
                                X509Certificate.CreateFromCertFile(certPath));
```

```
     long lngResult = 0;
     try
     {
        lngResult = mathservice.Add(operand1, operand2);
     }
     catch(Exception ex)
     {
        if(ex is WebException)
        {
           WebException we = ex as WebException;
           WebResponse webResponse = we.Response;
           throw new Exception("Exception calling method. " + ex.Message);
        }
     }
     ProfileManager.UnloadUserProfile(WindowsIdentity.GetCurrent().Token,
                                      profile.hProfile);
     CloseHandle(dupeTokenHandle);
     return lngResult;
  }

  private IntPtr DupeToken(IntPtr token, int Level)
  {
     IntPtr dupeTokenHandle = new IntPtr(0);
     bool retVal = DuplicateToken(token, Level, ref dupeTokenHandle);
     if (false == retVal)
     {
        return IntPtr.Zero;
     }
     return dupeTokenHandle;
  }
} // end class
```

9. On the **Build** menu, click **Build Solution**.

8. Configure and Install the Serviced Component

This procedure configures the service component, generates a strong name, installs it in the global assembly cache and registers it with COM+.

1. Open assemblyinfo.cs and add the following **using** statement beneath the existing **using** statements.

   ```
   using System.EnterpriseServices;
   ```

2. Add the following assembly level attribute to assemblyinfo.cs to configure the serviced component to run within a COM+ server application.

   ```
   [assembly: ApplicationActivation(ActivationOption.Server)]
   ```

3. Open a command prompt window and change to the current project directory.

4. Use the sn.exe utility to generate a key file that contains a public-private key pair.

```
sn.exe -k WebServiceRequestor.snk
```

5. Return to Visual Studio .NET.

6. Locate the [**AssemblyKeyFile**] attribute within assemblyinfo.cs and modify it to reference the key file in the project directory as follows.

```
[assembly: AssemblyKeyFile(@"..\..\WebServiceRequestor.snk")]
```

7. On the **Build** menu, click **Build Solution**.

8. Return to the command prompt and run the following command to add the assembly to the global assembly cache.

```
gacutil.exe /i bin\debug\webservicerequestor.dll
```

9. Run the following command to register the assembly with COM+.

```
regsvcs bin\debug\webservicerequestor.dll
```

10. Start **Component Services** (located beneath the **Administrative Tools** program group).

11. Expand the **Component Services**, **Computers**, and **My Computer** nodes.

12. Expand the **COM+ Applications** folder.

13. Right-click **WebServiceRequestor**, and then click **Properties**.

14. Click the **Identity** tab.

15. Select the **This user:** option and enter the account details corresponding to the custom account that you created earlier.

    This configures the COM+ application to run using your custom account.

16. Click **OK** to close the **Properties** dialog box.

17. Close Component Services.

9. Develop a Web Application to Call the Serviced Component

This procedure creates a simple ASP.NET Web application that you will use as the client application to call the Web service (via the serviced component).

▶ **To develop a Web application to call the serviced component**

1. On the Web service client computer, create a new C# ASP.NET Web application called **SecureMathClient**.

2. Add a reference to System.EnterpriseServices

3. Add a reference to the **WebServiceRequestor** serviced component.

   Browse to WebServiceRequestor.dll located within the bin\debug folder beneath the **WebServiceRequestor** project directory.

4. Open WebForm1.aspx.cs and add the following **using** statement beneath the existing **using** statements.

```
using WebServiceRequestor;
```

5. View WebForm1.aspx in Designer mode and create the form shown in Figure 3 using the following IDs:
   - operand1
   - operand2
   - result
   - add

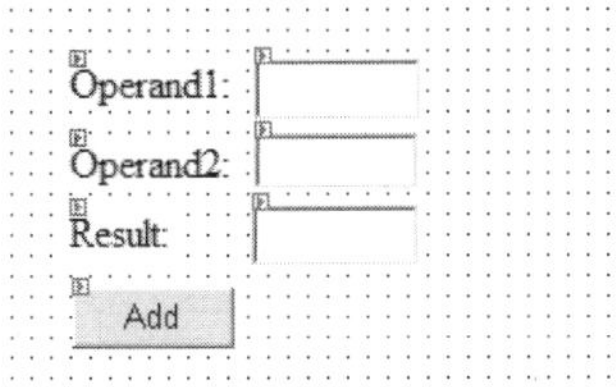

Figure 3
Web Form control arrangement

6. Double-click **Add** to create a button-click event hander.

7. Add the following code to the event handler.

Note: Set the **certPath** string to the location of the certificate file that you exported during Procedure 6, "Export the Client Certificate to a File."

Set the **url** string with the HTTPS URL to your Web service.

```
private void add_Click(object sender, System.EventArgs e)
{
  // TODO: Replace with a valid path to your certificate
  string certPath = @"C:\CustomAccountCert.cer";
  // TODO: Replace with a valid URL to your Web service
  string url = "https://wsserver/securemath/math.asmx";
  MathServiceComponent mathComp = new MathServiceComponent();

  long addResult = mathComp.CallMathWebService( certPath,
                                                url,
                                                Int32.Parse(operand1.Text),
                                                Int32.Parse(operand2.Text));
  result.Text = addResult.ToString();
}
```

8. On the **Build** menu, click **Build Solution**.

9. Run the application. Enter two numbers to add, and then click **Add**.

The Web application will call the serviced component which will call the Web service using SSL and passing the client certificate.

Additional Resources

For more information, see "How To: Set Up SSL on a Web Server" in the Reference section of this book.

How To:
Call a Web Service Using SSL

You can configure a Web service to require Secure Sockets Layer (SSL) to protect sensitive data sent between the client and the service. SSL provides:

- **Message integrity**. This ensures that messages are not modified while in transit.
- **Message confidentiality**. This ensures that messages remain private while in transit.

This How To describes how to configure a Web service to require SSL and how to call the Web service from an ASP.NET client application by using the HTTPS protocol.

Note: The information in this How To also applies to remote objects hosted by ASP.NET and IIS (using .NET Remoting technology). For information about how to create a remote component hosted by IIS, see article Q312107, "HOW TO: Host a remote object in Internet Information Services" in the Microsoft Knowledge Base.

Requirements

The following items describe the recommended hardware, software, network infrastructure, skills and knowledge, and service packs you will need:

- Microsoft® Windows® 2000 Server operating system
- Microsoft Visual Studio® .NET development system
- A Web server with an installed server certificate

  For more information about installing Web server certificates, see "How To: Set Up SSL on a Web Server."

The procedures in this article also require that you have knowledge of ASP.NET Web development with Microsoft Visual C#™ development tool.

Summary

This article includes the following procedures:

1. Create a Simple Web Service
2. Configure the Web Service Virtual Directory to Require SSL
3. Test the Web Service Using a Browser

4. Install the Certificate Authority's Certificate on the Client Computer

5. Develop a Web Application to Call the Serviced Component

1. Create a Simple Web Service

▶ **To create a simple Web service on the Web service host computer**

1. Start Visual Studio .NET and create a new C# ASP.NET Web Service application called **SecureMath**.

2. Rename service1.asmx as math.asmx.

3. Open math.asmx.cs and rename the **Service1** class as **math**.

4. Add the following Web method to the **math** class.

```
[WebMethod]
public long Add(long operand1, long operand2)
{
    return (operand1 + operand2);
}
```

5. To create the Web service, click **Build Solution** on the **Build** menu.

2. Configure the Web Service Virtual Directory to Require SSL

Your Web service runs on Internet Information Services (IIS) and relies on IIS to provide SSL support.

This procedure assumes that you have a valid server certificate installed on your Web server. For more information about installing Web server certificates, see "How To: Set Up SSL on a Web Server."

▶ **To use IIS to configure your Web service's virtual directory for SSL**

1. On the Web service host computer, start **IIS**.

2. Navigate to the **SecureMath** virtual directory.

3. Right-click **SecureMath**, and then click **Properties**.

4. Click the **Directory Security** tab.

5. Under **Secure communications**, click **Edit**.

   If **Edit** is unavailable, it is likely that a Web server certificate is not installed.

6. Select the **Require secure channel (SSL)** check box.

7. Click **OK**, and then **OK** again.

8. In the **Inheritance Overrides** dialog box, click **Select All**, and then click **OK** to close the **SecureMath** properties dialog box.

This applies the new security settings to all subdirectories in the virtual directory root.

3. Test the Web Service Using a Browser

This procedure ensures that the Web server certificate is valid and has been issued by a Certification Authority (CA) that is trusted by the client computer.

▶ **To call the Web service using SSL from Internet Explorer**

1. Start Internet Explorer on the client computer and browse (using HTTPS) to the Web service. For example:

   ```
   https://WebServer/securemath/math.asmx
   ```

   The Web service test page should be displayed by the browser.

2. If the Web service test page is displayed successfully, close Internet Explorer and go to Procedure 5, "Develop a Web Application to Call the Serviced Component."

3. If the **Security Alert** dialog box, as illustrated in Figure 1, is displayed, click **View Certificate** to see the identity of the issuing CA for the Web server certificate. You must install the CA's certificate on the client computer. This is described in Procedure 4, "Install the Certificate Authority's Certificate on the Client Computer."

4. Close Internet Explorer.

Figure 1
Security Alert dialog box

4. Install the Certificate Authority's Certificate on the Client Computer

This procedure installs the issuing CA's certificate on the client computer as a trusted root certificate authority. The client computer must trust the issuing CA in order to accept the server certificate without displaying the **Security Alert** dialog box.

▶ **If you use Microsoft Certificate Services as a CA within your Windows domain**

Perform this procedure only if your Web server certificate was issued by a Microsoft Certificate Services CA. Otherwise, if you have the CA's .cer file, go to Step 8.

1. Start Internet Explorer and browse to http://*hostname*/certsrv, where *hostname* is the name of the computer where Microsoft Certificate Services that issued the server certificate is located.

2. Click **Retrieve the CA certificate or certificate revocation list**, and then click **Next**.

3. Click **Install this CA certification path**.

4. In the **Root Certificate Store** dialog box, click **Yes**.

5. Browse to Web service using HTTPS. For example:

```
https://WebServer/securemath/math.asmx
```

The Web service test page should now be correctly displayed by the browser, without a **Security Alert** dialog box.

You have now installed the CA's certificate in your personal trusted root certificate store. To be able to call the Web service successfully from an ASP.NET page, you must add the CA's certificate to the computer's trusted root store.

6. Repeat Steps 1 and 2, click **Download CA certificate**, and then save it to a file on your local computer.

7. Now perform the remaining steps.

If you have the CA's .cer certificate file

8. On the taskbar, click **Start**, and then click **Run**.

9. Type **mmc**, and then click **OK**.

10. On the **Console** menu, click **Add/Remove Snap-in**.

11. Click **Add**.

12. Select **Certificates**, and then click **Add**.

13. Select **Computer account**, and then click **Next**.

14. Select **Local Computer: (the computer this console is running on)**, and then click **Finish**.

15. Click **Close**, and then **OK**.

16. Expand **Certificates (Local Computer)** in the left pane of the MMC snap-in.

17. Expand **Trusted Root Certification Authorities**.

18. Right-click **Certificates**, point to **All Tasks**, and then click **Import**.

19. Click **Next** to move past the **Welcome** dialog box of the Certificate Import Wizard.

20. Enter the path and filename of the CA's .cer file.

21. Click **Next**.

22. Select **Place all certificates in the following store**, and then click **Browse**.

23. Select **Show physical stores**.

24. Expand **Trusted Root Certification Authorities** within the list, and then select **Local Computer**.

25. Click **OK**, click **Next**, and then click **Finish**.

26. Click **OK** to close the confirmation message box.

27. Refresh the view of the **Certificates** folder within the MMC snap-in and confirm that the CA's certificate is listed.

28. Close the MMC snap-in.

5. Develop a Web Application to Call the Web Service

This procedure creates a simple ASP.NET Web application. You will use this ASP.NET Web application as the client application to call the Web service.

▶ **To create a simple ASP.NET Web application**

1. On the Web service client computer, create a new C# ASP.NET Web application called **SecureMathClient**.

2. Add a Web reference (by using HTTPS) to the Web service.

   a. Right-click the **References** node within Solution Explorer, and then click **Add Web Reference**.

   b. In the **Add Web Reference** dialog box, enter the URL of your Web service. Make sure you use an HTTPS URL.

   Note: If you have already set a Web reference to a Web service without using HTTPS, you can manually edit the generated proxy class file and change the line of code that sets the **Url** property from an HTTP URL to an HTTPS URL.

   ---

   c. Click **Add Reference**.

3. Open WebForm1.aspx.cs and add the following **using** statement beneath the existing **using** statements.

```
using SecureMathClient.WebReference1;
```

4. View WebForm1.aspx in Designer mode and create a form like the one illustrated in Figure 2 using the following IDs:
   - operand1
   - operand2
   - result
   - add

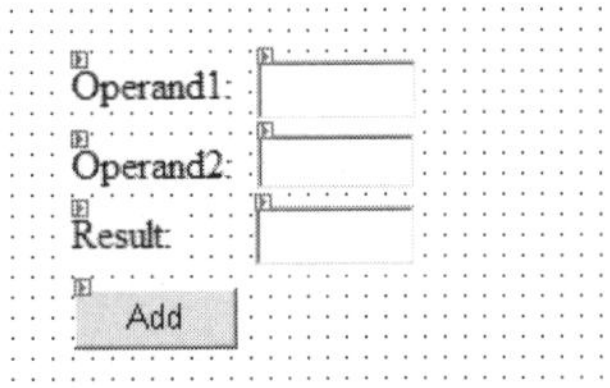

Figure 2
WebForm1.aspx form

5. Double-click the **Add** button to create a button-click event hander.

6. Add the following code to the event handler.

```
private void add_Click(object sender, System.EventArgs e)
{
  math mathService = new math();
  int addResult = (int) mathService.Add( Int32.Parse(operand1.Text),
                                          Int32.Parse(operand2.Text));
  result.Text = addResult.ToString();
}
```

7. On the **Build** menu, click **Build Solution**.

8. Run the application. Enter two numbers to add, and then click the **Add** button. The Web application will call the Web service using SSL.

Additional Resources

- "How To: Set Up SSL on a Web Server"
- "How To: Call a Web Service Using Client Certificates from ASP.NET"

How To:
Host a Remote Object
in a Windows Service

This How To describes how to host a remote object in a Windows service and call it from an ASP.NET Web application.

Notes

- Remote objects (that is, .NET objects accessed remotely using .NET Remoting technology) can be hosted in Windows services, custom executables, or ASP.NET.
- Clients communicate with remote objects hosted in custom executables or Windows services by using the TCP channel.
- Clients communicate with remote objects hosted in ASP.NET by using the HTTP channel.
- If security is the prime concern, host objects in ASP.NET and use the HTTP channel. This allows you to benefit from the underlying security features of ASP.NET and IIS.

  For information about how to host a remote object in ASP.NET (with IIS), see article Q312107, "HOW TO: Host a Remote Object in IIS," in the Microsoft Knowledge Base.
- If performance is the prime concern, host objects in a Windows service and use the TCP channel. This option provides no built-in security.

Requirements

The following items describe the recommended hardware, software, network infrastructure, skills and knowledge, and service packs you will need.

- Microsoft® Windows® 2000 operating system
- Microsoft Visual Studio® .NET development system

The procedures in this article also require that you have knowledge of the Microsoft Visual C#™ development tool.

Summary

This How To includes the following procedures.

1. Create the Remote Object Class
2. Create a Windows Service Host Application
3. Create a Windows Account to Run the Service
4. Install the Windows Service
5. Create a Test Client Application

1. Create the Remote Object Class

This procedure creates a simple remote object class. It provides a single method called **Add** that will add two numbers together and return the result.

▶ **To create the remote object class**

1. Start Visual Studio .NET and create a new Visual C# Class Library project called **RemoteObject**.
2. Use Solution Explorer to rename class1.cs as Calculator.cs.
3. In Calculator.cs, rename **Class1** as **Calculator** and rename the default constructor accordingly.
4. Derive the **Calculator** class from **MarshalByRefObject** to make the class remotable.

```
public class Calculator : MarshalByRefObject
```

5. Add the following public method to the **Calculator** class.

```
public int Add( int operand1, int operand2 )
{
   return operand1 + operand2;
}
```

6. On the **Build** menu, click **Build Solution**.

2. Create a Windows Service Host Application

This procedure creates a Windows service application, which will be used to host the remote object. When the service is started it will configure the TCP remoting channel to listen for client requests.

Note: This procedure uses an Installer class and the Installutil.exe command line utility to install the Windows service. To uninstall the service, run Installutil.exe with the **/u** switch. As an alternative, you could use a Setup and Deployment Project to help install and uninstall the Windows service.

▶ **To create a Windows Service host application**

1. Add a new Visual C# Windows Service project called **RemotingHost** to the current solution.

2. Use Solution Explorer to rename Service1.cs as RemotingHost.cs.

3. In RemotingHost.cs, rename the **Service1** class as **HostService** and rename the default constructor accordingly.

4. At the top of the file, add the following **using** statement beneath the existing **using** statements.

```
using System.Runtime.Remoting;
```

5. Locate the **Main** method and replace the existing line of code that initializes the **ServicesToRun** variable with the following.

```
ServicesToRun = new System.ServiceProcess.ServiceBase[] {
                                        new HostService() };
```

6. Locate the **InitializeComponent** method and set the **ServiceName** property to **RemotingHost.**

```
this.ServiceName = "RemotingHost";
```

7. Locate the **OnStart** method and add the following line of code to configure remoting. The fully qualified path to the configuration file will be passed as a start parameter to the service.

```
RemotingConfiguration.Configure(args[0]);
```

8. Add a new C# class file to the project and name it **HostServiceInstaller**.

9. Add an assembly reference to the System.Configuration.Install.dll assembly.

10. Add the following **using** statements to the top of **HostServiceInstaller** beneath the existing **using** statement.

```
using System.ComponentModel;
using System.ServiceProcess;
using System.Configuration.Install;
```

11. Derive the **HostServiceInstaller** class from the **Installer** class.

```
public class HostServiceInstaller : Installer
```

12. Add the **RunInstaller** attribute at the class level as follows.

```
[RunInstaller(true)]
public class HostServiceInstaller : Installer
```

13. Add the following two private member variables to the **HostServiceInstaller** class. The objects will be used when installing the service.

```
private ServiceInstaller HostInstaller;
private ServiceProcessInstaller HostProcessInstaller;
```

14. Add the following code to the constructor of the **HostServiceInstaller** class.

```
HostInstaller = new ServiceInstaller();
HostInstaller.StartType = System.ServiceProcess.ServiceStartMode.Manual;
HostInstaller.ServiceName = "RemotingHost";
HostInstaller.DisplayName = "Calculator Host Service";
Installers.Add (HostInstaller);
HostProcessInstaller = new ServiceProcessInstaller();
HostProcessInstaller.Account = ServiceAccount.User;
Installers.Add (HostProcessInstaller);
```

15. Within Solution Explorer, right-click **RemotingHost**, point to **Add**, and then click **Add New Item**.

16. In the **Templates** list, click **Text File** and name the file **app.config**.

    Configuration files with the name app.config are automatically copied by Visual Studio .NET as part of the build process to the output folder (for example, *<projectdir>*\bin\debug) and renamed as *<applicationname>*.config.

17. Click **OK** to add the new configuration file.

18. Add the following configuration elements to the new configuration file.

```
<configuration>
<system.runtime.remoting>
  <application name="RemoteHostService">
    <service>
      <wellknown type="RemoteObject.Calculator, RemoteObject"
                 objectUri="RemoteObject.Calculator" mode="Singleton" />
    </service>
    <channels>
      <channel ref="tcp" port="8085">
        <serverProviders>
          <formatter ref="binary" />
        </serverProviders>
      </channel>
    </channels>
  </application>
</system.runtime.remoting>
</configuration>
```

19. On the **Build** menu, click **Build Solution**.

3. Create a Windows Account to Run the Service

This procedure creates a Windows account used to run the Windows service.

▶ **To create a Windows account to run the service**

1. Create a new local user account called **RemotingAccount**. Enter a password and select the **Password never expires** check box.

2. In the **Administrative Tools** programs group, click **Local Security Policy**.

3. Use the **Local Security Policy** tool to give the new account the **Log on as a service** privilege.

4. Install the Windows Service

This procedure installs the Windows service using the installutil.exe utility and then start the service.

▶ **To install the Windows service**

1. Open a command window and change directory to the Bin\Debug directory beneath the **RemotingHost** project folder.

2. Run the installutil.exe utility to install the service.

```
installutil.exe remotinghost.exe
```

3. In the **Set Service Login** dialog box, enter the user name and password of the account created earlier in procedure 3 and click **OK**.

   View the output from the installutil.exe utility and confirm that the service is installed correctly.

4. Copy the RemoteObject.dll assembly into the **RemotingHost** project output directory (that is, RemotingHost\Bin\Debug).

5. From the **Administrative Tools** program group, start the **Services** MMC snap-in.

6. In the **Services** list, right-click **Calculator Host Service**, and then click **Properties**.

7. Enter the full path to the service's configuration file (remotinghost.exe.config) into the **Start parameters** field.

Note: A quick way to do this is to select and copy the **Path to executable** field and paste it into the **Start parameters** field. Then append the ".config" string.

---

8. Click **Start** to start the service.

9. Confirm that the service status changes to **Started**.

10. Click **OK** to close the **Properties** dialog box.

5. Create a Test Client Application

This procedure creates a test console application that is used to call the remote object within the Windows service.

▶ **To create a test client application**

1. Add a new Visual C# Console application called **RemotingClient** to the current solution.

2. Within Solution Explorer, right-click **RemotingClient**, and then click **Set as StartUp Project**.

3. Add an assembly reference to the System.Runtime.Remoting.dll assembly.

4. Add a project reference to the **RemoteObject** project.

5. Add the following **using** statements to the top of class1.cs beneath the existing **using** statements.

```
using System.Runtime.Remoting.Channels;
using System.Runtime.Remoting.Channels.Tcp;
using RemoteObject;
```

6. Add the following test code to the **Main** method to call and invoke the **Calculator** object hosted by the Windows service.

```
TcpChannel chan = new TcpChannel();
ChannelServices.RegisterChannel(chan);
Calculator calc = (Calculator)Activator.GetObject(
                    typeof(RemoteObject.Calculator),
                    "tcp://localhost:8085/RemoteObject.Calculator");
if (calc == null)
   System.Console.WriteLine("Could not locate server");
else
   Console.WriteLine("21 + 21 is : " + calc.Add(21,21) );
```

7. On the **Build** menu, click **Build Solution**.

8. Run the client application and confirm that the correct result is displayed in the console output window.

References

For information about how to host a remote object in ASP.NET (with IIS), see article Q312107, "HOW TO: Host a Remote Object in IIS," in the Microsoft Knowledge Base.

How To:
Set Up SSL on a Web Server

Secure Sockets Layer (SSL) is a set of cryptographic technologies that provides authentication, confidentiality, and data integrity. SSL is most commonly used between Web browsers and Web servers to create a secure communication channel. It can also be used between client applications and Web services.

Requirements

The following items describe the recommended hardware, software, network infrastructure, skills and knowledge, and service packs you will need.

- Microsoft® Windows® 2000 Server operating system (Service Pack 2)
- Microsoft Certificate Services (required if you need to generate your own certificates).

The procedures in this How To also require that you have some knowledge of IIS configuration.

Summary

This How To includes the following procedures:

1. Generate a Certificate Request
2. Submit a Certificate Request
3. Issue the Certificate
4. Install the Certificate on the Web server
5. Configure Resources to Require SSL Access

1. Generate a Certificate Request

This procedure creates a new certificate request, which can be sent to a Certificate Authority (CA) for processing. If successful, the CA will send you back a file containing a validated certificate.

► **To generate a certificate request**

1. Start the IIS Microsoft Management Console (MMC) snap-in.

2. Expand your Web server name and select the Web site for which you want to install a certificate.

3. Right-click the Web site, and then click **Properties**.

4. Click the **Directory Security** tab.

5. Click the **Server Certificate** button within **Secure communications** to launch the Web Server Certificate Wizard.

Note: If **Server Certificate** is unavailable, you probably selected a virtual directory, directory, or file. Go back to Step 2 and select a Web site.

---

6. Click **Next** to move past the welcome dialog box.

7. Click **Create a New Certificate**, and then click **Next**.

8. The dialog box has the following two options:

   ● Prepare the request now, but send it later

   This option is always available.

   ● Send the request immediately to an online certification authority

   This option is available only if the Web server can access one or more Microsoft Certificate servers in a Windows 2000 domain configured to issue Web server certificates. Later on in the request process, you are given the opportunity to select an authority from a list to send the request to.

   Click **Prepare the request now, but send it later**, and then click **Next**.

9. Type a descriptive name for the certificate in the **Name** field, type a bit length for the key in the **Bit length** field, and then click **Next**.

   The wizard uses the name of the current Web site as a default name. It is not used in the certificate but acts as a friendly name to help administrators.

10. Type an organization name (such as Contoso) in the **Organization** field and type an organizational unit (such as Sales Department) in the **Organizational unit** field, and then click **Next**.

Note: This information will be placed in the certificate request, so make sure it is accurate. The CA will verify this information and will place it in the certificate. A user browsing your Web site will want to see this information in order to decide if they should accept the certificate.

---

11. In the **Common name** field, type a common name for your site, and then click **Next**.

> **Important:** The common name is one of the most significant pieces of information that ends up in the certificate. It is the DNS name of the Web site (that is, the name that users type in when browsing your site). If the certificate name doesn't match the site name, a certificate problem will be reported when users browse to the site.
>
> If your site is on the Web and is named www.contoso.com, this is what you should specify for the common name.
>
> If your site is internal and users browse by computer name, enter the NetBIOS or DNS name of the computer.

12. Enter the appropriate information in the **Country/Region**, **State/province**, and **City/locality** fields, and then click **Next**.

13. Enter a file name for the certificate request.

    The file contains information similar to the following.

    ```
    -----BEGIN NEW CERTIFICATE REQUEST-----
    MIIDZjCCAs8CAQAwgYoxNjA0BgNVBAMTLW1penJvY2tsYXB0b3Aubm9ydChbWVy…
    -----END NEW CERTIFICATE REQUEST-----
    ```

    This is a Base 64 encoded representation of your certificate request. The request contains the information entered into the wizard and also your public key and information signed with your private key.

    This request file is sent to the CA. The CA then uses your public key information from the certificate request to verify information signed with your private key. The CA also verifies the information supplied in the request.

    After you submit the request to a CA, the CA sends back a certificate contained in a file. You would then restart the Web Server Certificate Wizard.

14. Click **Next**. The wizard displays a summary of the information contained in the certificate request.

15. Click **Next**, and then click **Finish** to complete the request process.

    The certificate request can now be sent to a CA for verification and processing. After you receive a certificate response from the CA, you can continue and install the certificate on the Web server, once again by using the IIS Certificate Wizard.

2. Submit a Certificate Request

This procedure uses Microsoft Certificate Services to submit the certificate request generated in the previous procedure.

▶ **To submit a certificate request**

1. Use Notepad to open the certificate file generated in the previous procedure and copy its entire contents to the clipboard.

2. Start Internet Explorer and navigate to http://*hostname*/CertSrv, where *hostname* is the name of the computer running Microsoft Certificate Services.

3. Click **Request a Certificate**, and then click **Next**.

4. On the **Choose Request Type** page, click **Advanced request**, and then click **Next**.

5. On the **Advanced Certificate Requests** page, click **Submit a certificate request using a base64 encoded PKCS#10 file**, and then click **Next**.

6. On the **Submit a Saved Request** page, click in the **Base64 Encoded Certificate Request (PKCS #10 or #7)** text box and press **CTRL+V** to paste the certificate request you copied to the clipboard earlier.

7. In the **Certificate Template** combo box, click **Web Server**.

8. Click **Submit**.

9. Close Internet Explorer.

3. Issue the Certificate

▶ **To issue the certificate**

1. Start the **Certification Authority** tool from the **Administrative Tools** program group.

2. Expand your certificate authority, and then select the **Pending Requests** folder.

3. Select the certificate request you just submitted.

4. On the **Action** menu, point to **All Tasks**, and then click **Issue**.

5. Confirm that the certificate is displayed in the **Issued Certificates** folder, and then double-click it to view it.

6. On the **Details** tab, click **Copy to File**, and save the certificate as a Base-64 encoded X.509 certificate.

7. Close the properties window for the certificate.

8. Close the Certificate Authority tool.

4. Install the Certificate on the Web Server

This procedure installs the certificate issued in the previous procedure on the Web server.

▶ **To install the certificate on the Web server**

1. Start Internet Information Services, if it's not already running.

2. Expand your server name and select the Web site for which you want to install a certificate.

3. Right-click the Web site, and then click **Properties**.

4. Click the **Directory Security** tab.

5. Click **Server Certificate** to launch the Web Server Certificate Wizard.

6. Click **Process the pending request and install the certificate**, and then click **Next**.

7. Enter the path and file name of the file that contains the response from the CA, and then click **Next**.

8. Examine the certificate overview, click **Next**, and then click **Finish**.

   A certificate is now installed on the Web server.

5. Configure Resources to Require SSL Access

This procedure uses Internet Services Manager to configure a virtual directory to require SSL for access. You can require the use of SSL for specific files, directories, or virtual directories. Clients must use the HTTPS protocol to access any such resource.

▶ **To configure resources to require SSL access**

1. Start Internet Information Services, if it's not already running.

2. Expand your server name and Web site. (This must be a Web site that has an installed certificate.)

3. Right-click a virtual directory, and then click **Properties**.

4. Click the **Directory Security** tab.

5. Under **Secure communications**, click **Edit**.

6. Click **Require secure channel (SSL)**.

   Client's browsing to this virtual directory must now use HTTPS.

7. Click **OK**, and then click **OK** again to close the **Properties** dialog box.

8. Close Internet Information Services.

How To:
Set Up Client Certificates

Web services often need to be able to authenticate their callers (other applications) in order to perform authorization. Client certificates provide an excellent authentication mechanism for Web services. When you use client certificates, your application also benefits from the creation of a secure channel (using Secure Sockets Layer [SSL]) between the client application and Web service. This allows you to securely send confidential information to and from the Web service. SSL ensures message integrity and confidentiality.

This How To includes step-by-step instructions to call a Web service that is configured to require client certificates.

Note: The information in this How To also applies to remote components hosted by IIS.

Requirements

The following items describe the recommended hardware, software, network infrastructure, skills and knowledge, and service packs you will need.

- Microsoft® Windows® 2000 Server operating system with Service Pack 2
- Microsoft Visual Studio® .NET development system
- Access to a Certificate Authority (CA) to generate new certificates
- A Web server with an installed server certificate

  For more information about installing Web server certificates, see "How To: Set Up SSL on a Web Server" in the Reference section of this book.

The procedures in this How To also require that you have knowledge of ASP.NET Web development with the Microsoft Visual C#™ development tool.

Summary

This How To includes the following procedures:

1. Create a Simple Web Application
2. Configure the Web Application to Require Client Certificates
3. Request and Install a Client Certificate
4. Verify Client Certificate Operation

1. Create a Simple Web Application

► **To create a simple Web application**

1. Start Visual Studio .NET and create a new C# ASP.NET Web application called **SecureApp**.

2. Drag a label control from the toolbox onto the WebForm1.aspx Web form, and then set its ID property to **message.**

3. Drag a second label onto WebForm1.aspx and set its ID property to **certData**.

4. Add the following code to the **Page_Load** event procedure.

```
string username;
username = User.Identity.Name;
message.Text = "Welcome " + username;
HttpClientCertificate cert = Request.ClientCertificate;
if (cert.IsPresent)
{
    certData.Text = "Client certificate retrieved";
}
else
{
    certData.Text = "No client certificate";
}
```

5. On the **Build** menu, click **Build Solution**.

6. Start Internet Explorer and navigate to *http://localhost/SecureApp/WebForm1.aspx.*

   The page should be displayed with the messages "Welcome" (no user name is displayed because the user has not been authenticated) and "No client certificate."

7. Close Internet Explorer.

2. Configure the Web Application to Require Client Certificates

This procedure uses Internet Information Services (IIS) to configure your Web application's virtual directory to require certificates.

This procedure assumes that you have a valid certificate installed on your Web server. For more information about installing Web server certificates, see "How To: Set Up SSL on a Web Server."

► **To configure your Web application's virtual directory to require certificates**

1. On the Web service host computer, start IIS.

2. Navigate to the **SecureApp** virtual directory.

3. Right-click **SecureApp**, and then click **Properties**.

4. Click the **Directory Security** tab.

5. Under **Secure communications**, click **Edit**.

   If **Edit** is unavailable, it is likely that a Web server certificate is not installed.

6. Select the **Require secure channel (SSL)** check box.

7. Select the **Require client certificates** option.

8. Click **OK**, and then click **OK** again.

9. In the **Inheritance Overrides** dialog box, click **Select All**, and then click **OK** to close the **SecureApp** properties dialog box.

   This applies the new security settings to all subdirectories in the virtual directory root.

10. To confirm that the Web site is configured correctly, start Internet Explorer and browse (using HTTPS) to *https://localhost/secureapp/webform1.aspx.*

11. A **Client Authentication** dialog box is displayed by Internet Explorer asking you to select a client certificate. Because you have not yet installed a client certificate, click **OK**, and confirm that an error page is displayed informing you that the page requires a client certificate.

12. Close Internet Explorer.

3. Request and Install a Client Certificate

This procedure installs a client-side certificate. You can use a certificate from any certificate authority, or you can generate your own certificate using Microsoft Certificate Services as described in the following sections.

This procedure assumes that Microsoft Certificate Services is configured for pending requests, which require an administrator to explicitly issue the certificate. It can also be configured to automatically issue certificates in response to certificate requests.

▶ **To check the certificate request status setting**

1. On the Microsoft Certificate Services computer, select **Certification Authority** from the **Administrative Tools** programs group.

2. Expand **Certification Authority (Local)**, right-click the certification authority and click **Properties**.

3. Click the **Policy Module** tab, and then click **Configure**.

4. Check the default action.

   The following procedure assumes that **Set the certificate request status to pending. Administrator must explicitly issue the certificate** is selected.

▶ **To request a client-side certificate**

1. Start Internet Explorer and navigate to *http://*hostname*/certsrv*, where *hostname* is the name of the computer on which Microsoft Certificate Services is installed.

2. Click **Request a certificate**, and then click **Next**.

3. On the **Choose Request Type** page, click **User Certificate**, and then click **Next**.

4. Click **Submit** to complete the request.

5. Close Internet Explorer.

▶ **To issue the client-side certificate**

1. From the **Administrative Tools** program group, start the **Certification Authority** tool.

2. Expand your certificate authority, and then select the **Pending Requests** folder.

3. Select the certificate request you just submitted, point to **All Tasks** on the **Action** menu, and then click **Issue**.

4. Confirm that the certificate is displayed in the **Issued Certificates** folder, and then double-click it to view it.

5. On the **Details** tab, click **Copy to File** to save the certificate as a Base-64 encoded X.509 certificate.

6. Close the properties window for the certificate.

7. Close the Certification Authority tool.

▶ **To install the client-side certificate**

1. To view the certificate, start Windows Explorer, navigate to the .cer file saved in the previous procedure, and then double-click it.

2. Click **Install Certificate**, and then click **Next** on the first page of the **Certificate Import Wizard**.

3. Select **Automatically select the certificate store based on the type of certificate**, and then click **Next**.

4. Click **Finish** to complete the wizard. Dismiss the confirmation message box, and then click **OK** to close the certificate.

4. Verify Client Certificate Operation

This procedure verifies that you can access the **SecureApp** application using a client certificate.

▶ **To verify client certificate operation**

1. Start Internet Explorer and navigate to *https://localhost/secureapp/webform1.aspx*.

2. Confirm that the Web page displays successfully.

Additional Resources

For more information, see "How to Set Up SSL on a Web Server" in the Reference section of this guide.

How To:
Use IPSec to Provide Secure Communication Between Two Servers

Internet Protocol Security (IPSec) can be used to secure the data sent between two computers, such as an application server and a database server. IPSec is completely transparent to applications because encryption, integrity, and authentication services are implemented at the transport level. Applications continue to communicate with one another in the normal manner using TCP and UDP ports.

Using IPSec you can:

- Provide message confidentiality by encrypting all of the data sent between two computers.
- Provide message integrity between two computers (without encrypting data).
- Provide mutual authentication between two computers. For example, you can help secure a database server by establishing a policy that permits requests only from a specific client computer (for example, an application or Web server).
- Restrict which computers can communicate with one another. You can also restrict communication to specific IP protocols and TCP/UDP ports.

This How To shows you how to secure the communication channel between an application server and a database server running SQL Server 2000. The application server uses the recommended TCP/IP client network library to connect to SQL Server and uses the default SQL Server TCP port 1433. The configuration is shown in Figure 1 on the next page.

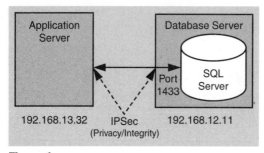

Figure 1
How To solution configuration

This How To describes how to use a simple IPSec policy to enforce the following:

- Allow communications with SQL Server only from the application server using TCP through port 1433.
- Drop all other IP packets, including ICMP (ping).
- Encrypt all data sent between the two computers to guarantee confidentiality.

The advantages of this approach are:

- Data confidentiality is provided for all data sent between the two computers.
- The attach surface on SQL Server is significantly reduced. The only remaining points of attack are to interactively log on to the database server or to gain control of the application server and try to attack SQL Server via TCP port 1433.
- The IPSec policy is extremely simple to define and implement.

This particular policy suffers from the following drawbacks:

- SQL Server cannot communicate with domain controllers and as a result:
  - Group policy cannot be applied (the database server should be a standalone server).
  - Windows authentication between the application server and database server requires synchronized local accounts (with the same user name and password) on both computers.
  - You cannot use more robust methods of applying IPSec (Windows 2000 default / Kerberos).
- SQL Server will not be able to communicate with other computers, including DNS servers.
- The approach presented in this How To uses pre-shared key authentication, which is not recommended for production scenarios. Production systems should use certificates or Windows 2000 domain authentication. IPSec policies that use pre-shared secrets are suitable for use in development or test environments only.
- Both computers must have static IP addresses.

Notes

- An IPSec policy consists of a set of filters, filter actions, and rules.
- A **filter** consists of:
  - A source IP address or range of addresses.
  - A destination IP address or range of addresses.
  - An IP protocol, such as TCP, UDP, or "any."
  - Source and destination ports (for TCP or UDP only).
- Filters can also be mirrored on two computers. A mirrored filter applies the same rule on client and server computer (with the source and destination addresses reversed).
- A **filter action** specifies actions to take when a given filter is invoked. It can be one of the following:
  - **Permit**. The traffic is not secured; it is allowed to be sent and received without intervention.
  - **Block**. The traffic is not permitted.
  - **Negotiate security**. The endpoints must agree on and then use a secure method to communicate. If they cannot agree on a method, the communication does not take place. If negotiation fails, you can specify whether to allow unsecured communication or to whether all communication should be blocked.
- A **rule** associates a filter with a filter action.
- A **mirrored** policy is one that applies rules to all packets with the exact reverse of the specified source and destination IP addresses. A mirrored policy is created in this How To.

Requirements

The following items describe the recommended hardware, software, network infrastructure, skills and knowledge, and service packs you will need.

- Two computers running Microsoft® Windows® 2000 Server operating system
  You must know their IP addresses
- Microsoft® SQL Server™ 2000 on the database server computer

Summary

This How To includes the following procedures:

1. Create an IP Filter
2. Create Filter Actions
3. Create Rules
4. Export the IPSec Policy to the Remote Computer
5. Assign Policies
6. Verify that it Works

1. Create an IP Filter

▶ **To create a new IP filter on the database server computer**

1. Log on to the database server as an administrator.
2. Start the **Local Security Policy** Microsoft Management Console (MMC) snap-in from the **Administrative Tools** program group.
3. In the left pane, right-click **IP Security Policies on Local Machine**, and then click **Manage IP filter lists and filter actions**.

   You will see that two filter lists are already defined for all ICMP traffic and all IP traffic.
4. Click **Add**.
5. In the **IP Filter List** dialog box, type **SQL Port** in the **Name** field.
6. Click **Add**, and then click **Next** to move past the welcome dialog of the IP Filter Wizard.
7. In the **IP Traffic Source** dialog box, select **A specific IP Address** from the **Source address** drop-down list, and then enter the IP address of your application server computer.
8. Click **Next**.
9. In the **IP Traffic Destination** dialog box, select **A specific IP Address** from the **Destination address** drop-down list, and then enter the IP address of your database server computer.
10. Click **Next**.
11. In the **IP Protocol Type** dialog box, select **TCP** as the protocol type, and then click **Next**.
12. In the **IP Protocol Port** dialog box, select **From any port**, and then select **To this port**. Enter **1433** as the port number.
13. Click **Next**, and then click **Finish** to close the wizard.
14. Click **Close** to close the **IP Filter List** dialog box.

2. Create Filter Actions

This procedure creates two filter actions. The first will be used to block all communications from specified computers and the second will be used to enforce the use of encryption between application server and database server computers.

▶ **To create filter actions**

1. Click the **Manage Filter Actions** tab.

   Note that several predefined actions are already defined.

2. Click **Add** to create a new filter action.

   In the next few steps, you will create a block action that can be used to block all communications from selected computers.

3. Click **Next** to move past the initial dialog box of the Filter Action Wizard.

4. In the **Name** field, type **Block**, and then click **Next**.

5. In the **Filter Action General Options** dialog box, select **Block**, and then click **Next**.

6. Click **Finish** to close the wizard.

7. Click **Add** to start the Filter Action Wizard again.

   In the next few steps, you will create a filter action to force the use of encryption between application server and database server computers.

8. Click **Next** to move past the initial dialog box of the Filter Action Wizard.

9. In the **Name** field, type **Require High Security**, and then click **Next**.

10. Select **Negotiate security**, and then click **Next**.

11. Select **Do not communicate with computers that do not support IPSec**, and then click **Next**.

12. Select **Custom**, and then click **Settings**.

13. Make sure that the **Data integrity and encryption (ESP)** check box is selected.

14. Select **SHA1** from the **Integrity algorithm** drop-down list.

15. Select **3DES** from the **Encryption algorithm** drop-down list.

16. Select the two check boxes within the **Session Key Settings** group to generate a new key every 100000 Kb and 3600 seconds respectively.

17. Click **OK** to close the **Custom Security Method Settings** dialog box, and then click **Next**.

18. Select the **Edit Properties** check box, and then click **Finish**.

19. Clear the **Accept unsecured communication, but always respond using IPSec** check box.

20. Select the **Session key Perfect Forward Secrecy** check box, and then click **OK**.

21. Click **Close** to close the **Manage IP filter lists and filter actions** dialog box.

3. Create Rules

This procedure creates two new rules that will be used to associate the filter that you created in Procedure 1, with the two filter actions you created in Procedure 2.

▶ **To create rules**

1. In the left pane, right-click **IP Security Policies on Local Machine**, and then click **Create IP Security Policy**.

2. Click **Next** to move past the initial dialog box of the IP Security Policy Wizard.

3. In the **Name** field, type **Secure SQL**, and then click **Next**.

4. Clear the **Activate the default response rule** check box, and then click **Next**.

5. Leave the **Edit properties** check box selected, and then click **Finish**.

6. Click **Add** to start the Security Rule Wizard.

7. Click **Next** to move past the initial dialog box of the Security Rule Wizard.

8. Click **This rule does not specify a tunnel**, and then click **Next**.

9. Click **All network connections**, and then click **Next**.

10. Click **Use this string to protect the key exchange (preshared key)**.

11. Enter **MySecret** as a "secret" key in the text box.

> **Note:** This key must be the same for both computers in order for them to successfully communicate. You should use a long random number, but for the purposes of this How To, "MySecret" will suffice.

12. Click **Next**.

13. Select the **SQL Port** option.

> **Note:** You must click the circle (radio button) and not the text for the option to be selected.

14. Click **Next**.

15. Select the **Require High Security** option, and then click **Next**.

16. Click **Finish** to return to the **Secure SQL Properties** dialog box.

17. Click **Add** to start the Security Rule Wizard again, and then click **Next** to move past the initial dialog box.

18. Click **This rule does not specify a tunnel**, and then click **Next**.

19. Click **All network connections**, and then click **Next**.

20. In the **Authentication Method** dialog box, leave **Windows 2000 default (Kerberos V5 Protocol)** selected, and then click **Next**.

> **Note:** This rule will specify the **Block** filter action, so no authentication will be needed.

22. In the **IP Filter List** dialog box, click **All IP Traffic**, and then click **Next**.

23. In the **Filter Action** dialog box, select the **Block** option, and then click **Next**.
24. Click **Finish**.
25. Click **Close** to close the **Secure SQL Properties** dialog box.

4. Export the IPSec Policy to the Remote Computer

The IPSec policy that you have created on the database server must now be exported and copied to the application server computer.

▶ **To export the IPSec policy to the application server computer**

1. In the left pane, right-click the **IP Security Policies on Local Machine** node, point to **All Tasks**, and then click **Export Policies**.
2. In the **Name** field, type **Secure SQL**, and then click **Save** to export the file to the local hard disk.
3. Either copy the .ipsec file across to the application server or make it available by using a file share.

Important: Because the exported policy file contains a pre-shared key in clear text, the file must be properly secured. It should not be stored on the hard disk of either computer.

---

4. Log on to the Application Server as an administrator and start the **Local Security Policy** MMC snap-in.
5. Select and right-click **IP Security Policies on Local Machine**, point to **All Tasks**, and then click **Import Policies**.
6. Browse for the previously exported .ipsec file and click **Open** to import the policy.

5. Assign Policies

An IPSec policy must be assigned before it becomes active. Note that only one policy may be active at any one time on a particular computer.

▶ **To assign the Secure SQL policy on the application server and database server computers**

1. On the application server computer, right-click the newly imported Secure SQL policy, and then click **Assign**.
2. Repeat the previous step on the database server computer.

   The mirrored policy is now assigned on both computers.

   The policies ensure that only the application server can communicate with the database server. Furthermore, only TCP connections using port 1433 are permitted and all traffic sent between the two computers is encrypted.

6. Verify that it Works

This procedure uses Network Monitor to verify that data sent between the application server and database server is encrypted.

▶ **To verify that it works**

1. On the application server computer, use Visual Studio .NET to create a new C# Console Application called **SQLIPSecClient**.

2. Copy the following code to class1.cs replacing all of the existing code.

Note: Replace the IP address in the connection string with the IP address of your database server.

```csharp
using System;
using System.Data;
using System.Data.SqlClient;

namespace SQLIPSecClient
{
  class Class1
  {
    [STAThread]
    static void Main(string[] args)
    {
      // Replace the IP address in the following connection string with the IP
      // address of your database server
      SqlConnection conn = new SqlConnection(
        "server=192.168.12.11;database=NorthWind;Integrated Security='SSPI'");

      SqlCommand cmd = new SqlCommand(
                      "SELECT ProductID, ProductName FROM Products");
      try
      {
        conn.Open();
        cmd.Connection = conn;
        SqlDataReader reader = cmd.ExecuteReader();
        while (reader.Read())
        {
          Console.WriteLine("{0} {1}",
                  reader.GetInt32(0).ToString(),
                  reader.GetString(1) );
        }
        reader.Close();
      }
      catch( Exception ex)
      {
      }
      finally
      {
        conn.Close();
      }
    }
  }
}
```

3. On the **Build** menu, click **Build Solution**.

4. In order for Windows authentication to succeed between the two computers, you must duplicate the account that you are currently interactively logged on to the application computer with, on the database server computer. Ensure that the user name and password matches.

   You must also use SQL Server Enterprise Manager to create a database login for the newly created account and add a new database user for this logon to the Northwind database.

5. Temporarily un-assign the Secure SQL IPSec policy on both computers:

   a. Start Local Security Settings on the application server computer.

   b. Click **IP Security Policies on Local Machine**.

   c. In the right pane, right-click **Secure SQL**, and then click **Un-assign**.

   d. Repeat Steps a–c on the database server computer.

6. On the database server computer, click **Network Monitor** in the **Administrative Tools** program group.

   Note: A limited version of Network Monitor is available with Windows 2000 Server. A full version is available with Microsoft SMS.

   If you do not have Network Monitor installed, go to **Add/Remove Programs** in Control Panel, click **Add/Remove Windows Components**, select **Management and Monitoring Tools** from the **Windows Components** list, click **Details**, and then click **Network Monitor Tools**. Click **OK**, and then click **Next** to install the limited version of Network Monitor. You may be prompted for a Windows 2000 Server CD.

   ---

7. On the **Capture** menu, click **Filter** to create a new filter configured to view TCP/IP network traffic sent between the application server and database server.

8. Click the **Start Capture** button.

9. Return to the application server computer and run the test console application. A list of products from the Northwind database should be displayed in the console window.

10. Return to the database server and click the **Stop and View Capture** button within Network Monitor.

11. Double-click the first captured frame to view the captured data.

12. Scroll down through the captured frames. You should see the SELECT statement in clear text followed by the list of products retrieved from the database.

13. Assign the Secure SQL IPSec policy on both computers:

    a. Start Local Security Settings on the application server computer.

    b. Click **IP Security Policies on Local Machine**.

    c. In the right pane, right-click **Secure SQL**, and then click **Assign**.

    d. Repeat Steps a–c on the database server computer.

14. In Network Monitor, close the capture window.

15. Click the **Start Capture** button, and then click **No** in the **Save File** message box.

16. Return to the application server computer and run the test console application once again.

17. Return to the database server computer and click **Stop and View Capture** within Network Monitor.

18. Confirm that the data is now unintelligible (because it is encrypted).

19. Close Network Monitor.

Additional Resources

For more information about IPSec, see "IP Security and Filtering" on TechNet (*http://www.microsoft.com/technet/treeview/default.asp?url=/technet/prodtechnol /winxppro/reskit/prcc_tcp_erqb.asp?frame=true>*).

For more information about Network Monitor, see the "Network Monitor" section of the Microsoft Platform SDK on MSDN (*http://msdn.microsoft.com/library /default.asp?url=/library/en-us/netmon/netmon/network_monitor.asp*).

How To:
Use SSL to Secure Communication with SQL Server 2000

You can use the Secure Sockets Layer (SSL) protocol to secure the communication link between clients (direct callers) and Microsoft® SQL Server™ 2000. When you configure SQL Server for SSL, all of the data transmitted between client and server (and vice versa) may be encrypted to ensure that the data remains confidential while in transit between the client and SQL Server.

Notes

- SSL is an alternative to using IPSec to secure database traffic.

  For more information about how to use IPSec to secure database traffic, see "How To: Use IPSec to Provide Secure Communication Between Two Servers" in the Reference section of this book.

- Unlike IPSec, configuration changes are not required if the client or server IP addresses change.

- For SSL to work, you must install a server certificate on the database server computer. The client computer must also have a root certificate authority (CA) certificate from the same authority.

- Clients must have the SQL Server 2000 connectivity libraries installed. Earlier versions or generic libraries will not work.

- SSL only works for TCP/IP (the recommended communication protocol for SQL Server) and named pipes.

- You can configure the server to force the use of encryption for all connections.

- On the client, you can:

  - Force the use of encryption for all outgoing connections.

  - Allow client applications to choose whether or not to use encryption on a per-connection basis, by using the connection string.

Requirements

The following items describe the recommended hardware, software, network infrastructure, skills and knowledge, and service packs you will need.

- Two computers running the Microsoft Windows® 2000 Server operating system.
- SQL Server 2000 on the database server computer. For this example, the SQL Server service is assumed to be running as Local System. If the certificate is in the Local Machine store, SSL should work no matter which account SQL runs under.
- Microsoft Data Access Components (MDAC) 2.6 or later, or SQL Server 2000 client connectivity libraries on the client computer.
- This example requires access to Microsoft Certificate Services running on Windows 2000 to allow the creation of server authentication certificates; however, this is not a requirement.

Summary

This How To includes the following procedures:

1. Install a Server Authentication Certificate
2. Verify that the Certificate Has Been Installed
3. Install the Issuing CA's Certificate on the Client
4. Force All Clients to Use SSL
5. Allow Clients to Determine Whether to Use SSL
6. Verify that Communication Is Encrypted

1. Install a Server Authentication Certificate

SSL requires that the server possess a server authentication certificate issued by a certificate authority (CA) that is trusted by connecting clients.

▶ **To install a server certificate**

1. Logon to the database server computer using an administrator account.
2. Start Internet Explorer and browse to Microsoft Certificate Services, for example:

   ```
   http://MyCA/certsrv
   ```

3. Click **Request a certificate**, and then click **Next**.
4. Click **Advanced request**, and then click **Next**
5. Click **Submit a certificate request to this CA using a form**, and then click **Next**.
6. Fill out the certificate request form noting the following:

a. Enter the fully-qualified domain name of the computer running SQL Server into the **Name** field. For example:

```
sql01.nwtraders.com
```

b. In the **Intended Purpose** (or **Type of Certificate Needed**) field, click **Server Authentication Certificate**.

c. For the Cryptographic Service Provider (CSP), click **Microsoft RSA SChannel Cryptographic Provider**.

Note: Microsoft Base Cryptographic Provider version 1.0 and Microsoft Enhanced Cryptographic providers also work. Microsoft Strong Cryptographic Provider does not.

---

d. Select the **Use local machine store** check box.

Note: Do NOT select **Enable strong private key protection**.

---

7. Click **Submit** to submit the request.

   If the certificate server automatically issues certificates, you can install the certificate now. Otherwise, you can install the certificate after it has been issued by the CA administrator by browsing to Microsoft Certificate Services and selecting **Check on a pending certificate**.

2. Verify that the Certificate Has Been Installed

This procedure verifies that the server certificate has been installed successfully.

▶ **To verify that the certificate has been installed**

1. On the taskbar, click the **Start** button, and then click **Run**.

2. Enter **mmc**, and then click **OK**.

3. On the **Console** menu, click **Add/Remove Snap-in**.

4. Click **Add**.

5. Click **Certificates**, and then click **Add**.

6. Click **Computer account**, and then click **Next**.

7. Ensure that **Local computer: (the computer this console is running on)** is selected, and then click **Finish**

8. Click **Close**, and then click **OK**.

9. In the left-pane tree view, expand **Certificates (Local Computer)**, expand **Personal**, and then select **Certificates**.

10. Verify that there is exactly one certificate with the fully qualified domain name that you specified in the previous procedure.

    You can double-click the certificate to view its details.

3. Install the Issuing CA's Certificate on the Client

After the certificate has been installed and the SQL Server service has been restarted, SQL Server can negotiate SSL with clients. Clients that use SSL to connect to SQL Server must:

- Have MDAC 2.6 or SQL Server 2000 connectivity libraries installed.
- Trust the issuer of the SQL Server's certificate.

▶ **To install the certificate of the issuing CA on the client computer**

1. Log on to the client computer as an administrator.
2. Start Internet Explorer and browse to Microsoft Certificate Services, for example:

   `http://MyCA/certsrv`

3. Click **Retrieve the CA certificate or certificate revocation list**, and then click **Next**.
4. Click **Install this CA certification path**, and then click **Yes** in response to the confirmation dialog to install the root certificate.

4. Force All Clients to Use SSL

You can configure the server to force all clients to use SSL (as described in this procedure), or you can let clients choose whether or not to use SSL on a per-connection basis (as described in the next procedure). The advantages of configuring the server to force clients to use SSL are:

- All communications are guaranteed to be secure.
- Any unsecured connections are rejected.

The disadvantages are:

- All clients must have MDAC 2.6 or SQL Server 2000 connectivity libraries installed; earlier or generic libraries will fail to connect.
- Connections that you do not need to secure suffer a slight performance overhead due to the added encryption.

▶ **To force all clients to use SSL**

1. On the computer running SQL Server, click **Server Network Utility** in the **Microsoft SQL Server** program group.
2. Click to select **Force protocol encryption**.
3. Verify that TCP/IP and/or named pipes are enabled.

   SSL is not supported with other protocols.
4. Click **OK** to close the SQL Server Network Utility, and then click **OK** in response to the **SQL Server Network Utility** message box.
5. Restart the SQL Server service.

   All subsequent client connections will be required to use SSL, whether they specify secure connections or not.

5. Allow Clients to Determine Whether to Use SSL

This procedure shows you how to configure SSL to allow clients to choose whether or not to use SSL. You can either configure the client libraries to enforce the use of SSL on all connections, or you can let individual applications choose on a per-connection basis. The advantages of configuring the client are:

- The overhead of SSL is incurred only for connections that truly require it.
- Clients that do not support SSL with SQL Server can still connect.

If you adopt this approach, make sure that you are willing to allow unsecured connections.

▶ **To reconfigure the server**

1. On the computer running SQL Server, run the **Server Network Utility**.
2. Clear the **Force protocol encryption** check box.
3. Restart the SQL Server service.
4. Return to the client computer.

▶ **To use SSL for all client connections**

With this approach, you configure the client libraries to use SSL for all connections. This means that SQL Servers that do not support encryption and SQL Servers earlier than SQL Server 2000 will not be accessible.

1. In the **Microsoft SQL Server** program group, click **Client Network Utility**.
2. Ensure that TCP/IP and/or named pipes are enabled.
3. Select **Force protocol encryption**.

► **To allow applications to choose whether or not to use encryption**

With this approach applications use the connection string to determine whether or not to use encryption. This allows each application to only use encryption when it is needed.

1. If you are using the OLE-DB data provider to connect to SQL Server, set **Use Encryption for Data** to **true** as shown in the following sample OLE-DB connection string.

```
"Provider=SQLOLEDB.1;Integrated Security=SSPI;Persist Security
Info=False;Initial Catalog=Northwind;Data Source=sql01;Use Encryption for
Data=True"
```

2. If you are using the SQL Server .NET data provider to connect to SQL Server, set **Encrypt** to true as shown in the following example.

```
"Server=sql01;Integrated Security=SSPI;Persist Security
Info=False;Database=Northwind;Encrypt=True"
```

6. Verify that Communication is Encrypted

In this procedure you will use Network Monitor to verify that data sent between the application server and database server is encrypted. You will start by sending data in clear text form and then enable encryption first by configuring the server and then by configuring the client.

► **To verify that communication is encrypted**

1. On the client computer, use Visual Studio.NET to create a new C# Console Application called **SQLSecureClient**.

2. Copy the following code to class1.cs replacing all of the existing code.

Note: Replace server name in the connection string with the name of your database server.

```
using System;
using System.Data;
using System.Data.SqlClient;

namespace SQLSecureClient
{
  class Class1
  {
    [STAThread]
    static void Main(string[] args)
    {
```

```
// Replace the server name in the following connection string with the
// name of your database server
SqlConnection conn = new SqlConnection(
  "server='sql01';database=NorthWind;Integrated Security='SSPI'");

SqlCommand cmd = new SqlCommand("SELECT * FROM Products");
try
{
  conn.Open();
  cmd.Connection = conn;
  SqlDataReader reader = cmd.ExecuteReader();
  while (reader.Read())
  {
    Console.WriteLine("{0} {1}",
              reader.GetInt32(0).ToString(),
              reader.GetString(1) );
  }
  reader.Close();
}
catch( Exception ex)
{
}
finally
{
  conn.Close();
}
}
}
}
```

3. On the **Build** menu, click **Build Solution**.

4. In order for Windows authentication to succeed between the two computers, you must duplicate the account that you are currently interactively logged on to the client computer with, on the database server computer. Ensure that the user name and password matches. An alternative is to use a domain account that is recognized by both computers.

   You must also use SQL Server Enterprise Manager to create a database logon for the newly created account and add a new database user for this logon to the Northwind database.

5. On the database server computer, use the SQL Server Network Utility to disable the use of encryption by ensuring that the **Force protocol encryption** option is not selected.

6. On the database server computer, click **Network Monitor** in the **Administrative Tools** program group.

Note: A limited version of Network Monitor is available with Windows 2000 Server. A full version is available with Microsoft SMS.

If you do not have Network Monitor installed, go to **Add/Remove Programs** in Control Panel, click **Add/Remove Windows Components**, select **Management and Monitoring Tools** from the **Windows Components** list, click **Details** and select **Network Monitor Tools**. Click **OK**, and then click **Next**, to install the limited version of Network Monitor. You may be prompted for a Windows 2000 Server CD.

---

7. On the **Capture** menu, click **Filter** to create a new filter configured to view TCP/IP network traffic sent between the database server and database server.

8. Click the **Start Capture** button.

9. Return to the client computer and run the test console application. A list of products from the Northwind database should be displayed in the console window.

10. Return to the database server and click the **Stop and View Capture** button within Network Monitor.

11. Double-click the first captured frame to view the captured data.

12. Scroll down through the captured frames. You should see the SELECT statement in clear text followed by the list of products retrieved from the database.

13. Now force the use of encryption for all connections by configuring the server with the SQL Server Network Utility:

    a. Use the SQL Server Network Utility to select **Force protocol encryption**.

    b. Stop and restart the SQL Server service.

14. Return to Network Monitor and click the **Start Capture** button. In the **Save File** dialog box, click **No**.

15. Return to the client computer and run the test console application once again.

16. Return to the database server computer and click **Stop and View Capture** within Network Monitor.

17. Confirm that the data is now unintelligible (because it is encrypted).

18. Reconfigure the server to no longer force encryption:

    a. Use the SQL Server Network Utility and clear the **Force protocol encryption** check box.

    b. Stop and restart the SQL Server service.

19. Start a new capture within Network Monitor and rerun the client application. Confirm that the data is once again in clear text.

20. Return to the client computer and select **Client Network Utility** from the **Microsoft SQL Server** program group.

21. Select **Force protocol encryption**, and then click **OK** to close the Client Network Utility.

22. Return to Network Monitor and click the **Start Capture** button. In the **Save File** dialog box, click **No**.

23. Return to the client computer and run the test console application once again.

24. Return to the database server computer and click **Stop and View Capture** within Network Monitor.

25. Confirm that the data is now unintelligible (because it is encrypted).

26. Note that, in all cases, SQL Server sends its server authentication certificate in the clear to the client at the beginning of the communication sequence. This is part of the SSL protocol. Note that this occurs even when neither the server nor the client requires encryption.

Additional Resources

For information about how to install Network Monitor in Windows 2000, go to the Microsoft Knowledge Base and search for the following articles:

- "HOW TO: Install Network Monitor in Windows 2000 (Q243270)"
- "HOW TO: Enable SSL Encryption for SQL Server 2000 with Certificate Server"(Q276553)"

For more information about Network Monitor, see the "Network Manager" section of the Microsoft Platform SDK on MSDN (*http://msdn.microsoft.com/library /default.asp?url=/library/en-us/netmon/netmon/network_monitor.asp*).

Base Configuration

The following table illustrates the base software configuration used during the development and testing of *Building Secure ASP.NET Applications*.

Base Configuration	Notes
Windows 2000 SP3 .NET Framework SP2	For more information, see the following Knowledge Base article: "INFO: Determining Whether Service Packs Are Installed on .NET Framework" (*http://support.microsoft.com /default.aspx?scid=kb;en-us;Q318785*) The .NET Framework Service Pack 2 can be downloaded from: *http://msdn.microsoft.com/netframework/downloads/sp /default.asp*

ASP.NET	Notes
Running ASP.NET on a domain controller	In general, it's not advisable to run your Web server on a domain controller, because a compromise of the machine is a compromise of the domain. If you need to run ASP.NET on a domain controller, you need to give the ASP.NET process account appropriate privileges as outlined in the following Knowledge Base article: "BUG: ASP.NET Does Not Work with the Default ASPNET Account on a Domain Controller" (*http://support.microsoft.com /default.aspx?scid=kb;en-us;q315158*)
ASP.NET Session State Security Update	*http://www.microsoft.com/Downloads/Release.asp?ReleaseID=39298*

MDAC	Notes
MDAC 2.6 is required by the .NET Framework	Visual Studio .NET installs MDAC 2.7

SQL Server 2000	Notes
SQL Server 2000 SP2	

Configuration Stores and Tools

The combined authentication, authorization, and secure communication services available to .NET Web applications are summarized in the following tables. The tables show the various security services available to each of the core .NET Web application technologies and for each one indicates where the related security configuration settings are maintained and what tools are available to edit the settings.

Note: Settings within the Internet Information Services (IIS) metabase are configured using the IIS MMC snap-in, or programmatically via script. Settings maintained within machine.config or web.config can be edited with any text editor (such as Notepad) or XML editor (such as the Microsoft Visual Studio® .NET XML editor).

Table 1: IIS security configuration

Authentication	Configuration	Tools
Anonymous Basic Digest Windows Integrated Client Certificates	IIS metabase	IIS MMC snap-in Script Makecert.exe can be used to create test certificates

Authorization	Configuration	Tools
NTFS permissions (Windows ACLs)	Windows (NTFS) file system	Windows Explorer Cacls.exe Security templates Secedit.exe
IP and DNS restrictions	IIS metabase	Group Policy

Secure Communication	Configuration	Tools
SSL	Windows (NTFS) file system	IIS MMC snap-in Script
IPSec	Machine's local policy (registry) or Microsoft Active Directory® directory service	Local Security Policy MMC snap-in Domain security Policy MMC snap-in Ipsecpol.exe

Table 1: IIS security configuration *(continued)*

Additional Gatekeepers	Configuration	Tools
IP address and domain name restrictions	IIS metabase	IIS MMC snap-in Script

Table 2: ASP.NET security configuration

Authentication	Configuration	Tools
Windows Forms Passport None (Custom)	<**authentication**> element of machine.config or web.config	Notepad.exe Visual Studio .NET Any XML editor

Authorization	Configuration	Tools
URL authorization	<**authorization**> element of Machine.config or Web.config	Notepad.exe Visual Studio .NET Any XML editor
File authorization	Windows (NTFS) file system Active Directory – or – SAM database – or – Custom data store (for example, SQL Server)	Windows Explorer Calcs.exe Security templates Secedit.exe Group Policy For Windows groups, use the Active Directory Users and Computers MMC snap-in or (for local settings) use the Computer Management tool
.NET roles		ADSI script Net.exe For custom groups – depends on custom data store

Table 3: Enterprise Services security configuration*

Authentication	Configuration	Tools
DCOM/RPC authentication	COM+ Catalog **Note**: Computer-wide settings for serviced component (and regular DCOM) proxies is maintained in Machine.config.	Component Services MMC snap-in Script (Catalog automation objects)

Authorization	Configuration	Tools
Enterprise Services (COM+) roles	COM+ Catalog	Component Services MMC snap-in Script (Catalog automation objects)
Windows ACLs (when using impersonation in serviced component)	Windows (NTFS) file system	Windows Explorer Cacls.exe Security templates Secedit.exe Group Policy

Secure Communication	Configuration	Tools
RPC encryption (packet privacy)	COM+ Catalog **Note**: Computer-wide settings for serviced component (and regular DCOM) proxies is maintained in Machine.config.	Component Services Script (Catalog automation objects)
IPSec	Machine's local policy (registry) or Active Directory	Local Security Policy MMC snap-in Ipsecpol.exe

* The security services for Enterprise Service components apply both to components hosted by server and library applications. However, certain restrictions apply for library applications because many of the security defaults are inherited from the host process and as a result are not directly configurable. Process-wide authentication may also be explicitly switched off by library applications. For more details, see Chapter 9, "Enterprise Services Security."

Table 4: Web Services (Implemented using ASP.NET) security configuration

Authentication	Configuration	Tools
Windows	<**authentication**> element of Machine.config or Web.config	Notepad Visual Studio .NET Any XML editor
Custom	Custom data store (for example. SQL Server or Active Directory)	Depends on custom store.

Table 4: Web Services (Implemented using ASP.NET) security configuration *(continued)*

Authorization	Configuration	Tools
URL Authorization	Web.config	Notepad Visual Studio .NET Any XML editor
File Authorization	Windows (NTFS) file system	Windows Explorer Cacls.exe Security templates Secedit.exe Group Policy
.NET roles	Active Directory – or – SAM database – or – Custom data store (for example, SQL Server)	For Windows groups, use the Active Directory Users and Computers MMC snap-in or (for local settings) use the Computer Management tool ADSI script Net.exe For custom groups – depends on custom store

Secure Communication	Configuration	Tools
SSL	IIS metabase	IIS MMC snap-in Script
IPSec	Machine's local policy (registry) or Active Directory	Local Security Policy MMC snap-in Ipsecpol.exe

Table 5: .NET Remoting security configuration (When hosted by ASP.NET using HTTP Channel)

Authentication	Configuration	Tools
Windows	IIS metabase	IIS MMC snap-in Script
Custom	Custom data store (for example SQL Server)	Depends on custom store

Authorization	Configuration	Tools
URL authorization	Web.config	Notepad Visual Studio .NET Any XML editor
File authorization	Windows (NTFS) file system	Windows Explorer Cacls.exe Security templates Secedit.exe Group Policy
.NET roles	Active Directory – or – SAM database – or – Custom data store (for example, SQL Server	For Windows groups, use the Active Directory Users and Computers MMC snap-in or (for local settings) use the Computer Management tool ADSI script, Net.exe For custom groups – depends on custom store

Secure Communication	Configuration	Tools
SSL	IIS metabase	IIS MMC snap-in Script
IPSec	Machine's local policy (registry) or Active Directory	Local Security Policy MMC snap-in Ipsecpol.exe

** The security services shown for .NET Remoting assumes that the .NET remote component is hosted within ASP.NET and is using the HTTP channel. No default security services are available to .NET remote components hosted outside of IIS (for example, in a custom Win32 process or Win32 service) using the TCP channel. For more details, see Chapter 11, ".NET Remoting Security."

Table 6: .SQL Server security configuration

Authentication	Configuration	Tools
Integrated Windows	SQL Server	SQL Server Enterprise Manager
		SQL Server Enterprise Manager
SQL Server standard authentication	SQL Server	

Authorization	Configuration	Tools
Object permissions	SQL Server	SQL Server Enterprise Manager
Database roles		Osql.exe (Database script)
Server roles		
User defined database roles		
Application roles		

Secure Communication	Configuration	Tools
SSL	Server's machine certificate store	Certificates MMC snap-in
	Client and server registry settings	Server Network Utility
	Connection string	Client Network Utility
IPSec	Machine's local policy (registry) or Active Directory	Local Security Policy snap-in
		Ipsecpol.exe

Reference Hub

This section provides a series of reference links to articles, support roadmaps, and technology hubs that relate to the core areas covered by *Building Secure ASP.NET Applications*. Use this section to help locate additional background reading and useful articles. This section has a consolidated set of pointers for the following:

- MSDN articles and hubs from MSDN (*http://msdn.microsoft.com/*)
- Knowledge Base articles and roadmaps for support (*http://support.microsoft.com/*)
- Articles and hubs from Microsoft.com (*http://www.microsoft.com/*)
- Seminars from Microsoft Online Seminars (*http://www.microsoft.com/seminar/*)
- Support WebCasts (*http://support.microsoft.com/default.aspx?scid=/webcasts*)
- How To articles on MSDN (*http://msdn.microsoft.com/howto/*)
  For security specific How Tos, see *http://msdn.microsoft.com/howto/security.asp*.
- Articles and resources on GotDotNet (*http://www.gotdotnet.com/*)

Searching the Knowledge Base

You can search the Microsoft Knowledge Base from two locations:

- Directly from Microsoft's Support site (*http://support.microsoft.com/*)
- Indirectly from MSDN's search facility (*http://msdn.microsoft.com/*)

When you search the Knowledge Base, you can supplement your search with keywords to help refine the articles that appear as a result of your search.

The following example uses the support search site, but similar concepts apply when searching from MSDN.

▶ To search the Knowledge Base, from http://support.microsoft.com

1. In the **Search the Knowledge Base** box, select **All Microsoft Search Topics** (the default selection).
2. In the **For solutions containing (optional)** box, type your search criteria. You can use a combination of Knowledge Base keywords and search criteria.

The following list shows some example Knowledge Base keywords:

- **kbAspNet** – Returns ASP.NET articles.
- **kbAspNet kbSecurity** – Returns ASP.NET articles that discuss *security* issues.
- **kbAspNet impersonation** – Returns ASP.NET articles that discuss *impersonation*. Note that *impersonation* is not a keyword; it is simply an additional search criterion, which helps to refine the search.

Tips

- To access additional search options, click **Show options**.
- To make sure the search includes all of the words you enter, click **All of the words entered** in the **Using** field.
- To limit the age of articles returned from the search, select a value from the **Maximum Age** field.
- To show more search results than the default 25, enter a value into the **Results Limit** field.

You may find the following Knowledge Base keywords helpful:

- Security: kbSecurity
- Roadmaps: kbArtTypeRoadmap
- How Tos: kbHowToMaster

You can use the preceding keywords in conjunction with the following technology and product keywords:

- ADO.NET: kbAdoNet
- ASP.NET: kbAspNet
- Enterprise Services: kbEntServNETFRAME
- Web Services: kbWebServices
- Remoting: kbRemoting

.NET Security

Hubs

- MSDN: .NET Security Hub: *http://msdn.microsoft.com/library/default.asp?url=/nhp /Default.asp?contentid=28001369*
- GotDotNet: .NET Security: *http://www.gotdotnet.com/team/clr/about_security.aspx*

Active Directory

Hubs

- Microsoft.com: Active Directory information: *http://www.microsoft.com/ad/*
- MSDN Active Directory information: *http://msdn.microsoft.com/library /default.asp?url=/nhp/Default.asp?contentid=28000413*

Key Notes

- Transitive trust is always available between domains in the same forest. Only "external trusts," which are not transitive, are available in separate forests in Windows 2000.

- Active Directory installations in perimeter networks (also known as DMZ, demilitarized zones, and screened subnets) should always be in a separate forest, not just a separate domain. The forest is the security boundary. This concept is illustrated in Chapter 6, "Extranet Security."

- If you need more than 5,000 members in a group then you need either .NET Server (which supports direct group membership of arbitrary sizes) or nested groups. The Commerce Server 2000 Software Development Kit (SDK) uses nested groups. However, the SDK is not required.

Articles

- Active Directory Extranet Adoption Fueled by Internet Scalability and Rapid Return on Investment: *http://www.microsoft.com/PressPass/press/2002/May02/05-08ADMomentumPR.asp*

- Netegrity SiteMinder 4.61 with Microsoft Active Directory AuthMark Performance: *http://www.mindcraft.com/whitepapers/sm461ad/sm461ad.html*

ADO.NET

Roadmaps and Overviews

- INFO: Roadmap for Using ADO in .NET: *http://support.microsoft.com/default.aspx?scid=kb;EN-US;Q308044*

- INFO: Roadmap for ADO.NET DataSet Objects and XML Web Services (Q313648): *http://support.microsoft.com/default.aspx?scid=kb;en-us;Q313648*

Seminars and WebCasts

- Advanced ADO.NET Online Seminars: *http://www.microsoft.com/seminar/*

ASP.NET

Hubs

- MSDN : ASP.NET Developer Center: *http://msdn.microsoft.com/library/default.asp?url=/nhp/default.asp?contentid=28000440*

- Support: ASP.NET Support Center: *http://support.microsoft.com/default.aspx?scid=fh;EN-US;aspnet*

Roadmaps and Overviews

- INFO: ASP.NET Roadmap:
  http://support.microsoft.com/default.aspx?scid=kb;en-us;Q305140
- INFO: ASP.NET Security Overview:
  http://support.microsoft.com/default.aspx?scid=kb;EN-US;Q306590
- INFO: ASP.NET HTTP Modules and HTTP Handlers Overview:
  http://support.microsoft.com/default.aspx?scid=kb;EN-US;Q307985
- INFO: ASP.NET Configuration Overview:
  http://support.microsoft.com/default.aspx?scid=kb;EN-US;Q307626

Knowledge Base

The following keywords help retrieve ASP.NET articles:

- Show ASP.NET articles: kbAspNet
- Show ASP.NET articles related to security: kbAspNet kbSecurity

Articles

- Managed Security Context in ASP.NET: *http://msdn.microsoft.com/library /default.asp?url=/nhp/Default.asp?contentid=28000440*

How Tos

- HOW TO: Implement Forms-Based Authentication in Your ASP.NET Application by Using C# .NET:
  http://support.microsoft.com/default.aspx?scid=kb;en-us;Q301240
- HOW TO: Secure ASP.NET Application Using Client-Side Certificate:
  http://support.microsoft.com/default.aspx?scid=kb;EN-US;Q315588
- HOW TO: Secure an ASP.NET Application by Using Windows Security:
  http://support.microsoft.com/default.aspx?scid=kb;EN-US;Q315736
- HOW TO: Implement Role-Based Security in ASP.NET App by Using C#:
  http://support.microsoft.com/default.aspx?scid=kb;EN-US;Q311495
- HOW TO: Create Keys with VB .NET for Use in Forms Authentication:
  http://support.microsoft.com/default.aspx?scid=kb;EN-US;Q313091
- HOW TO: Create Keys w/ C# .NET for Use in Forms Authentication:
  http://support.microsoft.com/default.aspx?scid=kb;EN-US;Q312906
- HOW TO: Control Authorization Permissions in ASP.NET Application:
  http://support.microsoft.com/default.aspx?scid=kb;EN-US;Q316871

- HOW TO: Authenticate Against the Active Directory by Using Forms:
  http://support.microsoft.com/default.aspx?scid=kb;EN-US;Q316748

- HOW TO: Implement Role-Based Security with Forms-Based Authentication in Your ASP.NET Application by Using Visual Basic .NET:
  http://support.microsoft.com/default.aspx?scid=kb;en-us;Q306238

For more ASP.NET related How Tos, you can search using the following KB keywords:

- kbAspNet
- kbHowToMaster

Seminars and WebCasts

- Support WebCast: Microsoft ASP.NET Security:
  http://support.microsoft.com/default.aspx?scid=http://support.microsoft.com /servicedesks/webcasts/wc112001/wcblurb112001.asp

Enterprise Services

Knowledge Base

- HOW TO: Search for Enterprise Services in the Knowledge Base and MSDN:
  http://support.microsoft.com/default.aspx?scid=kb;en-us;Q316816

- HOWTO: Search for COM+ Knowledge Base Articles:
  http://support.microsoft.com/default.aspx?scid=kb;EN-US;Q252318

Roadmaps and Overviews

- INFO: Roadmap for .NET Enterprise Services: *http://support.microsoft.com /default.aspx?scid=kb;en-us;Q308672*

- Serviced Component Overview:
  http://msdn.microsoft.com/library/default.asp?url=/library/en-us/cpguide/html /cpconservicedcomponentoverview.asp

- COM+ Integration: How .NET Enterprise Services Can Help You Build Distributed Applications:
  http://msdn.microsoft.com/library/default.asp?url=/library/en-us/dnmag01/html /complus0110.asp

- Understanding Enterprise Services (COM+) in .NET:
  http://msdn.microsoft.com/library/default.asp?url=/library/en-us/dndotnet/html /entserv.asp

How Tos

- Q305683 – BETA-HOWTO: Create a Simple Serviced Component that Uses Transactions in C#: *http://kbtools/PreviewWEB/PreviewQ.asp?Q=305683*
- Q305679 – HOWTO: Sign Your Assembly with a Strong Name Using SN.EXE: *http://kbtools/PreviewWEB/PreviewQ.asp?Q=305679*

FAQs

- Enterprise Services FAQ:

  http://www.gotdotnet.com/team/xmlentsvcs/

Seminars and WebCasts

- Support WebCast: Microsoft COM+ and the Microsoft .NET Framework:

  http://support.microsoft.com/default.aspx?scid=http://support.microsoft.com /servicedesks/webcasts/wc032202/wcblurb032202.asp
- Support WebCast: COM Threading and Application Architecture in COM+ Applications:

  http://support.microsoft.com/default.aspx?scid=http://support.microsoft.com /servicedesks/webcasts/wc051801/wcblurb051801.asp

IIS (Internet Information Server)

Hubs

- Microsoft.com: IIS : *http://www.microsoft.com/iis/*
- Support: IIS 5 Support Center: IIS *http://support.microsoft.com /default.aspx?scid=fh;EN-US;iis50*

Remoting

Roadmaps and Overviews

- An Introduction to Microsoft .NET Remoting Framework:

  http://msdn.microsoft.com/library/default.asp?url=/library/en-us/dndotnet/html /introremoting.asp?frame=true
- Microsoft .NET Remoting: A Technical Overview:

  http://msdn.microsoft.com/library/default.asp?url=/library/en-us/dndotnet/html /hawkremoting.asp

How Tos

- Remoting Basic and Advanced samples:

  http://msdn.microsoft.com/library/default.asp?url=/library/en-us/cpsamples/html/remoting.asp

- **IPrincipal** remoting sample:

  http://staff.develop.com/woodring/dotnet/#remprincipal

Seminars and WebCasts

- Develop Distributed Applications using Microsoft .NET Remoting: *http://www.microsoft.com/Seminar/Includes/Seminar.asp?Url=/Seminar/en/Developers/20020531devt1-54/Portal.xml*

- Support WebCast: Microsoft .NET Framework: .NET Remoting Essentials

  http://support.microsoft.com/default.aspx?scid=http://support.microsoft.com/servicedesks/webcasts/wc040402/wcblurb040402.asp

SQL Server

Hubs

- MSDN: SQL Server: *http://msdn.microsoft.com/library/default.asp?url=/nhp/Default.asp?contentid=28000409*

- Support: SQL Server Support Center:

  http://support.microsoft.com/default.aspx?scid=fh;EN-US;sql

Seminars and WebCasts

- Microsoft SQL Server 2000: How to Configure SSL Encryption

  http://support.microsoft.com/default.aspx?scid=http://support.microsoft.com/servicedesks/webcasts/wc042302/wcblurb042302.asp

Visual Studio .NET

Hubs

- Support: Visual Studio .NET Support Center: *http://support.microsoft.com/default.aspx?scid=fh;EN-US;vsnet*

Roadmaps and Overviews:

- HOW TO: Use the Key Productivity Features in Visual Studio .NET:

  http://support.microsoft.com/default.aspx?scid=kb;en-us;Q318205

Web Services

Hubs

- MSDN.Microsoft.Com: Web Services:

  *http://msdn.microsoft.com/library/default.asp?url=/nhp
  /Default.asp?contentid=28000442*

Roadmaps and Overviews

- INFO: Roadmap for ADO.NET DataSet Objects and XML Web Services
  (Q313648):

  http://support.microsoft.com/default.aspx?scid=kb;en-us;Q313648
- INFO: Roadmap for XML Serialization in the .NET Framework:

  http://support.microsoft.com/default.aspx?scid=kb;EN-US;Q314150
- INFO: Roadmap for XML in the .NET Framework:

  http://support.microsoft.com/default.aspx?scid=kb;EN-US;Q313651
- XML Web Services Technology Map:

  *http://msdn.microsoft.com/library/default.asp?url=/library/en-us/dndotnet/html
  /Techmap_websvcs.asp?frame=true*
- House of Web Services:

  *http://msdn.microsoft.com/msdnmag/issues/01/11/webserv/webserv0111.asp ;
  http://msdn.microsoft.com/msdnmag/issues/02/02/WebServ/WebServ0202.asp*

How Tos

- HOW TO: Secure XML Web Services with SSL in Windows 2000:

  http://support.microsoft.com/default.aspx?scid=kb;EN-US;Q307267

Seminars and WebCasts

- Support WebCast: Microsoft ASP.NET: Advanced XML Web Services Using
  ASP.NET:

  *http://support.microsoft.com/default.aspx?scid=http://support.microsoft.com
  /servicedesks/webcasts/wc032802/wcblurb032802.asp*
- Support WebCast: Microsoft .NET: Introduction to Web Services:

  *http://support.microsoft.com/default.aspx?scid=http://support.microsoft.com
  /servicedesks/webcasts/wc012902/wcblurb012902.asp*

Search Online Seminars at *http://www.microsoft.com/seminar/* for:

- How to Migrate Windows DNA Applications to .NET and XML Web Services
- XML Web Services – Authoring, Consuming, Testing and Deploying

- Best Practices for Building Web Services with Microsoft Visual Studio .NET
- Advanced Web Services

Windows 2000

Hubs

- Microsoft.com: Windows 2000 :
  http://www.microsoft.com/windows2000/default.asp
- Support.Microsoft.Com: Windows 2000 Support Center:
  http://support.microsoft.com/default.aspx?scid=fh;EN-US;win2000
- MSDN.Microsoft.Com:
  http://msdn.microsoft.com/library/default.asp?url=/nhp
  /Default.asp?contentid=28000458
- TechNet.Microsoft.Com:
  http://www.microsoft.com/technet/treeview/default.asp?url=/technet/prodtechnol
  /windows2000serv/Default.asp

How Does It Work?

This appendix provides additional material to explain in more detail how certain key concepts and processes discussed within the main body of the book actually work.

IIS and ASP.NET Processing

Note: The information in this section applies to Internet Information Services (IIS) 5, running on Windows 2000.

ASP.NET Web applications and Web services are processed by code that executes in a single instance of the ASP.NET worker process (aspnet_wp.exe), although on multi-processor computers, you can configure multiple instances, one per processor.

IIS authenticates callers and creates a Windows access token for the caller. If anonymous access is enabled within IIS, then a Windows access token for the anonymous Internet user account (typically, IUSR_MACHINE) is created by IIS.

Requests for ASP.NET file types are handled by an ASP.NET ISAPI extension (aspnet_isapi.dll), which runs in the IIS (inetinfo.exe) process address space. This uses a named pipe to communicate with the ASP.NET worker process as shown in Figure 1. IIS passes the Windows access token that represents the caller to the ASP.NET worker process. The ASP.NET Windows authentication module uses this to construct a **WindowsPrincipal** object and the ASP.NET File authorization module uses it to perform Windows access checks to ensure the caller is authorized to access the requested file.

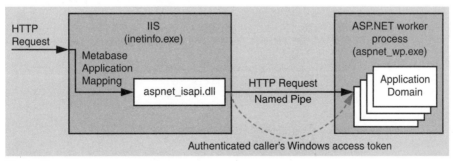

Figure 1
IIS and ASP.NET communication

Note: Access tokens are process relative. As a result, the ASP.NET ISAPI DLL running in inetinfo.exe calls **DuplicateHandle** to duplicate the token handle into the aspnet_wp.exe process address space and then passes the handle value through the named pipe.

Application Isolation

Separate application domains within the worker process (one per IIS virtual directory, or in other words, one per ASP.NET Web application or Web service) are used to provide isolation.

This is in contrast to classic ASP, where the application protection level, configured within the IIS metabase determined whether the ASP application should execute in process with IIS (inetinfo.exe), out of process in a dedicated instance of Dllhost.exe, or in a shared (pooled) instance of Dllhost.exe.

Important: The process isolation level setting within IIS has no affect on the way ASP.NET Web applications are processed.

The ASP.NET ISAPI Extension

The ASP.NET ISAPI extension (aspnet_isapi.dll) runs in the IIS process address space (inetinfo.exe) and forwards requests for ASP.NET file types to the ASP.NET worker process through a named pipe.

Specific ASP.NET file types are mapped to the ASP.NET ISAPI extension by mappings defined within the IIS metabase. Mappings for standard ASP.NET file types (including .aspx, .asmx, .rem, .soap) are established when the .NET Framework is installed.

▶ **To view application mappings**

1. From the **Administrative Tools** programs group, start Internet Information Services.
2. Right-click the default Web site on your Web server computer, and then click **Properties**.
3. Click the **Home Directory** tab, and then click **Configuration**.

   A list of mappings is displayed. You can see which file types are mapped to Aspnet_isapi.dll

IIS 6.0 and Windows .NET Server

IIS 6.0 on Windows .NET Server will introduce some significant changes to the current process arrangement.

- You will be able to configure multiple application pools, each served by one or more process instances (w3wp.exe). This will provide additional fault tolerance and manageability benefits and will allow you to isolate separate applications in separate processes.

- ASP.NET is integrated with the IIS 6.0 Kernel mode HTTP listener, which will allow requests to be passed directly from the operating system to the ASP.NET worker process.

More Information

For more information about IIS6, see the "IIS 6 Overview" article on TechNet (*http://www.microsoft.com/technet/treeview/default.asp?url=/TechNet/prodtechnol/iis /evaluate/iis6ovw.asp*).

ASP.NET Pipeline Processing

ASP.NET authentication and authorization mechanisms are implemented using HTTP module objects, which are invoked as part of the standard ASP.NET pipeline processing. Individual Web requests and responses pass through a pipeline of objects as shown in Figure 2.

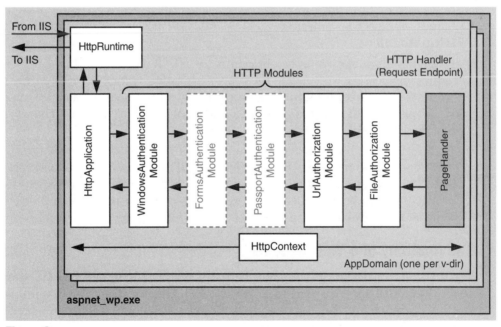

Figure 2
ASP.NET pipeline processing

The ASP.NET pipeline model consists of an **HttpApplication** object, various HTTP module objects, and an HTTP handler object, together with their associated factory objects, which have been omitted from Figure 2 for clarity. An **HttpRuntime** object is used at the start of the processing sequence and an **HttpContext** object is used throughout the lifecycle of a request to convey details about the request and response.

The following list explains the responsibilities and operations performed by the objects associated with the HTTP processing pipeline:

- The **HttpRuntime** object examines the request received from IIS and dispatches it to an appropriate instance of the **HttpApplication** object to process the request. There is a pool of **HttpApplication** objects in each application domain in Aspnet_wp.exe. There is a one-to-one mapping between application domains, **HttpApplication** objects and IIS virtual directories. In other words, ASP.NET treats separate IIS virtual directories as separate applications.

Note: There is one instance of **HttpRuntime** in every Web application domain.

- The **HttpApplication** objects control the pipeline processing. An individual **HttpApplication** object is created to handle each simultaneous HTTP request. **HttpApplication** objects are pooled for performance reasons.

- HTTP module objects are filters that process HTTP request and response messages as they flow through the pipeline. They can view or alter the content of the request and response messages. HTTP modules are classes that implement **IHttpModule**.

- HTTP handler objects are the endpoints for HTTP requests and provide the request processing for specific file types. For example, one handler processes requests for *.aspx files while another processes requests for *.asmx files. The HTTP response message is generated and returned from the HTTP handler. HTTP handlers are classes that implement **IHttpHandler**.

- An **HttpContext** object is used throughout the pipeline to represent the current Web request and response. It is available to all modules in the pipeline and the handler object at the end of the pipeline. The **HttpContext** object exposes various properties including the **User** property which contains an **IPrincipal** object that represents the caller.

The Anatomy of a Web Request

The ASP.NET ISAPI library (Aspnet_isapi.dll) runs inside the IIS process address space (Inetinfo.exe). It dispatches requests to the **HttpRuntime** object within the ASP.NET worker process (Aspnet_wp.exe). The following set of actions occurs in response to each Web request received by ASP.NET:

- The **HttpRuntime** object examines the request and forwards it to an instance of an **HttpApplication** object.

  There is at least one **HttpApplication** object instance per application domain (the objects are pooled) and one application domain per IIS virtual directory. The initial request for a file in a particular virtual directory results in a new application domain and a new **HttpApplication** object being created.

- A list of HTTP modules is read from Machine.config (they are contained within the **<httpModules>** element). Additional custom HTTP modules can be added to Web.config for a specific application. The default **<httpModules>** element within Machine.config is shown in the following code snippet.

```
<httpModules>
  <add name="OutputCache"
       type="System.Web.Caching.OutputCacheModule"/>
  <add name="Session"
       type="System.Web.SessionState.SessionStateModule"/>
  <add name="WindowsAuthentication"
       type="System.Web.Security.WindowsAuthenticationModule"/>
  <add name="FormsAuthentication"
       type="System.Web.Security.FormsAuthenticationModule"/>
  <add name="PassportAuthentication"
       type="System.Web.Security.PassportAuthenticationModule"/>
  <add name="UrlAuthorization"
       type="System.Web.Security.UrlAuthorizationModule"/>
  <add name="FileAuthorization"
       type="System.Web.Security.FileAuthorizationModule"/>
</httpModules>
```

  The authentication modules hook the **AuthenticateRequest** event, while the authorization modules hook the **AuthorizeRequest** event.

  The request passes through every module in the pipeline, although only a single authentication module is loaded. This depends on the configuration of the **<authentication>** element in Web.config. For example, the **<authentication>** element that follows results in the **WindowsAuthenticationModule** being loaded.

```
<authentication mode="Windows" />
```

- The activated authentication module is responsible for creating an **IPrincipal** object and storing it in the **HttpContext.User** property. This is vital, because the downstream authorization modules use this **IPrincipal** object in order to make authorization decisions.

In the absence of authentication (for example, where anonymous access is enabled within IIS and ASP.NET is configured with <authentication mode="None" />), there's a special non configured module that puts a default anonymous principal into the **HttpContext.User** property. As a result, **HttpContext.User** is always non-null after authentication.

If you implement a custom authentication module, code within the custom module must create an **IPrincipal** object and store it in **HttpContext.User**,

---

Note: ASP.NET also wires up **Thread.CurrentPrincipal** based on **HttpContext.User** after the **AuthenticateRequest** event.

- The **HttpApplication** fires the **AuthenticateRequest** event, which can be hooked in global.asax. This allows you to inject custom processing code; for example, to load the set of roles associated with the current user. However, note that the **WindowsAuthenticationModule** does this automatically. The role list is obtained from the set of Windows groups in which the authenticated Windows user is a member.

- After the appropriate authentication module has finished its processing, the authorization modules are called if the request hasn't been aborted.

- When the **UrlAuthorizationModule** is called, it checks for an **<authorization>** tag in Machine.config and Web.config. If present, it retrieves the **IPrincipal** object from **HttpContext.User** and checks to see whether the user is authorized to access the requested resource using the specified verb (GET, POST, and so on).

  If the user is not authorized, the **UrlAuthorizationModule** calls **HttpApplication.CompleteRequest**, which aborts normal message processing. The **UrlAuthorizationModule** returns an HTTP 401 status code.

- Next, the **FileAuthorizationModule** is called. It checks whether the **IIdentity** object in **HttpContext.User.Identity** is an instance of the **WindowsIdentity** class.

  If the **IIdentity** object is not a **WindowsIdentity**, the **FileAuthorizationModule** performs no further processing.

  If a **WindowsIdentity** is present, the **FileAuthorizationModule** calls the **AccessCheck** API (through P/Invoke) to see if the authenticated caller (whose access token has been passed to ASP.NET by IIS and is exposed by the **WindowsIdentity** object) is authorized to access the requested file. If the file's security descriptor contains at least a Read ACE in its DACL, the request is allowed to proceed. Otherwise the **FileAuthorizationModule** calls **HttpApplication.CompleteRequest** and returns a 401 status code.

Forms Authentication Processing

The **FormsAuthenticationModule** is activated when the following element is in Web.config.

```
<authentication mode="Forms" />
```

Remember that for Forms authentication, you implement the **Application_Authenticate** event in Global.asax. For Forms authentication, the following sequence occurs:

- Within this code, you can construct an **IPrincipal** object and store it in **HttpContext.User**. This typically contains the role list retrieved from a custom data store (normally a SQL Server database or Active Directory). The **IPrincipal** object is typically an instance of the **GenericPrincipal** class but could also be a custom **IPrincipal** class.

  The **FormsAuthenticationModule** checks to see if you have created an **IPrincipal** object. If you have, it is used by the downstream authorization modules. If you haven't, the **FormsAuthenticationModule** constructs a **GenericPrincipal** (with no roles) and stores it in the context.

  If there is no role information, any authorization checks (such as **PrincipalPermssion** demands) that demand role membership, will fail.

- The **UrlAuthorizationModule** handles the **AuthorizeRequest** event. Its authorization decisions are based on the **IPrincipal** object contained within **HttpContext.User**.

Windows Authentication Processing

The **WindowsAuthenticationModule** is activated when the following element is in Web.config.

```
<authentication mode="Windows" />
```

For Windows authentication, the following sequence occurs:

1. The **WindowsAuthenticationModule** creates a **WindowsPrincipal** object using the Windows access token passed to ASP.NET by IIS.
2. It uses P/Invoke to call Win32 functions to obtain the list of Windows group that the user belongs to. These are used to populate the **WindowsPrincipal** role list.
3. It stores the **WindowsPrincipal** object in **HttpContext.User**, ready to be used by the downstream authorization modules.

Event Handling

The **HttpApplication** object fires the set of events shown in Table 1. Individual HTTP modules can hook these events (by providing their own event handlers).

Table 1: Events fired by HttpApplication objects

Event	Notes
BeginRequest	Fired before request processing starts
AuthenticateRequest	To authenticate the caller
AuthorizeRequest	To perform access checks
ResolveRequestCache	To get a response from the cache
AcquireRequestState	To load session state
PreRequestHandlerExecute	Fired immediately before the request is sent to the handler object
PostRequestHandlerExecute	Fired immediately after the request is sent to the handler object
ReleaseRequestState	To store session state
UpdateRequestCache	To update the response cache
EndRequest	Fired after processing ends
PreSendRequestHeaders	Fired before buffered response headers are sent
PreSendRequestContent	Fired before buffered response body sent

Note: The HTTP handler executes in between the **PreRequestHandlerExecute** and **PostRequestHandlerExecute** events.

The last two events are non-deterministic and could occur at any time (for example, as a result of a **Response.Flush**). All other events are sequential.

You do not need to implement an HTTP module simply in order to hook one of these events. You can also add event handlers to Global.asax. In addition to the events listed in Table 1 (which can all be hooked by individual HTTP module objects), the **HttpApplication** object fires **Application_OnStart** and **Application_OnEnd** handlers, which will be familiar to ASP developers. These can be handled only within Global.asax. Finally, you can also implement custom event handlers within Global.asax for events fired by individual HTTP module objects. For example, the session state module fires **Session_OnStart** and **Session_OnEnd** events.

Implementing a Custom HTTP Module

▶ **To create your own HTTP module and insert it into the ASP.NET processing pipeline**

1. Create a class that implements **IHttpModule**.

2. Place the assembly that contains the module in your application's \bin subdirectory or you can install it into the Global Assembly Cache.

3. Add an **<HttpModules>** element to your application's web.config, as shown below.

```
<system.web>
  <httpModules>
    <add name="modulename"
         type="namespace.classname,assemblyname" />
  </httpModules>
</system.web>
```

Implementing a Custom HTTP Handler

You may need to implement a custom HTTP handler, for example to handle the processing of files with the .data file extension.

▶ **To implement a custom HTTP handler**

1. Add a mapping to the IIS metabase to map the .data file extension to the ASP.NET ISAPI extension (Aspnet_isapi.dll).

   Right-click your application's virtual directory in the IIS MMC snap-in, click the **Configuration** button, and then click **Add** to create a new mapping for .data files to C:\Winnt\Microsoft.NET\Framework\v1.0.3705\aspnet_isapi.dll.

   Note: If you select the **Check that file exists** check box when adding the mapping, then the file must be physically present. This is usually what is wanted unless you have virtualized paths that don't map to a physical file. Virtualized paths ending with .rem or .soap are used by .NET Remoting.

   ---

2. Create a class that implements **IHttpHandler** (and optionally **IHttpAsyncHandler** if you want to handle requests asynchronously).

3. Place the assembly that contains the handler in your application's \bin subdirectory or you can install it into the Global Assembly Cache.

4. Add the handler to the processing pipeline by adding an **<httpHandlers>** section to your application's Web.config file.

```
<system.web>
  <httpHandlers>
    <add verb="*" path="*.data" type="namespace.classname, assemblyname" />
  </httpHandlers>
</system.web>
```

ASP.NET Identity Matrix

Principal objects implement the **IPrincipal** interface and represent the security context of the user on whose behalf the code is running. The principal object includes the user's identity (as a contained **IIdentity** object) and any roles to which the user belongs.

ASP.NET provides the following principal and identity object implementations:

- **WindowsPrincipal** and **WindowsIdentity** objects represent users who have been authenticated with Windows authentication. With these objects, the role list is automatically obtained from the set of Windows groups to which the Windows user belongs.

- **GenericPrincipal** and **GenericIdentity** objects represent users who have been authenticated using Forms authentication or other custom authentication mechanisms. With these objects, the role list is obtained in a custom manner, typically from a database.

- **FormsIdentity** and **PassportIdentity** objects represent users who have been authenticated with Forms and Passport authentication respectively.

The following tables illustrate, for a range of IIS authentication settings, the resultant identity that is obtained from each of the variables that maintain an **IPrincipal** and/ or **IIdentity** object. The following abbreviations are used in the table:

- **HttpContext = HttpContext.Current.User**, which returns an **IPrincipal** object that contains security information for the current Web request. This is the authenticated Web client.

- **WindowsIdentity = WindowsIdentity.GetCurrent()**, which returns the identity of the security context of the currently executing Win32 thread.

- **Thread = Thread.CurrentPrincipal** which returns the principal of the currently executing .NET thread which rides on top of the Win32 thread.

Table 1: IIS Anonymous Authentication

Web.config Settings	Variable Location	Resultant Identity
<identity impersonate="true"/> <authentication mode="Windows" />	HttpContext WindowsIdentity Thread	- MACHINE\IUSR_MACHINE -
<identity impersonate="false"/> <authentication mode="Windows" />	HttpContext WindowsIdentity Thread	- MACHINE\ASPNET -
<identity impersonate="true"/> <authentication mode="Forms" />	HttpContext WindowsIdentity Thread	Name provided by user MACHINE\IUSR_MACHINE Name provided by user
<identity impersonate="false"/> <authentication mode="Forms" />	HttpContext WindowsIdentity Thread	Name provided by user MACHINE\ASPNET Name provided by user

Table 2: IIS Basic Authentication

Web.config Settings	Variable Location	Resultant Identity
<identity impersonate="true"/> <authentication mode="Windows" />	HttpContext WindowsIdentity Thread	Domain\UserName Domain\UserName Domain\UserName
<identity impersonate="false"/> <authentication mode="Windows" />	HttpContext WindowsIdentity Thread	Domain\UserName MACHINE\ASPNET Domain\UserName
<identity impersonate="true"/> <authentication mode="Forms" />	HttpContext WindowsIdentity Thread	Name provided by user Domain\UserName Name provided by user
<identity impersonate="false"/> <authentication mode="Forms" />	HttpContext WindowsIdentity Thread	Name provided by user MACHINE\ASPNET Name provided by user

Table 3: IIS Digest Authentication

Web.config Settings	Variable Location	Resultant Identity
<identity impersonate="true"/> <authentication mode="Windows" />	HttpContext WindowsIdentity Thread	Domain\UserName Domain\UserName Domain\UserName
<identity impersonate="false"/> <authentication mode="Windows" />	HttpContext WindowsIdentity Thread	Domain\UserName MACHINE\ASPNET Domain\UserName
<identity impersonate="true"/> <authentication mode="Forms" />	HttpContext WindowsIdentity Thread	Name provided by user Domain\UserName Name provided by user
<identity impersonate="false"/> <authentication mode="Forms" />	HttpContext WindowsIdentity Thread	Name provided by user MACHINE\ASPNET Name provided by user

Table 4: IIS Integrated Windows

Web.config Settings	Variable Location	Resultant Identity
<identity impersonate="true"/> <authentication mode="Windows" />	HttpContext WindowsIdentity Thread	Domain\UserName Domain\UserName Domain\UserName
<identity impersonate="false"/> <authentication mode="Windows" />	HttpContext WindowsIdentity Thread	Domain\UserName MACHINE\ASPNET Domain\UserName
<identity impersonate="true"/> <authentication mode="Forms" />	HttpContext WindowsIdentity Thread	Name provided by user Domain\UserName Name provided by user
<identity impersonate="false"/> <authentication mode="Forms" />	HttpContext WindowsIdentity Thread	Name provided by user MACHINE\ASPNET Name provided by user

Cryptography and Certificates

Keys and Certificates

Asymmetric encryption uses a public/private key pair. Data encrypted with the private key can be decrypted only with the corresponding public key and vice versa.

Public keys (as their name suggests) are made generally available. Conversely, a private key remains private to a specific individual. The distribution mechanism by which public keys are transported to users is a certificate. Certificates are normally signed by a certification authority (CA) in order to confirm that the public key is from the subject who claims to have sent the public key. The CA is a mutually trusted entity.

The typical implementation of digital certification involves a process for signing the certificate. The process is shown in Figure 1.

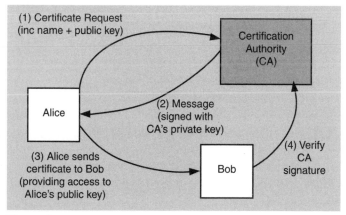

Figure 1
Digital certification process

The sequence of events shown in Figure 1 is as follows:

1. Alice sends a signed certificate request containing her name, her public key, and perhaps some additional information to a CA.

2. The CA creates a message from Alice's request. The CA signs the message with its private key, creating a separate signature. The CA returns the message and the signature, to Alice. Together, the message and signature form Alice's certificate.

3. Alice sends her certificate to Bob to give him access to her public key.

4. Bob verifies the certificate's signature, using the CA's public key. If the signature proves valid, he accepts the public key in the certificate as Alice's public key.

As with any digital signature, any receiver with access to the CA's public key can determine whether a specific CA signed the certificate. This process requires no access to any secret information. The preceding scenario assumes that Bob has access to the CA's public key. Bob would have access to that key if he has a copy of the CA's certificate that contains that public key.

X.509 Digital Certificates

X.509 digital certificates include not only a user's name and public key, but also other information about the user. These certificates are more than stepping stones in a digital hierarchy of trust. They enable the CA to give a certificate's receiver a means of trusting not only the public key of the certificate's subject, but also that other information about the certificate's subject. That other information can include, among other things, an e-mail address, an authorization to sign documents of a given value, or the authorization to become a CA and sign other certificates.

X.509 certificates and many other certificates have a valid time duration. A certificate can expire and no longer be valid. A CA can revoke a certificate for a number of reasons. To handle revocations, a CA maintains and distributes a list of revoked certificates called a Certificate Revocation List (CRL). Network users access the CRL to determine the validity of a certificate.

Certificate Stores

Certificates are stored in safe locations called a certificate stores. A certificate store can contain certificates, CRLs, and Certificate Trust Lists (CTLs). Each user has a personal store (called the "MY store") where that user's certificates are stored. The MY store can be physically implemented in a number of locations including the registry, on a local or remote computer, a disk file, a data base, a directory service, a smart device, or another location.

While any certificate can be stored in the MY store, this store should be reserved for a user's personal certificates, that is the certificates used for signing and decrypting that particular user's messages.

In addition to the MY store, Windows also maintains the following certificate stores:

- **CA and ROOT**. This store contains the certificates of certificate authorities that the user trusts to issue certificates to others. A set of trusted CA certificates are supplied with the operating system and others can be added by administrators.

- **Other**. This store contains the certificates of other people to whom the user exchanges signed messages.

The CryptoAPI provides functions to manage certificates. These APIs can be accessed only through unmanaged code. Also, CAPICOM is a COM-based API for the CryptoAPI, which can be accessed via COM Interop.

More Information

For more information, see "Cryptography, CryptoAPI, and CAPICOM" on MSDN (*http://msdn.microsoft.com/library/default.asp?url=/library/en-us/security/Security /cryptography_cryptoapi_and_capicom.asp*).

Cryptography

Cryptography is used to provide the following:

- **Confidentiality**. To ensure data remains private. Confidentiality is usually achieved using encryption. Encryption algorithms (that use encryption keys) are used to convert plain text into cipher text and the equivalent decryption algorithm is used to convert the cipher text back to plain text. Symmetric encryption algorithms use the same key for encryption and decryption, while asymmetric algorithms use a public/private key pair.

- **Data integrity**. To ensure data is protected from accidental or deliberate (malicious) modification. Integrity is usually provided by message authentication codes or hashes. A hash value is a fixed length numeric value derived from a sequence of data. Hash values are used to verify the integrity of data sent through insecure channels. The hash value of received data is compared to the hash value of the data as it was sent to determine if the data was altered.

- **Authentication**. To assure that data originates from a particular party. Digital certificates are used to provide authentication. Digital signatures are usually applied to hash values as these are significantly smaller than the source data that they represent.

Technical Choices

- Use a hash when you want a way of verifying that data has not been tampered with in transit.

- Use a keyed hash when you want to prove that an entity knows a secret without sending the secret back and forth, or you want to defend against interception during transit by using a simple hash.

- Use encryption when you want to hide data when being sent across an insecure medium or when making the data persistent.

- Use a certificate when you want to verify the person claiming to be the owner of the public key.

- Use symmetric encryption for speed and when both parties share the key in advance.
- Use asymmetric encryption when you want to safely exchange data across an insecure medium.
- Use a digital signature when you want authentication and non-repudiation.
- Use a salt value (a cryptographically generated random number) to defend against dictionary attacks.

Cryptography in .NET

The **System.Security.Cryptography** namespace provides cryptographic services, including secure encoding and decoding of data, hashing, random number generation, and message authentication.

The .NET Framework provides implementations of many standard cryptographic algorithms and these can be easily extended because of the well defined inheritance hierarchy consisting of abstract classes that define the basic algorithm types — symmetric, asymmetric and hash algorithms, together with algorithm classes.

Table 1: Algorithms for which the .NET Framework provides implementation classes "out of the box"

Symmetric Algorithms	Asymmetric Algorithms	Hash Algorithms
DES (Data Encryption Standard)	DSA (Digital Signature Algorithm)	HMAC SHA1 (Hash-based Message Authentication Code using the SHA1 hash algorithm)
TripleDES (Triple Data Encryption Standard)	RSA	MAC Triple DES (Message Authentication Code using Triple DES)
Rijndael		MD5
RC2		SHA1, SHA256, SHA384, SHA512 (Secure Hash Algorithm using various hash sizes)

Symmetric Algorithm Support

.NET provides the following implementation classes that provide symmetric, secret key encryption algorithms:

- DESCryptoServiceProvider
- RC2CryptoServiceProvider
- RijndaelManaged
- TripleDESCryptoServiceProvider

Note: The classes that end with "CryptoServiceProvider" are wrappers that use the underlying services of the cryptographic service provider (CSP) and the classes that end with "Managed" are implemented in managed code.

Figure 2 shows the inheritance hierarchy adopted by the .NET Framework. The algorithm type base class (for example, **SymmetricAlgorithm**) is abstract. A set of abstract algorithm classes derive from the abstract type base class. Algorithm implementation classes provide concrete implementations of the selected algorithm; for example DES, Triple-DES, Rijndael and RC2.

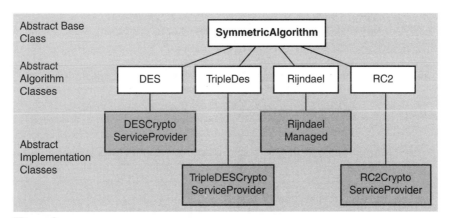

Figure 2
The symmetric crypto class inheritance hierarchy

Asymmetric Algorithm Support

.NET provides following asymmetric (public/private key) encryption algorithms through the abstract base class
(**System.Security.Crytography.AsymmetricAlgorithm**):

- DSACryptoServiceProvider
- RSACryptoServiceProvider

These are used to digitally sign and encrypt data. Figure 3 shows the inheritance hierarchy.

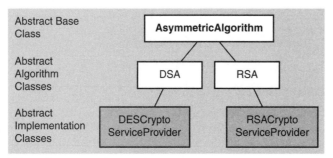

Figure 3
The asymmetric crypto class inheritance hierarchy

Hashing Algorithm Support

.NET provides following hash algorithms:

- SHA1, SHA256, SHA384, SHA512
- MD5
- HMACSHA (Keyed Hashed algorithm)
- MACTripleDES (Keyed Hashed algorithm)

Figure 4 shows the inheritance hierarchy for the hash algorithm classes.

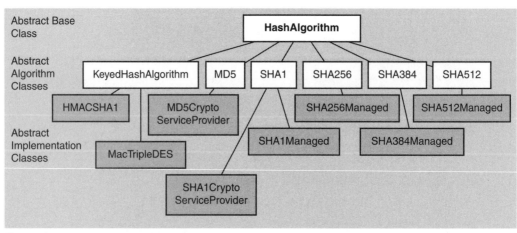

Figure 4
The hash crypto class inheritance hierarchy

Summary

Cryptography is an important technology for building secure Web applications. This appendix has covered some of the fundamentals of certificates and cryptography and has introduced some of the classes exposed by the **System.Security.Cryptography** namespace, which enable you to more easily incorporate cryptographic security solutions into your .NET applications.

For more information about cryptography in .NET, search MSDN for the page entitled ".NET Framework Cryptography Model."

.NET Web Application Security

The technologies that fall under the umbrella of the .NET security framework include:

- IIS
- ASP.NET
- Enterprise Services
- Web Services
- .NET Remoting
- SQL Server

These are illustrated in Figure 1.

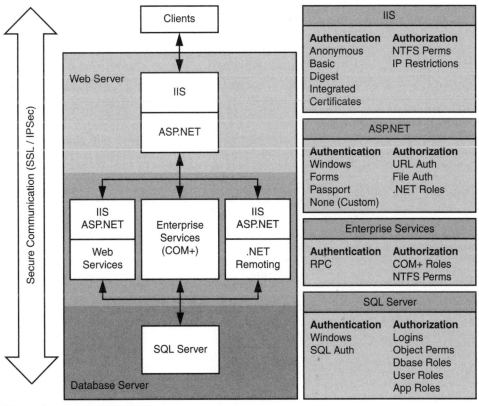

Figure 1

The .NET Web application security framework

Glossary

A

access control entry (ACE)

An access control entry (ACE) identifies a specific user or user group within an access control list and specifies the access rights for the user or user group. An individual ACE may explicitly deny or permit rights.

access control list (ACL)

An access control list (ACL) is an ordered list of access control entries (ACEs) attached to a securable object. The Windows operating system uses two types of ACL; a discretionary access control list (DACL) used to specify the access rights of a user or user group and a system access control list (SACL) used to determine when specific types of access should generate audit messages.

access right

An access right is an attribute of an access token that determines the type of operation that a particular Windows group or user can perform on a secured object. Example access rights include read, write, delete, execute, and so on.

access token

An access token is a data structure attached to every Windows process. It maintains security context information for the process, which includes a user SID identifying the principal whom the logon session represents, and authorization attributes including the user's group SIDs and privileges.

Every access token is associated with exactly one logon session, while a logon session may contain multiple access tokens; one for each process started within the logon session and optionally, additional thread tokens attached to individual threads.

account

An account is an entry in the security database that maintains the security attributes of an individual principal. The security database may either be the SAM database or Active Directory.

Accounts may either be domain accounts or local accounts.

Active Directory

Active Directory is the LDAP directory service used by the Windows 2000 operating system.

anonymous authentication

Anonymous authentication is a form of IIS authentication in which IIS makes no attempt to prove the identity of its clients. Anonymous authentication is akin to no authentication. It is often used in conjunction with ASP.NET Forms authentication which uses an HTML form to capture the client's credentials.

application server

An application server is a dedicated server computer, separate from a front-end Web server. The application server typically hosts Web services, remote components, and/or Enterprise Services applications that contain the majority of an application's business logic.

authentication

Authentication is the process of proving identity. For example, when you log on to Windows, the operating system authenticates you by requesting your credentials; a user name and password. When a process (a type of principal), acting on your behalf connects to a remote computer, it uses a cached set of credentials to answer network authentication requests.

authority

An authority is a trusted entity (organization or computer) that is used to provide authentication services.

authorization

Authorization is the process of determining whether or not an authenticated identity is allowed to access a requested resource or perform a requested operation.

B

Base 64 encoding

Base 64 encoding is a well-defined method for rendering binary data as printable ASCII text, suitable for use with text-based protocols such as HTTP. It is not encryption.

Basic authentication

Basic authentication is part of the HTTP 1.0 protocol. It is widely used because it is implemented by virtually all Web servers and Web browsers. Basic authentication is a simple authentication mechanism that does not involve cryptography or challenge/response handshaking. Instead, a principal's credentials (user name and password) are passed directly from client to server. Basic authentication is insecure unless combined with SSL, because the password is not encrypted before it is passed across the network. It is transmitted using Base 64 encoding, so the clear text password is easily obtainable.

C

certificate

A certificate is a digitally signed data structure that contains information about a subject (person or application) and the subject's public key. Certificates are issued by trusted organizations called certification authorities (CAs) after the CA has verified the identity of the subject.

certificate authentication

Certificate authentication is a form of IIS authentication in which IIS accepts client-certificates used to prove the client's identity. Using this form of authentication, IIS can optionally map a client certificate to a Windows user account by using an internal mapping table or Active Directory.

certificate revocation list (CRL)

A CRL is a document that is maintained and published by a certification authority (CA) that lists certificates issued by the CA that are no longer valid.

certificate store

A certificate store is a storage location for certificates, certificate revocation lists (CRLs) and certificate trust lists (CTL).

certification authority (CA)

A CA is a trusted organization or entity that issues certificates.

code access security

Code access security is a form of .NET security that is used to control the access that code has to protected resources.

clear text

Clear text is data that has not been encrypted.

cipher

Cipher is a cryptographic algorithm used to encrypt data.

cipher text

Cipher text is data that has been encrypted.

client certificate

A client certificate is a certificate used by clients to provide positive identification of their identity to server applications.

confidentiality

See privacy.

credentials

Credentials are the set of items that a principal uses to prove its identity. A user name and password are a common example of a set of credentials.

cryptography

Cryptography is the art and science of information security. It encompasses confidentiality, integrity, and authentication.

D

declarative authorization

Declarative authorization is a form of authorization applied through the use of attributes. For example, .NET provides the **PrincipalPermissionAttribute** class which can be used to annotate methods to provide declarative authorization.

For example, the following declarative authorization ensures that the method **DoPrivMethod** can only be executed by members of the Manager or Teller role.

```
[PrincipalPermissionAttribute(SecurityAction.Demand, Role="Teller"),
 PrincipalPermissionAttribute(SecurityAction.Demand, Role="Manager")]
public void DoPrivMethod()
{
}
```

delegation

Delegation is an extended form of impersonation that allows a server process that is performing work on behalf of a client, to access resources on a remote computer. This capability is natively provided by Kerberos on Windows 2000 and later operating systems. Conventional impersonation (for example, that provided by NTLM) allows only a single network hop. When NTLM impersonation is used, the one hop is used between the client and server computers, restricting the server to local resource access while impersonating.

DES (data encryption standard)

DES is a block cipher that encrypts data in 64-bit blocks. DES is a symmetric algorithm that uses the same algorithm and key for encryption and decryption. DES has been superceded by triple DES.

dictionary attack

A dictionary attack is a brute-force attack in which the attacker tries every possible secret key to decrypt encrypted data. You can mitigate against this form of attack by using a salt value in conjunction with encrypted (or hashed) data.

Digest authentication

Digest authentication is defined by the HTTP 1.1 protocol although it is not widely used. With this form of authentication a clear text password is not passed across the network. A password hash or digest is passed instead. While more secure than Basic authentication, it requires Internet Explorer 5.0 or later on the client, and a Windows 2000 computer running IIS 5.0 with Active Directory on the server.

digital signature

A digital signature is used for message authentication; to ensure the validity of the sender of the message and also for message integrity; to ensure that data is not modified while in transit. Signing data does not alter it; it simply generates a digital signature string which is transmitted with the data.

Digital signatures are created using public-key signature algorithms such as the RSA public-key cipher.

digest

See hash.

discretionary access control list (DACL)

A DACL is associated with a securable object (using a security descriptor) and specifies the set of access rights granted to users and groups of users. The DACL is controlled by the owner of an object and it consists of an ordered list of access control entries (ACEs) that determine the types of operation a user or user group can perform against the object.

domain accounts

Domain accounts are a Windows or group account centrally maintained and administered in a domain controller's SAM database or in Active Directory.

DPAPI (data protection API)

DPAPI is a Win32 API available on Windows 2000 and later operating systems used to encrypt and decrypt data. DPAPI passes the key management issue associated with encryption techniques to the operating system, as it uses Windows account passwords to generate encryption keys.

E

EFS (encrypting file system)

The encrypting file system (EFS) is provided by Windows 2000 and later operating systems, to provide file-encryption capabilities on an NTFS volume.

encryption

Encryption is the process of converting data (plain text) into something that appears to be random and meaningless (cipher text), which is difficult to decode without a secret key. Encryption is used to provide message confidentiality.

entropy

Entropy is a measure of uncertainty. It is used in association some encryption technologies to introduce a degree of randomness into the encryption process. An entropy value used in addition to a key to encrypt data must also be used to decrypt data.

F

fixed principal impersonation

Fixed principal impersonation is a form of impersonation used by ASP.NET in which the impersonated identity remains constant regardless of the authenticated caller's identity. Usually, the impersonated identity is determined by the identity of the caller. The identity used for fixed principal impersonation is specified by using the **userName** and **password** attributes of the <**identity**> element in web.config. An example follows.

```
<identity userName="Bob" password="password" />
```

Forms authentication

Forms authentication is a type of authentication supported by ASP.NET that requires users to log on by supplying logon credentials through an HTML form.

G

gatekeeper

A gatekeeper is a technology or subsystem used to provide access control. Example gatekeepers include IIS, the ASP.NET **UrlAuthorizationModule**, and the ASP.NET **FileAuthorizationModule**.

GenericIdentity

GenericIdentity is an implementation of the **IIdentity** interface, used by ASP.NET in conjunction with Forms, Passport (and sometimes custom) authentication mechanisms. The **GenericPrincipal** object contains a **GenericIdentity** object.

GenericPrincipal

GenericPrincipal is an implementation of the **IPrincipal** interface, used by ASP.NET in conjunction with Forms and Passport (and possibly custom) authentication mechanisms. It contains the list of roles (retrieved by the application from a custom data store) that the user belongs to.

The **GenericPrincipal** object is attached to the context of Web requests and is used for authorization. It contains a **GenericIdentity** object.

H

hash

A hash is a fixed length numeric value that uniquely identifies data. Hash values are useful to verify the integrity of data sent through insecure channels. The hash value of received data can be compared to the hash value of data as it was sent to determine if the data was altered.

Hash values are also used with digital signatures. Because small hash values can be used to represent much large amounts of data, only the hash of a message needs to be signed; rather than the entire message data.

HTTP context

HTTP context is the context or property collection associated with (and describing) the current Web request.

HTTP module

An HTTP module is a module used by ASP.NET to process Web requests. An HTTP module is an assembly that implements the **IhttpModule** interface and handles events. ASP.NET uses a series of built-in modules such as authentication modules, the session state module and the global cache module. Custom HTTP modules can be developed and plugged into the ASP.NET HTTP processing pipeline.

HTTP handler

ASP.NET maps HTTP requests to HTTP handlers. ASP.NET maps individual URLs or groups of URL extensions to specific HTTP handlers. HTTP handlers are functionality equivalent to ISAPI extensions but with a much simpler programming model. An HTTP handler is an assembly that implements the **IHttpHandler** and **IHttpAsyncHandler** interfaces.

I

identity

Identity refers to a characteristic of a user or service that can uniquely identify it. For example, this is often a display name, which often takes the form "authority/username".

imperative authorization

Imperative authorization is a form of authorization applied within method code. For example, .NET provides the **PrincipalPermissionAttribute** class which can be used to provide imperative authorization as shown in the code that follows. The code demands that the caller belong to the Teller role. If the caller doesn't belong to this role, a security exception is generated and the privileged code (the code that follows the **Demand** method call) is not executed.

```
public UsePrivilege()
{
   PrincipalPermission permCheck = new PrincipalPermission(null,"Teller");
   permCheck.Demand();
   // privileged code
}
```

impersonation

Impersonation is the technique used by a server application to access resources on behalf of a client by using a copy of the client's access token. To facilitate the generation of a client's access token on a server computer, the client must pass its identity across the network to the server application.

Also see fixed principal impersonation.

impersonation/delegation model

An impersonation/delegation model is a resource access model that flows the security context of the original caller through successive application tiers and onto back-end resource managers. This allows resource managers to implement authorization decisions based on the identity of the original caller.

This is in contrast to the trusted subsystem model that uses fixed "trusted" identities for resource access.

impersonation token

See thread token.

integrity

Secure communication channels must also ensure that data is protected from accidental or deliberate (malicious) modification while in transit. Integrity is usually provided by using message authentication codes (MACs).

IPSec (Internet Protocol Security)

IPSec is a form of transport level security. IPSec is designed to encrypt data as it travels between two computers, protecting the data from modification and interpretation.

K

Kerberos

Kerberos is an authentication protocol supported by Windows 2000 and later operating systems. Kerberos supports the extended form of impersonation called delegation, which allows a caller's security context to access network resources in addition to resources local to the server's operating system.

key

A key is a value supplied to an encryption or decryption algorithm used to encrypt and decrypt data. Symmetric encryption algorithms use the same key to encrypt and decrypt data, while asymmetric algorithms use a public/private key pair.

key pair

A key pair is a public and private pair of keys that belong to an entity and are used to encrypt and decrypt data.

key store

A key store is where the Microsoft Cryptography API (CryptoAPI) stores key pairs (usually in a file or registry key). Key stores are specific to either a user or the computer the keys were generated on.

L

LDAP (Lightweight Directory Access Protocol)

LDAP is a protocol used to access directory services including Active Directory.

local account

A local account is a Windows account maintained and stored within the SAM database local to a specific computer. Local accounts (unlike domain accounts) cannot be used to access network resources, unless a duplicate local account (with the same name and password) is created on the remote computer.

logon session

A logon session defines the security context in which every process runs. When you interactively log on to a computer, an interactive logon session is created to host the Windows shell and any process that you may start interactively. When a process connects on your behalf to a remote computer, your credentials (which are cached in your local logon session) are used to handle authentication requests from the remote computer. Assuming the authentication process is successful, a network logon session is established on the remote computer to represent the work performed on your behalf on the remote computer.

LogonUser

LogonUser is a Win32 API used to create a logon session (and access token) for a specified Windows account. Code that calls **LogonUser** must be part of the computer's TCB, which means that it must be running within a process whose Windows account has been granted the "Act as part of the operating system" privilege.

LSA (Local Security Authority)

The Local Security Authority (LSA) is a local Windows subsystem responsible for providing authentication services.

M

MAC (message authentication code)

Message authentication code is a hash value appended to a message to provide integrity. When using a MAC algorithm to generate a hash, the receiving application must also posses the session key to re-compute the hash value so it can verify that the message data has not changed.

mutual authentication

Mutual authentication is a form of authentication where the client authenticates the server in addition to the server authenticating the client. Mutual authentication is not supported by NTLM but is supported by Kerberos. Mutual authentication is also possible with SSL when the server accepts or requires client certificates.

N

non-repudiation

Non-repudiation is the ability to identify users who performed certain actions, thus irrefutably countering any attempts by a user to deny responsibility. For example, a system may log the ID of a user whenever a file is deleted.

NTLM

NTLM (which stands for Windows NT LAN Manager) is a challenge/response authentication protocol used on networks that include systems running versions of the Microsoft Windows NT operating system earlier than Windows 2000 and on stand-alone systems.

P

PKCS (public-key cryptography standards)

PKCS is a set of syntax standards for public-key cryptography covering security functions, including methods for signing data, exchanging keys, requesting certificates, public-key encryption and decryption, and other security functions.

plain text

See clear text.

principal

A principal is an entity (typically a human, computer, application or service) that attempts to access a secured resource or application. A principal has a unique name and some way of proving its Identity to other principals in a system.

principle of least privilege

Principle of least privilege is the notion of running executable code using the weakest possible process identity. This is to limit the potential damage that can be done should the process be compromised.

If a malicious user manages to inject code into a server process, the privileges granted to that process determine to a large degree the types of operations the user is able to perform.

privacy

Privacy is concerned with ensuring that data remains private and confidential, and cannot be viewed by eavesdroppers who may be armed with network monitoring software. Privacy is usually provided by means of encryption.

private key

A private key is the secret half of a key pair used in a public key algorithm. Private keys are typically used to encrypt a symmetric session key, digitally sign a message, or decrypt a message that has been encrypted with the corresponding public key.

privilege

Privilege is the right of a user to perform various system-related operations, such as shutting down the system, loading device drivers, or changing the system time. A user's access token contains a list of the privileges held by either the user or the user's groups.

process identity

Process identity is determined by the Windows account used to run an executable process. For example, the default process identity of the ASP.NET worker process (aspnet_wp.exe) is ASPNET (a local, least privileged Windows account).

The process identity determines the security context used when code within the process accesses local or remote resources. If the code is impersonating, the thread identity (determined by the thread token) provides the security context for resource access.

proxy account

See service account.

public key

A public key is the public half of a public/private key pair. It is typically used when decrypting a session key or a digital signature. The public key can also be used to encrypt a message, guaranteeing that only the person with the corresponding private key can decrypt the message.

public-private key encryption

Public-private key encryption is an asymmetric form of encryption that relies on a cryptographically generated public/private key pair. Data encrypted with a private key can only be decrypted with the corresponding public key (and vice-versa).

R

RC2

RC2 is the CryptoAPI algorithm name for the RC2 algorithm.

RC4

RC4 is the CryptoAPI algorithm name for the RC4 algorithm.

roles

Roles are logical identifiers (such as "Manager" or "Employee") used by an application to group together users who share the same security privileges within the application. Example role types include .NET roles, Enterprise Services (COM+) roles, and database roles used by SQL Server.

RSA

RSA Data Security, Inc., is a major developer and publisher of public-key cryptography standards. RSA stands for the names of the company's three developers and the owners: Rivest, Shamir, and Adleman.

S

SACL (system access control list)

An SACL is associated with a securable object (using a security descriptor) and specifies the types of operations performed by particular users that should generate audit messages.

salt value

Salt value is random data that can be used in conjunction with encrypted or hashed data in order to increase the work required to mount a brute-force dictionary attack against the protected data. It is usually placed in front of the encrypted or hashed data.

SAM database

The SAM database is the database used by Windows NT and Windows 2000 (without Active Directory) to maintain user and group accounts.

secure communication

Secure communication is concerned with providing message integrity and privacy, while data flows across a network. Technologies that provide secure communication include SSL and IPSec.

security context

Security context is a generic term used to refer to the collection of security settings that affect the security-related behavior of a process or thread. The attributes from a process' logon session and access token combine to form the security context of the process.

security descriptor (SD)

A security descriptor (SD) contains security information that is associated with a securable object such as a file or process. A security descriptor contains attributes that includes an identification of the object's owner, the security groups the owner belongs to, and two access control lists (ACLs); the discretionary access control list (DACL) which defines the access rights for individual users and groups of users, and the system access control list (SACL) which defines the types of operation performed on the object that should result in the generation of audit messages.

service account

A service account is a specifically configured account (also known as a proxy account) used solely for the purposes of accessing a downstream resource (often a database) in a multi-tier distributed application. Middle tier components often use a limited number of service accounts to connect to a database to support connection pooling. Service accounts may be Windows accounts maintained in Active Directory or the SAM database, or SQL accounts maintained within SQL Server.

session key

Session key is a randomly-generated symmetric key used to encrypt data transmitted between two parties. Session keys are used once (for a single session) and then discarded.

SHA (secure hash algorithm)

SHA is an algorithm used to generate a message digest or hash. The original SHA algorithm has been replaced with the improved SHA1 algorithm.

SID (security identifier)

A security identifier (SID) uniquely identifies a user or user group within a domain. A SID is a variable length value and consists of a revision level, an authenticating authority value (the SID issuer, typically Windows), a set of sub-authority values (typically representing the network domain) and a relative ID (RID) which is unique within the authenticating authority / sub-authority combination.

SIDs are never reused even when a user account is deleted and then recreated with the same name and password combination.

SOAP

SOAP is a lightweight, XML-based protocol for the exchange of information in a distributed environment. Used by Web services

SOAP extension

A SOAP extension is an extensibility mechanism supported by ASP.NET that allows you to extend SOAP message processing. With a SOAP extension, you can inspect or modify a message at specific stages during the processing lifecycle on either the client or server.

SSL (secure sockets layer)

SSL is a protocol for secure network communications using a combination of public and secret key technology.

SSPI (security support provider interface)

SSPI is a common interface between transport-level applications, such as Microsoft Remote Procedure Call (RPC), and security providers, such as the Windows Integrated authentication provider. SSPI allows a transport application to call one of several security providers to obtain an authenticated connection in a uniform fashion.

symmetric encryption

Symmetric encryption is a form of encryption that uses the same (single) key to encrypt and decrypt data. Both the sender and the recipient of the encrypted data must have the same key.

T

TCB (trusted computing base)

A TCB is a boundary that defines the portion of a system that is trusted to enforce security policy. Executable code that runs within the TCB is able to perform operations without being subjected to normal security checks. Device drivers run within the TCB. User code runs within the TCB if the associated process account is granted the "Act as part of the operating system" privilege. User code that runs under the local SYSTEM account also runs within the boundaries of the TCB.

temporary token

See thread token.

thread token

A thread token is a temporary access token associated with a specific thread. When a thread is created, it has no access token and any secure operations performed by the thread, use information obtained from the process token. A classic situation in which a thread acquires an access token is when a thread in a server process wants to perform work on behalf of a client. In this situation the thread impersonates the client by acquiring an access token to represent the client.

Thread tokens are also referred to as temporary tokens and impersonation tokens.

token

See access token.

transitive trust

Transitive trust is a bidirectional form of trust relationship between computers or domains. Transitive means that if authority A trusts authority B and authority B trusts authority C then authority A implicitly trusts authority C (without an explicit trust relationship having to exist between A and C). Transitive trust relationships are supported by Active Directory on Windows 2000.

triple DES

This is the triple DES (3DES) encryption cipher. It is a variation of the DES block cipher algorithm that encrypts plain text with one key, encrypts the resulting cipher text with a second key, and finally, encrypts the result of the second encryption with a third key. Triple DES is a symmetric algorithm that uses the same algorithm and keys for encryption and decryption.

trust

Secure systems rely on the notion of trust to one degree or another. For example, users who have administrative privileges (that is, administrators) must be trusted to correctly administer a system and not to deliberately perform malicious acts. Similarly, code that runs with extended privileges, such as device drivers and code that runs as LocalSystem must be trusted. Code that implicitly requires trust such as this, runs within the computer's Trusted Computing Base (TCB). Code that cannot be fully trusted must not be allowed to run within the TCB.

The notion of trust is also important for the trusted subsystem model, which places trust in an application or service.

trusted subsystem model

A trusted subsystem model is a resource access model adopted by Web applications in which the application uses a fixed "trusted" identity to access downstream resource managers such as databases.

A database administrator defines security roles and permissions for the specific "trusted" identity within the database. This model supports database connection pooling which greatly helps an application's ability to scale. This is in contrast to the impersonation/delegation model.

U

user profile

User profiles maintain a user's configuration information. This includes desktop arrangement, personal program groups, program items, screen colors, screen savers, network connections and so on. When a user logs on interactively, the system loads the user's profile and configures the environment according to the information in the profile.

The **LoadUserProfile** API can be used to programmatically load a user profile. Non-interactive accounts such as the local ASPNET account used to run ASP.NET Web applications do not have a user profile.

W

WindowsIdentity

WindowsIdentity is an implementation of the **IIdentity** interface, used by ASP.NET in conjunction with Windows authentication. A **WindowsIdentity** object exposes the Windows access token of the user together with user name information. The **WindowsPrincipal** object contains a **WindowsIdentity** object.

WindowsPrincipal

WindowsPrincipal is an implementation of the **IPrincipal** interface, used by ASP.NET in conjunction with Windows authentication. ASP.NET attaches a **WindowsPrincipal** object to the context of the current Web request to represent the authenticated caller. It is used for authorization.

The **WindowsPrincipal** object contains the set of roles (Windows groups) that the user belongs to. It also contains a **WindowsIdentity** object that provides identity information about the caller.

X

XML digital signature

An XML digital signature is a digital signature applied to an XML document.

Index

Symbols and Numbers

-- (double dash), 320
% (percent sign), 322
; (semicolon), 320
' (single quotation), 320
3 Data Encryption Standard (3DES), 185, 190, 425

A

access checks. *See* authorization
accounts. *See also* identities
  anonymous domain, at Web servers, 125
  anonymous Internet, 178–80, 300–301
  creating custom, for serviced component, 453–54
  creating database for. *See* SQL Server 2000, Forms
    authentication with
  default ASPNET. *See* ASPNET default account
  duplicate, 64, 101, 118
  IUSR_MACHINENAME, 14, 24, 330, 332
  Kerberos delegation and, 382
  least privileged, 4–5, 168. *See also* least privileged
    accounts
  mirrored, 176–77, 296–98, 347–48
  SQL Server, 302–3, 324
  Web services client certificates and, 255
  Windows, 416–17, 441, 473. *See also* Windows ACLs
  Windows group, 16, 204–5, 357–58
ACLs. *See* Windows ACLs
Active Directory
  delegation and, 381
  extranet settings, 106, 112
  Forms authentication with. *See* Active Directory,
    Forms authentication with
  reference information, 514–15
  SPNs, 331
Active Directory, Forms Authentication with, 124, 133,
    146, 353–62
  authenticating users and creating authentication
    ticket, 358–60
  configuring Web application for, 355–56
  creating Web application with logon page, 354
  developing LDAP authentication code, 356–57
  developing LDAP group retrieval code, 357–58
  implementing authentication request handler to
    construct GenericPrincipal object, 360–61
  requirements, 353

testing, 362
administration effort, 37
administrators, rogue, 182
ADO.NET
  gates, 19
  as implementation technology, 10
  reference information, 515
  user account database and, 368–70
algorithms, 425, 540–42. *See also* cryptography;
    encryption
Anonymous authentication
  configuring IIS, 162
  configuring impersonation, 149
  data access security and, 300–301
  disabling, 19
  network resources and, 178–80
  troubleshooting, 330
  Web.config settings, 534
  Windows authentication and, 14
anonymous domain accounts at Web servers, 125
apartment model objects, 174–75
application isolation, 524
application level identity flow, 31, 38
application level security
  IPSec, 56, 306
  Web services, 227
application roles, 304
application servers
  configuring, for .NET remoting, 275–76, 279–80, 283
  configuring, for Web services, 244–45, 247–48, 250
  Internet settings, 130
  intranet settings, 80–81, 87–88, 96–97
  secure communication, 59–60
  Web servers as, 9
application tiers, remote, 9
applications, Web. *See* Web applications
articles. *See* reference hub
AspCompat directive, 174, 251
ASP.NET
  applications, 7–9. *See also* Web applications
  as implementation technology, 10, 11
  reference information, 515–17
  security. *See* ASP.NET security

ASPNET default account
  duplicated, 64, 101, 118
  as interactive user account, 255
  as least privileged account, 5, 450
  mirrored, 297–98
  process identity and, 169–72, 332, 347. *See also*
    process identity
  troubleshooting, 332
ASP.NET security, 135–91. *See also* ASP.NET; Web
    applications security
  accessing COM objects, 174–75
  accessing network resources, 176–82
  accessing system resources, 173–74
  architecture, 135–39
  ASP.NET settings, 149–52
  authentication and authorization strategies, 139–47
  authentication modes, 13–15
  authorization options, 16–17. *See also* explicit role
    checks; File authorization; .NET roles; principal
    permission demands; URL authorization
  base configuration, 505
  configuration stores and tools, 508
  configuring, 147–55
  configuring for custom accounts, 352
  configuring for Forms authentication, 162
  configuring for .NET remoting, 275, 276, 278, 280,
    282, 283
  configuring for Passport authentication, 167
  configuring for Web services, 237, 244–45, 247,
    248, 249, 250
  creating custom accounts, 347–52
  custom authentication, 168. *See also* custom
    authentication
  default account, 5, 169–72. *See also* ASPNET default
    account
  extranet settings, 106, 112
  Forms authentication, 160–66. *See also* Forms
    authentication
  gatekeepers and gates, 18, 137–39, 230, 264–65
  HTTP channel and, 263–64
  identity matrix, 24, 533–35
  IIS settings, 149
  impersonation, 172
  Internet settings, 121, 129–30. *See also* Internet
    security
  intranet settings, 66–67, 74, 80–81, 87–88, 95–96.
    See also Intranet security
  ISAPI extension, 150, 154–55, 170, 262, 523–24
  least privileged accounts, 5. *See also* least
    privileged accounts
  .NET remoting requests and, 262–63
  options, 4, 12, 545

Passport authentication, 167. *See also* Passport
    authentication
  pipeline processing, 525–31
  process identity, 168–72. *See also* process identity
  processing and IIS, 523–25
  programming, 155–59
  remote object hosting, 262–63, 265–66, 276, 280,
    283, 285–86
  resetting default configuration, 298
  secure communication, 155, 182
  securing resources, 152–55
  securing session and view state, 185–87
  storing secrets, 182–84
  troubleshooting, 333
  using DPAPI directly, 313–14
  Web farm considerations, 188–90
  Windows authentication, 159–60, 187. *See also*
    Windows authentication
aspnet_regiis.exe tool, 298
aspnet_setreg.exe tool, 64, 101, 171, 186, 298, 352
Aspnet_wp.exe worker process, 168, 170. *See also*
    process identity
assemblies
  building and adding, to global assembly cache, 445
  strong names for, 402–3, 444
  versioning, 214–15
asymmetric encryption, 55, 537, 540, 541–42
auditing
  authentication and, 30
  Enterprise Services, 212
  extranet scenario, 108
  IIS authentication and, 330
  impersonation/delegation model and, 35–36
  intranet scenarios, 69, 84
  logon, 323–24, 339–40
  troubleshooting with logging and, 339–41
  trusted subsystem model and, 37
  Windows authentication and, 142
authenticated clients. *See* principals
authentication
  ASP.NET modes, 13–15. *See also* custom
    authentication; Forms authentication; Passport
    authentication; Windows authentication
  ASP.NET processing, 135–37
  authorization pattern and, 156
  choosing mechanisms for, 30–31, 47–51
  client application, 206
  comparison of mechanisms, 51
  configuration stores and tools, 507–12
  configuring, 149, 199, 206
  credentials. *See* credentials
  cryptography and, 539

data access security and, 294, 295–303
database stores and, 317–18
delegation and, 39–40, 180–81. *See also* delegation; Kerberos delegation
Enterprise Services, 193–95, 199, 206, 219, 221–22
extranet. *See* extranet security
Internet. *See* Internet security
intranet. *See* Intranet security
IPSec and, 56, 61
level negotiation, 221–22
level promotion, 221
library application, 197
Machine.config and, 216
.NET remoting, 263, 265–66, 270–73, 276–80, 286
non-SQL Server databases and, 303
passing credentials for, to Web services, 238–42
proxy server, 242
server application, 199
SQL. *See* SQL authentication
strategies, 2. *See also* authentication and authorization strategies
technologies and principles, 3–6, 12
troubleshooting, 329–31
URL authorization and, 151–52
Web services, 226, 229–30, 237, 245–48
Web.config settings, 533–35
Windows service features, 286
authentication and authorization strategies, 2–3, 27–52, 139–47. *See also* authentication; authorization
authentication mechanisms, 47–51
authorization approaches, 31–38
authorization options, 140
designing, 27–31
flowing identity, 38–40. *See also* identity flow
Forms authentication, 145–47
implementing Kerberos delegation, 381–83
.NET remoting, 268–69
Passport authentication, 147
role-based authorization, 40–47
User Services layer and, 8
Web services, 231–35
Windows authentication, 141–45
authorization
approaches, 31–38
configuration stores and tools, 507–12
configuring, 150, 199–200
data access security and, 304–5
Enterprise Services, 193–95, 199–200, 219. *See also* role-based authorization, Enterprise Services
extranet. *See* extranet security
Internet. *See* Internet security
intranet. *See* Intranet security
.NET remoting, 264, 267–68, 286–87

.NET roles for Internet, 124–25
options, 16–17, 140
pattern, 156–58
programming, 155–59
resource access models and, 33–38
resource-based, 32–33
role-based, 31–32. *See also* role-based authorization
strategies, 2–3, 28–29. *See also* authentication and authorization strategies
technologies and principles, 3–6, 12
troubleshooting, 331–32
Windows service features, 286–87
<authorization> element, 150, 332

B

base configuration, 505
Base64 encoding, 58
Basic authentication
delegation and, 180–81
identity flow and, 31
intranet original caller identity flow and, 92
.NET remoting and, 276–77, 286
SSL and, 58
Web services and, 241, 245
Web.config settings, 534
Windows authentication and, 13
BinaryFormatter class, 261–62
browsers
authentication and, 30, 48
Basic authentication and, 13
certificate authentication and, 252
exporting client certificate to file, 455–56
Internet Explorer, 13, 48, 455–56, 465
intranet scenarios and, 70
non-Internet Explorer, 13, 70
proxy server authentication, 242
secure communication from, to Web servers, 58
testing client certificates, 455, 484
testing Web services using SSL, 465
troubleshooting authentication, 329–30
buffer overflow attacks, 5
business applications, 1
Business Services layer, 8

C

C#
class libraries, 396–402, 426–32, 442
objects in COM+, 175
callers. *See* identities; identity flow
CAPICOM objects, 184
CAS. *See* Code Access Security
case sensitivity, 303

Certificate authentication
  browsers and, 252
  certificate stores, 538–39
  cryptography and, 539. *See also* cryptography
  IIS settings, 149
  issuing certificates, 478
  keys and certificates, 537–39
  setting up client certificates, 481–84. *See also* client
    certificates
  SSL and, 475–79, 495–503. *See also* server certificates;
    SSL
  troubleshooting, 338
  trusted subsystem model and, 252–55
  Windows authentication and, 14
  X.509 digital certificates, 538
Certificate Authority certificates, 60, 466–67, 475–84,
    496–98, 537–39. *See also* client certificates; server
    certificates
channel security. *See* secure communication
channels, .NET remoting and, 259–61, 263–64, 285
check points. *See* gatekeepers and gates
classes. *See also* .NET Framework security
  adding roles to, 201
  assigning roles to, 197
  creating dummy, to launch serviced component, 416
  creating remote object, 470
  cryptography, 540–42
  interfaces. *See* interfaces
  IPrincipal interface. *See* IPrincipal interface
    implementations
  methods. *See* methods
  principal and identity, 23
client applications
  allowing, to choose whether to use SSL, 499–500
  calling Web services from, 238–42
  configuring, 205–6
  forcing, to use SSL, 498–99
  specifying credentials to remote objects, 270–73
  test, for Web services, 237
client certificates, 251–55, 481–84. *See also* Certificate
    authentication; server certificates
  configuring Web application to require, 482–83
  creating simple Web application, 482
  IIS settings, 149
  installing, 466–67
  requesting and installing, 483–84
  requirements, 481
  SSL and, 60, 338, 449. *See also* SSL
  verifying operation of, 484
  Web services and. *See* client certificates, Web services
    security using
  Web services proxies and, 239

client certificates, Web services security using, 251–55,
    449–62
  authenticating browser clients, 252
  configuring and installing serviced component,
    459–60
  configuring Web services virtual directory to require
    client certificates, 452
  creating custom account for serviced component, 453
  creating simple Web services, 451–52
  creating Web application to call serviced component,
    460–62
  developing serviced component to call Web services,
    456–59
  exporting client certificate to file, 455–56
  requesting client certificate for custom account,
    453–54
  requirements, 451
  testing client certificate using browser, 455
  user profiles and, 450
  using serviced component, 449–50
  using trusted subsystem model, 252–55
clients. *See* principals; users
client-side proxies, .NET remoting, 275, 279, 283
cloaking, 223
CoCopyProxy, 217–18
Code Access Security (CAS), 20–21
  Enterprise Services and, 197
  evidence and security policies, 20–21
  Web applications and, 21
CoImpersonateClient, 210, 211, 212, 222–23
COM, distributed. *See* DCOM
COM objects
  accessing, 174–75, 251
  cryptography and, 184
  determining identity in Visual Basic 6, 336–37
COM+
  C# and VB .NET objects in, 175
  catalog. *See* COM+ catalog
  constructor strings for storing secrets, 184, 316–17
  roles. *See* role-based authorization, Enterprise
    Services
  services, 193. *See also* Enterprise Services
COM+ catalog
  configuration settings, 199, 219
  Enterprise Services authorization and, 17
  storing connection strings in, 316–17
communication, secure. *See* secure communication
Component Services tool
  assigning Windows accounts to roles, 205
  configuring security, 199, 219
  examining configured applications, 445
  preventing COM+ catalog access, 316

role membership, 17, 42
server settings, 57, 196
components
    adding roles to, 201
    authorization, 199–200
    disabling, 6
    serviced. *See* serviced components
confidentiality, 3, 53, 305, 463, 485, 539
configurable security. *See also* configuration;
        programmatic security
    ASP.NET, 149–52
    Forms authentication, 146
    .NET remoting, 264, 271
    Web services, 231–32, 233–34
    Windows authentication with impersonation, 141,
        231–33
    Windows authentication without impersonation,
        143–44, 233–35
configuration. *See also* configurable security;
        programmatic security
    ASP.NET account, 64. *See also* ASP.NET default
        account
    authentication level, 58
    data, 2
    default settings, 5, 298
    deployment time vs. development time, 199
    Enterprise Services security. *See* configuration,
        Enterprise Services security
    extranet scenarios, 104–7, 111–13
    files. *See* Global.asax files; Machine.config files;
        Web.config files
    Forms authentication, 146, 162, 355–56, 365–66,
        375, 387
    IIS security, 149
    Internet scenarios, 120–22, 128–31
    intranet scenarios, 66–67, 74–76, 79–82, 87–89, 95–98
    IPSec, 485–86
    locking, 153–54
    .NET remoting security, 274–80, 282–84
    Passport authentication, 167
    requiring client certificates, 482–83
    resetting ASP.NET default, 298
    resources to require SSL access, 479
    scenarios. *See* configuration scenarios
    secure communication, 155
    secure resource, 152–55
    SSL, 498–500
    stores and tools. *See* configuration stores and tools
    troubleshooting ASP.NET, 333
    troubleshooting authorization, 332
    Web application security, 147–55
    Web services security, 236–38, 242–50, 452, 464–65

configuration, Enterprise Services security, 198–207
    client applications, 205–6
    Enterprise Services (COM+) roles, 42
    impersonation levels, 206–7
    interface proxies, 216–18
    security blanket settings, 217–18
    server applications, 198–205
    serviced components, 417–18, 459–60
    Windows authentication and impersonation, 216–18
configuration scenarios
    base software, 505
    Enterprise Services and DPAPI, 411–13
    extranet, 104–5, 111. *See also* extranet security
    Internet, 120, 128. *See also* Internet security
    intranet, 65, 73, 79, 86, 92, 93–94. *See also* Intranet
        security
    IPSec, 487–86
configuration stores and tools, 507–12
    ASP.NET, 508
    Enterprise Services, 508–9
    IIS, 507–8
    .NET remoting, 510–11
    SQL Server, 512
    Web services, 509–10
connected landscape, 1
connection pooling, 37
connection strings
    reading encrypted, from Web.config file, 409–10,
        423–24
    secure storage of, 292, 310–17
    securing, 186–87, 303
    SQL authentication and, 183, 302
    storing, in COM+ catalog, 316–17
    storing, in configuration files, 314
    storing, in custom text files, 316
    storing, in UDL files, 314–15
    storing encrypted, in registry, 316, 435–40
    storing encrypted, with DPAPI, 310–14
connectiongroupname property, 241, 272–73
console applications
    creating, to test encryption library, 433–34
    creating, to test remote object hosting, 474
    remote object hosting in, 287–88
contexts, security
    ASP.NET. *See* HttpContext.User property
    delegating, 5. *See also* delegation
    flowing. *See* identity flow
    WindowsThread.CurrentPrincipal property, 21, 24,
        45, 266, 533
ContextUtil class, 142
cookie replay attacks, 165

cookies
  cookieless Forms authentication, 166
  Forms authentication tickets, 14, 161, 163, 358–60, 375–77, 388–90
  securing, 185
  troubleshooting, 331
CoQueryProxyBlanket, 217–18
CoRevertToSelf, 212, 223
corporate network extranet connectivity, 115
CoSetProxyBlanket, 217–18
credentials. *See also* authentication; identity flow
  data access, 292. *See also* connection strings
  default, with Kerberos delegation, 243–45, 274–76
  encrypting, 64
  explicit, with Basic or Forms authentication, 246–48, 276–80
  logon, 3
  in Machine.config file, 170–72
  passing, over networks, 303
  passing, to remote objects, 270–73
  passing, to Web services, 238–42
  retrieving and validating, 156, 162
  secret, 183
  specific, 171, 240, 271–72
  storing, 47–48
  troubleshooting .NET remoting, 337
  validating, against database stores, 317–18
Crypto API, 184, 395
cryptography, 537–43. *See also* DPAPI; encryption
  asymmetric algorithm support, 541–42
  certificate stores, 538–39
  certificates and keys, 537–39. *See also* Certificate authentication
  hashing alogorithm support, 542
  Integrated Windows authentication and, 13
  .NET Framework support, 184, 540–42
  password hashes with salt values, 317–18
  symmetric algorithm support, 541
  technical choices, 539–40
  X.509 digital certificates, 538
CryptProtectData and CryptUnprotectData, 310, 395
custom accounts. *See* least privileged accounts
custom authentication, 14, 158–59, 168, 266, 286
custom channels, 261
custom HTTP modules and HTTP handlers, 531
custom identities, 30
custom sinks, 261
custom text files, storing connection strings in, 316

D

data, sensitive. *See* secure communication
data access security, 291–325
  auditing, 323–24
  authentication, 15–16, 295–303
  authorization, 304–5
  creating least privileged accounts, 308–9
  Data Services layer, 8
  gates, 18–19
  intranet. *See* Intranet security
  key issues, 291–92
  least privileged connections, 307–8
  process identity for SQL Server, 324
  secure communication, 59–60, 305–6
  SQL injection attacks, 319–22
  SQL Server gatekeepers, 293
  SQL Server roles, 42
  storing connection strings, 310–17
  technologies, 10
  trusted subsystem vs. impersonation/delegation, 293–95
  validating user credentials against database stores, 317–18
  Web servers and, 9
Data Encryption Standard (DES), 189, 425
data integrity, 3, 53, 305, 463, 485, 539. *See also* secure communication
Data Services layer, 8
data stores. *See* stores
database, user account. *See* SQL Server 2000, Forms authentication with
database connection strings. *See* connection strings
database resources, 28
database servers. *See also* SQL Server 2000
  authentication, 2
  intranet configuration, 98
  secure communication from application servers to, 59–60
database trust, 307–8
db_owner role, 302, 307, 322
DCOM (Distributed COM)
  authentication levels, 199, 205, 221–22
  Enterprise Services and, 194
  firewalls and, 215
  Internet scenario and, 133
  RPC encryption and, 53, 57
declarative principal permission demands, 142, 144, 147, 232, 234
declarative role checks, 45
decryption. *See* cryptography; DPAPI; encryption
decryptionKey attribute, 189–90
default configuration, ASP.NET, 298
default credentials, 239, 243–44, 270–73, 274–76
default domain, 277
default security settings, 5
delegation. *See also* identity flow
  authentication and, 30

impersonation and, 38–40. *See also* impersonation/ delegation model
Kerberos. *See* Kerberos delegation
demilitarized zone (DMZ), 9, 515
deployment
configuration upon, 199
serviced component, 214–15
Web application, 9, 54
DES (Data Encryption Standard), 189, 425
design principles, 4–6
development time configuration, 199
Digest authentication, 13, 535
digests, password, 363
directory, active. *See* Active Directory
directory, virtual. *See* virtual directory
directory traversal bugs, 184
distributed Web applications. *See* Web applications
DLL locking problems, 213
Dllhost.exe, 195, 208
DllImport attribute, 212
DMZ (demilitarized zone), 9, 515
domain, default, 277
domain accounts
anonymous, 125
custom, 297
domain controllers, ASP.NET process account and, 169
double dash (--), 320
downloading of files, preventing, 154–55
DPAPI (Data Protection API)
libraries. *See* DPAPI libraries
LSA vs., 310
with machine store, 313–14, 405–10
machine store vs. user store, 310–11, 395–96
storing database connection strings using, 310–14
storing secrets, 184
with user store, 311–13, 411–24
Web farms and, 188
DPAPI libraries, 395–403
calling managed, 415–16
creating C# class library, 396–402
issues, 395–96
requirements, 396
strong naming assemblies, 402–3
duplicated accounts, 64, 101, 118
dynamic cloaking, 223

E

encryption. *See also* DPAPI
allowing applications to choose whether to use, 500
cookies, 185
credentials, 64, 145, 171–72
cryptography and, 539. *See also* cryptography libraries. *See* encryption libraries

privacy and, 3, 53
secure communication. *See* secure communication
session and view state, 185–87
storing encrypted connection strings in registry, 435–40
storing secrets, 184
verifying, 500–503
Web farms and, 188–90
encryption libraries, 425–34
algorithms, 425
creating C# class library, 426–32
creating console test application, 433–34
requirements, 425
end users. *See* users
end-to-end security, 59, 227–28, 256, 284, 305–6
Enterprise Manager, 309, 323, 339
Enterprise Services
as implementation technology, 10, 11
reference information, 517–18
security. *See* Enterprise Services security
serviced components. *See* serviced components
Enterprise Services security, 193–224. *See also* Enterprise Services
accessing network resources, 209–11
architecture, 193–97
authentication, 15, 221–22
authorization, 17
building serviced components, 213–15
calling serviced components from ASP.NET, 216–18
choosing process identities, 208–9
Code Access Security requirements, 197
concepts, 219–23
configuration stores and tools, 508–9
configuring, 42, 198–207
configuring ASP.NET client applications, 205–6
configuring impersonation levels for Enterprise Services applications, 206–7
configuring server applications, 198–205
creating Windows account, 416–17
DCOM and firewalls, 215
Enterprise Services (COM+) roles vs. .NET roles, 16, 43, 220
flowing original callers, 211–12
gatekeepers and gates, 18, 195–96
impersonation, 222–23
impersonation/delegation and, 36
Internet scenario, 125–34
intranet scenario, 71–77, 93–99
logon auditing, 339
options, 4, 12, 545
passing Web services client certificates, 254–55
programming, 207–8
role-based authorization, 441–47. *See also* role-based authorization, Enterprise Services

Enterprise Services security, *continued*
  RPC encryption, 213
  secure communication, 59
  for server and library applications, 197
  server applications and, 196
  using DPAPI, 311–13, 411–24
entropy parameter, 311, 313–14, 396
errors
  minimizing exposure, 5–6
  Query Interface, 215
  SQL, 322
event handling, ASP.NET, 530
event logs
  accessing, 173
  troubleshooting and, 339
evidence, 20–21
exceptions. *See* errors
explicit credentials
  .NET remoting, 276–80
  Web services, 246–48
explicit role checks. *See also* role-based authorization
  ASP.NET gatekeeper, 139, 230
  Forms authentication, 147
  .NET Remoting, 264, 265
  Windows authentication with impersonation, 142, 232
  Windows authentication without impersonation, 144, 234
exporting IPSec policies, 491
exposure, reducing, 5
Extensible Markup Language (XML), 1
external systems, 5
extranet security, 101–15
  authentication scenarios, 50
  connected landscape and, 1
  exposing Web applications, 109–15
  exposing Web services, 102–9
  scenarios, 101

F

failures. *See* errors
FAQs. *See* reference hub
farms. *See* Web farms
File authorization
  ASP.NET security, 16, 20, 137–38, 141, 143, 160
  gatekeeper, 137–38
  .NET remoting, 264–65, 267–68
  Web services, 230, 231
file canonicalization bugs, 184
File Monitor (FileMon.exe), 341
files, 2. *See also* stores
  accessing, on UNC shares, 181
  configuration. *See* Global.asax files; Machine.config files; Web.config files

database. *See* SQL Server 2000
exporting client certificates to, 455–56
preventing access to, 182
preventing downloading of, 154–55
resource-based authorization and, 33
storing connection strings in custom text, 316
storing connection strings in UDL, 314–15
storing secrets in, on separate logical volumes, 184
troubleshooting access, 331, 341
UNC, 153, 181
Web services, 231, 233
filtering user input, 5, 319–22
filters, IP, 487, 488–89
firewalls
  data access security and, 297, 301, 306
  DCOM and, 215
  Internet scenario and, 125–26
  secure communication and, 3, 57, 61, 306
  Web services and, 10
fixed database roles, 304
fixed identities
  ASP.NET and, 299–30
  impersonating, 348
  multiple, 34–35
  .NET remoting and, 270
  resources and, 29, 32
  as secrets, 183
  trusted subsystem model and, 34
  Web services and, 241
  Windows authentication using, 144, 145, 235
flow, identity. *See* identity flow
forests, 515
formatter sinks, 261–62
forms. *See* logon Web forms; Web pages
Forms authentication
  Active Directory and, 124, 133, 146, 353–62
  advantages and disadvantages, 47–48, 49
  ASP.NET security and, 14
  cookieless, 166
  development steps for, 162–65
  enabling, 145–47
  forms implementation guidelines, 165–66
  GenericPrincipal objects and, 373–80
  hosting multiple applications using, 166
  with IPrincipal implementations, 385–94
  .NET remoting and, 266, 277–80
  .NET roles and, 16
  processing, 529
  protecting passwords, 183
  sequence of events, 160–61
  SQL Server and, 363–72
  SSL and, 58
  tickets, 14, 161, 163, 358–60, 375–77, 388–90. *See also* cookies

FormsIdentity objects, 23, 373, 378–79 , 533
Fusion Log Viewer (Fuslogvw.exe), 341–42

G

Gacutil.exe tool, 204, 445, 460
gatekeepers and gates, 17–20
    ASP.NET Web application, 137–39
    check points and, 5
    Enterprise Services, 195–96
    IIS, 17–19, 137, 230, 264
    .NET remoting, 264–65
    SQL Server, 293
    technologies and, 17–20
    Web services, 230–31
GenericIdentity objects, 23, 533
GenericPrincipal objects, 385
    creating, 378–79
    creating, with authentication request handler, 360–61
    Forms authentication with. *See* GenericPrincipal
        objects, Forms authentication with
    identity flow and, 38
    identity objects and, 23, 533
    non-Windows authentication and, 41, 44, 139, 157–58
GenericPrincipal objects, Forms authentication with,
        369, 373–80
    configuring Web application for, 375
    constructing GenericPrincipal and FormsIdentity
        objects, 378–79
    creating Web application with logon page, 374–75
    generating an authentication ticket for
        authenticated users, 375–77
    requirements, 374
    testing, 379–80
global assembly cache, 204, 445, 460
Global XML Web Services Architecture (GXA) initiative,
        59, 225, 227–28, 241
Global.asax files, 167, 263, 360–61
granularity, 307, 315
group accounts
    assigning, to Enterprise Services roles, 204–5, 441
    .NET roles vs., 16
    retrieving, 357–58
GUIDs, generating, 214–15

H

handlers, custom HTTP, 168, 531
hash values
    cryptography and, 539
    generating, 366
    .NET Framework support, 542
    one-way password, 183, 317–18
help. *See* reference hub

homogenous intranets, 63
hosting remote objects. *See* remote object hosting
Hotfix Rollup, 381, 383
How To articles. *See* reference hub
HTML forms. *See* logon Web forms; Web pages
HTTP (Hypertext Transport Protocol), 1
    channel and .NET remoting, 259–61, 263–64, 265,
        281–82, 510–11
    disabling HTTP-GET and HTTP-POST, 237–38
    implementing custom HTTP modules and HTTP
        handlers, 168, 531
    modules, 153
    pipeline processing, 525–31
HttpContext.User property
    ASP.NET and, 24, 533
    .NET roles and, 41, 45
    putting IPrincipal objects into, 139, 157, 164, 332.
        See also IPrincipal interface implementations
HttpForbiddenHandler class, 154–55
hubs. *See* reference hub
Hypertext Transport Protocol. *See* HTTP

I

identities
    ASP.NET, 24, 533–35
    authentication and, 47
    authorization and, 157–58
    choosing, for resource access, 29–30
    data access, 292, 295
    determining, in Visual Basic 6 COM objects, 336–37
    determining, in Web pages, 334–36
    determining, in Web services, 336
    Enterprise Services, 208–9, 216, 219
    fixed. *See* fixed identities
    flowing. *See* identity flow
    GenericPrincipal objects, 23. *See also* GenericPrincipal
        objects
    multiple trusted, 34–35
    .NET Framework security and, 20
    Passport authentication, 167
    principals and, 21–22. *See also* principals
    process. *See* process identity
    SQL Server process, 324
    troubleshooting, 327–28, 331–32, 342–43
    WindowsIdentity, 23
<identity> element, 145, 150
identity flow
    application vs. operating system, 38
    authentication and, 48
    gatekeepers and, 5
    impersonation and delegation for, 38–40. *See also*
        impersonation/delegation   model

identity flow, *continued*
.NET remoting and, 281
original caller. *See* original caller identity flow
strategies for, 30, 31
identity matrix, ASP.NET, 533–35
IIdentity interface, 22, 30, 41
IIS (Internet Information Services)
ASP.NET processing and, 135–37, 523–25
authentication settings, 533–35
configuration stores and tools, 507–8
configuring, for anonymous access, 162
configuring, for .NET remoting, 274, 275, 278, 279,
282, 283
configuring, for Web services, 236, 243–44, 246,
247, 249, 250
configuring security, 148, 149
delegation, 39–40
extranet settings, 105, 111
gatekeepers and gates, 17–19, 137, 230, 264
Internet settings, 120, 129, 130
intranet settings, 66, 74, 80, 87, 95
logging, 340–41
reference information, 518
security options, 4, 12, 545
troubleshooting, 329–30, 343
Windows authentication and, 13, 39–40, 159–60
imperative principal permission demands, 142, 144,
146, 232, 234
imperative role checks, 45
impersonation. *See also* identity flow
of anonymous accounts, 179
ASP.NET security and, 172
authorization options and, 140
configuring, 149–50, 206
delegation and, 38–40. *See also* impersonation/
delegation model
Enterprise Services, 194, 197, 206–7, 219, 222–23
of fixed identities, 145, 299–300, 348
intranet security and, 69
library applications and, 197
serviced components and, 216
of specific Windows identity using LogonUser API,
180, 301
Web services, 237
Windows authentication with, 141–43, 216, 231–33
Windows authentication without, 143–45, 233–35
impersonation/delegation model, 35–37. *See also*
delegation; impersonation
advantages and disadvantages, 36–37
authentication and, 30
identity flow and, 31
.NET remoting and, 269
trusted subsystem model vs., 293–95

implementation solutions, 328–29. *See also* reference
hub; troubleshooting security issues
implementation technologies, 10. *See also* technologies
input, user
filtering, 5, 319–22
validating, 363
installing
applications, 173
client certificates, 466–67, 483–84, 498
server certificates, 478–79, 496–97, 498
Windows services, 471, 473
InstallUtil.exe tool, 173, 420, 471, 473
Integrated Windows authentication
intranet original caller identity flow and, 92–93
troubleshooting, 329–30
Web.config settings, 535
Windows authentication and, 13
integrity, 3, 53, 305, 463, 485, 539. *See also* secure
communication
interactive user, Enterprise Services and, 208–9
interfaces
adding roles to, 201–2
assigning roles to, 197
configuring proxies for, 216–18
IPrincipal and IIdentity, 22, 30, 41. *See also* IPrincipal
interface implementations
Internet Explorer, 13, 48, 455–56, 465. *See also* browsers
Internet Information Services. *See* IIS
Internet Protocol Security. *See* IPSec
Internet security, 117–34
anonymous user account, 178–80, 300–301
ASP.NET to Remote Enterprise Services to SQL Server,
125–34
ASP.NET to SQL Server, 118–25
authentication, 49–50
connected landscape and, 1
Forms authentication, 147
scenarios, 117–18
Intranet security, 63–99
ASP.NET to Enterprise Services to SQL Server, 71–77
ASP.NET to Remoting to SQL Server, 85–91
ASP.NET to SQL Server, 64–71
ASP.NET to Web Services to SQL Server, 77–85
authentication, 50
connected landscape and, 1
flowing original callers to database, 91–99
.NET remoting vs. Web services, 288–89
scenarios, 63–64
IPrincipal interface implementations, 385–94
configuring Forms authentication, 387
creating, 156–57, 164, 390–91
creating custom, 41, 158–59, 391–93
creating simple Web application, 386–87

custom identities and, 30
generating authentication ticket, 388–90
identity and, 533
IIdentity interface and, 22
.NET remoting and, 273, 287
.NET roles and, 40, 45
principal permission demands and, 139. *See also*
    principal permission demands
putting, into current HTTP context, 139, 157, 164, 332
reasons for, 385–86
requirements, 386
testing, 393–94
IPSec (Internet Protocol Security), 485–94. *See also*
    secure communication
ASP.NET security and, 182
assigning policies, 491
configuration for, 485–86
configuring, 155
creating filter actions, 489
creating IP filter, 488
creating rules, 490–91
exporting policy to remote computer, 491
as implementation technology, 10, 11
issues, 56–57, 306, 487
requirements, 487
SSL vs., 53, 61, 495
troubleshooting, 338
verifying, 492–94
IPSec Monitor (Ipsecmon.exe), 56
ISAPI extension, 150, 154–55, 170, 262, 523–24
isolation, application, 524
ISQL.exe, 342
IUSR_MACHINENAME account, 14, 24, 330, 332, 348

K

Kerberos delegation
    authentication and, 13, 15
    confirming client account configuration for, 382
    confirming server process account as trusted for,
        382–83
    default credentials with, 243–45, 274–76
    identity flow and, 31
    impersonation, remote resources, and, 172
    impersonation/delegation model and, 37
    implementing, 381–83
    intranet security, 91
    IPSec and, 56
    issues, 381
    original caller and, 180
    requirements, 382
    troubleshooting, 331
    as unconstrained, 40

Kerbtray.exe, 331
keys
    certificates and, 537–39
    DPAPI and, 395
    machine, 188–90
    as secrets, 183, 450
    user profiles and, 450
Klist.exe, 331
Knowledge Base. *See also* reference hub
    ASP.NET, 516
    Enterprise Services and, 517
    searching, 513–14
    troubleshooting and, 327, 329

L

LDAP (Lightweight Directory Access Protocol), 353.
    See also Active Directory
    authentication code, 356–57
    group retrieval code, 357–58
least privileged accounts
    ASP.NET worker process identity and, 168–72, 347
    assigning minimum privileges, 349
    assigning NTFS permissions, 350–51
    configuring ASP.NET for, 352
    creating custom, 177, 297, 347–52
    creating custom database, 308–9
    Enterprise Services and custom, 209
    impersonating fixed identities, 348
    issues, 348
    principle of, 4–5
    SQL code and, 322
library applications, Enterprise Services
    authentication and, 15, 196, 219
    authorization and, 200
    security for, 197
    server applications vs., 15, 196–97, 219
libraries. *See* DPAPI libraries; encryption libraries
Lightweight Directory Access Protocol. *See* LDAP
load balancing, 61, 288
local accounts
    ASPNET as, 169–72. *See also* ASPNET default account
    creating, 349
    mirrored, 297
local resources, impersonation and, 172
Local Security Authority (LSA), 169, 298, 310
Local Security Policy tool, 56, 349, 488
locking configuration settings, 153–54
logging. *See also* auditing
    event logs, 6, 173
    IIS, 340–41
    troubleshooting with, 339–41
logical tiers, 8

logical volumes, storing files on, 184
Login method, 266
logon auditing, 323–24, 339–40
logon credentials. *See* credentials
logon Web forms
  creating, 162, 354, 364–65, 374–75
  Forms authentication and, 14
  implementation guidelines, 165–66
  troubleshooting, 331
LogonUser API, 169, 178–80, 211, 235, 270, 299
LSA (Local Security Authority), 169, 298, 310

M

machine store, DPAPI with, 313–14, 405–10. *See also*
  DPAPI
  ASP.NET and, 313–14
  creating Web application, 406–8
  issues, 405–6
  modifying Web application to read encrypted
    connection string from Web.config file, 409–10
  requirements, 406
  testing, 408
  user store vs., 310–11, 395–96
Machine.config files, 149–52
  authentication level setting, 58
  default ASPNET account and, 64, 101, 118, 169–72,
    176, 298
  disabling HTTP-GET and HTTP-POST, 238
  encrypted connection strings, 313
  least privileged accounts, 352
  locking settings, 153–54
  machine key, 188–90
  process identity in, 183
  securing, 153
  serviced component authentication, 216
  SQL session state, 186
  storing, 184
  storing database connection strings in, 314
  troubleshooting and, 333
  view state, 185
<machineKey> element, 188–90
MACs (Message Authentication Codes), 3, 53, 185, 189
malicious Web users, 182, 237–38
manual role checks, 45
mapping, role, 32
Marshaler role, 201, 203, 447
master secrets, 450
MDAC, 498, 505
Message Authentication Codes (MACs), 3, 53, 185, 189
Message Digest 5 (MD5), 185, 190
message encryption, IPSec, 56
message integrity and confidentiality, 305, 463, 485
message level security, 59, 227–28, 256, 284, 305–6

methods
  adding roles to, 202–3
  assigning roles to, 197
  authorization and, 2
  creating encryption and decryption, 414–15
  identity flow and, 31, 281
  testing encryption and decryption, 420–23
Microsoft C#. *See* C#
Microsoft Certificate Services, 457, 466, 477–78, 483–84,
  496–98
Microsoft Internet Explorer, 13, 48, 455–56, 465. *See*
  also browsers
Microsoft Knowledge Base. *See* Knowledge Base
Microsoft Mobile Internet Toolkit, 166
Microsoft .NET Framework Configuration Tool, 204.
  See also .NET Framework security
Microsoft Online Seminars, 513. *See also* reference hub
Microsoft Passport, 14. *See also* Passport authentication
Microsoft SQL Server 2000. *See* SQL Server 2000
Microsoft Support Center, 328, 329
Microsoft Support site, 513–14. *See also* reference hub
Microsoft Visual Basic 6 COM objects, 336–37
Microsoft Visual Basic .NET objects in COM+, 175
Microsoft Visual Studio .NET. *See* Visual Studio .NET
Microsoft Windows 2000. *See* Windows 2000
Microsoft Windows .NET Server 2003, 180, 211
Microsoft.com site, 513
mirrored filters, IPSec, 487
mirrored local accounts, 297, 347
mirrored policy, IPSec, 487
mirrored process identity, 176–77, 296, 297–98
Mobile Forms authentication, 166
modules
  disabling, 6, 153
  implementing custom HTTP, 168, 531
MSDN, 328, 513. *See also* reference hub
multiple applications
  Forms authentication and, 166
  hosting, with anonymous access, 179–80
multiple trusted identities, 34–35. *See also* fixed
  identities

N

named pipes, 286
names, strong, 402–3, 417–18, 444, 459
names, user. *See* user names
negotiation, authentication level, 221–22
.NET Framework security, 20–25. *See also* Web
  applications security
  ASP.NET and security contexts, 24
  authentication classes, 23
  authentication options, 13–16. *See also* authentication
  authorization options, 16–17. *See also* authorization

Code Access Security (CAS), 20–21
cryptography support, 184, 540–42
implementing IPrincipal interface, 385–94
.NET Framework versions, 21, 145, 180, 235
.NET remoting and Web services, 24–25
principals and identities, 21–22. *See also* identities;
  principals
reference information, 514
.NET remoting
  as implementation technology, 10
  reference information, 518–19
  security. *See* .NET remoting security
.NET remoting security, 259–89. *See also* .NET remoting
  accessing network resources, 270
  accessing system resources, 269
  architecture, 259–64
  ASP.NET and HTTP channel, 263–64
  ASP.NET hosting and requests, 262–63
  authentication, 265–66
  authentication and authorization strategies, 268–69
  authorization, 267–68
  choosing host processes, 285–88
  client certificates and, 449. *See also* client certificates
  configuration stores and tools, 510–11
  configuring client-side proxy, 275, 279, 283
  flowing original callers, 273–80
  gatekeepers and gates, 19, 264–65
  hosting remote objects in Windows services, 469–74
  Internet scenario, 134
  intranet scenario, 85–91
  options, 12, 24–25, 545
  passing credentials for authentication to remote
    objects, 270–73
  remoting sinks, 260–62
  secure communication, 59, 284
  troubleshooting, 337
  trusted subsystem model and, 280–84
  Web services security vs., 288–89
.NET roles. *See also* role-based authorization
  ASP.NET security, 16
  checking. *See* explicit role checks
  Enterprise Services (COM+) roles vs., 43, 220
  Internet authorization and, 124–25
  IPrincipal objects and, 40–41
  role checking, 44–47, 157–58
  Windows authentication and, 41
Netscape Navigator, 13. *See also* browsers
Network Address Translation (NAT), 57
Network Monitor (NetMon.exe), 343, 492–94, 501–3
network resources, 176–82
  anonymous Internet user account and, 178–79
  Enterprise Services and, 209–11
  identifying, 28

impersonating specific Windows identity and, 180
.NET remoting and, 270
non-Windows resources, 181–82
original caller and, 180–81, 210
process identity and, 176–77, 210–11
serviced components and, 177–78
specific service account and, 211
UNC file shares, 181
Web services and, 250–51
networks
  deployment models, 9
  extranet connectivity, 115
  passing credentials over, 303
  resources. *See* network resources
  securing session state across, 187
  troubleshooting, 343
newsgroups, 328, 329
None authentication mode, 14, 168. *See also* custom
  authentication
NTFS permissions
  assigning, 149, 350–51
  file authorization and, 138
  IIS Web permissions vs., 17
NTLM authentication, 13, 15

O

obscurity, 5
OLE DB .NET Data Provider, 314–15
one-way password hashes, 317–18. *See also* hash values
operating system identity flow, 31, 32–33, 38
operations access, 31–32, 44. *See also* role-based
  authorization
original caller identity flow. *See also* delegation;
  identity flow
  ASP.NET to Enterprise Services to SQL Server, 93–99
  ASP.NET to SQL Server, 92–93
  data access security and, 301
  database trust and, 308
  Enterprise Services and, 211–12, 216
  impersonation/delegation model and, 35
  intranet databases and, 71, 91–99
  .NET remoting and, 270, 273–80
  resource access and, 29, 180–81, 210
  Web services and, 232–33, 241, 242–48, 249–50
  Windows authentication with impersonation and, 142
overviews. *See* reference hub

P

Packet Privacy authentication level, 213, 217–18, 221
packetmon.exe, 343
pages. *See* Web pages
Parameters collection, 321

partner applications, Web services, 105
Passport authentication
　advantages, 50
　ASP.NET security and, 14, 167
　.NET remoting and, 266
　Web services and, 230
PassportIdentity objects, 23, 533
passwords. *See also* credentials
　ASPNET account and, 169–72
　authentication and, 2. *See also* authentication
　digests, 363
　Forms authentication, 183. *See also* Forms
　　authentication
　one-way hashes, 317–18
　strong, 297–98, 349
pattern matching statements, 322
percent sign (%), 322
performance
　remote object hosting, 285
　SSL, 55
　UDL files, 315
permissions. *See also* principal permission demands;
　　privileges
　IIS Web, 17
　NTFS. *See* NTFS permissions
　registry, 173
　SQL Server, 292–93
　unmanaged code, 197
physical deployment. *See* deployment
P/Invoke, 212, 217
pipeline processing, ASP.NET, 525–31
　anatomy of Web requests, 526–29
　event handling, 530
　implementing custom HTTP handlers and HTTP
　　modules, 531
plain text, 1, 14
platform/transport level (point-to-point) security, 226.
　　See secure communication; Windows 2000
policies
　CAS, 20–21
　IPSec, 487, 490–91
preauthenticate property, 240–41, 272
pre-master secrets, 450
principal permission demands
　ASP.NET security, 16, 139, 230
　custom identities and, 30
　Forms authentication, 146–47
　.NET remoting, 264, 265
　.NET roles and, 40, 45
　Windows authentication with impersonation, 142, 232
　Windows authentication without impersonation,
　　144, 234

principals. *See also* users
　as authenticated clients, 2
　classes, 23
　identities and, 21–25. *See also* identities
privacy, 3, 53, 305, 463, 485, 539. *See also* secure
　　communication
private keys, 537–38
privileges. *See also* permissions
　assigning, 349
　library application, 197
process identity. *See also* identities
　accessing network resources, 176–77, 210–11
　avoiding SYSTEM account as, 169
　choosing, for Enterprise Services, 208–9
　data access security and, 296–99
　default ASPNET account for, 169–72. *See also* ASPNET
　　default account
　domain controllers and, 169
　as least privileged account, 168
　.NET remoting and, 270
　resource access and, 30
　as secret, 183
　SQL Server, 324
　troubleshooting, 331–32
　using current, 210–11
　Windows authentication and, 187
processes
　authentication levels and, 221–22
　certificate authentication and, 255
　choosing host, for .NET remoting, 285–88
　.NET remoting, 25
　server, and delegation, 382–83
<processModel> element, 58, 64, 101, 118, 169–72, 328
programmatic security. *See also* configurable security
　ASP.NET. *See* programmatic security, ASP.NET
　Enterprise Services role-based, 207–8
　Forms authentication, 146–47
　.NET remoting, 264, 271
　Web services, 232, 234
　Windows authentication with impersonation, 142, 232
　Windows authentication without impersonation,
　　144, 234
programmatic security, ASP.NET, 155–59
　authorization based on user identity and/or role
　　membership, 157–58
　authorization pattern, 156–58
　creating custom IPrincipal class, 158–59
　creating IPrincipal objects, 156–57
　putting IPrincipal objects in HTTP contexts, 157
　putting users in roles, 156
　retrieving and validating credentials, 156
promotion, authentication level, 221

proxies
    interface, 216–18
    .NET remoting, 260, 275, 279, 283
    Web services, 238–39, 244, 247, 250
proxy server authentication, 242
public keys, 537–38

Q

queries, ISQL.exe, 342
QueryInterface exceptions, 215
quotation mark ('), 320

R

RC2, 425
reference hub, 513–21
    Active Directory, 514–15
    ADO.NET, 515
    ASP.NET, 515–17
    Enterprise Services, 517–18
    IIS, 518
    .NET remoting, 518–19
    .NET security, 514
    searching Knowledge Base, 513–14. See also
        Knowledge Base
    SQL Server, 519
    troubleshooting and, 328–29
    Visual Studio .NET, 519
    Web services, 520–21
    Windows 2000, 521
Regedt32.exe, 316
registry
    accessing, 174
    enabling logon auditing, 323–24, 339–40
    event logs, 173
    Fusion logs, 341–42
    keys, 2
    manually registering serviced component, 445
    registering serviced components, 199, 417–18
    storing connection strings in, 186, 316, 435–40
    storing credentials in, 171–72
    time set setting, 55
    tools, 199, 204, 215, 316, 343, 417, 423
    troubleshooting, 331, 343
Registry Monitor (regmon.exe), 343
Regsvcs.exe tool, 199, 204, 215, 417, 423, 460
remote application servers
    configuring, for .NET remoting, 275–76
    configuring, for Web services, 244–45
    secure communication from Web servers to, 59
remote application tier, 9, 11
remote object hosting. See also .NET remoting security
    in ASP.NET Web applications, 262–63, 265–66, 276,
        280, 283, 285–86

    choosing hosts, 282, 285–88
    in console applications, 287–88
    creating remote object class, 470
    creating test console application, 474
    creating Windows accounts for Windows services,
        473
    creating Windows services, 470–72
    features, 286–87
    installing Windows services, 473
    issues, 469
    requirements, 469
    in Windows services, 266, 282, 286–87, 469–74
Remote Procedure Call. See RPC
remote resources. See also network resources
    anonymous access, 178–79
    delegation and, 39–40
    impersonation and, 172
Remoting. See .NET remoting
requests, client certificate, 475–78, 483–84
requests, Web. See pipeline processing, ASP.NET
resource-based authorization, 29, 32–33
resources
    access models, 33–38, 293–95
    authorization and, 2. See also authorization
    choosing identities for accessing, 29–30
    configuring, to require SSL access, 479
    configuring security for, 148, 152–55
    delegation and remote, 38–40
    gatekeepers, gates, and, 17–20. See also gatekeepers
        and gates
    identifying, 28
    impersonation and, 172
    impersonation/delegation access model, 35–37. See
        also impersonation/delegation model
    network. See network resources
    system. See system resources
    trusted subsystem access model, 33–35, 37–38. See
        also trusted subsystem model
    Web services and, 232, 233, 237
    Windows ACLs and, 141, 143–44, 146. See also
        Windows ACLs
Rijndael, 425
roadmaps. See reference hub
roaming user profiles, 188, 311, 396
rogue administrators, 182
role mapping, 32
role-based authorization, 2, 40–47. See also authorization
    data access, 294
    database trust and, 307–8
    Enterprise Services. See role-based authorization,
        Enterprise Services

role-based   authorization,   *continued*
  explicit role checks. *See* explicit role checks
  Forms authentication and, 165
  gatekeepers, gates, and, 18
  multiple database roles and, 304–5
  .NET roles, 40–41, 44–47. *See also* .NET roles
  .NET roles vs. Enterprise Services (COM+) roles,
    16, 43, 220
  Passport authentication and, 167
  programming security and, 156–58
  resource-based authorization vs., 28–29, 31–33
  retrieving role lists from data stores, 163
  SQL Server roles, 17, 42, 183, 304–5
role-based authorization, Enterprise Services, 441–47.
    See also Enterprise Services security
  assigning roles to classes, interfaces, and methods,
    197
  building and adding assembly to global assembly
    cache, 445
  concepts, 219
  configuring serviced component, 443–44
  creating and assigning roles, 200–203
  creating C# class library to host serviced component,
    442
  creating serviced component, 442–43
  creating test client application, 446–47
  DLL locking problems, 213
  Enterprise Services (COM+) roles vs., 16, 17, 42, 43,
    220
  examining configured application, 445–46
  gatekeepers, gates, and, 195–96
  generating strong name for assembly, 44
  issues, 441
  manually registering serviced component, 445
  populating roles, 204–5
  programmatic, 207–8
  QueryInterface exceptions, 215
  requirements, 441
  versioning, 214–15
  Windows authentication with impersonation and,
    142, 195
RPC (Remote Procedure Call)
  encryption, 53, 57–58. *See also* secure communication
  Enterprise Services and, 15, 194–95, 213, 221–22
rules, IPSec, 487, 490–91

S

sa account, 302, 307, 308, 322
salt values, generating, 183, 318, 366
scalability, 2, 37, 180, 210
scenarios, configuration. *See* configuration scenarios
screened subnets, 9, 515

script injection attacks, 5
secrets, 182–84, 450
secure communication, 53–62
  application server to database server, 59–60
  ASP.NET security, 182
  Basic authentication and, 13
  browser to Web server, 58
  configuration stores and tools, 507–12
  configuring, 148, 155
  data access security, 305–6
  Enterprise Services security, 193–95
  extranet security, 107, 113
  Internet security, 122, 131
  intranet security, 63, 67, 76, 82, 89
  IPSec, 56–57. *See also* IPSec
  IPSec vs. SSL, 53, 61
  .NET Framework security, 545
  .NET remoting security, 264, 284, 287
  RPC encryption, 57–58
  scenarios, 58–60
  setting up client certificates, 481–84
  SQL Server session state and, 187
  SSL, 55, 60. *See also* SSL
  technologies, 3–4, 10, 11–12, 53, 545
  troubleshooting, 338
  Web application deployment models, 54
  Web farming and load balancing, 61
  Web server to application server, 59
  Web services, 226, 229–31, 238, 255–56
  Windows service features, 287
Secure Hash Algorithm (SHA1), 185, 190
secure resources. *See* resources
Secure Sockets Layer. *See* SSL
SecureMethod attribute, 201–3
security. *See* Web applications security
security blanket settings, 217–18
security contexts. *See* contexts, security
security logs. *See* logging
security policies, CAS, 20–21
Security Service Provider Interface (SSPI), 15, 286
SecurityRole attribute, 200–203
semicolon (;), 320
seminars. *See* reference hub
sensitive data. *See* secure communication
server applications, Enterprise Services
  configuring, 198–205
  authentication, 199
  authorization, 199–200
  cloaking, 223
  creating and assigning roles, 200–203
  development time vs. deployment time, 199
  identity, 205

library applications vs., 15, 196–97, 219
populating roles, 204–5
registering serviced components, 204
server certificates. *See also* Certificate authentication;
   client certificates
configuring resources to require, 479
generating requests, 475–77
IIS settings, 149
installing, 478–79, 496–97, 498
issuing, 478
submitting requests, 477–78
SSL and, 55, 59–60, 475–79
verifying installation of, 497–98
server compromise, 38
server process account, delegation and, 382–83
servers. *See* application servers; database servers;
   secure communication; Web servers
service accounts, 30, 34, 211
Service Control Manager (SCM), 195
Service Principal Names (SPNs), 331
serviced components. *See* also Enterprise Services
   security
accessing network resources using, 177–78
authentication, 15
building, 213–15
caller identity, 216
calling, from ASP.NET Web applications, 216–18
client certificates and. *See* client certificates, Web
   services security using
configuring, 96–97, 443–44
configuring, strong naming, and registering, 417–18
configuring and installing, 459–60
configuring interface proxies, 216–18
creating, with encryption and decryption methods,
   414–15
creating Windows service to launch, 418–20
DLL locking problems, 213
QueryInterface exceptions, 215
registering, 204
role-based authorization with, 441–47
storing secrets with, 184
versioning, 214–15
Windows authentication and impersonation, 216, 300
session state
networks and, 187
as secret, 183
SQL, 185–87
Web farms and, 188
Setspn.exe, 331
settings. *See* configurable security; configuration
SHA1 (Secure Hash Algorithm), 185, 190
signing certificates, 537

single quotation ('), 320
sinks, .NET remoting, 260–62
custom, 261
formatter, 261–62
transport channel, 260–61
Sn.exe tool, 402, 417, 444, 459
SOAP headers, 227, 229, 241
SoapFormatter class, 262
software configuration, base, 505
specific credentials, 171, 240, 271–72
SQL authentication
choosing SQL accounts, 302–3
connection strings, 183, 186, 302, 303
data access security and, 301–3
intranet security and, 70–71, 84
ISQL.exe and, 342
options, 15–16
passing credentials over networks, 303
SSL and, 60
Windows authentication vs., 295–96
SQL injection attacks, 5, 319–22
SQL Server 2000. *See also* data access security
accounts, 302–3
application roles, 42, 183, 304
auditing, 323–24, 339–40
authentication, 15–16. *See also* SQL authentication
authorization, 17
base configuration, 505
configuration stores and tools, 512
database roles, 304–5
database trust, 307–8
Enterprise Manager, 309, 323, 339, 501
extranet settings, 107, 113
fixed identities, 34–35
Forms authentication with. *See* SQL Server 2000,
   Forms authentication with
gates and gatekeepers, 18–19, 293
as implementation technology, 10, 11
Internet settings, 122, 131. *See also* Internet security
intranet settings, 67, 75, 81–82, 88–89, 98. *See also*
   Intranet security
IPSec and, 485–94
Network Utility, 501–2
original caller identity flow, 91–99
process identity, 324
reference information, 519
security options, 4, 12, 545
session state, 183, 185–87
SQL injection attacks, 5, 319–22
SSL to, 59–60, 495–503. *See also* SSL
user defined database roles, 42, 304
Windows authentication and, 298–99

SQL Server 2000, Forms authentication with, 146, 363–72
authenticating user against database, 369–70
configuring Web application for, 365–66
creating user account database, 367–68
creating Web application with logon page, 364–65
developing functions to generate hash and salt values, 366
requirements, 364
storing credentials, 363
testing, 371–72
using ADO.NET to store account details in database, 368–69
SSL (Secure Sockets Layer). *See also* secure communication
ASP.NET security and, 182
browser to Web server scenario, 58
client certificates and, 449. *See also* client certificates
configuring, 155
configuring resources to require, 464–65, 479
configuring server to allow clients to choose whether to use, 499–500
configuring server to force clients to use, 498–99
Forms authentication and, 14
generating certificate request, 475–77
as implementation technology, 10, 11
installing certificate on client, 466–67, 498
installing certificate on Web server, 478–79
installing server authentication certificate, 496–97
IPSec vs., 53, 61, 495
issues, 55, 495
issuing certificate, 478
requirements, 463, 475, 496
setting up, on Web server, 475–79
SQL Server and, 60, 495–503
submitting certificate request, 477–78
testing, 465
troubleshooting, 338
verifying encryption, 500–503
verifying server certificate installation, 497–98
Web farming and load balancing and, 61
Web services security and, 463–68, 481–84
SSPI (Security Service Provider Interface), 15
state, securing session and view, 185–87
static cloaking, 223
stored procedures
identity flow and, 31, 38, 281
SQL injection attacks and, 319
stores. *See also* files
certificate, 538–39
configuration. *See* configuration stores and tools

DPAPI. *See* machine store, DPAPI with; user store, DPAPI with
role lists in custom data, 163
strings, connection. *See* connection strings
strong names, 20, 402–3, 417–18, 444, 459
strong passwords, 297–98, 349
Support Center, 328, 329
surface area, reducing, 5
symmetric encryption, 55, 540, 541
sysadmin role, 302, 307, 322
SYSTEM account, 5, 169, 171, 324, 348, 381–83
system resources
accessing event log, 173
accessing registry, 174
authorization and, 2
identifying, 28
.NET remoting and, 269
Web services and, 250

T

Task Manager, 342–43
TCP channel, 260–61, 263, 266, 281–82, 286–87, 469
tcptrace.exe, 343
technologies
gatekeepers, gates, and, 17–20
implementation, 10
secure communication, 53
security, 3–4, 11–12, 545
testing
client certificates, 484
DPAPI with machine store, 408
encryption, 500–503
encryption and decryption, 420–23
encryption library, 433–34
Forms authentication with Active Directory, 362
Forms authentication with GenericPrincipal objects, 379–80
Forms authentication with IPrincipal implementations, 393–94
Forms authentication with SQL Server, 371–72
installation of server authentication certificate, 497–98
IPSec security, 492–94
text, plain, 1, 14
text files, connection strings in custom, 316
threading
COM objects and, 174–75
impersonation and, 172
principals, identities, and, 21–22
Thread.CurrentPrincipal property, 21, 24, 45, 266, 533
tickets, Forms authentication, 14, 161, 163, 358–60, 375–77, 388–90. *See also* cookies

tiers
  authentication and, 2
  logical, 8
  remote application, 9, 10
  secure communication and, 3
  security and, 6, 12
TLS. *See* SSL
tools
  aspnet_setreg.exe tool, 64, 101, 171, 186, 298, 352
  Component Services. *See* Component Services tool
  configuration, 507–12
  DLL locking and, 213
  Gacutil.exe, 204, 445, 460
  InstallUtil.exe, 173, 420, 471, 473
  IPSec Monitor (Ipsecmon.exe), 56
  Kerberos, 331
  Local Security Policy, 56, 349, 488
  Network Monitor (NetMon.exe), 343, 492–94, 501–3
  Regedt32.exe, 316
  Regsvcs.exe, 199, 204, 215, 417, 423, 460
  Sn.exe, 402, 417, 444, 459
  troubleshooting, 341–44
  User Manager, 176, 179, 297
  Users and Computers Administration, 204–5
  Wsdl.exe, 239, 242
tracing
  enabling, 333
  network, 343
transport channel sinks, 260–61
Transport Layer Security. *See* SSL
transport level security. *See* secure communication
Triple DES (3DES), 189–90, 425
troubleshooting security issues, 327–44
  ASP.NET, 333
  auditing and logging, 339–41
  authentication issues, 329–31
  authorization issues, 331–32
  enabling tracing, 333
  identity determination, 334–37
  IPSec, 338
  .NET remoting, 337
  process for, 327–29
  searching for implementation solutions, 328–29
  SSL, 338
  tools, 341–44
trust, database, 307–8
trusted identities. *See* fixed identities
trusted query parameter approach, 38, 281
trusted subsystem model, 33–35
  advantages and disadvantages, 37–38
  fixed identities and, 34
  impersonation/delegation model vs., 293–95
  multiple trusted identities and, 34–35

.NET remoting security and, 269, 280–84
Web services security and, 248–50
Web services security with client certificates and, 252–55
types
  connection string, 302
  IIS authentication, 39–40
  specific authentication, 240, 272

U

UDL files, connection strings in, 314–15
UDP (User Data Protocol), 221
UNC (Universal Naming Convention) file shares, 153, 181
unmanaged code, 197
URL authorization
  ASP.NET security, 16, 20, 230, 136, 137
  configuring, 150–52
  Forms authentication, 146
  .NET remoting, 264
  .NET roles and, 44
  Windows authentication with impersonation, 141, 232
  Windows authentication without impersonation, 144, 234
User Data Protocol (UDP), 221
User Manager, 176, 179, 297
user names. *See also* credentials
  authentication and, 2. *See also* authentication
  authorization and, 165
  for ASPNET account, 169
user profiles, 188, 286, 310–11, 312, 396, 417
User Services layer, 8
user store, DPAPI with, 311–13, 411–24. *See also* DPAPI
  Enterprise Services and, 311–13
  calling managed DPAPI class library, 415–16
  configuring, strong naming, and registering serviced component, 417–18
  creating dummy class to launch serviced component, 416
  creating serviced components with encryption and decryption methods, 414–15
  creating Web application to test encryption and decryption, 420–23
  creating Windows account for Enterprise Services application and Windows service, 416–17
  creating Windows service to launch serviced component, 418–20
  installing and starting Windows service, 420
  issues, 411–13
  machine store vs., 310–11, 395–96
  modifying Web application to read encrypted connection string from Web.config file, 423–24
  requirements, 414

user store, DPAPI with, *continued*
  using Enterprise Services, 412–13
  using Windows service, 413
user-defined database roles, 304
users, 2. *See also* identities; principals
  accounts. *See* accounts
  anonymous Internet account, 178–80
  authenticating and authorizing, 2–3. *See also*
    authentication; authorization
  identifying authenticated, 160
  input. *See* input, user
  interactive, and Enterprise Services, 208–9
  malicious Web, 182, 237–38
  names. *See* user names
  profiles, 188, 286, 310–11, 312, 396, 417
  putting, into roles, 156
  unfiltered input, 319–22
  User Services layer, 8
Users and Computers Administration tool, 204–5

V

validating user input, 5, 319–22, 363
validation attributes, 189–90
versioning, 214–15
view state, 185, 189
virtual directory
  configuring, to require certificates, 482–83
  configuring anonymous Internet user account for,
    179–80
  configuring Web services, 452, 456
Visual Basic 6 COM objects, 336–37
Visual Basic .NET objects in COM+, 175
Visual Studio .NET
  reference information, 519
  tools, 344
  versioning, 214–15
  Web services proxies, 239
volumes, secrets in files on separate, 184

W

W3C Extended Logging, 340–41
Web applications, 7–10
  adding roles to, 200–201
  client. *See* client applications
  connected landscape of distributed, 1
  creating, to call Web services, 460–62, 467–68
  creating, to retrieve encrypted connection string
    from registry, 439–40
  creating, to test encryption and decryption, 420–32
  creating, to test serviced component security, 446–47
  creating, with logon page, 354, 364–65, 374–75
  creating simple, for client certificates, 482

  creating simple, for IPrincipal implementation, 386–87
  database trust of, 307
  hosting multiple, 166, 179–80
  logical tiers, 8
  physical deployment models, 9. *See also*
    application servers; Web servers
  remote object hosting, 262–63, 265–66, 276, 280,
    283, 285–86
  security. *See* Web applications security
  servers. *See* application servers; database servers;
    Web servers
  technologies, 3–4, 10, 12
  Web services partner applications, 105
Web applications security. *See also* Web applications
  architecture, 11–20
  ASP.NET security, 13–15, 16–17, 18, 24. *See also*
    ASP.NET security
  authentication, 2, 13–16. *See also* authentication
  authentication and authorization strategies. *See*
    authentication and authorization strategies
  authorization, 2–3, 16–17. *See also* authorization
  Code Access Security, 20–21
  configurable. *See* configurable security
  configuration. *See* configuration
  connected landscape and, 1
  data access security. *See* data access security
  design principles, 4–6
  Enterprise Services security, 15, 17, 18. *See also*
    Enterprise Services security
  extranet security. *See* extranet security
  gatekeepers and gates, 17–20. *See also* gatekeepers
    and gates
  Internet security. *See* Internet security
  intranet security. *See* Intranet security
  .NET Framework security, 20–25. *See also* .NET
    Framework security
  .NET remoting security, 19, 24–25. *See also* .NET
    remoting security
  programmatic. *See* programmatic security
  reference hub, 513–21
  secure communication, 3, 53–62. *See also* secure
    communication
  SQL Server security, 15–16, 17, 18–19. *See also* SQL
    Server 2000
  technologies, 3–4, 10, 11–12, 545
  troubleshooting. *See* troubleshooting security issues
  Web application characteristics, 7–9. *See also* Web
    applications
  Web services security, 19, 24–25. *See also* Web
    services security
  Windows security, 18. *See also* Windows 2000
Web browsers. *See* browsers

Web farms, 188–90
  DPAPI and, 188
  session state and, 188
  SSL, load balancing, and, 61
  using Forms authentication in, 188–90
Web gardens, 188
Web pages
  creating COM objects in, 175
  determining identity in, 334–36
  logon. *See* logon Web forms
Web requests. *See* pipeline processing, ASP.NET
Web Server Certificate Wizard, 476
Web servers
  anonymous domain accounts at, 125
  as application servers, 9
  extranet settings, 105–6, 111–12
  Internet settings, 120–21, 129–30
  intranet settings, 80, 87, 95–96
  .NET remoting settings, 274–75, 278–79, 282–84
  original caller identity flow and, 92–93
  proxy server authentication, 242
  resources and, 28
  secure communication and, 58–59
  setting up SSL on, 475–79
  Web services settings, 243–45, 246–47, 249–50
Web services
  creating application to call, 467–68
  creating simple, 464
  Development Toolkit, 59, 225, 228
  Enterprise Services and, 215
  as implementation technology, 10
  reference information, 520–21
  security. *See* Web services security
Web services security, 225–57. *See also* Web services
  accessing COM objects, 174, 251
  accessing network resources, 250–51
  accessing system resources, 250
  architecture, 226, 229–31
  authentication and authorization strategies, 231–35
  calling Web services from non-Windows clients, 241
  configuration stores and tools, 509–10
  configuring, 236–38
  connected landscape and, 1
  determining identity in, 336
  extranet scenario, 102–9
  flowing original callers, 242–48
  gatekeepers and gates, 19
  intranet scenario, 77–85
  model, 225–28
  .NET remoting security vs., 288–89
  options, 12, 24–25, 545
  passing credentials for authentication, 238–42
  secure communication, 59, 255–56

troubleshooting, 344
trusted subsystem model, 248–50
using client certificates, 251–55, 449–62, 481–84
using SSL, 463–68
Web sites, 329, 477, 513. *See also* reference hub
WebCasts. *See* reference hub
Web.config files
  ASP.NET security, 149–52
  authorization, 136, 137, 143–44, 146
  connection strings in, 314
  custom authentication, 168
  encrypted connection strings, 313–14, 409–10, 423–24
  Enterprise Services (COM+) roles, 42
  fixed identities, 183
  Forms authentication, 145
  HTTP-GET and HTTP-POST support, 238
  IIS security, 533–35
  impersonation, 178, 180
  locking settings in, 153–54
  .NET remoting security, 268
  Passport authentication, 147, 167
  preventing download of files, 154–55
  securing, 153
  troubleshooting and, 328, 333
  Windows authentication, 141, 143–44, 145, 231
WebServiceStudio, 344
<wellknown> element, 268
WFetch.exe, 343
Windows 2000
  accounts, 416–17, 441, 473. *See also* Windows ACLs
  authentication. *See* Integrated Windows authentication; Windows authentication
  base configuration, 505
  calling Web services from non-Windows clients, 241
  certificate stores, 538–39
  event log, 6
  gatekeepers and gates, 18
  groups, 204–5, 357–58
  groups vs. .NET roles, 16
  High Encryption Pack, 189–90
  identities vs. .NET Framework identities, 21
  identity flow, 38
  Installer, 173
  IPSec and, 56
  Kerberos. *See* Kerberos delegation
  .NET remoting and, 284
  reference information, 521
  Resource Kit, 331, 344
  RPC for DCOM, 221
  security logs, 339
  security options, 12
  services. *See* Windows services
  SSPI, 15, 286
  Task Manager, 342–43

Windows ACLs
  authorization and, 2, 37
  configuring, for secure resources, 152–55
  Enterprise Services and, 194
  Forms authentication and, 146
  registry keys and, 316
  resource-based authorization and, 29, 32
  troubleshooting, 331
  UDL files and granularity of, 315
  Windows authentication with impersonation, 141, 231–32
  Windows authentication without impersonation, 143–44, 233
Windows authentication
  with anonymous Internet user account, 300–301
  ASP.NET process identity and, 187, 296–99
  ASP.NET security and, 13–14, 159–60
  authorization options and, 140
  data access security and, 295–301
  delegation and, 39–40
  with fixed identities, 145, 235, 299–300
  with impersonation, 141–43, 216, 231–33, 301
  without impersonation, 143–45, 233–35
  ISQL.exe and, 342
  mechanisms, 13–14. *See also* Anonymous
    authentication; Basic authentication; Certificate
    authentication; Digest authentication; Integrated
    Windows authentication

  .NET remoting and, 263
  .NET roles with and without, 41, 44
  original caller identity and, 301
  principals and identities, 23
  processing, 529
  scenarios that prevent, 301
  serviced components and, 216, 300
  SQL authentication vs., 295–96
  SQL Server and, 15–16, 60, 298–99
  troubleshooting, 330
  Web services and, 231–35, 239–41
Windows .NET Server 2003, 180, 524–25
Windows services
  creating, to launch serviced component, 418–20
  creating Windows account for, 416–17
  installing and starting, 420
  passing Web services client certificates using, 254–55
  remote object hosting in, 266, 282, 286–87, 469–74
  TCP channel and, 469
  using, with DPAPI, 413
WindowsIdentity objects, 23, 27, 533
WindowsPrincipal objects, 23, 41, 139, 157, 385, 533
Wsdl.exe tool, 239, 242
WS-Security specification, 59, 225, 227–28

X

X.509 digital certificates, 478, 538
XML (Extensible Markup Language), 1

Microsoft®
patterns & practices

Proven practices for predictable results

Patterns & practices are Microsoft's recommendations for architects, software developers, and IT professionals responsible for delivering and managing enterprise systems on the Microsoft platform. Patterns & practices are available for both IT infrastructure and software development topics.

Patterns & practices are based on real-world experiences that go far beyond white papers to help enterprise IT pros and developers quickly deliver sound solutions. This technical guidance is reviewed and approved by Microsoft engineering teams, consultants, Product Support Services, and by partners and customers. Organizations around the world have used patterns & practices to:

Reduce project cost

- Exploit Microsoft's engineering efforts to save time and money on projects
- Follow Microsoft's recommendations to lower project risks and achieve predictable outcomes

Increase confidence in solutions

- Build solutions on Microsoft's proven recommendations for total confidence and predictable results
- Provide guidance that is thoroughly tested and supported by PSS, not just samples, but production quality recommendations and code

Deliver strategic IT advantage

- Gain practical advice for solving business and IT problems today, while preparing companies to take full advantage of future Microsoft technologies.

To learn more about *patterns & practices* visit: *msdn.microsoft.com/practices*

To purchase *patterns & practices* guides visit: *shop.microsoft.com/practices*

patterns & practices
Proven practices for predictable results

patterns & practices

Proven practices for predictable results

Patterns & practices are available for both IT infrastructure and software development topics. There are four types of patterns & practices available:

Reference Architectures

Reference Architectures are IT system-level architectures that address the business requirements, operational requirements, and technical constraints for commonly occurring scenarios. Reference Architectures focus on planning the architecture of IT systems and are most useful for architects.

Reference Building Blocks

References Building Blocks are re-usable sub-systems designs that address common technical challenges across a wide range of scenarios. Many include tested reference implementations to accelerate development.

Reference Building Blocks focus on the design and implementation of sub-systems and are most useful for designers and implementors.

Operational Practices

Operational Practices provide guidance for deploying and managing solutions in a production environment and are based on the Microsoft Operations Framework. Operational Practices focus on critical tasks and procedures and are most useful for production support personnel.

Patterns

Patterns are documented proven practices that enable re-use of experience gained from solving similar problems in the past. Patterns are useful to anyone responsible for determining the approach to architecture, design, implementation, or operations problems.

To learn more about *patterns & practices* visit: *msdn.microsoft.com/practices*

To purchase *patterns & practices* guides visit: *shop.microsoft.com/practices*

patterns & practices current titles

December 2002

Reference Architectures

Microsoft Systems Architecture—Enterprise Data Center *2007 pages*
Microsoft Systems Architecture—Internet Data Center *397 pages*
Application Architecture for .NET: Designing Applications and Services *127 pages*
Microsoft SQL Server 2000 High Availability Series: Volume 1: Planning *92 pages*
Microsoft SQL Server 2000 High Availability Series: Volume 2: Deployment *128 pages*
Enterprise Notification Reference Architecture for Exchange 2000 Server *224 pages*
Microsoft Content Integration Pack for Content Management Server 2001
      and SharePoint Portal Server 2001 *124 pages*
UNIX Application Migration Guide *694 pages*
Microsoft Active Directory Branch Office Guide: Volume 1: Planning *88 pages*
Microsoft Active Directory Branch Office Series Volume 2: Deployment and
      Operations *195 pages*
Microsoft Exchange 2000 Server Hosting Series Volume 1: Planning *227 pages*
Microsoft Exchange 2000 Server Hosting Series Volume 2: Deployment *135 pages*
Microsoft Exchange 2000 Server Upgrade Series Volume 1: Planning *306 pages*
Microsoft Exchange 2000 Server Upgrade Series Volume 2: Deployment *166 pages*

Reference Building Blocks

Data Access Application Block for .NET *279 pages*
.NET Data Access Architecture Guide *60 pages*
Designing Data Tier Components and Passing Data Through Tiers *70 pages*
Exception Management Application Block for .NET *307 pages*
Exception Management in .NET *35 pages*
Monitoring in .NET Distributed Application Design *40 pages*
Microsoft .NET/COM Migration and Interoperability *35 pages*
Production Debugging for .NET-Connected Applications *176 pages*
Authentication in ASP.NET: .NET Security Guidance *58 pages*
Building Secure ASP.NET Applications: Authentication, Authorization, and
      Secure Communication *608 pages*

Operational Practices

Security Operations Guide for Exchange 2000 Server *136 pages*
Security Operations for Microsoft Windows 2000 Server *188 pages*
Microsoft Exchange 2000 Server Operations Guide *113 pages*
Microsoft SQL Server 2000 Operations Guide *170 pages*
Deploying .NET Applications: Lifecycle Guide *142 pages*
Team Development with Visual Studio .NET and Visual SourceSafe *74 pages*
Backup and Restore for Internet Data Center *294 pages*

For current list of titles visit: *msdn.microsoft.com/practices*

To purchase *patterns & practices* guides visit: *shop.microsoft.com/practices*

patterns & practices
Proven practices for predictable results

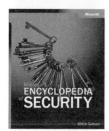

Get a **Free**
e-mail newsletter, updates,
special offers, links to related books,
and more when you

register on line!

Register your Microsoft Press® title on our Web site and you'll get a FREE subscription to our e-mail newsletter, *Microsoft Press Book Connections*. You'll find out about newly released and upcoming books and learning tools, online events, software downloads, special offers and coupons for Microsoft Press customers, and information about major Microsoft® product releases. You can also read useful additional information about all the titles we publish, such as detailed book descriptions, tables of contents and indexes, sample chapters, links to related books and book series, author biographies, and reviews by other customers.

Registration is easy. Just visit this Web page and fill in your information:

http://www.microsoft.com/mspress/register

Microsoft®
